Black Rednecks
and
White Liberals

Black Rednecks
and
White Liberals

Thomas Sowell

ENCOUNTER BOOKS
SAN FRANCISCO

First edition published in 2005 by Encounter Books, an activity of Encounter for Culture and Education, Inc., a nonprofit corporation.

Encounter Books website address: www.encounterbooks.com

Manufactured in the United States and printed on acid-free paper.

The paper used in this publication meets the minimum requirements of ANSI/NISO Z39.48-1992 (R 1997)(*Permanence of Paper*).

FIRST EDITION

Library of Congress Cataloging-in-Publication Data

Sowell, Thomas.
    Black rednecks and white liberals / Thomas Sowell.
        p. cm.
    Includes bibliographical references and index.
    ISBN 1-59403-086-3 (alk. paper)
Stereotype (Psychology). 2. Ethnic relations—History. 3. Race relations—History. I. Title.
HM1096 .S683 2005
305.8'00973—dc22
2005041506

10 9 8 7 6 5 4 3 2 1

We do not live in the past, but the past in us.

— U. B. Phillips

Contents

Preface

RACE AND RHETORIC HAVE GONE TOGETHER for so long that it is easy to forget that facts also matter—and these facts often contradict many widely held beliefs. Fantasies and fallacies about racial and ethnic issues have had a particularly painful and deadly history, so exposing some of them is more than an academic exercise. The history of intergroup strife has been written in blood in many countries around the world and across centuries of human history.

The purpose of this book is to expose some of the more blatant misconceptions poisoning race relations in our time. The reasons for these misconceptions range from simple, innocent ignorance to reasons that are far from simple and far from innocent. Many of the facts cited here may be surprising or even startling to some readers, but they are not literally unknown to scholars; they have simply not been widely discussed in the media or even in academia. Too much has been assumed for too long and too little has been scrutinized.

It may be optimistic merely to suggest that racial or ethnic issues can be discussed rationally. Evidence to the contrary is all too abundant in the strident and sweeping condemnations directed against many who have tried to do so. Yet there is also evidence in recent years of a growing willingness to consider views that differ from the racial orthodoxy that has prevailed largely unchallenged from the 1960s onward in intellectual circles and in the popular media. In any event, these essays summarize the conclusions of more than a quarter of a century of my research on racial and cultural issues, as well as drawing on the work of innumerable other scholars around the world.

These writings do not pretend to be definitive. If they provoke thoughts on a subject where clichés and dogmas too often prevail, then this book will have achieved one of its major goals.

However, even a work seeking primarily to untangle a complex set of historic social issues can provoke the fashionable question: "But what is *your* solution?" Yet there is not the slightest danger that there will be a shortage of solutions. On the contrary, an abundance of uninformed solutions has been one of our biggest social problems.

Any serious consideration of social problems is likely to involve trade-offs rather than neat "solutions," and trade-offs depend on values which can vary from one individual to the next. What trade-offs others might make after considering what these essays have to offer is not something that can be predicted, nor is such a prediction necessary. There is still much to be said for the ancient adage: "With all your getting, get understanding." If this book can contribute to understanding on a subject where misunderstandings abound, then it will have done its work.

Because this book is written for the general public, it does not feature long, convoluted sentences with escape clauses designed to prevent words from being twisted to mean something that they were never intended to mean. Common sense can be more readily expected when writing for the general public than when writing for the intelligentsia. To prevent the words in the essays that follow from being stretched, twisted, or given clever meanings, let me state here and now that these essays do *not* mean that (1) all Southern whites were or are rednecks, that (2) all black Americans today or in the past were or are black rednecks, that (3) Jews are exactly the same as the other groups with whom they are compared, or that (4) slavery is somehow morally acceptable because everyone was guilty of it. One cannot predict, much less forestall, all the clever misinterpretations that others might put on one's words. The most that can be done is to alert honest people to the problem.

While this book is not particularly large in bulk, its scope is worldwide and it goes back through centuries. No one can write a book of such scope without incurring many debts to others. These include scholars who devoted much of their careers to the study of some particular specialty, such as the history of agriculture in the Southern United States or the origins in Britain of various social groups in America. Such debts are too numerous to list here, quite aside from the danger of implicating other writers in conclusions which are my own. What must be acknowledged is my debt to the Hoover Institution, which has provided the conditions and the support which have facilitated my research and writing for more than two decades. For much of that time, my research assistant Na Liu has been an indispensable part of my work and, for this particular book, she has been very ably assisted by the dedicated work of Elizabeth Costa. In the end, however, I must and will take full responsibility for the conclusions reached in the essays that follow.

THOMAS SOWELL
Hoover Institution
Stanford University

Black Rednecks and White Liberals

These people are creating a terrible problem in our cities.
They can't or won't hold a job, they flout the law constantly
and neglect their children, they drink too much and their
moral standards would shame an alley cat. For some reason
or other, they absolutely refuse to accommodate themselves
to any kind of decent, civilized life.

THIS WAS SAID IN 1956 IN INDIANAPOLIS, not about blacks or other minorities, but about poor whites from the South. Nor was Indianapolis unique in this respect. A 1951 survey in Detroit found that white Southerners living there were considered "undesirable" by 21 percent of those surveyed, compared to 13 percent who ranked blacks the same way. In the late 1940s, a Chicago employer said frankly, "I told the guard at the plant gate to tell the hillbillies that there were no openings." When poor whites from the South moved into Northern cities to work in war plants during the Second World War, "occasionally a white southerner would find that a flat or furnished room had 'just been rented' when the landlord heard his southern accent."[1]

More is involved here than a mere parallel between blacks and Southern whites. What is involved is a common subculture that goes back for centuries, which has encompassed everything from ways of talking to attitudes toward education, violence, and sex—and which originated not in the South, but in those parts of the British Isles from which white Southerners came. That culture long ago died out where it originated in Britain, while surviving

1

in the American South. Then it largely died out among both white
and black Southerners, while still surviving today in the poorest
and worst of the urban black ghettos.

It is not uncommon for a culture to survive longer where it is
transplanted and to retain characteristics lost in its place of origin.
The French spoken in Quebec and the Spanish spoken in Mexico
contain words and phrases that have long since become archaic in
France and Spain.[2] Regional German dialects persisted among Germans living in the United States after those dialects had begun to
die out in Germany itself.[3] A scholar specializing in the history of
the South has likewise noted among white Southerners "archaic
word forms,"[4] while another scholar has pointed out the continued
use in that region of "terms that were familiar at the time of the
first Queen Elizabeth."[5] The card game whist is today played almost
exclusively by blacks, especially low-income blacks, though in the
eighteenth century it was played by the British upper classes, and
has since then evolved into bridge. The history of the evolution of
this game is indicative of a much broader pattern of cultural evolution in much more weighty things.

Southern whites not only spoke the English language in very
different ways from whites in other regions, their churches, their
roads, their homes, their music, their education, their food, and
their sex lives were all sharply different from those of other
whites. The history of this redneck or cracker culture is more than
a curiosity. It has contemporary significance because of its influence on the economic and social evolution of vast numbers of
people—millions of blacks and whites—and its continuing influence on the lives and deaths of a residual population in America's
black ghettos which has still not completely escaped from that
culture.

From early in American history, foreign visitors and domestic
travelers alike were struck by cultural contrasts between the white
population of the South and that of the rest of the country in general—and of New England in particular. In the early nineteenth
century, Alexis de Tocqueville contrasted white Southerners with
white Northerners in his classic *Democracy in America* and Frederick Law Olmsted did the same later in his books about his travels
through the antebellum South, notably *Cotton Kingdom*. De Toc-

queville set a pattern when he concluded that "almost all the differences which may be noticed between the Americans in the Southern and in the Northern states have originated in slavery."[6] Olmsted likewise attributed the differences between white Southerners and white Northerners to the existence of slavery in the South.[7] So did widely read antebellum Southern writer Hinton Helper, who declared that "slavery, and nothing but slavery, has retarded the progress and prosperity of our portion of the Union."[8]

Just as they explained regional differences between whites by slavery, so many others in a later era would explain differences between blacks and whites nationwide by slavery. Plausible as these explanations might seem in both cases, they will not stand up under a closer scrutiny of history.

It is perhaps understandable that the great, overwhelming moral curse of slavery has presented a tempting causal explanation of the peculiar subculture of Southern whites, as well as that of blacks. Yet this same subculture had existed among Southern whites and their ancestors in those parts of the British Isles from which they came, long before they had ever seen a black slave. The nature of this subculture, among people who were called "rednecks" and "crackers" in Britain before they ever saw America, needs to be explored before turning to the question of its current status among ghetto blacks and how developments in the larger society have affected its evolution.

REDNECK CULTURE

Emigration from Britain, like other migrations around the world, was not random in either its origins or its destinations. Most of the Britons who migrated to colonial Massachusetts, for example, came from within a 60-mile radius of the town of Haverhill in East Anglia. The Virginia aristocracy came from different localities in southern and western England. Most of the common white people of the South came from the northern borderlands of England—for centuries a no-man's land between Scotland and England—as well as from the Scottish highlands and from Ulster County, Ireland. All these fringe areas were turbulent, if not lawless, regions, where none of the contending forces was able to establish full control and create a stable order. Whether called a "Celtic fringe" or "north Britons," these were people from outside the cultural heartland of England, as their behavior on both sides of the Atlantic showed. Before the era of modern transportation and communication, sharp regional differences were both common and persistent.

In some of the counties of colonial Virginia, from nearly three-quarters to four-fifths of the people came from northern Britain and similar proportions were found in some of the counties of Kentucky and Tennessee, as well as in parts of both the Carolinas.[9] Although they predominated in many parts of the South, such people also had some Northern enclaves in colonial America, notably western Pennsylvania, where Ulster Scots settled. What is at least equally important as where particular peoples settled is *when* they emigrated from the borderlands, Ulster, and the Scottish highlands.

Scotland in particular progressed enormously in the eighteenth century. The level from which it began may be indicated by the fact that a visitor to late eighteenth-century Edinburgh found it noteworthy that its residents no longer threw sewage from their chamber pots out their windows into the street—something that passersby had long had to be alert for, to avoid being splattered.[10] Such crude and unsanitary living had long been characteristic of earlier times, when rural Scots lived in the same primitive shelters with their animals, and vermin abounded.[11] A similar lack of concern with cleanliness was found among others in the borderlands of Britain—and among their descendants on the other side of the Atlantic in the antebellum South.[12] For example, a nineteenth-century politician "built up a political machine in the poor white districts of Mississippi" by such practices as this:

> He did not resort to any conventional tactics of kissing dirty babies, but he pleased mothers and fathers in log cabins by taking their children upon his lap and searching for red bugs, lice, and other vermin.[13]

Back in the British Isles, the life of the Scottish people was transformed dramatically, from the masses to the elites, as they advanced from being one of the least educated to one of the most educated peoples in Europe. However, what is significant here is that much of the migration to the American South occurred *before* these sweeping social transformations. This timing was crucial, as Professor Grady McWhiney has pointed out in his book *Cracker Culture:*

> ...had the South been peopled by nineteenth-century Scots, Welshmen, and Ulstermen, the course of Southern history would doubtless have been radically different. Nineteenth-century Scottish and Scotch-Irish immigrants did in fact fit quite comfortably into northern American society. (Significantly the Irish, who retained their Celtic ways, did not.) But only a trickle of the flood of nineteenth-century immigrants came into the South; the ancestors of the vast majority of Southerners arrived in America before the Anglicization of Scotland, Wales, and Ulster had advanced very far.[14]

In earlier centuries, Scotland was a poor and backward country, like Wales and Ireland—and like the turbulent northern borderlands of England, where the Scots and the English fought wars and committed atrocities against each other for centuries. Local feuding clans and freebooting marauders kept this region in an uproar, even when there were no military hostilities between the English and Scottish kingdoms. Ulster County had a different kind of turbulence, as the English and Scottish settlers there encountered the hostility and terrorist activities of the conquered, dispossessed, and embittered indigenous Irish population.

These were the parts of Britain from which most people migrated to the American South, before the political and cultural unification of the British Isles or the standardization of the English language. The rednecks of these regions were what one social historian has called "some of the most disorderly inhabitants of a deeply disordered land."[15]

In this world of impotent laws, daily dangers, and lives that could be snuffed out at any moment, the snatching at whatever fleeting pleasures presented themselves was at least understandable. Certainly prudence and long-range planning of one's life had no such pay-off in this chaotic world as in more settled and orderly societies under the protection of effective laws. Books, businesses, technology, and science were not the kinds of things likely to be promoted or admired in the world of the rednecks and crackers.

Manliness and the forceful projection of that manliness to others—an advertising of one's willingness to fight and even to put one's life on the line—were at least plausible means of gaining whatever measure of security was possible in a lawless region and a violent time. The kinds of attitudes and cultural values produced by centuries of living under such conditions did not disappear very quickly, even when social evolution in North America slowly and almost imperceptibly created a new and different world with different objective prospects.

What the rednecks or crackers brought with them across the ocean was a whole constellation of attitudes, values, and behavior patterns that might have made sense in the world in which they had lived for centuries, but which would prove to be counterproductive in the world to which they were going—and counterproductive to the blacks who would live in their midst for centuries before emerging into freedom and migrating to the great urban centers of the United States, taking with them similar values.

The cultural values and social patterns prevalent among Southern whites included an aversion to work,[16] proneness to violence,[17] neglect of education,[18] sexual promiscuity,[19], improvidence,[20] drunkenness,[21] lack of entrepreneurship,[22] reckless searches for excitement,[23] lively music and dance,[24] and a style of religious oratory marked by strident rhetoric, unbridled emotions, and flamboyant imagery.[25] This oratorical style carried over into the political oratory of the region in both the Jim Crow era and the civil rights era, and has continued on into our own times among black politicians, preachers, and activists. Touchy pride, vanity, and boastful self-dramatization were also part of this redneck culture[26] among people from regions of Britain "where the civilization was the least developed."[27] "They boast and lack self-restraint," Olmsted said, after observing their descendants in the American antebellum South.[28]

While Professor Grady McWhiney's *Cracker Culture* is perhaps the most thorough historical study of the values and behavioral patterns of white Southerners, many other scholarly studies have turned up very similar patterns, even when they differed in some ways as to the causes. Professor David Hackett Fischer's *Albion's Seed,* for example, challenges the Celtic connection thesis put forth by Professor McWhiney, but shows many of the same cultural patterns among the same people, both in Britain and in the American South. Popular writings of the nineteenth and twentieth centuries have likewise described similar behavior, including the Indianapolis resident's comments on white Southern migrants to that city, which sound so much like what many have said about ghetto blacks.

None of this is meant to claim that these patterns have remained rigidly unchanged over the centuries or that there are literally no differences between whites and blacks in any aspects of this subculture. However, what is remarkable is how pervasive and how close the similarities have been.

Pride and Violence

Centuries before "black pride" became a fashionable phrase, there was cracker pride—and it was very much the same kind of pride. It was not pride in any particular achievement or set of behavioral standards or moral principles adhered to. It was instead a touchiness about anything that might be even remotely construed as a personal slight, much less an insult, combined with a willingness to erupt into violence over it. New Englanders were baffled about this kind of pride among crackers. Observing such people, the Yankees "could not understand what they had to feel proud about."[29] However, this kind of pride is perhaps best illustrated by an episode reported in Professor McWhiney's *Cracker Culture:*

> When an Englishman, tired of waiting for a Southerner to start working on a house he had contracted to build, hired another man to do the job, the enraged Southerner, who considered himself dishonored, vowed:"to-morrow morn, I will come with men, and twenty rifles, and I will have your life, or you shall have mine."[30]

In the vernacular of our later times, he had been "dissed"—and he was not going to stand for it, regardless of the consequences for himself or others. The history of the antebellum South is full of episodes showing the same pattern, whether expressed in the highly formalized duels of the aristocracy or in the no-holds-barred style of fighting called "rough and tumble" among the common folk, a style that included biting off ears and gouging out eyes. It was not simply that particular isolated individuals did such things; *social approval* was given to these practices, as illustrated by this episode in the antebellum South:

> A crowd gathered and arranged itself in an impromptu ring. The contestants were asked if they wished to "fight fair" or "rough and tumble." When they chose "rough and tumble," a roar of approval rose from the multitude.

This particular fight ended with the loser's nose bitten off, his ears torn off, and both his eyes gouged out, after which the "victor, himself maimed and bleeding, was 'chaired round the grounds,' to the cheers of the crowd." This "rough and tumble" style of fighting was also popular in the southern highlands of Scotland, where grabbing an opponent's testicles and attempting to castrate him by hand was also an accepted practice.[31] Scottish highlanders were, in centuries past, part of the "Celtic fringe" or "north Britons," outside the orbit of English culture, not only as it existed in England but also in the Scottish lowlands.

The highlanders lagged far behind the lowlanders in education and economic progress, as well as in the speaking of the English language, for Gaelic was still widely spoken by highlanders in the nineteenth century, not only in Scotland itself but also in North Carolina and in Australia, where immigrants from the Scottish highlands were unable to communicate with English-speaking people, including lowland Scots who had also immigrated. In the Hebrides Islands off Scotland, Gaelic had still not completely died out in the middle of the twentieth century.[32]

What is important in the pride and violence patterns among rednecks and crackers was not that particular people did particular things at particular times and places. Nor is it necessary to attempt to quantify such behavior. What is crucial is that violence growing out of such pride had *social approval.* As Professor McWhiney pointed out:

> Men often killed and went free in the South just as in earlier times they had in Ireland and Scotland. As one observer in the South noted, enemies would meet, exchange insults, and one would shoot the other down, professing that he had acted in

self-defense because he believed the victim was armed. When
such a story was told in court, "in a community where it is not a
strange thing for men to carry about their persons deadly
weapons, [each member of the jury] feels that he would have
done the same thing under similar circumstances so that in condemning him they would but condemn themselves."[33]

"The actions of southern courts often amazed outsiders," Professor McWhiney said. But what may be even more revealing of
widespread attitudes were the cases that never even went to trial. As
another study of white Southerners put it:

> To many rural southerners, rather than a set of legal statutes, jus-
> tice remained a matter of societal norms allowing for respect of
> property rights, individual honor, and a maximum of personal
> independence. Any violation of this pattern amounted to a
> breach of justice requiring a specific response from the injured
> party. Upon learning that a youthful neighbor had approached
> his wife in an overly friendly manner, Robert Leard of Tangipa-
> hoa, Louisiana, promptly tracked the young man down and killed
> him. Under the piney-woods code of justice, anything less would
> have invited shame and ridicule upon the Leard family.[34]

"Intensity of personal pride" was connected by Olmsted with
the "fiend-like street fights of the South."[35] He mentioned an
episode of public murder with impunity:

> A gentleman of veracity, now living in the South, told me that
> among his friends he had once numbered two young men, who
> were themselves intimate friends, till one of them, taking
> offence at some foolish words uttered by the other, challenges
> him. A large crowd assembled to see the duel, which took place
> on a piece of prairie ground. The combatants came armed with
> rifles, and at the first interchange of shots, the challenged man
> fell disabled by a ball in the thigh. The other, throwing down his
> rifle, walked toward him, and kneeling by his side, drew a bowie
> knife, and deliberately butchered him. The crowd of bystanders
> not only permitted this, but the execrable assassin still lives in
> the community, has since married, and, as far as my informant
> could judge, his social position has been rather advanced then
> otherwise, from thus dealing with his enemy.[36]

Again, what is important here is not the isolated incident itself but the set of social attitudes which allowed such incidents to take place publicly with impunity, the killer knowing in advance that what he was doing had community approval. Moreover, such attitudes went back for centuries, on both sides of the Atlantic, at least among the particular people concerned.

During the era when dueling became a pattern among upper-class Americans—between the Revolutionary War and the Civil War—it was particularly prevalent in the South. As a social history of the United States noted: "Of Southern statesmen who rose to prominence after 1790, hardly one can be mentioned who was not involved in a duel."[37] Editors of Southern newspapers became involved in duels so often that cartoonists depicted them with a pen in one hand and a dueling pistol in the other.[38] Most duels arose not over substantive issues but over words considered insulting.[39] At lower social levels, Southern feuds such as that between the Hatfields and the McCoys—which began in a dispute over a pig and ultimately claimed more than 20 lives[40]—became legendary.

It has been estimated that, while at least three-quarters of the settlers in colonial New England originated in the lowland southeastern half of Britain, a similarly large proportion of the population of the South originated in the Scottish highlands, Ireland, Wales, or the northern and western uplands of England.[41] Those arriving from Ireland in colonial times would have been from Ulster County, where Scots and Englishmen settled, since substantial immigration of the indigenous Irish did not begin until near the middle of the nineteenth century. Radically different cultures could develop and persist during this era before transportation and communication developed to the point of promoting widespread interactions among people in different regions.

In colonial America, the people of the English borderlands and of the "Celtic fringe" were seen by contemporaries as culturally quite distinct, and were socially unwelcome. Mob action prevented a shipload of Ulster Scots from landing in Boston in 1719[42] and the Quaker leaders of eastern Pennsylvania encouraged Ulster Scots to settle out in western Pennsylvania,[43] where they acted as a buffer to the Indians, as well as being a constant source of friction and conflict with the Indians. It was not just in the North that crackers and rednecks were considered to be undesirables. Southern plantation owners with poor whites living on adjoining land would often offer to buy their land for more than it was worth, in order to be rid of such neighbors.[44]

Because there were no racial differences to form separate statistical categories for these north Britons and for other whites who settled in the South or in particular enclaves elsewhere, indirect indicators must serve as proxies for these cultural differences. Names are among these indicators. Edward, for example, was a popular name in Virginia and in Wessex, England, from which many Virginians had emigrated, but the first forty classes of undergraduates at Harvard College contained only one man named Edward. It would be nearly two centuries before Harvard enrolled anyone named Patrick, even though that was a common name in western Pennsylvania, where the Ulster Scots settled.[45] This says something not only about the social and geographic differences of the times, but also about how regionalized the naming patterns were then, in contrast to the fact that no one today finds it particularly strange when an Asian American has such non-Asian first names as Kevin or Michelle.

Even where there was no conflict or hostility involved, Southerners often showed a reckless disregard for human life, including their own. For example, the racing of steamboats that happened to encounter each other on the rivers of the South often ended with exploding boilers, especially when the excited competition led to the tying down of safety valves, in order to build up more pressure to generate more speed.[46] An impromptu race between steamboats that encountered each other on the Mississippi illustrates the pattern:

> On board one boat "was an old lady, who, having bought a winter stock of bacon, pork, &c., was returning to her home on the banks of the Mississippi. Fun lovers on board both boats insisted upon a race; cheers and drawn pistols obliged the captains to cooperate. As the boats struggled to outdistance each other, excited passengers demanded more speed. Despite every effort, the boats raced evenly until the old lady directed her slaves to

throw all her casks of bacon into the boilers. Her boat then moved ahead of the other vessel, which suddenly exploded: "clouds of splinters and human limbs darken[ed] the sky." On the undamaged boat passengers shouted their victory. But above their cheers could "be heard the shrill voice of the old lady, crying, 'I did it, I did it—it's all my bacon!' "[47]

On the Mississippi and other "western" rivers of the United States as it existed in the early nineteenth century, it has been estimated that 30 percent of all the steamboats were lost in accidents. Part of this may have been due to deficiencies in the early steamboats themselves but much of it was due to the recklessness with which they were operated on Southern rivers. The comments of a fireman on a Mississippi steamboat of that era may suggest why a river voyage was considered more dangerous than crossing the Atlantic—at a time when sinkings in the Atlantic were by no means rare:

"Talk about *Northern* steamers," the fireman of a Mississippi steamboat sneered to an eastern traveler in 1844, "it don't need no spunk to navigate them waters. You haint bust a biler in five years. But I tell you, stranger, it takes a man to ride one of these half alligator boats, head on a snag, high pressures, valve soldered down, 600 souls on board & in danger of going to the devil."[48]

This was not mere idle talk. Among the steamboat explosions in the South, one on the Mississippi in 1838 killed well over a hundred people, and another near Baton Rouge in 1859 killed more than half of the 400 people on board and badly injured more than half the survivors.[49] Southerners were just as reckless on land, whether in escapades undertaken for the excitement of the moment or in the many fights and deaths resulting from some insult or slight among people "touchy about their honor and dignity."[50] Again, all of this went back to a way of life in the turbulent regions of Britain from which white Southerners came.[51] Nor is it hard to recognize in these attitudes clear parallels to the behavior and attitudes of ghetto gangs today, who kill over a look or a word, or any action that can be construed as "dissing" them.

Pride had yet another side to it. Among the definitions of a "cracker" in the Oxford dictionary is a "braggart"[52]—one who "talks trash" in today's vernacular—a wise*cracker.* More than mere wisecracks were involved, however. The pattern is one said by Professor McWhiney to go back to descriptions of ancient Celts as "boasters and threateners, and given to bombastic self-dramatisation."[53] Examples today come readily to mind, not only from ghetto life and gangsta rap, but also from militant black "leaders," spokesmen or activists. What is painfully ironic is that such attitudes and behavior are projected today as aspects of a distinctive "black identity," when in fact they are part of a centuries-old pattern among the whites in whose midst generations of blacks lived in the South.

Any broad-brush discussion of cultural patterns must, of course, not claim that all people—whether white or black—had the same culture, much less to the same degree. There are not only changes over time, there are cross-currents at a given time. Nevertheless, it is useful to see the outlines of a general pattern, even when that pattern erodes over time and at varying rates among different subgroups.

The violence for which white Southerners became most lastingly notorious was lynching. Like other aspects of the redneck and cracker culture, it has often been attributed to race or slavery. In fact, however, most lynching victims in the antebellum South were white.[54] Economic considerations alone would prevent a slaveowner from lynching his own slave or tolerating anyone else's doing so. It was only after the Civil War that the emancipated blacks became the principal targets of lynching. But, by then, Southern vigilante violence had been a tradition for more than a century in North America[55] and even longer back in the regions of Britain from which crackers and rednecks came, where "retributive justice" was often left in private hands.[56] Even the burning cross of the Ku Klux Klan has been traced back to "the fiery cross of old Scotland" used by feuding clans.[57]

Economic Activity

Observers of the white population of the antebellum South often commented not only on their poverty but also on their lack of industriousness or entrepreneurship. A contemporary characterized many white Southerners as "too poor to keep slaves and too proud to work."[58] A landmark history of agriculture in the antebellum South described the poor whites this way:

They cultivated in a casual and careless fashion small patches of corn or rice, sweet potatoes, cowpeas, and garden products. Women and children did a large part of the work.The men spent their time principally in hunting or idleness....The men were inveterate drunkards and sometimes the women joined them in drinking inferior whisky. Licentiousness was prevalent among them....Among their equals, the men were quarrelsome and inclined to crimes of violence....The poor whites were densely ignorant.[59]

Their labors tended to be intermittent—often when they were pressed for money, rather than a steady employment career.[60] Frederick Law Olmsted called it "lazy poverty," with whatever work they did being done in a "thoughtless manner."[61] Summarizing his observations in the antebellum South, Olmsted said:

...I know that while men seldom want an abundance of coarse food in the Cotton States, the proportion of the free white men who live as well in any aspect as our working classes in the North, on an average, is small, and that the citizens of the cotton States, as a whole, are poor.They work little, and that little, badly; they earn little; they sell little; they buy little, and they have little—very little—of the common comforts and consolations of civilized life.Their destitution is not material only; it is intellectual and it is moral.[62]

When Olmsted found work done efficiently, promptly, and well during his travels through the South—when he found well-run businesses, good libraries, impressive churches, and efficiently functioning institutions in general—he almost invariably found them to be run by Northerners, foreigners, or Jews.[63] Nor was he the only visiting observer to reach such conclusions. Another observed that "nearly all of the Old South's successful storekeepers were either Yankees or Yankee-trained Southerners."A French visitor said that, when you saw a plantation in better condition than others, you would often discover that it was owned by someone from the North.[64] A history of Southern agriculture presented this picture of North Carolina in the early eighteenth century:

Many of the inhabitants were rough borderers who lived a crude, half savage existence. Some were herdsmen, dependent mainly on the product of the range and "under the necessity of eating meat without bread." There were also many thriftless and lazy families who had been attracted to the country by the mild climate and the ease with which a bare livelihood could be obtained by hunting and fishing, raising a little corn, and keeping a few head of swine and possibly a cow or two on the range. On the other hand, there were small farmers, many of Northern or European extraction, living industrious and thrifty lives amidst a rude abundance and considerable diversity of food supplies. They maintained good-sized herds of cattle, swine, and sheep, and the women made butter and cheese.[65]

"Borderers" at that point would refer to people from the borderlands of Britain, those included in what Professor McWhiney and others have called the "Celtic fringe" and what Professor Fischer called "north Britons." While the making of butter and cheese might seem to be an unremarkable activity in most rural communities, butter- and cheese-making by these farmers of non-Southerner origins was in fact exceptional in the South. One of Frederick Law Olmsted's complaints during his travels through the antebellum South was the scarcity of butter, despite all the cows he saw.[66] Even among plantation owners, he said, "as for butter, some have heard of it, some have seen it, but few have eaten it."[67] Hard data support his conclusions about the scarcity of butter in the antebellum South, despite an abundance of cows. In 1860, the South had 40 percent of all the dairy cows in the country but produced just 20 percent of the butter and only one percent of the cheese.[68] As a study of antebellum Southern agriculture noted, "attempts to stimulate greater attention to commercial production were futile" and even the bluegrass regions "imported a large proportion of the cheese consumed." The study concluded:

> In short, while the South abounded in cattle, the reported production of dairy products was very small. A table based on census statistics shows that some of the Southern States, such as Texas and Florida, had far more cattle per capita than important dairy states like Vermont and New York, and in most of the Southern States cattle per capita were nearly or quite as numerous as in the Northern States. Yet the production of butter and cheese per capita in most of the Southern States was insignifi-

cant as compared with per capita production in the principal Northeastern States.[69]

A speaker before an agricultural society in Orange County, North Carolina, said: "It is a reproach to us as farmers, and no little deduction from our wealth, that we suffer the population of our towns and villages to supply themselves with butter from another Orange County in New York."[70] In colonial times, butter was imported from as far away as Ireland. Where butter was not imported, it was often produced locally by people of non-Southern origins. As a scholarly history of Southern agriculture reported:

> In 1858 the dairies producing whole milk for the city of Louisville, Kentucky, were described as "probably as well conducted as any in the country," but almost without exception managed by Swiss or German operatives.[71]

Meanwhile, a newspaper in South Carolina said in 1857: "Good butter is indeed a luxury to almost every planter in the Southern country, and there is, perhaps, no one article of food that is more eagerly sought after."[72] In antebellum Virginia, a Richmond newspaper likewise complained of the scarcity of good butter, saying that the quality of butter available in the local market "would hardly be thought good enough to grease a cart-wheel." When considering legislation to try to remedy the situation, a member of the Virginia legislature attributed the poor quality of that state's butter to the carelessness with which Virginia farmers prepared it.[73]

One reason for the contrast between the abundance of butter and cheese produced by German farmers in states like Wisconsin, for example, and the scarcity of butter and cheese in the South was that German farmers, wherever they were located, tended to build fences and huge barns for their livestock, and to feed them there during the winter. Southerners more often let their cows and hogs roam freely during the winter, even though this meant that "in the spring they turned up half starved and it took the summer for them to put on normal weight."[74] This too was a continuation of patterns found among their ancestors in the British Isles,[75] and was part of a more general pattern of carelessness:

Many other observers noticed the broken fences and the stunted cattle running at large, unfed and unprotected. Their manure was put to no use. Artificial pasture long remained a rarity, and few farmers stored feed for the winter. In Virginia a French traveler of the late 17th century saw "poor beasts of a morning all covered with snow and trembling with the cold, but no forage was provided for them. They eat the bark of the trees because the grass was covered." Wild animals—wolves, bears, and savage dogs—attacked the helpless cattle, and made the raising of sheep difficult.[76]

Germans were better able than Southerners to milk their cows regularly and prepare dairy products, while cows owned by Southerners were more likely to run dry after calves were weaned. A contemporary observer said that even Southern farmers with many cows "will not give themselves the trouble of milking more than will maintain their Family."[77] As late as the 1930s, a scholar studying the geography and economy of the South wrote: "The close attention to duty, the habits of steady skillful routine accepted by butter fat producers of Wisconsin as a matter of fact, are traits not yet present in southern culture."[78] At that point, the Southern states, with 26 percent of the country's dairy cows, produced just 7 percent of processed dairy products such as butter, cheese, ice cream and condensed milk.[79]

There was a similar contrast between German farmers and Southern farmers when it came to clearing land for farming back in pioneering days. Germans cleared frontier land by both chopping down trees and laboriously removing their stumps and roots, so that all the land could be plowed thereafter. Southerners more often cut down the tree, or even simply girdled it and left it to die and rot, but in any case leaving the stump in the ground and plowing around it.[80] Although the erosion-prone soils of the Southern uplands have been blamed for the poverty of the whites living on them, nevertheless on that same land Germans "were able to cultivate the hill soil, so as to avoid erosion and were willing to expend upon it the additional labor which its topography required" so that these soils in their hands "yielded excellent regular returns."[81]

Comments on the lack of enterprise by Southern whites were made by numerous observers in various parts of the South.

In Alexis de Tocqueville's classic *Democracy in America,* he contrasted the attitudes toward work among Southern and Northern whites as being so great as to be visible to the casual observer sailing down the Ohio River and comparing the Ohio side with the Kentucky side.[82] These were not just the prejudices of outsiders. "No southern man," South Carolina's famed Senator John C. Calhoun said, "not even the poorest or the lowest, will, under any circumstances…perform menial labor…. He has too much pride for that." General Robert E. Lee likewise declared: "Our people are opposed to work. Our troops officers community & press. All ridicule & resist it."[83] "Many whites," according to a leading Southern historian, "were disposed to leave good enough alone and put off changes till the morrow."[84]

Very similar kinds of comments were made about these Southerners' ancestors in the parts of the British Isles from which they came.[85] Although the term "lazy" appears frequently in comments on these people on both sides of the Atlantic, there has been no evidence of any such aversion on their part to strenuous physical activity in dancing, fighting, hunting and other recreational activities, so sloth was not the real issue. Nor have rednecks or crackers been prominent in such less physically demanding activities as entrepreneurship or scholarship. It is the nature of the particular activities in which they have taken an active interest and on which they have expended their energies, rather than the physical demands of those activities, that seems to have been crucial.

Not only did many of the groups who settled in the South disdain business as a career, as their ancestors had in those parts of Britain from which they came, they typically lacked the kinds of habits necessary to be successful in business. Among the habits needed to run a business, none is more basic than a steady application to the tasks at hand, doing things in a "business-like" way. But those relatively few Southerners who did run businesses often displayed no such business-like attitudes.

Even when there was business to transact, Southerners would often stop to go watch a cockfight or a parade, or visit a saloon or go hunting.[86] "In traveling in the South," a Northern visitor commented in the 1850s, "you become astonished at the little

attention men pay to their business."[87] Such views were not confined to Northerners, however, nor to urban businesses. According
to a noted history of the antebellum South, the Richmond
Enquirer "attributed the success of Northern farmers where
Southerners had failed to the social nature of the latter, which led
them to gather around the courthouse and country stores to
smoke, chew, talk politics, and, in general, to waste time."[88] Many
Southern businessmen were unreliable about either paying their
bills or delivering goods and services when promised.[89]

Among Southerners in general, their improvident spending,
and the indebtedness to which it often led, was widely commented on in the United States and in the places from which their
ancestors came in Britain.[90] Even large Southern plantation owners
with lavish lifestyles were often deeply in debt. Among the Virginia
gentry, "extravagant and even ruinous bets on horses" were common, according to a scholarly study.[91]

Nor were Southerners alert to profitable investment
prospects, according to observers in the antebellum South. For
example, although there were large coal deposits and "a beautiful
quality of marble" near Tuscaloosa, Alabama, the people there
bought coal from Philadelphia, and marble for tombstones was
imported from Italy.[92] In antebellum Virginia, as well, Olmsted
observed "the natural resources of the land were strangely unused,
or were used with poor economy."[93] Nor was he alone in that conclusion. A twentieth century scholar also commented on the coal
available in Alabama:

> The Alabama iron district is one of the cheapest, if not the
> cheapest, iron district in the entire world. It possesses a phe-
> nomenal natural equipment. Jutting out of the hillsides that
> flank one side of the broad open valley are thick deposits of iron
> ore. On the other side of the valley are the coal mines and coke
> ovens, and the limestone is at hand. Instead of carrying ore a
> thousand miles, as at Pittsburgh and the English furnaces, or fuel
> 600 miles as at Lake Champlain, the raw materials for these
> Southern furnaces are shifted across the valley by switching
> engines, and the local supply of cheap black labor helps to give
> a wonderfully low cost.[94]

Yet it was more than 20 years after the Civil War before Birmingham became an iron and steel production center. As for the reasons for the belated development of such a promising combination of natural resources:

> In spite of the favors of geography, the iron and steel industry in the South was slow in its beginnings and development. Like everything southern, the industry was retarded by lack of capital and technical skill.[95]

Capital was available from outside the South, or indeed from outside the country, as foreign capital was used to finance the building of the Pennsylvania Railroad and the Illinois Central during the same era. But the other factors had to be there to create a promising prospect of profitability that would attract investment. The difficulties of developing those other factors in Alabama was shown by the fact that in 1888 "Birmingham saw its first ton of steel run through the furnaces of the Henderson Steel Company and burn out the crude furnace linings in the process."[96]

Early explorers and settlers in the antebellum South "wrote in glowing terms of the wild fruits, especially the wild grapes of unusual size which excited extravagant hopes of the development of wine industries."[97] Yet early attempts to find a market for Southern wine in Britain were ruined by the fact that a sample of wine that was sent across the Atlantic spoiled in the musty casks in which Southerners had carelessly shipped it.[98] Later efforts to establish a wine industry in the South were undertaken by foreigners—French, German, and Portuguese. A German settlement in Missouri created a wine industry with an annual output of about 100,000 gallons.[99] But the South as a whole produced less than one-fifth of the wine in the United States in 1849[100]—and this was long before the development of the California wine industry.

As late as the beginning of the twentieth century, there were still laments about the opportunities in the South missed by Southerners and put to use by outsiders with different patterns of behavior. Landowners in Alabama were said to have "cheated themselves out of millions of dollars by failing to see the opportunities within their grasp" which "lumbermen from the North and East" seized by cutting trees and shipping the lumber around the world. Some Southerners along the Gulf coast likewise spoke of "the golden opportunities which they failed to grasp, of the numerous successes of Northern and Eastern men and lamented the passing of the old school of gentlemen, the midday mint juleps, and the easy-going business methods." Some of these Southerners, however, seemed to prosper "working shoulder to shoulder with the Yankees."[101]

Not only in the South, but in the communities from which white Southerners had come in the Scottish highlands, in Ulster, and in Wales of an earlier era, most of the successful businessmen were outsiders.[102] Even the poorest highland Scots would not skin their horses when they died. Instead, "Scots sold their dead horses for three pence to English soldiers who in turn got six pence for the skinned carcass and another two shillings for the hide."[103] This was not due to a lack of knowledge of skinning. In earlier times, when Scotland and England were at war, one of the atrocities committed by the Scots was skinning captured English officers alive.[104] During the sixteenth century border feuds, the "Johnston-Johnson clan adorned their houses with the flayed skins of their enemies the Maxwells."[105] It was not the skill that was lacking, but the enterprise.

Contemporary observers commented on another peculiarity of antebellum Southerners—fording rivers and streams, instead of building bridges over them. Nor was this due simply to poverty. A biography of famed nineteenth-century congressman John Randolph of Virginia referred to the "bridgeless streams" in the area where elite families like his lived.[106] Thomas Jefferson noted that he had to cross eight rivers between Monticello and Washington, "five of which had neither bridges nor boats."[107] This peculiarity was noted in other parts of the South and by observers in those parts of Britain from which Southerners came:

> Commenting on just how lazy Southerners were, one man noted that "no Northern farmer" would neglect to build a bridge over a stream that crossed his property; indeed, two "live Yankees" would complete the work in a single day, but "the Southern planter will ford the creek lying between his house & stable a whole lifetime." The same complaint was made about Highland Scots, whose roads were equally bad as those of Ireland and the Old South. In the 1790s a minister, noting that fords rather than

bridges crossed streams on one of the most heavily traveled road in the Highlands, wrote:"From a desire to save labour or time, the ford is often attempted, when the...river [is] too high, and the consequence is frequently fatal."[108]

Again, it is necessary to emphasize that the culture which Southerners brought over from the parts of Britain from which they came changed in Britain in the years after they left. But all this happened after the ancestors of rednecks and crackers had immigrated to the American South from the outer regions of British society, rather than from central England.

Intellectual Activity

Given the historical background of crackers and rednecks in Britain, it could hardly be expected that intellectual activity would be a major interest of theirs in the United States. A study of 18,000 county records from seventeenth-century colonial Virginia showed that nearly half of all the white male Virginians "were so illiterate that they could not sign their names" and simply made a mark on legal documents. While the small Virginia aristocracy were often well educated and had impressive collections of books in their homes, these books were typically imported from England rather than purchased from local bookstores. Thomas Jefferson complained that the area where he lived was "without a single bookstore."[109] As late as the census of 1850, more than one-fifth of Southern whites were still illiterate, compared to less than one percent of New Englanders.[110]

In the Southern backcountry, levels of schooling "were lower here than in any other part of the United States," according to a landmark historical study, and "there were no institutions comparable to New England's town schools."[111] Although the white population of the South was only one-half as large as that of the North, the total number of illiterate whites in the South in 1850 was larger than the total number of illiterates in the North. In the antebellum era, the total circulation of Northern newspapers was more than four times the total circulation of Southern newspapers.[112] Moreover, many editors of Southern newspapers were themselves from the North.[113] The North had four times as many schools, attended by more than four times as many pupils.[114] Children in Massachusetts spent more than twice as many years in school as children in Virginia.[115]

When it came to inventions, only 8 percent of the patents issued in 1852 went to residents of the Southern states, whose white population was approximately one-third of the white population of the country. Even in agriculture, the main economic activity of the region, only 9 out of 62 patents for agricultural implements went to Southerners.[116] The cotton gin, perhaps the most crucial invention for the antebellum South, was invented by a Northerner.

A Southerner said to Frederick Law Olmsted: "The fact is, sir, the people here are not like you northern people; they don't reason out everything so."[117] Olmsted himself likewise concluded from his travels in the antebellum South that Southerners were "greatly disinclined to exact and careful reasoning."[118] As late as the First World War, white soldiers from Georgia, Arkansas, Kentucky, and Mississippi scored lower on mental tests than black soldiers from Ohio, Illinois, New York, and Pennsylvania.[119] At higher levels of achievement, the contrast between the South and other regions was even more stark. A study of leading American figures in the arts and sciences in the first half of the nineteenth century found most clustered in the Northeast, while vast regions of the South—Virginia alone excepted—were without a single one.[120]

The kinds of statistical disparities found between Southern whites and Northern whites in the past are today often taken as evidence or proof of racial discrimination when such disparities are found between the black and white populations of the country as a whole, while others have taken such disparities as signs of genetic deficiencies. Yet clearly neither racial discrimination nor racial inferiority can explain similar differences between whites in the North and the South in earlier centuries.[121] This should at least raise questions about such explanations when applied to blacks of a later era who inherited the culture of white Southerners.

Sexual Activity

Southern whites were as different from Northern whites when it came to sexual patterns as they were in other ways. Widespread casual sex was commented on by outside observers in both the American South and in those parts of Britain from which Southerners had come.[122] Here again, the greatest contrast is with New England. While pregnant brides were very rare in seventeenth-century New England,[123] they were more common in the Southern backcountry than anywhere else in the United States. A missionary estimated that more than nine-tenths of the backcountry women at whose weddings he officiated were already pregnant. In this, as in other respects, the "sexual customs of the southern backcountry were similar to those of northwestern England."[124] Meanwhile, the region of England from which New Englanders came "had the lowest rates of illegitimacy in England," just as their descendants had the lowest rates of illegitimacy in the United States.[125]

Women dressed more revealingly in the South and both sexes spoke more freely about sex than was common in New England. In the seventeenth century, "most Virginia girls found a husband by the age of seventeen," while in Massachusetts, the average age at which women married was twenty-three.[126] In that era, fornication and rape were acts severely punished in New England. Rape was a hanging offense in New England, while in the Chesapeake Bay colonies it was sometimes punished less severely than petty theft.[127]

As with other North-South differences, differences in sexual behavior have often been attributed to the existence of slavery in the South—due, in this case, to the opportunities which this presented for sexual exploitation of slave women. But, again, history shows the same patterns among the same people and their ancestors in Britain, before they had ever seen a black woman. In colonial Virginia as well, the sexual exploitation of white indentured servant girls was common before the slave population had grown large enough for white servant girls to be replaced by black women.[128]

Religion

Religious denominations, practices, and churches differed as between the crackers and rednecks of the South and those of the white population in the rest of the country. As in other things, the greatest contrast was with the role of religion in New England. This did not mean that there was uniformity across the South, for the Virginia elite tended to be Anglicans and there were also Quakers in the South, for example, but most Southerners were either Baptists or Methodists. Those Northerners or foreigners who visited the South found the style and manner of religion among most white Southerners distinct—and distasteful. These visitors "viewed with contempt people who whooped and hollered, chewed and spit tobacco in church."[129] Many Southern religious gatherings were not held in churches but at outdoor "camp meetings"—a style that went back to practices of these Southerners' ancestors in Britain.[130] So too did the oratorical style of Southern preachers and the behavior of their congregations, whether in churches or outdoors.

Frederick Law Olmsted's description of a typical preacher in the antebellum South noted that "the speaker nearly all the time cried aloud at the utmost stretch of his voice, as if calling to some one a long distance off," that "he was gifted with a strong imagination, and possessed of a good deal of dramatic power," that he "had the habit of frequently repeating a phrase," and that he exhibited "a dramatic talent" that included "leaning far over the desk, with his arms stretched forward, gesticulating violently, yelling at the highest key, and catching his breath with an effort."[131] Similar scenes were described a century earlier in Virginia and at a camp meeting in Scotland, where the preacher was "sweating, bawling, jumping and beating the desk."[132]

This melodramatic and emotional oratorical style could still be seen in twentieth-century America, not only in religious services but also in politics, both among white Southern politicians of the Jim Crow era and among black leaders of the civil rights movement in the South and community activists in the Northern ghettos.

By contrast, religious services in colonial Massachusetts developed what has been called the "meeting and lecture" approach, where the "style of preaching was a relentless cultivation of the plain style." These "addresses tended to be closely argued statements of great density, in which Puritans reasoned as relentlessly with their maker as they did with one another."[133] This intellectual approach to religion carried over into their daily lives:

Even more than most people in their time, they searched constantly for clues to God's purposes in the world. It was this impulse which led so many English Puritans to study nature with that extraordinary intensity which played a central part in the birth of modern science.[134]

There was a dark side to this intensity as well. The vast majority of the persecutions and executions of women for witchcraft occurred in New England.[135] Quakers did not have the persecuting intolerance of the Puritans but they too had plain-spoken religious meetings, also in contrast to melodramatic services among the rednecks and crackers of the South. The Anglican services were likewise less emotional and dramatic, but Anglicanism in the South was largely confined to the Tidewater region.[136] Catholics too had a quieter service, though more formal than the Quakers, but there was little Catholicism in the South, where even Irish immigrants tended to become absorbed into the Protestant religions, just as the Scots tended to become absorbed into Southern fundamentalist religions. The South was a region lacking the prerequisites for maintaining an educated clergy, as required by both Presbyterians and Catholics. Anyone familiar with religious practices among black Americans today will recognize the clear imprint of the white Southern pattern.

It was not just the Southern preachers who behaved differently from their counterparts in other parts of the country. So did the congregations. While many of those listening to hellfire-and-damnation sermons were moved to extreme emotional reactions of fear, confession, and repentance, many others took these sermons as dramatic performances or spectacles, and the young women and men often treated these religious gatherings as occasions for socializing and preludes to romantic encounters later.[137] This pattern too went back to earlier centuries in Scotland where, while some at the camp meetings were "groaning, sighing and weeping" for their sins, there was usually also "a knot of young fellows and girls making assignations to go home together in the evening, or to meet in some ale-house."[138]

While the keeping of the Sabbath as a day free of worldly activities and amusements was a common practice in many parts of the United States in centuries past, that was not the practice among the rednecks and crackers of the antebellum South. Southerners "had fun on Sundays," to the consternation of Northern observers:

> "One of the strangest sights to a New England man, on visiting Southern states, is the desecration of the Sabbath," wrote a Yankee. " In some of the cities, especially if a good number of the business men are from the North, the churches are tolerably well attended, — there being but one sermon for the day. But even here the afternoon and evening are much devoted to amusements." Another Northerner declared that in the south "there is no Sabbath ... they work, run, swear, and drink here on Sundays just as they do on any other day of the week."[139]

Many Southerners did not go to church at all, or did so intermittently, or when not distracted by other activities.[140] Again, this was a pattern found among their ancestors in Britain.[141] Among the reasons given by contemporaries for low church-attendance among Southerners was that they often got drunk on Saturday night and were in no condition to go to church on Sunday morning.[142]

BLACK REDNECKS

Much of the cultural pattern of Southern rednecks became the cultural heritage of Southern blacks, more so than survivals of African cultures, with which they had not been in contact for centuries. (Even in colonial times, most blacks on American soil had been born on American soil.) Moreover, such cultural traits followed blacks out of the Southern countrysides and into the urban ghettos— North and South—where many settled. The very way of talking, later to be christened "black English," closely followed dialects brought over from those parts of Britain from which many white Southerners came, though these speech patterns died out in Britain while surviving in the American South,[143] as such speech patterns would later die out among most Southern whites and among middle-class blacks, while surviving in the poorer black ghettos around the country. For example:

> Where a northerner said, "I am," "You are," "She isn't," "It doesn't," and "I haven't," a Virginian even of high rank preferred to say

"I be," "You be," "She ain't," "It don't," and "I hain't." ...These Virginia speechways were not invented in America.They derived from a family or regional dialects that had been spoken throughout the south and west of England during the seventeenth century.[144]

From these same regions of England came such words as "yaller for "yellow," "ax" for ask, "acrost" for "across," "y'awl" for "you," "bile" for "boil," "do' " for "door," "dis" for "this" and "dat" for "that."[145] Many of these usages have long since died out in England, though the word "chittlins" for hog entrails continued to be used in some localities in England, even in the twentieth century,[146] as such usage remained common among black Americans. But no such words came from Africa. Nor did the holiday Kwaanza, which originated in Los Angeles.The slaves' custom of marking their marriages by jumping over a broomstick—a custom resurrected at a posh wedding among blacks in twentieth-century New York, as a mark of racial identity[147]—was in fact a pagan custom in Europe in centuries past and survived for a time among Southern whites.[148]

Complaints about the improvidence of whites in the South, and of their ancestors in Britain before that, were echoed in W. E. B. Du Bois' picture of his fellow blacks in the 1890s:

> Probably few poor nations waste more money by thoughtless and unreasonable expenditure than the American Negro, and especially those living in large cities.Thousands of dollars are annually wasted...in amusements of various kinds, and in miscellaneous ornaments and gewgaws....The Negro has much to learn of the Jew and the Italian, as to living within his means and saving every penny from excessive and wasteful expenditures.[149]

It was not, however, from Jews or Italians that blacks had absorbed their culture. Du Bois' description of the spending habits of blacks in the 1890s was echoed by a contemporary observer, Jacob Riis, who said that the Negro "loves fine clothes and good living a good deal more than he does a bank account."[150] Similar observations have been made by many others over the years, inside and outside the black community.

For the lower socioeconomic classes among blacks, Gunnar

Myrdal's descriptions of them near the middle of the twentieth century still bore a remarkable resemblance to descriptions of Southern whites and their regional forebears in Britain, including "less resourcefulness,""disorganized" family life,"lax" sexual morals, and "recklessness," with tendencies toward aggression and violence.[151] Despite a generally sympathetic approach to the study of blacks in his landmark book *An American Dilemma,* which has often been credited with a major influence on the advancement of civil rights, Myrdal also noted the "low standards of efficiency, reliability, ambition, and morals actually displayed by the average Negro."[152] He observed "something of the 'devil-may-care' attitude in the pleasure-seeking of Negroes" and a general attitude in which "life becomes cheap and crime not so reprehensible."[153]

Like other observers, Myrdal tended to attribute to slavery such aspects of black culture as "the low regard for human life," when in fact antebellum whites had exhibited this same reckless disregard of lethal dangers and so had their ancestors in Britain. Unlike many others, however, Myrdal also recognized the influence of the Southern white culture on the culture of blacks, pointing out that "the general Southern pattern of illegality maintained this low regard for human life."[154] He also noted that "the so-called 'Negro dialect' is simply a variation on the ordinary Southern accent,"[155] that religious "emotionalism was borrowed from and sanctioned by religious behavior among whites"[156] in the South, and that the "Negro trait of audaciousness is characteristic of white Southerners too." He quoted black scholar (and, later, statesman) Ralph Bunche:"White Southerners employ many of the defense mechanisms characteristic of the Negro. They often carry a 'chip on the shoulder'; they indulge freely in self-commiseration, they rather typically and in real Negro fashion try to overcome a feeling of inferiority by exhibitionism, raucousness in dress, and exaggerated self-assertion."[157]

Although Dr. Bunche presented these as parallels, historically it was of course the Southern whites who first had these patterns, reflecting patterns among their ancestors in Britain. In much of the literature on black culture, however, the supposed influence of slavery has been far more sweepingly assumed and the cultural influence of white Southerners and their forebears in Britain largely ignored. Attempts to derive the black manner of speaking from slavery and its parallel among whites as an influence from black speech were answered by a Southern historian who asked, "from whence came the drawl of the people of the upper Great Plains and of the Blue Ridge, Smoky, and Cumberland Mountains, who have had little or no contact with the Negro?"[158] Another cultural historian of Southerners aptly observed that "southerners white and black share the bonds of a common heritage, indeed a common tragedy, and often speak a common language, however seldom they may acknowledge it."[159]

Half a century after Myrdal, another study of racial attitudes noted "the intimidating ethnic style of many underclass black males,"[160] and noted that nearly half of all murder victims in America were black, and that 94 percent of them were killed by other blacks.[161] Many of these killings were due to gang members who killed for such reasons as "Cause he look at me funny," "Cause he give me no respect,"[162] and other reasons reminiscent of the touchy pride and hair-trigger violence of rednecks and crackers in an earlier era.

The neglect and disdain of education found among antebellum white Southerners has been echoed not only in low performance levels among ghetto blacks but perhaps most dramatically in a hostility toward those black students who are conscientious about their studies, who are accused of "acting white"—a charge that can bring anything from social ostracism to outright violence.[163] So much attention has been paid to questions of ability that few have looked at cultural attitudes. One of those who has is black professor and best-selling author Shelby Steele, who "sees in many of these children almost a determination not to learn," even though, once outside the school and in their own neighborhoods, "these same children learn everything."[164] He drew on his own experiences teaching at a university:

> For some years I have noticed that I can walk into any of my classes on the first day of the semester, identify the black students, and be sadly confident that on the last day of the semester a disproportionate number of them will be at the bottom of the class, far behind any number of white students of equal or even lesser ability.[165]

Statistical data substantiate these impressions. Black students typically perform academically below the level of those white students *with the same mental test scores,*[166] in contrast to Asian American students, who perform better than white students with the same test scores as themselves.[167] In short, even though black students average lower test scores than either white or Asian American students, those test scores are not necessarily the sole, nor perhaps even the predominant, reason for lower black academic achievement. Indeed, it is possible that the lower test scores may be a *result* of cultural attitudes—and of actions or inactions over a period of years, based on those attitudes—more so than a *cause* of academic failures.

While it has long been known that, historically, the average IQ of blacks has been about 85, compared to a national average of 100, what has not been so widely known is that the average IQ of blacks in the North was for years consistently higher than that of blacks in the South.[168] A 1942 study of freshmen at black colleges found:"The superiority of freshmen from northern schools over those from southern schools was found to persist throughout the colleges."[169] As already noted, black soldiers from some Northern states scored higher on mental tests than whites from some Southern states during the First World War. From that same era, European immigrants from cultures where education was not a high priority for ordinary people—parts of Eastern and Southern Europe, for example—scored no higher on mental tests than American blacks[170] and, in some communities, their children scored lower than Northern black children attending the same schools.[171]

The low test scores of some European immigrant children cannot be automatically attributed to their being new to the United States. There have been settled communities of whites with test scores similar to those of blacks, where these have been culturally isolated people such as the inhabitants of the Hebrides Islands off Scotland or people living in Tennessee mountain communities ("hillbillies") or inhabitants of canal boat communities in Britain.[172] In short, some kinds of cultures tend to produce lower mental test scores, whether the people in those cultures are black or white, American or European.[173] As someone has aptly said:"The tests are not unfair. *Life* is unfair and the tests measure the results."

No one chooses which culture to be born into or can be blamed for how that culture evolved in centuries past.

In business-ownership, as in other ways, the pattern among black Americans has followed the pattern of rednecks in earlier times, with people from other groups owning most of the businesses in black neighborhoods. Some may try to explain the lack of locally-owned businesses in the ghettos by racial discrimination or poverty but, as early as the 1920s, there were numerous black-owned businesses in Harlem—the majority of which were owned by blacks from the Caribbean, not blacks from the American South, who were the majority population of Harlem.[174] Although New York was the principal destination of blacks from the Caribbean, then as now, the 1930 census showed that there were more than four times as many native-born blacks in Manhattan as there were foreign-born blacks.[175]

In a parallel to differences between Southern and non-Southern whites, a study of West Indian blacks in the United States noted that "the Negro immigrants, particularly the British West Indians, bring a zest of learning that is not typical of the native-born population."[176] While black Americans have long been over-represented among people in prison, a study of the racial composition of New York State's Sing Sing prison in the early 1930s found that black West Indians were *under*-represented relative to their share of the population, at a time when native-born black Americans were over-represented several-fold among Sing Sing inmates.[177] During that same era, when American-born black women and West Indian black women both worked in New York City's garment district, the latter were "more frequently found at the skilled tasks."[178] More generally, the study found that the black immigrant "brings a cultural heritage that is vastly different from that of the American Negro."[179]

The first black borough presidents of Manhattan were West Indians. As late as 1970, the highest ranking blacks in New York's police department were West Indians, as were all the black federal judges in the city.[180] The 1970 census showed that black West Indian families in the New York metropolitan area had 28 percent higher incomes than the families of American blacks.[181] The incomes of second-generation West Indian families living in the same area exceeded that of black families by 58 percent.[182] Neither race nor racism can explain such differences.[183] Nor can slavery, since native-born blacks and West Indian blacks both had a history of slavery. Studies published in 2004 indicated that an absolute majority of the black alumni of Harvard were either West Indian or African immigrants, or the children of these immigrants. Somewhat similar findings have emerged in studies of some other elite colleges.[184] With blacks as with whites, the redneck culture has been a less achieving culture. Moreover, that culture has affected a higher proportion of the black population than of the white population, since only about one-third of all whites lived in the antebellum South, while nine-tenths of all blacks did.

From the 1960s onward, much of the transplanted Southern culture would—like "black English"—be seen as sacrosanct features of a distinctive black "identity," despite their mirroring very similar cultural patterns among Southern whites in times past. Not all black Americans, of course, retained this anachronistic culture, for the spread of education and the growing experience of the counterproductive effects of the Southern redneck way of life eroded it over time for many blacks, as happened also among the whites who brought this culture over from Britain. Even during the era of slavery, those blacks who were house servants in more educated homes tended to pick up a different culture, giving their descendants enduring advantages over the descendants of field hands.

Contemporary black ghetto culture in the United States is not, however, a simple linear extrapolation from the culture of Southern whites. First of all, most black Americans today are no longer part of the ghetto culture. Moreover, aside from influences peculiar to the circumstances of blacks, profound changes in the larger American society around them have also had an influence, both positive and negative. The burgeoning of the American welfare state in the second half of the twentieth century and the declining effectiveness of the American criminal justice system at the same time allowed borrowed and counterproductive cultural traits to continue and flourish among those blacks who had not yet moved beyond that culture, thereby prolonging the life of a chaotic, counterproductive, dangerous, and self-destructive subculture in many urban ghettos.

Crime and violence were among the features of this subculture that were artificially prolonged. Prior to the 1960s, while black males had a higher murder rate than other males, their murder rate was also *declining* more sharply than the general murder rate. Subsequently, the general murder rate in the United States and the murder rate for black males both reversed and began rising sharply—that of black males more sharply than others.[185] In short, the drastic changes in law enforcement and social morality during the 1960s had particularly adverse effects on the behavior and actions of blacks—and on black victims of the criminals in their midst. Intellectuals have also played a role, along with the welfare state, in prolonging and legitimizing a counterproductive culture among blacks.

Nowhere was the effect of the white liberalism of the 1960s on the social evolution of black culture more devastating than in the disintegration of the black family. The raw facts are these: As of 1960, 51 percent of black females between the ages of 15 and 44 were married and living with their husbands, another 20 percent were divorced, widowed, or separated, and only 28 percent had never been married. Twenty years later, only 31 percent of black women in these age brackets were married and living with their husbands, while 48 percent had never married. By 1994, an absolute majority—56 percent—of black women in these age brackets were never married and only 25 percent were married and living with their husbands.[186] Accordingly, while two-thirds of black children were living with both parents in 1960, only one-third were by 1994.[187] While only 22 percent of black children were born to unmarried women in 1960, 70 percent were by 1994.[188]

White liberals, instead of comparing what has happened to the black family since the liberal welfare state policies of the 1960s were put into practice, compare black families to white families and conclude that the higher rates of broken homes and unwed motherhood among blacks are due to "a legacy of slavery." But why the large-scale disintegration of the black family should have begun a hundred years after slavery is left unexplained. Whatever the situation of the black family relative to the white family, in the past or the present,[189] it is clear that broken homes were far more common among blacks at the end of the twentieth century than they were in the middle of that century or at the beginning of that century[190]—even though blacks at the beginning of the twentieth century were just one generation out of slavery. The widespread and casual abandonment of their children, and of the women who bore them, by black fathers in the ghettos of the late twentieth century was in fact a painfully ironic contrast with what had happened in the immediate aftermath of slavery a hundred years earlier, when observers in the South reported desperate efforts of freed blacks to find family members who had been separated from them during the era of slavery. A contemporary journalist reported meeting black men walking along the roads of Virginia and North Carolina, many of whom had walked across the state—or across more than one state—looking for their families.[191] Others reported similar strenuous and even desperate efforts of newly freed blacks to find members of their families.[192]

New England Enclaves

It should be noted again that not all blacks today are part of the redneck culture—far from it—nor has that culture been the only culture in which blacks lived in the past. There were small but significant enclaves of New England culture introduced into Southern black communities by teachers from New England who poured into the South immediately after the end of the Civil War, to establish schools and to teach and acculturate the children of freed slaves. Often these were the only schools available for black children, because the South was slow to begin establishing public schools, especially for blacks. W. E. B. Du Bois called the work of these dedicated missionaries "the finest thing in American history."[193]

By 1866—just one year after the Civil War ended—there were about 1,400 Northern white teachers from dozens of religious missionary associations teaching black children in 975 Southern schools—the numbers suggesting that these were mostly the kinds of one-room school houses common at the time in rural areas, which is where most Southern blacks lived. Just a few years later, at the end of the decade, there were more than 2,500 Northern teachers in just over 2,000 schools for black children.[194] A sample of about a thousand of these teachers whose origins could be traced showed that more than 500 came directly from New England, and the others are believed to include people born in New England but who came South directly from some other location. To put this in perspective, only 17 percent of the Northern population lived in New England at the time, so this was a wholly disproportionate representation of New Englanders among those who began to educate newly emancipated blacks. This was a New England-led crusade, much like the pre-war abolitionist movement, and many of those who went into the post-bellum South were former abolitionists.[195]

These teachers brought a wholly different culture into the South. In the words of distinguished black scholar E. Franklin Frazier: "The missionaries from New England who founded the first schools for Negroes in the South left the imprint of their Puritan background upon Negro education."[196] In addition to strict morality, these missionaries "taught the Yankee virtues of industry and thrift."[197] This cultural transformation was not incidental. The avowed purpose of the American Missionary Association was to transplant a different culture into the school and college enclaves which they established among young blacks in the South, in order to deliberately supplant the existing culture. These were deeply religious institutions, but in the New England sense, so that black students "were not to indulge in the religious emotionalism of the black masses" in the South. They were to be different in many other ways, as E. Franklin Frazier noted:

> First, students were taught to speak English correctly and thus avoid the ungrammatical speech and dialect of the Negro masses. They were expected to be courteous, speak softly and never exhibit the spontaneous boisterousness of ordinary Negroes.[198]

The casual Southern attitude toward sex was not tolerated: "To be detected in immoral sex behavior, especially if the guilty person was a woman, meant expulsion from the school."[199]

The American Missionary Association was quite explicit in their desire to remove black youngsters from their existing culture and place them in enclaves of the culture transplanted from the North. In an 1882 essay titled "Change of Environment," Dr. W. W.

Patton, president of the A.M.A., lamented that many black children "grow up in communities of prevailing ignorance, superstition and immorality, where they live in miserable hovels, see only examples of coarseness and rudeness and hear only a negro dialect," when what was needed was "a total change of environment" by removing young people to places "where morals are pure; where manners are refined; where language is grammatical."[200] Far from celebrating the existing culture of the black community, Dr. Patton declared: "All improvement must be by an influence from without, which shall quicken and inspire, which shall teach and guide"—this being the purpose of "planting and strengthening the educational institutions which operate to change for the better the environment of the colored race in this country."[201]

Although there was another educational tradition established at the Hampton Institute in Virginia and transplanted to Tuskegee Institute in Alabama by Booker T. Washington, a graduate of Hampton, this tradition as well was based on replacing the existing culture of Southern blacks with a new imported culture. Hampton Institute's founder, General Samuel Chapman Armstrong, declared that the "average Negro student" needed a residential boarding school that could "control the entire twenty-four hours of each day—only thus can old ideas and ways be pushed out and new ones take their place."[202] Addressing the American Missionary Association in 1877, the Principal of Hampton Institute said: "There is no lack of those who have mental capacity. The question with him is not one of brains, but of right instincts, of morals, and of hard work."[203] Contrary to later caricatures, neither Hampton Institute nor Tuskegee Institute was based on an assumption that blacks had the capacity to be only hewers of wood and drawers of water.

In short, however divergent the different schools of thought were on educational philosophy, as between the Hampton-Tuskegee approach and the approach of the founders of other institutions for blacks, they were agreed that what was most needed for the advancement of blacks in the post-bellum South was the replacement of the culture prevailing around them and among them by a new imported culture. However, the greatest obstacle to creating this new culture was the existing black redneck culture:

For many missionaries the physical problems of overwork, illness and poor facilities were less frustrating than their everyday dealing with the freedmen. A constant problem for teachers was student absenteeism; a pupil would attend school for a few days, disappear for a time, then come back again; multiplied by a factor of 40 or 50, this made classroom continuity difficult. This "irregularity," said one teacher, was a "positive vice" of the freedmen. A related weakness was unreliability: "You can…never depend on any thing promised" went a typical complaint. Another "general failing among the colored people," according to many teachers, was their tardiness at meetings, classes, church services, and so on….

More serious were sexual offenses, theft, and lying.[204]

Many of the teachers blamed such behavior on slavery but, as we have already seen, similar behavior was common among white rednecks on both sides of the Atlantic, people who had never been enslaved. Remarkably, the Northern teachers persisted in the face of difficult students and a hostile white Southern society, from which they were excluded and by which they were sometimes terrorized.[205]

Although many teachers burned out in a few years, new teachers continued to arrive from New England and other parts of the North—thousands in the postwar decades. When black colleges were founded, New Englanders were again disproportionately represented among their teachers and college presidents, and much of these colleges' philosophy was that of New England. These institutions introduced strict behavioral standards, as well as high academic standards, imposing stern discipline and developing self-discipline in a region where such was not the norm for either blacks or whites. Noted black scholar and educator Charles S. Johnson said, "No less stern rectitude could have broken the grip of habits adjusted to a now out-moded life of irresponsibility and reshaped them to a new and serious purpose."[206]

W. E. B. Du Bois, himself a New Englander and with the first Ph.D. from Harvard earned by a black man, declared the movement "to plant the New England college in the South" to be "the salvation of the South and the Negro."[207] Perhaps even more remarkable than these dedicated efforts, was the fact that such efforts began to produce educational results, early on:

In 1871, the Georgia legislature created a board of visitors to attend public examinations at Atlanta University. The chairman of the first board of visitors was ex-slaveholder Joseph Brown, who reportedly said that he expected the examinations to confirm the Negro's inferiority. But the recitations of former slaves in Latin, Greek, and geometry forced from him the confession that "we were impressed with the fallacy of the popular idea...that the members of the African race are not capable of a high grade of intellectual culture." And the Atlanta Constitution could hardly "believe what we witnessed. To see colored boys and girls fourteen to eighteen years of age, reading in Greek and Latin, and demonstrating correctly problems in Algebra and Geometry...appears almost wonderful."[208]

However discordant the philosophy of the American Missionary Association may have been with "multicultural" views prevailing today, the crucial fact is that it worked—as so many of today's notions do not.

There was yet another route by which New England culture reached some blacks in the nineteenth century. Oberlin College was founded by New Englanders in 1833 and it functioned as a New England college transplanted to Ohio—"an outpost of New England culture beyond the Appalachians," as one scholar put it.[209] It was also one of the few colleges to which blacks were admitted before the Civil War, as well as being a station on the Underground Railroad through which Southern blacks escaped from slavery. Although blacks were no more than 5 percent of the students at Oberlin College, Oberlin was a much more significant factor in the higher education of blacks. Of the 309 blacks who were known to have received a degree from a white college in America up through 1899, nearly half (149) received their degrees from Oberlin.[210]

The first black woman to receive a college degree in America received it in Oberlin's class of 1862. She became the principal of a remarkable high school for blacks in Washington, D.C., discussed in a later essay as Dunbar High School. Of that school's first ten principals, three were graduates of Oberlin, two graduated from Harvard and one each from Amherst and Dartmouth. In essence, most of this highly successful school's principals during its early formative period had New England educations in a New England culture, whether or not they received that education in New England itself.

A wholly disproportionate share of future black leaders came out of the schools and colleges established by New Englanders in the South, not even counting Oberlin College or Dunbar High School. These alumni of institutions founded as New England enclaves in the South included W. E. B. Du Bois, James Weldon Johnson, Langston Hughes, Walter White, Mary McLeod Bethune, A. Philip Randolph, James Farmer, Thurgood Marshall, and Martin Luther King Jr.[211] In addition to these individuals from these Southern institutions, the first black man to graduate from Annapolis, the first black woman to earn a Ph.D., the first black general, the first black Cabinet member, and the first black federal judge all came from the same public high school—Dunbar High School in Washington, with its culturally New England-educated principals in its formative years.

Such concentrations of black pioneers and leaders in a few highly atypical cultural enclaves suggests that their achievements were not solely a matter of individual ability—"cream rising to the top"—but were also a result of a culture very unlike that in which most blacks were raised and educated. However much the achievements of these individuals have been celebrated, the culture behind those achievements has not been. Today, the culture that is celebrated in much of the media and in the schools is not the culture that succeeded, but the culture that has failed—the black redneck culture. When white couples who adopt black children are warned to be sure to put those children in touch with their "cultural heritage," all too often that means the black redneck culture.

Internal Cultural Differences

Internal cultural differences among blacks have long been extreme, ranging from such things as urbanization, education, and regional distribution to rates of crime, economic achievement, and general acculturation to the norms of the surrounding society.

Historically, the most fundamental difference for many generations was between those blacks who were slaves and those who were free. They differed not only in their legal status but also in their regional distribution, their degree of urbanization, and even biologically. There were free blacks as far back as the seventeenth century. In fact, there were free blacks before there were slaves in America. The first Africans brought in captivity to colonial Virginia in 1619 became indentured servants, like the white indentured servants who were common in colonial America.[212] Only later, with the mass importation of Africans, did this change. The first law in America recognizing perpetual slavery appeared in 1661 in Virginia.[213]

The small class of free blacks in colonial America had fewer restrictions than other free blacks would have in the nineteenth century—and many of them and their descendants made use of their opportunities. There was a black writer named Gustavus Vassa whose book was popular enough to go through eight editions[214] at a time when the vast majority of blacks were still illiterate slaves in the South. Benjamin Banneker was a publisher of almanacs and was also one of those who designed the lay-out of the city of Washington—again, long before most blacks were either free or able to read and write.

There were not just isolated individual blacks who were culturally more advanced than other blacks, but whole classes of blacks who had achieved cultural levels that most blacks would not achieve until many generations later. The size of the free black population increased after the United States came into existence as an independent nation, as the ideology of freedom associated with the American revolution led most Northern states to abolish slavery, and even in the South, enough white slaveowners freed their slaves to cause the free black population there to nearly double and then redouble between 1790 and 1810.[215]

Both the regional distribution and the degree of urbanization of free and enslaved blacks differed greatly. After the invention of the cotton gin in 1793, the cotton plantations of the Deep South began to draw slaves away from upper South states like Virginia and North Carolina toward more southerly states like Mississippi and Alabama, sometimes as individuals "sold down the river" and often as part of whole plantations that relocated. Thus the geographic center of the black population moved steadily southwestward at an average of about 50 miles per decade.[216] Meanwhile, the "free persons of color" were moving in the directly opposite direction. While more than 90 percent of the antebellum black population lived in the South, the "free persons of color" were evenly divided between the states of the North and South and, within the South, they tended to leave the Deep South and gravitate toward that region's less oppressive places farther north.[217]

The difference in geographic distribution was so extreme that in 1860 there were more free blacks living in the city of Washington alone than in the states of Mississippi, Alabama, and Georgia combined—these states having huge concentrations of slaves.[218] The slave and the free also differed greatly in urbanization. While most black slaves worked in rural settings, by 1860 the "free persons of color" were more urbanized than even the white population.[219]

There were cultural consequences to these historic and geographic differences. While the vast majority of slaves could neither read nor write, the census of 1850 showed that most "free persons of color" were literate, but it would be half a century later—two generations after emancipation—before the same would be true of the black population as a whole.[220] It would be 1940 before the black population as a whole became as urbanized as the "free persons of color" were in 1850.[221] The cultural head starts of this segment of the black population had enduring consequences. The descendants of the antebellum "free persons of color" remained predominant among black leaders in many fields, well into the twentieth century, and they included W. E. B. Du Bois, Thomas Fortune, Charles Waddell Chestnutt, Thurgood Marshall, John Hope Franklin, and many others. Most black holders of doctoral degrees in the middle of the twentieth century, as well as most Negroes working in the professions in the nation's capital at that time, were by all indications descendants of the antebellum "free persons of color"—a group that was never more than 14 percent of the black population.[222]

As a group, the "free persons of color" also differed from the slaves in racial mixture. As in most of the Western Hemisphere, freed slaves were often the offspring of those who freed them, and the adults freed were more often female than male. While only 8 percent of slaves met the stringent U.S. Census requirement of half or more white ancestry to be classified as mulatto, 37 percent of the "free persons of color" did. This is not to say that all the others in either category were of pure African ancestry. But there were very noticeable skin color differences between the more acculturated descendants of those freed before the Civil War and those freed as a result of the Emancipation Proclamation. The noticeably greater success of the former was often attributed to their white ancestry, both by whites and by some of the Negro elite themselves.[223] But the historical and cultural antecedents of that success are undeniable. Moreover, the later rise of other blacks to similar levels of achievement undermines the biological explanation of these internal differences among blacks.

The point here is that cultural differences led to striking socioeconomic differences among blacks, as they did among whites. In both races, those who lived within the redneck culture lagged far behind those who did not. That these cultural differences among blacks also coincided with biological differences did not mean that biology explained the differences in performance. The offspring of white slaveowners not only had a better chance of being freed, they also tended to have better opportunities while still enslaved—being more likely to be house servants rather than field hands and, in some cases, living the lives of de facto free persons while still legally in bondage.[224] Reconstruction-era black Senator Blanche K. Bruce, for example, was during the era of slavery tutored alongside his owner's son—or other son, as many believed.[225]

During the antebellum era, there were other mulatto offspring of white slaveowners who were given special consideration and aid.[226] Some were sent to Oberlin College, sometimes with an intermediary handling financial arrangements,[227] apparently to conceal the identity of the white father. This is not to say that most slaveowners freed their mulatto offspring but that, of those blacks freed voluntarily, mulattoes were far more common than among the slave population in general, and that women were freed more often than men. Moreover, this pattern prevailed throughout the Western Hemisphere. The point here is that the descendants of "free persons of color" had a cultural history that served them better than the cultural history of the descendants of slaves, even after the abolition of slavery ended differences in their legal status.

Whether by individual escapes from slavery, by voluntary manumissions in the antebellum South, or by general emancipation by law in the Northern states, a black class of "free persons of color" emerged long before the Emancipation Proclamation. The more prosperous of these families were able to educate their own children, sometimes through college, and these were typically lighter-skinned people, as well as people with generations of a head start in freedom and acculturation, as compared to the mass of enslaved blacks. The net result was that the elite among American Negroes tended to be, and to remain for generations after emancipation, a racially mixed group that married among themselves and formed a socially exclusive class.[228]

Among nineteenth-century Negroes in Philadelphia, for example, 85 percent of mulatto men married mulatto women and 93 percent of black men married black women.[229] This was not solely a matter of color prejudice, for there were major behavioral differences between the two groups. The mulatto neighborhoods had lower crime rates and a higher percentage of their children attending school, as compared to the black neighborhoods, even though it can hardly be claimed that school attendance or crime rates are genetically predetermined.[230] In short, there were major cultural differences—and these differences in turn produced other differences, such as a higher occupational status, better housing, and more wealth among the mulattoes.[231] Nor was this pattern confined to Philadelphia. All across the country, North and South, the elite of the Negro community were lighter in complexion than the masses—and very self-conscious, and sometimes snobbish, about that fact.[232] This remained so through at least the first half of the twentieth century.

Among the consequences of the extreme range of education and acculturation within the Negro community has been the larger society's erection of racial barriers provoked by black rednecks, which barriers then deeply offended those individuals at the other end of the cultural spectrum. These barriers based on race prevented cultural elites from separating themselves as much as they would like from lower-class blacks, with whom they were forced to live in proximity and to share institutions. Yet protests against racial barriers had to be made in the name of all—light or dark—leading to charges of hypocrisy against the elites who spear-headed protests against white social and economic barriers, while maintaining their own social and economic barriers against the black lower class.

That internal social barriers within the black community became more pronounced at the same time as white barriers against blacks in general suggests that more than coincidence was involved, since both occurred in the wake of the mass arrival of black rednecks from the South. Among the behavioral differences between the black elites and the black masses was that the elites had more stable families, with separation or divorce being rare among them.[233] It took more than money or a light complexion to enter the social circles of the black elite. Behavioral standards were also essential—and individuals who met these standards could be admitted with little money and regardless of complex-ion,[234] though the history of black rednecks meant that few would rise to elite levels.

External Relations

Cultural differences affected not only the internal development of the black community but also the way that the black community as a whole was treated by the larger surrounding white commu-nity—and the way in which that treatment varied over time. The small number of blacks who were free in colonial times were joined over the generations by increasing numbers of blacks who were either released from bondage or who escaped on their own. The growth of this largely unacculturated population—"fugitives in the rough," in the words of black historian Carter G. Woodson[235]—in Northern cities during the first half of the nine-teenth century brought both social barriers and discriminatory laws barring black children from schools and black adults from equal access to public accommodations.[236] Yet, as these black com-munities grew more acculturated over time, and began to rise economically, these laws and practices began to be relaxed in many Northern cities in the latter part of the nineteenth century.

Writing in 1899, W. E. B. Du Bois noted "a growing liberal spirit toward the Negro in Philadelphia," in which "the community was disposed to throw off the trammels, brush away petty hindrances and to soften the harshness of race prejudice"—leading, among other things to blacks being able to live in white neighborhoods. Jacob Riis noted similar changes in New York, and similar trends emerged in other Northern cities in the last quarter of the nineteenth century. In Detroit, blacks who had been denied the vote in 1850 were voting in the 1880s, and in the 1890s blacks were being elected to public office by a predominantly white electorate in Michigan. The black upper class in Detroit at that time had regular social interactions with whites and their children attended high schools and colleges with whites. In Illinois during this same era, legal restrictions on access to public accommodations for blacks were removed from the law, even though there were not enough black voters at the time to influence public policy, so that this represented changes in white public opinion.[237]

By all indications, Northern black urban communities were themselves becoming cleaner, safer, and more orderly during this era of improving race relations, so changes in white public opinion were not merely inexplicable mood swings. Neither were the later retrogressions in race relations in the North which followed a massive influx of black migrants from the South—black rednecks—at the beginning of the twentieth century. As late as 1890, nine-tenths of all blacks in the United States still lived in the South, but those who lived in northern urban communities were largely from families long settled there. Most blacks living in New York State, for example, were born in New York State. In short, there were settled communities in both regions, and by all indications the Northern black communities at that time were acculturating to the norms of the Northern white society around them. But all of that changed radically within a relatively few years, as massive migrations from the South not only enlarged Northern black communities but transformed them culturally.

In 1900, for the first time, more than half of all blacks living in New York State had been born outside that state. Newcomers from the South became growing majorities in Northern urban black communities in other states as well. The record-breaking migrations of blacks from the South to the North during the first decade of the twentieth century was nearly tripled during the second decade—and that in turn was almost doubled again during the decade of the 1920s. Moreover, the proportion of these migrants coming from the Deep South, as distinguished from the Upper South, increased over time[238]—which meant that the least educated and least acculturated became a growing proportion of the black migrant population moving into the Northern cities. There were about 30,000 blacks living in Chicago in 1900 but this grew to well over 100,000 by 1920 and more than 277,000 by 1940. In Detroit, the black population grew from a little more than 4,000 in 1900 to more than 40,000 in 1920 and over 149,000 by 1940. New York City's black population was a little more than 60,000 in 1900, but grew to more than 150,000 by 1920 and more than 450,000 by 1940.[239] Writing in the midst of these massive migrations, historian Carter G. Woodson predicted, "The maltreatment of the Negro will be nationalized by this exodus."[240] That is what had happened a hundred years earlier and now it happened again.

The sheer numbers of these new black migrants from the South not only overwhelmed the relatively small black populations in Northern cities demographically in the early twentieth century, their very different behavior patterns shocked both blacks and whites at the time, as witnessed by adverse comments from earlier black settlers and the black press, denouncing the new arrivals from the South as vulgar, rowdy, unwashed, and criminal.[241] Nor were these conclusions without foundation. For example, a study in early twentieth century Pennsylvania found that the rate of violent crimes by blacks who had migrated there was nearly five times the rate of such crimes by blacks born in Pennsylvania.[242] In Washington, the rate of births out of wedlock more than doubled with a large influx of Southern blacks during the late nineteenth century.[243]

One indication of the white reaction was that blacks no longer remained as free to live in white neighborhoods. This represented a major retrogression in race relations. In the late nineteenth century, racial segregation in housing in Northern cities was no longer what it had once been—or what it would become again in the years ahead. In Detroit, as early as 1860, no neighborhood was even 50 percent black.[244] In Chicago, as late as 1910, more than two-thirds of the black population lived in neighborhoods where most residents were white[245] but, after the mass migrations of blacks from the South, attempts by blacks to move into white neighborhoods in Chicago were met with violence, including bombings. New York, Philadelphia, and Washington were also cities which began to restrict blacks to ghettoes only after the massive influx of Southern blacks and their redneck culture.[246] In many cities, blacks were prevented from moving into existing white neighborhoods but, in other cases, whites simply moved out when blacks moved in. Harlem, the first of the great Northern black ghettoes, was still predominantly white as late as 1910.[247] Racial segregation in housing became an explicit law in Baltimore in 1911.[248] In one way or another, residential segregation became the norm in Northern cities.

Residential segregation was not the only retrogression in race relations during this period. In some Northern and Midwestern cities where schools had been racially integrated for years, black children were now segregated from white children after the mass influx of blacks from the South.[249] Blacks in Washington were no longer allowed in white theaters, restaurants, or hotels, and their opportunities to work in white-collar occupations shrank.[250]

W. E. B. Du Bois summarized these retrogressions this way:

> Yet it has everywhere been manifest in the long run that while a part of the negroes were native-born and trained in the culture of the city, the others were immigrants largely ignorant and unused to city life. There were, of course, manifold exceptions, but this was the rule. Thus the history of the negro in Northern cities is the history of the rise of a small group by accretion from without, but at the same time periodically overwhelmed by them and compelled to start over again when once the material had been assimilated.[251]

In Philadelphia, for example, the native-born blacks had advanced but, according to Du Bois, they were "overwhelmed and dragged back" by black migrants from the South. He added: "In New York the native-born have been perhaps even more completely overwhelmed."[252]

This pattern is confirmed in places where the retrogression

in race relations took place at a different time because of local differences in the timing of large-scale in-migration of blacks from the South. In San Francisco, for example, that mass influx took place during the Second World War, as blacks from the South were attracted by jobs in new war production facilities, notably the Kaiser shipyards. Henry Kaiser recruited Southern blacks and brought them to the San Francisco Bay Area by the trainloads. The black population of San Francisco, which had been less than 5,000 in 1940, rose to more than 40,000 by the time of the 1950 census, and the black populations of Oakland and Berkeley also rose several-fold during the same decade.[253]

In the San Francisco Bay Area, as in the Northern cities half a century earlier, there was a long-settled black population which lived free of the Jim Crow laws and practices of the South, and which had been able to get civil service jobs as far back as the 1920s. But although the newcomers were skilled workers more often than the local black residents, culturally the newcomers lagged far behind. Native-born blacks in the Bay Area described the newcomers as "foreign" in the way they talked and in their behavior—for example, "eating hamburgers openly on the bus; and baloney, and loud talking and fighting on the busses....That never happened in the old days."[254] Some of the new blacks from the South were described as having "a little more of a chip on their shoulder than the people out here did."[255] Many local blacks thought that white racism increased after World War II, when both Southern blacks and Southern whites began arriving in large numbers.[256]

A similar retrogression in race relations on the Pacific coast during the Second World War occurred in Portland, Oregon, where again there were large influxes of black workers to take jobs in the growing war industries. These new black arrivals "with little education" were "resented by the small group of law-abiding and self-sustaining Negroes" already living in Portland. As in other places and times, a ghetto now developed in Portland "and discriminations in regard to civil rights were instituted."[257]

On the national scene, the much later receding of racism and the socioeconomic advancement of blacks in the second half of the twentieth century cannot be attributed simply to the passage of time, for the passage of time had produced major retrogressions in race relations before. Nor can these advances be attributed to the civil rights laws that began in the 1960s, for the advancement of blacks antedated any serious civil rights legislation by years and was in fact more dramatic in the years *preceding* such legislation. Between 1940 and 1960, the percent of black families with incomes below the official poverty line fell from 87 percent to 47 percent.[258] In various skilled trades, the income of blacks relative to whites more than doubled between 1936 and 1959.[259] The principal factor that raised black incomes during that period, both absolutely and relative to white income, was migration—from low-income areas to higher-income areas.[260] However much these migrations set back those blacks who were already living in Northern cities, this movement from the South put millions of blacks into places where their children would get better education, while their parents had better job opportunities.

With the passing years and generations, more and more of these migrant families ceased to be black rednecks, acculturating themselves in new surroundings, as minority groups tend to do in countries around the world. Once again, racial barriers began to erode after World War II—and before the civil rights legislation of the 1960s. Perhaps the most dramatic example was the crumbling of racial barriers in professional sports, exemplified by Jackie Robinson's becoming the first black major league baseball player in 1947, seventeen years before the Civil Rights Act of 1964. A poll that year showed his popularity to be second only to long-time entertainment idol Bing Crosby.[261]

The process of ending racial segregation in American military services was also begun during the Truman administration, years before segregation was declared unlawful in civilian life. In 1948, President Harry Truman ran for re-election on a platform that included civil rights for blacks, which some thought would doom his candidacy, but the fact that he won suggests that white public opinion had already begun to change.

The Civil Rights Act of 1964 and the Voting Rights Act of 1965 dealt major blows to racial restrictions, especially in the South, and had dramatic effects on the number of black elected officials. Economically, however, the upward trends in black income and occupations that had begun decades earlier simply continued, *but at no accelerated rate.* The rise of blacks into professional and other high-level occupations was in fact greater in the years *preceding* the Civil Rights Act of 1964 than in the years afterward,[262] and was greater in the 1940s than in the 1950s.[263] Behind such developments was the fact that blacks were closing the gap between themselves and whites in years of schooling during this era.[264]

In short, major social transformations within the black community were having an impact in their economic condition. It would hardly be surprising if it also had an impact on how whites viewed blacks, as had happened in the nineteenth century. The civil rights legislation of the 1960s may well have been an *effect* of the rise of blacks, rather than the sole or predominant cause of that rise, as it has been represented as being, by those leaders— black and white—with incentives to magnify their own role in racial progress.

The difference between cultural explanations of changing race relations and explanations based on political acts or swings of the pendulum in white public opinion is not just a matter of intellectual preference. There are wholly different implications, not only about the past, but especially about the future. The question is whether the advancement of blacks is helped or hindered by promoting a black "identity" built around a redneck culture whose track record has been largely negative for both blacks and whites.

WHITE LIBERALS

White liberals in many roles—as intellectuals, politicians, celebrities, judges, teachers—have aided and abetted the perpetuation of a counterproductive and self-destructive lifestyle among black rednecks. The welfare state has made it economically possible to avoid many of the painful consequences of this lifestyle that forced previous generations of blacks and whites to move away from the redneck culture and its values. Lax law enforcement has enabled the violent and criminal aspects of this culture to persist, and non-judgmental intellectual trends have enabled it to escape moral condemnation. As far back as 1901, W. E. B. Du Bois, while complaining of racial discrimination against blacks, also condemned "indiscriminate charity" for its bad effects within the black community.[265] In a later era, the burgeoning welfare state, especially since the 1960s, has spread an indiscriminate charity—in both money and attitudes—that has given the black redneck culture a new lease on life.

Intellectuals have been particularly prominent among those who have turned the black redneck culture into a sacrosanct symbol of racial identity. This includes both black and white intellectuals, though the latter predominate numerically and in terms of influence through the media and academia. Intellectuals have promoted misconceptions of history, misreadings of contemporary life, and counterproductive notions of how to prepare for the future.

By projecting a vision of a world in which the problems of blacks are consequences of the actions of whites, either immediately or in times past, white liberals have provided a blanket excuse for shortcomings and even crimes by blacks. The very possibility of any *internal* cultural sources of the problems of blacks have been banished from consideration by the fashionable phrase "blaming the victim." But no one can be blamed for being born into a culture that evolved in centuries past, even though moving beyond such a culture may do more for future advancement than blaming others or seeking special dispensations.

Blaming Others

Blaming others for anything in which blacks lag has become standard operating procedure among white liberals. If blacks do not pass bar exams or medical board tests as often as whites or Asians, then that shows that something is wrong with those tests, as far as many white liberals are concerned. Best-selling author Andrew Hacker, for example, says that academic problems in general are created for black students in white colleges because such colleges use curricula that "are white in logic and learning, in their conceptions of scholarly knowledge and demeanor."[266] Why this does not seem to be a problem for Asian students remains unexplained, even though blacks have lived in this white society for centuries longer than either Asian Americans or contemporary immigrants from Asia. Why it is not a problem for blacks from the Caribbean is another un-explained contradiction of such white liberal excuses for American-born blacks.

If black attorneys are not elevated to partnerships in law firms in proportion to their numbers, then to the *New York Times* this shows, in the words of their front page headline: "Law Firms are Slow in Promoting Minority Lawyers to Partner Role."[267] Apparently there can only be external reasons for anything negative that happens to blacks. According to Andrew Hacker, the fact that white taxi drivers often pass up black males seeking a ride, especially at night, shows these drivers to be "patently racist"[268]—even though black taxi drivers do the same, in order to avoid becoming victims of crime.[269]

White liberals long denied that there were higher crime rates among blacks by pointing to the imperfections of crime statistics in general or, more specifically, claiming that blacks are simply arrested more often for things that whites would not be arrested for. But if the imperfections of crime statistics were the real problem, then discussions could be limited to murder statistics, since dead bodies are not ignored, whether they are black or white, and neither are murderers, whatever their race. But murder statistics show the same disproportionate number of crimes by blacks as other statistics do. While murder statistics might provide more accuracy, they would not provide white liberals with a means of evading the obvious.

Riots by blacks are almost automatically blamed on whites, whether in the Kerner Report on the riots of the 1960s or in the reactions among white liberals to the Los Angeles riots of 1992. In some white liberal circles—the *New York Times,* for example—the police are almost automatically at fault in confrontations with black criminals, hoodlums, or rioters. When the police arrive on a scene of crime or violence in black communities, whatever they do is likely to be categorized later as either having let the situation get out of hand or as having used excessive force. Any force sufficient to prevent the situation from getting out of hand is almost certain to be called excessive force by white liberals in the media, so that—by definition—the police will have acted badly, no matter what they did or failed to do. Should the police arrive in such overwhelming numbers as to bring the disorder to a quick halt without any need to use force at all, then they will often be said to have "over-reacted" by sending so many cops to deal with unresisting people.

One of the reactions of the police to such predictable scape-goating in the media has been to "de-police" some of the most violent black neighborhoods, looking the other way rather than risk seeing a whole career ruined by media charges of racism. This gives criminals, hoodlums and rioters a freer hand—at the expense of law-abiding blacks, who may be the great majority, even in a high-crime neighborhood. There is evidence that this is in fact what happens after a barrage of adverse media coverage against the police.[270]

The incorrigibility of white society—and the corresponding futility of black efforts to improve their situation by improving their own education and other qualifications—is another leitmo-tif of much white liberal writing. After the U.S. Supreme Court struck down some racially gerrymandered congressional districts, forcing some black members of Congress to run in districts where most voters were white, *New York Times* columnist Anthony Lewis said, "the reality in the South is that black men and women, how-ever well qualified, have little chance of winning in white districts."[271] But these Southern black candidates were in fact re-elected.

The fact that black rednecks exhibit the same hostility and violence toward other minorities long associated with bigoted white rednecks in the South presents white liberals with another challenge to find a way to evade the obvious. Black anti-Semitism, for example, is not recognized by Andrew Hacker, who claims that "no one really knows if blacks and whites differ markedly in their feelings about Jews" —despite survey after survey showing greater hostility to Jews among blacks.[272] Black hostility to other minori-ties, such as the Koreans, has likewise often been ignored by such liberal publications as the *New York Times*[273] or even defined out of existence by a variety of white liberal writers on grounds that racism requires power, which blacks do not have.

Following that logic, Nazis were not anti-Semites until they gained control of the German government and the Ku Klux Klan today would not be called racist any more because it has lost the power it once had. But the arbitrary proviso of "power" was never part of the definition of racism until racism among blacks became widespread enough to require a convenient evasion.

The thuggish gutter words and brutal hoodlum lifestyle of "gangsta rap" musicians are not merely condoned but glorified by many white intellectuals—and "understood" by others lacking the courage to take responsibility for siding with savagery. The National Council of Teachers urged the use of hip hop in urban classrooms.[274] The cultural editor of the *San Francisco Chronicle* characterized rapper Tupac Shakur as "a lightning rod of insurrection in the name of social justice."[275] *USA Today* said, "gangsta rap is rooted in part in underfunded school systems which fail to equip students with the skills to speak out effectively and intersect with larger communities."[276] An article in the *New Republic* said that rap music "has become the nearest thing to a political voice of the poor."[277] Mikal Gilmore of *Rolling Stone* wrote of "all the terrible forces" responsible for "such a wasteful, unjustifiable end"[278] to the life of rapper Tupac Shakur by the very lawless violence he had sung of and lived, not by some mysterious "forces."

The blaming of gangsta rap barbarism on social conditions takes many forms, such as that of a *Boston Globe* columnist who depicted it as deriving from "the institutional indifference that thrives wherever poor people assemble in America: struggling schools, dangerous streets, long-gone factories, hospital emergency rooms or EMTs substituting for family doctors, futures measured by sunsets and sunrises and the dull feeling that nearly everything is against you."[279] A *New York Times* essay dismissing critics of gangsta rap referred to "the poverty and hopelessness that foster vicious behavior."[280]

The general orientation of white liberals has been one of "What can *we* do for *them*?" What blacks can do for themselves has not only been of lesser interest, much of what blacks have in fact already done for themselves has been overshadowed by liberal attempts to get them special dispensations—whether affirmative action, reparations for slavery, or other race-based benefits—even when the net effect of these dispensations has been much less than the effects of blacks' own self-advancement. For example, although the greatest reduction in poverty among blacks occurred *before* the civil rights revolution of the 1960s, the liberal vision in which black lags are explained by white oppression requires black advances to be explained by the fight against such oppression, symbolized by the civil rights legislation of the 1960s. This scenario has been repeated so often, through so many channels, that it has become a "well-known fact" by sheer repetition. Moreover, this protest-and-government-action model has become the liberals' preferred, if not universal, model for future black advancement.

Misconceptions of History

Many of the prevailing misconceptions of the histories of both blacks and whites in America derive from trying to amalgamate morality and causation, so as to make the moral evil of slavery a causal explanation of contemporary negative social phenomena which have in fact had entirely different historical bases.

The touchy "pride" of white Southerners, ready to explode into deadly violence, has often been explained as being a result of whites being used to unbridled domination over slaves. But the very same attitudes existed among their ancestors in Britain, where slavery did not exist, as those attitudes also existed in those parts of the South where slaves were virtually nonexistent and among people who were in no economic condition to buy slaves. When discussing both blacks and Southern whites, slavery has served as an all-purpose explanation of many social phenomena, ranging from broken families to poor education, lower labor force participation rates, and high rates of crime and violence. Often evidence has been neither asked for nor given. Not surprisingly, many of these explanations do not stand up under scrutiny. Census data, for example, show that labor force participation rates were higher among non-whites than among whites in 1920 and 1930.[281]

No matter what the origin of counterproductive behavior, such behavior must be changed if progress is the goal. On the other hand, if the real agenda is to score points against American society, then blacks can be used as a means to that end. More generally, a pro-black stance by white intellectuals enhances the latter's moral standing and self-esteem, whether or not the particular manifestation of that stance helps or harms blacks on net balance.

The chafing restrictions of civilization, which can at times become irksome to people of any color, may be vicariously thrown off by those white intellectuals who cheer on outlandish and even lawless behavior by black hoodlums or entertainers. Blacks in effect become the mascots of these intellectuals, symbolizing and acting out the latter's resistance to "society"—or, more accurately, civilization.[282] But, while mascots may be indulged, more fundamentally mascots exist for the sake of those who adopt them, and the actual well-being of the mascot is seldom a high priority. By cheering on counterproductive attitudes, making excuses for self-defeating behavior, and promoting the belief that "racism" accounts for most of blacks' problems, white intellectuals serve their own psychic, ideological, and political interests. They are the kinds of friends who can do more harm than enemies.

A crucial fact about white liberals must be kept in mind: They are *not* simply in favor of blacks in general. Their solicitude is poured out for blacks as *victims*, blacks as welfare mothers, criminals, political activists against the larger society, as well as those blacks who serve as general counter-cultural symbols against the larger society. White liberals have nothing approaching the same interest in blacks as the principal victims of black criminals or as people advancing themselves within the existing framework of American society, including many who have risen within the military, nor do they get particularly worked up over blacks who build up their own human capital or business capital. None of the many reports of black schools that excel academically seems to arouse any great interest among white liberals. It was not the liberals in Washington, but the Reagan administration, which offered successful black educator Marva Collins an appointment as Secretary of Education.

The "Identity" Fetish

Intellectuals in the 1960s began promoting the idea that those blacks who exhibited a culture different from the ghetto or black redneck culture were not "really" authentic blacks. This issue was strikingly demonstrated in a controversy between Irving Howe and Ralph Ellison, growing out of Howe's 1963 article criticizing such black writers as Ellison, whom Howe considered insufficiently authentic or militant. For Howe, the central character in Richard Wright's novel *Native Son*—a ghetto black epitomizing the black redneck culture—was authentic and the more sophisticated central character in Ellison's novel *Invisible Man* was not. Ellison rejected and derided the idea of a white man defining what a black man should be and attempting to confine individual blacks to that stereotype.[283]

The notion that the ghetto black was the authentic black not only spread among both white and black intellectuals, it had social repercussions far beyond the intellectual community. Rooting black identity in a counterproductive culture not only reduced incentives to move beyond that culture, it cut off those within that culture from other blacks who had advanced beyond it, who might otherwise have been sources of examples, knowledge, and experience that could have been useful to those less fortunate. But more successful blacks were increasingly depicted as either irrelevant non-members of the black community or even as traitors to it. In turn, this meant that many blacks who had a wider cultural exposure and greater socioeconomic success felt a need to conform, to some degree or another, to a more narrow ghetto view of the world, perhaps using ghetto language, in order to prove their "identity" with their own race.

Such social pressures become especially acute for young blacks in the schools and colleges. One consequence of this has been that counterproductive attitudes toward education have filtered upward into black middle-class young people raised in racially integrated middle-class communities such as Shaker Heights, who spend less time on their studies than their white or Asian American classmates—under the overhanging threat of being accused of "acting white" if they devote themselves to their studies, instead of to various social activities in which other black students indulge.

The painful irony is that those who make this accusation are themselves "acting white" when they perpetuate a redneck culture from a bygone era. Even such a modern ghetto creation as gangsta rap echoes the violence, arrogance, loose sexuality, and self-dramatization common for centuries in white redneck culture, and speaks in exaggerated cadences common in the oratory of rednecks in both the antebellum South and those parts of Britain from which their ancestors came.[284]

It is not only the cultural peculiarities of the black ghetto culture which has been perpetuated by the identity fetish developed in the post-1960s era. What has also been promoted has been a conformity of beliefs and affirmations among blacks, with those with different viewpoints being banished from consideration intellectually and ostracized socially—at least in so far as "identity" advocates succeed in imposing their straitjacket on others. Not only behavioral litmus tests but ideological litmus tests have been used by those promoting a black identity fetish, with those who do not pass such litmus tests being dismissed as not "really" black.

This post-1960s black identity intolerance—promoted by white intellectuals as well as black leaders and activists—is a painful parallel to the post-1830s intolerance among white Southerners against anyone who questioned slavery in any way. Maintaining what has been aptly called an "intellectual blockade"[285] against ideas differing from those prevailing in the South, antebellum Southerners not only insulated themselves from ideas and viewpoints originating outside the region but, at the same time, in effect drove out of the South independent-minded people who would not march in lockstep. The resulting narrow and unquestioning conformity of that era led the South into the blind alley of a Civil War that devastated wide sections of the region and left a legacy of bitterness that lasted for generations. It can only be hoped that today's narrow intolerance promoted by a black identity fetish will not lead into similarly disastrous blind alleys.

SUMMARY AND IMPLICATIONS

It would be good to know what proportion of either the black or the white population, past or present, could be considered culturally rednecks. While it is undoubtedly true that the South was not "a monolithic region,"[286] the issue here is how it differed from other regions, not its internal variations. What is known is that the white population of the antebellum South as a whole was strikingly different from the white population of the North, not only in the eyes of contemporary observers, but also in objective statistics that are an undeniable part of the historical record. What is also known is that, while about one-third of the white population of the United States lived in the antebellum South, nine-tenths of the black population lived there at that time. Thus a culture which produced lower levels of achievements for both blacks and whites, compared to other members of their respective races from different cultures, was more pervasive among blacks. The lesser educational and other opportunities for blacks are consistent with the longer persistence of this counterproductive culture among those who have not yet risen out of low-income ghettos.

In addition to the negative effect of the redneck culture on the achievements of both blacks and whites, it has also, for generations, provoked adverse reactions to rednecks of either race by others. Calling all adverse reactions "racism" in the case of blacks explains nothing when people of that same race have been treated very differently at different periods of American history, as well as in different parts of the country at the same time. There is no reason to rule out, *a priori*, the possibility that different subgroups of blacks were themselves different in behavior, attitudes, skills, and performances. That has already become apparent when comparing blacks from the Caribbean with blacks from the South, or when comparing blacks from the New England enclaves in the South with blacks from the redneck culture.

Easy recourse to slavery as an explanation of either North-South differences or black-white differences fails empirical tests. Not only did the main features of the redneck culture exist in Britain, centuries before blacks and whites encountered each other in the antebellum South, if slavery was the reason for the South's lags behind the North, then emancipation should have led to a narrowing of the economic and other gaps between the two regions. Contemporaries who drew this logical conclusion were subsequently disappointed by what actually happened in the wake of the end of slavery. Per capita real income in the South, which had been 81 percent of the national average in 1860, fell to 51 percent by 1880 and remained at about that level for another generation,[287] long past the time when the decline might have been plausibly explained by the damage suffered during the Civil War. However obtrusive and morally salient slavery might be, it failed to carry the heavy burden placed on it as an explanatory factor—then or now.

The counterproductive redneck culture that eroded away over the generations, among both whites and blacks, has been rescued after the 1960s by a "multicultural" ideology that has made this residual survival among ghetto blacks a sacrosanct badge of racial identity, not to be tampered with by teachers or criticized by others, under pain of being labeled "racist." It should also be noted that both cultural transformations within the South and a large return migration of blacks to the South in the late twentieth century make the redneck culture no longer a regional phenomenon but a largely urban ghetto phenomenon, North and South, with a certain amount of outward diffusion, to middle-class black youngsters especially.

Blanket application of the term "racism" as a *causal* explanation—as distinguished from simply an epithet—cannot explain why blacks who were living in white neighborhoods at the beginning of the twentieth century could no longer do so two decades later or five decades later. After all, those who lived interspersed among whites in the earlier period were of the same race as those who could not do so in the middle of the twentieth century. The Ku Klux Klan was certainly a racist organization but that description cannot explain why it began to make major inroads among whites in Northern states after a mass migration of blacks from the South had moved into those states. Like the ghettoization of blacks in Northern cities, where they had once lived dispersed among the white population, the spread of the Klan's racist organizations into Northern communities had to have some causal explanation. It is hard to see these two major retrogressions in race relations as mere coincidences that just happened to occur after the migrations of Southern blacks into Northern cities.

In short, cultural differences have had a major economic and social impact. Despite a tendency to attribute black-white differences in the United States to "a legacy of slavery," blacks from the West Indies also had a history of enslavement but brought with them to the United States a very different culture that was reflected in such things as differences from the native-born black population in entrepreneurship, education, and imprisonment rates. In short, what the two groups of blacks shared was a history of enslavement but what they did not share was the redneck culture. The disproportionate number of prominent blacks who came out of small enclaves of transplanted New England culture in the South likewise underscores the impact of cultural differences.

While only circumstantial evidence is possible on the connection between the cultural characteristics of Southern rednecks or crackers in the past and those of ghetto blacks today, that evidence is considerable. However, even if one were to dismiss all of that evidence as sheer coincidence, the redneck culture would still not be irrelevant, for it provides a demonstration of the counterproductive effects of such a way of life.

External explanations of black-white differences—discrimination or poverty, for example—seem to many to be more amenable to public policy than internal explanations such as culture. Those with this point of view tend to resist cultural explanations but there is yet another reason why some resist understanding the counterproductive effects of an anachronistic culture: Alternative explanations of economic and social lags provide a more satisfying ability to blame all such lags on the sins of others, such as racism or discrimination. Equally important, such external explanations require no painful internal changes in the black population but leave all changes to whites, who are seen as needing to be harangued, threatened, or otherwise forced to change.

In short, prevailing explanations provide an alibi for those who lag—and an alibi is for many an enormously valuable asset that they are unlikely to give up easily. As Eric Hoffer put it:

> There are many who find a good alibi far more attractive than an achievement. For an achievement does not settle anything permanently. We still have to prove our worth anew each day: we have to prove that we are as good today as we were yesterday. But when we have a valid alibi for not achieving anything we are fixed, so to speak, for life.[288]

However, as he said elsewhere:

America is the worst place for alibis. Sooner or later the most solid alibi begins to sound hollow.[289]

Those who provide black rednecks with alibis do no favor to them, to other blacks, or to the larger society in which we all live. In American society, achievement is what ultimately brings respect, including self-respect. Only for those who have written off blacks' potential for achievement will alibis be an acceptable substitute. The liberal vision of blacks' fate as being almost wholly in the hands of whites is a debilitating message for those blacks who take it seriously, however convenient it may be for those who are receptive to an alibi.

Whether black redneck values and lifestyle are a lineal descendant of white redneck values and lifestyle, as suggested here, or a social phenomenon arising independently within the black community and only coincidentally similar, it is still a way of life that has been tested before and found wanting, as shown by its erosion over the generations among whites who experienced its counterproductive consequences. By making black redneck behavior a sacrosanct part of black cultural identity, white liberals and others who excuse, celebrate, or otherwise perpetuate that lifestyle not only preserve it among that fraction of the black population which has not yet escaped from it, but have contributed to its spread up the social scale to middle class black young people who feel a need to be true to their racial identity, lest they be thought to be "acting white." It is the spread of a social poison, however much either black or white intellectuals try to pretty it up or try to find some deeper meaning in it.

Are Jews Generic?

I N ANY GIVEN COUNTRY, A PARTICULAR MINORITY may be hated for any of a number of reasons peculiar to that country or that group. However, in a worldwide perspective, the most hated kinds of minorities are often not defined by race, color, religion, or national origin. Often they are generically "middleman minorities," who can be of any racial or ethnic background, and in fact are of many. Many of the historic outbreaks of inter-ethnic mob violence on a massive scale have been against the Jews in Europe, the Chinese minorities in various Southeast Asian countries, against the Armenians in the Ottoman Empire, the Ibos in Nigeria, and against other middleman minorities in other times and places.

While many kinds of minorities have been persecuted and subjected to violence, the sheer magnitude and duration of the persecution and violence unleashed against middleman minorities eclipses that unleashed against other kinds of groups. Conquered aborigines or formerly enslaved groups, for example, might be held in greater contempt but lethal animosities on a mass scale have been particularly often directed at middleman minorities. The mass slaughter of tens of thousands of Ibos in mob attacks in Nigeria, and the horrors inflicted on the Vietnamese "boat people" (most of whom were ethnically Chinese) have been reminiscent of the pogroms against the Jews in Eastern Europe, and the term "genocide" has been used to characterize what happened to the Armenians in the Ottoman Empire during the First World War, as well as to the Jews under the Nazis a generation later. Smaller violent rampages against the businesses, homes, or persons of middleman minorities have been common around the world, whether directed against the Lebanese in Sierra Leone, the Japanese in Peru, the Indians in Burma, or the Chinese in Southeast Asia.

Other kinds of minorities have of course also suffered violence, but the scale of lethal mass violence against middleman minorities has been unequalled.[1] All the blacks lynched in the entire history of the United States[2] do not add up to as many people as the number of Chinese slaughtered by mobs near Saigon in 1782,[3] or the Jews killed by mobs in Central Europe in 1096 or in the Ukraine in 1648,[4] much less the slaughters of Armenians by mobs in the Ottoman Empire during the 1890s or during the First World War.[5] Only the Nazi Holocaust exceeded the slaughter of Armenians and, while the Holocaust was the ultimate catastrophe for Jews, it was also the culmination of a long history of lethal mass violence unleashed against middleman minorities around the world.

What do all these groups have in common and why have they been hated so much? Partly the resentments and animosities against these groups have derived from the economic role they play, a role that has been widely misunderstood and widely resented—in very disparate societies, over a period of many centuries—even when this economic role has been played by people not ethnically different from those around them. Differences of race, religion or ethnicity, added to the resentments arising from the economic role itself, have produced explosive mixtures in many times and places.

THE ECONOMIC ROLE

Middleman minorities have been intermediaries between producers and consumers, whether in the role of retailers or money-lenders. The retailing has ranged from the modest level of street peddlers to that of grand merchants owning chains of stores and money-lending has likewise ranged from the level of the small neighborhood pawnbroker to that of international financiers. Jews have historically been the classic middleman minority, to whom others have often been analogized—the overseas Chinese as "the Jews of Southeast Asia," the Lebanese as "the Jews of West Africa," the Parsees as "the Jews of India," and the Ibos as "the Jews of Nigeria," for example. Shakespeare's merchant of Venice was a Jew and

the story revolved around his money-lending. Numerically, however, the 36 million overseas Chinese are more than twice as
numerous as all the Jews in the world.

Among other prominent middleman minorities have been
the Gujaratis from India, who have played the middleman role in
countries ranging from the South Pacific islands of Fiji to the
United States and South Africa. Armenians have been another
prominent middleman minority in countries around the world,
and the Chettiars from India have specialized in the middleman
occupation of money-lending in many times and places. In addition to these international middleman minorities, there have been
ethnic groups who played this role in particular countries or
regions, such as the Marwaris in India's state of Assam or Koreans
in America's black ghettos.

Middleman minorities have often been middlemen in a social
sense, as well as an economic sense. They have often served as
intermediaries between social groups who, for one reason or
another, interact better through third parties than they do directly.
Sometimes there are differences in language and culture, as
between members of a colonial establishment and the indigenous
population that they rule—such as between the European over-
lords in colonial Africa and the African population with whom
they had economic and other transactions via the Lebanese as
intermediaries in West Africa. Sometimes there are vast differences
in status, which make both groups uncomfortable in dealing
directly with one another, as for example, Polish noblemen who
used Jews to collect rents from the peasants.

None of this is new. In ancient times, Milesians played the
middleman role in this sense:

> The Milesians not only were familiar with the Greek culture of
> the mainland, but also were conversant with the Near Eastern
> cultures of Lydia, of Cappadocia, of Phrygia, of the Phoenician
> lands, of Egypt, of the whole Levantine world. Traders they were,
> wandering about, speaking with great facility this, that, or the
> other tongue that they found necessary to transact their busi-
> ness.[6]

Armenians in the Ottoman Empire were likewise middlemen
in this social sense, as well as in the economic sense:

Armenians, although persecuted, possessed wealth and influence to a considerable degree because they had succeeded, in the course of centuries, in making themselves indispensable to their overlords. The Turk, after all, was not familiar with the intricate web of seaborne traffic, with the many languages of the Near East, with commercial accounting even when elementary—in short, was not able to get along without his despised Christian slave (because that's what the Armenian was, at least a semi-slave).[7]

During the centuries of Mongol domination in Central Asia, Armenians likewise served as trade envoys, interpreters, and soldiers.[8] In modern Sierra Leone, the Lebanese were often middlemen between the Europeans and the native Africans, investing the time to become better acquainted with local African languages and the African way of doing things, as well as with individual Africans.[9] The Chinese played a similar role during the colonial era in French Indochina and, of what were then called the Dutch East Indies, it was said: "All that the natives sold to Europeans they sold through Chinese, and all that the natives bought from Europeans they bought through Chinese."[10]

Such intermediary roles are not without their hazards. High prices, for example, may be caused by others but it is the middleman minorities who directly charge these prices who are likely to be blamed. The manufacturer may be raising his prices, or the government may be raising taxes, or the costs of doing business in a given neighborhood may be higher because theft, vandalism, and violence raise the cost of insurance, or for other reasons. But, in any case, those who charge the customers these higher prices are more likely to be blamed than those who caused the prices to be higher. Where those who cause the higher prices are of the same ethnic background as the customers, and the middleman is ethnically different, then it is a virtual certainty that the middleman will be blamed by the customers and by their political and other leaders.

In the case of aristocratic or colonial overlords, where a middleman minority collects the rents or taxes that these overlords impose, or otherwise serves as an economic or social intermediary, the resentments of the masses may again be directed at the middleman who is seen face to face, more so than at distant over-lords. What was said of the Chinese in the days of the Dutch East Indies could be said of other middlemen in other places and times: "the natives detested the Chinese, for they saw in them the active agents of a system of oppression by which they were frequently reduced to beggary."[11] Because the middleman is essential to the overlords, these rulers may protect him when necessary from overt violence. On the other hand, during periods when resent-ments reach the point where the governing powers themselves are at some risk, nothing is easier than to throw the middleman minority to the wolves and not only withdraw protection but even incite the mobs in order to direct their anger away from the over-lords.

Although there have been many middleman minorities over the centuries and around the world, the tragic history of the Jews, as a people without a country for two thousand years, climaxed by the Holocaust in which one-third of all the Jews in the world were murdered, is unique. Yet the history of many other groups in other times and places has borne a remarkable similarity to that of the Jews in a number of ways, though of course no two groups are the same in all ways. These similarities include their economic pat-terns, their social patterns, and the pattern of responses they have evoked from others.

Some observers have seen the resentments toward middle-man minorities as being due to their prosperity, but truly wealthy people have seldom provoked the kind of rage and bitterness directed at middleman minorities, even in times and places where most middlemen were far from rich. It is not just what these minorities have achieved, but how they have achieved it, that evokes suspicions and resentments.

Throughout most of the history of the human race, most peo-ple have made a living in agriculture—typically through arduous labor. The beginning of the industrial revolution meant, for most people, the transfer of the scene of that arduous labor from farm to factory. To such people, those who earned their livings without vis-ible toil, with clean hands, and by simply selling things that others had produced at higher prices than the producers had charged, were ready targets of resentments, especially when these nonproducers enjoyed a higher standard of living than those who worked in factories or on farms. It did not have to be a dramatically higher standard of living. Those nearby on the socioeconomic scale are often more hotly resented than distant rich people.

Just as there are those who believe that only workers who handle tangible physical objects in the production process are "really" producing output, so they believe that middlemen who physically produce nothing are merely parasites who insert themselves gratuitously between the "real" producers and the consumers. If this crude misconception seems like too little to account for so many centuries of hostility and violence against so many groups that are typically non-violent themselves, it is nevertheless at the core of animosities that have endured even after most members of middleman minorities have moved on to professional careers in medicine, law, and other fields.

The Economic Fallacy

Even in the absence of differences in toil or reward, the seeming conjuring of wealth out of thin air, apparently by "overcharging" others or making them pay back more money than was lent, has been seen as parasitic activity, rather than as a contribution to the well-being of the community. Suspicions are readily aroused against an occupation where an income is generated, in Friedrich Hayek's words, "'out of nothing,' without physical creation and by merely rearranging what already exists," an operation that to the uninitiated seems to "stink of sorcery." [12] Demagogues can easily supply theories that play upon this pre-existing suspicion and misapprehension. However, even in the absence of demagogues or of ethnic differences, the economic role alone can generate negative reactions.

An often-cited economist's account of rudimentary economic activities within a prisoner-of-war camp in Germany during World War II showed the economic and social role of middlemen among the men in the camp. Prisoners of war were fed by their captors, while monthly shipments of Red Cross packages supplemented their food and provided a few amenities like chocolates and cigarettes. All prisoners received the same material goods but of course they valued different items differently. Non-smokers traded cigarettes for chocolates. Sikhs among the prisoners traded away canned beef for jam or margarine.

On days when the Red Cross packages arrived, direct one-on-one trades created chaos in a camp with more than a thousand prisoners. Camp authorities sought to bring some order into the situation by setting up bulletin boards on which prisoners could make their offers of trades. But what proved to be even more efficient arose spontaneously among the prisoners themselves: Particular prisoners would circulate around the camp, trading back and forth—playing the role of middleman among their numerous fellow prisoners, who traded with one another without coming into direct contact. The other prisoners saved themselves the bother and the middlemen ended up with more material goods, in effect charging for their services.

The middlemen who emerged in this informal economy were not necessarily ethnically different. Those individuals who played the middleman role in the camp ranged from a Catholic chaplain to a Sikh. Moreover, the needs they met, though seemingly trivial from the perspective of a larger and more affluent society, were matters of "urgency," according to a British economist who was one of these prisoners.[13] Things like cigarettes, jam, razor blades and writing paper meant a lot in the grim conditions of a prisoner-of-war camp.

The other function of middlemen—lending and charging interest—also arose in the camp. As prisoners' supplies of cigarettes or sugar ran low near the end of the month, those who had saved these items would provide them to those had run out—in exchange for a pledge to pay back more than was lent when the next Red Cross packages arrived. The economist among them was fascinated to see many of the economic phenomena associated with a complex market economy appearing spontaneously in these primitive conditions. But he also noted social and political phenomena generated by the work of middlemen:

> Taken as a whole, opinion was hostile to the middleman. His function, and his hard work in bringing buyer and seller together, were ignored; profits were not regarded as a reward for labor, but as the result of sharp practices. Despite the fact that

his very existence was proof to the contrary, the middleman was held to be redundant...[14]

Here, in microcosm, was the fundamental problem of the middleman down through the centuries and around the world. In the prisoner-of-war camp, at least these misconceptions were not compounded by the additional factor of ethnically different middlemen and there was no market for political demagoguery.

Social Prerequisites

In the larger world, the economic role of a middleman *minority,* as distinguished from that of isolated individuals, implies various social patterns. For a particular minority group to become dominant in retailing or money-lending, whether at a high or a low economic level, means that their behavior pattern must be fundamentally different from that of the surrounding population. Otherwise, the majority population would supply the majority of the middlemen in their own society. This crucial difference cannot be simply that the middleman minority has more money. Again and again, in different ages and in various countries, the middleman minority has arrived on the scene as destitute immigrants, owning virtually nothing and barely able to speak a few words of the language of the country.

This was the situation of the vast numbers of Eastern European Jews who arrived in the United States in the late nineteenth and early twentieth centuries.[15] The greatest concentration of Jews in the world was on New York's lower east side, where a 1908 study showed that about half the families slept three or four people to a room, nearly one-fourth slept five or more to a room, and fewer than one-fourth slept two to a room.[16] During the same era, Chinese immigrants typically arrived in Southeast Asian countries in similar rock-bottom poverty. For example: "Immigrant Chinese arriving in Indonesia usually brought nothing but a bundle of clothes, a mat, and a pillow."[17] It was much the same story with Lebanese immigrants to colonial Sierra Leone and, in a later era, Korean immigrants and Vietnamese refugees to the United States. Whatever economic progress such people could make would come slowly and as a result of a long uphill struggle.

How could middleman minorities rise from such beginnings? More to the point, how could they eventually rise above the native-born population around them? Clearly, their values, their discipline, and their culture had to be different. Moreover, if they wanted their children to succeed, they had to make sure to keep these crucial intangible assets different. Accordingly, middleman minorities around the world have distanced themselves and their children from social involvement with the very different people around them—whose differences were the basis of their livelihood—and have therefore often been accused of being "clannish." This term has been applied not only to the Jews in Europe and America but also, on the other side of the world, to the Parsees of India[18]—and to other middleman minorities in between.

Even when middlemen have lived in the slums, their children have worked harder and succeeded more often in the same schools where other children were failing. That was not only the history of Jewish children in the United States but also of Chinese children in Southeast Asia, children of the Tamil middleman minority in Sri Lanka, of Korean immigrant children in the United States, and other offspring of middleman minorities elsewhere.

Middleman minorities, struggling up from the bottom, could not afford to have their children absorb the values of the society around them. Clannishness was all but inevitable.

This social differentness, compounded by social withdrawal from the larger society, creates additional sources of resentment and hostility faced by a middleman *minority*, besides the resentments growing out of the middleman economic role, as such. Yet, if the middleman minorities were not different, they would be of little use to others. People who do not save, for example, are able to get loans or to buy on credit from middleman minorities precisely because the latter do save. If middleman minorities were as improvident as their customers or clients, they would have nothing to offer them and their businesses would be very short-lived.

The ability to save has played a key role in the rise of middleman minorities. An observer in India noted: "Gujaratis were rigorous savers, and their families worked endless hours and lived abstemiously to ensure their success."[19] The same thing could be said of the Jews, the Koreans, the Lebanese and many other mid-

dleman minorities. Although middleman minorities often began at
the bottom, it was typically at the bottom in entrepreneurial activities, often as peddlers with packs on their backs, the more
fortunate ones with pushcarts, and—usually somewhat later—
small shops. Even such large enterprises as Macy's, Bloomingdale's,
and Levi Strauss among the Jews, and Haggar and Farah among
the Lebanese, began at the level of the lowly peddler.

According to a history of the Jews in the United States, "staggering numbers of Jews in the decades before and after the Civil
War first experienced America through peddling," which became
"the nearly universal American Jewish male experience."[20] While
Jewish peddlers worked as isolated individuals, their supplies
came from a wider network:

> Each peddler functioned in a long Jewish economic chain link-
> ing shopkeepers to Jewish wholesalers in the larger cities on
> whom they depended for credit. The Jewish peddler on the road
> served as the agent of the Jewish town shopkeeper and the big
> city jobber. This trading network depended on intracommunal
> trust. Wholesaler and peddler understood each other, spoke the
> same language, and knew the same people.[21]

Jewish wholesalers in port cities from New York to San Francisco supplied Jewish peddlers with merchandise which they
carried on their backs into the hinterlands—to farmers, miners,
railroad crews and others working far from the big cities and often
in places where there were few or no stores.[22] Peddlers of course
also worked in cities and in every region of the country—from the
Southern plantations to the California mining camps where Levi
Strauss first began to sell the rugged trousers that were to make
his name famous. While Jewish peddlers often worked in isolation
among a non-Jewish population, they were nevertheless tied to a
wider Jewish community, not only by commercial ties to Jewish
wholesalers and manufacturers, but also to family members in
Europe and America. They often saved money to pay for transatlantic passage for relatives in Europe to come and join them.

These savings at some point also allowed the peddler to set
up a little shop in town, settle down, get married, and raise a family. The wives and children then worked in the same little business.

Often the Jewish shopkeeper or other small businessman and his family lived above or behind the store.[23] Milton Friedman's family lived this way when he was growing up, a pattern that he described as common among the immigrants to America in that era.[24] Yet this pattern was by no means confined to Jews or to America. Similar economic and social patterns could be found among the Lebanese in Sierra Leone[25] and among other middleman minorities in other parts of the world. The overseas Chinese store-keeper in the Philippines was likewise "willing to live in a small corner of his store."[26]

As among the Jews, Lebanese children were initiated into their family businesses in the United States, as were the children of other middleman minorities in other countries:

> Whereas a minority of sons and daughters peddled at an early age, many, perhaps the majority of store owners' children were prepared for life behind a counter. School-age children, when not in school, were at their parents' elbows, waiting on customers, making change, stocking shelves, and imbibing the shrewdness of operating an independent business on meagre resources. They were inculcated with the parents' work and thrift ethics and the lesson that family unity and self-denial was essential to the family's goals.[27]

Lebanese children were likewise initiated into their families' stores, and into its economic culture, in Sierra Leone.[28]

A similar pattern could be found among Korean shopkeepers in late twentieth-century New York, where family members contributed many hours of unpaid labor toward the family business. For example:

> Mr. Kim...and his son daily purchase vegetables: at four o'clock every morning when the dawn is coming, they get up and drive to Hunts Point in the Bronx, where a city-run wholesale market is located....
>
> In the market they run and run in order to buy at low prices as many as one hundred and seventy different kinds of vegetables and fruits. All the transactions are made in cash. At 7 o'clock they return to the store and mobilize the rest of the family members in order to wash and trim vegetables.[29]

While Korean greengrocers in New York worked long hours by doing wholesale shopping early in the morning at Hunts Point, other greengrocers waited for a delivery service to bring fruits and vegetables to them. The Koreans not only saved the cost of the delivery service, they were able to pick the best quality fruits and vegetables available and, by having the family wash, clip, and sort them, reduce the rate of spoilage. But it took a toll: "They use expressions such as 'bloody urine,' 'drastic loss of weight,' and 'benumbed fingers like a leper's' when they describe the daily struggle of operating their businesses."[30] In Atlanta, Korean store-owners worked an average of 63 hours per week, with one-fifth working 80 hours or more."[31]

Early Lebanese businesses in the United States were noted for "opening 16 to 18 hours daily," utilizing "the assistance of the whole family."[32] During the earlier rise of Chinese shopkeepers in Southeast Asia, sixteen-to-eighteen-hour days were also common,[33] and market gardeners from India who settled in nineteenth-century South Africa, peddling produce, could be seen weeding their gardens by moonlight after hawking fruits and vegetables in the cities during the day.[34]

Because being a peddler or even a small storeowner does not require any large amount of capital, these are occupations open to innumerable people, so that widespread competition has been common—and that in turn means that profits cannot come easily or without long hours of work and much attention to the business, as well as living within limited means. Nevertheless, such sacrifices tend eventually to pay off. In eighteenth-century Russia's province of Astrakhan, people from India arrived "with very small means, which they then increase in Astrakhan by trade, and living there continuously for ten, twenty or thirty years, become extremely wealthy, so that some among them have now one or more hundred thousand roubles in their possession."[35]

While some observers might regard such determination and resourcefulness as admirable or inspiring, to others the rise of middleman minorities from poverty to prosperity has been like a slap across the face. If accepted as an achievement, it raises painful questions about others who have achieved nothing comparable, despite in some cases being initially more fortunate. Someone who was born rich represents no such assault on the ego and creates no such resentment or hostility. Anyone who can offer an alternative explanation of these middlemen's successes—such as calling them "parasites" or "bloodsuckers" who have prospered at the expense of others—has been popular in many countries and some have built entire careers and whole movements on such popularity. When people are presented with the alternatives of hating themselves for their failure or hating others for their success, they seldom choose to hate themselves. More commonly they will listen to even inconsistent or irrational arguments against middlemen, as for example against the Chinese in the Philippines:

> Pressed as to his case against the Chinese, the Filipino politician would say that the Chinese were too numerous, that they had more than half of the retail business in their hands, that they charged too high prices, cheated in weights and measures, and made high profits. Should it be objected that if this were so all the Filipino has to do was to open up a *tienda* of his own and put the Chinese out of business in the village, the politician would probably shift his ground. He would now say that the Chinese standard of living is deplorably low; the owner of a Chinese *tienda* is willing to live in a small corner of his store, that he eats almost nothing and works day and night; so does his family and his assistant if he has one. The Chinese in Manila, he says, persistently disregard the eight-hour law. In fine, the charge now is that the Chinese runs his business with too little, not with too great, overhead expenses and profits. If this is true, then the Chinese gives excellent service to the community as distributors. The Filipino can buy cheaply because the Chinese live so meagerly.[36]

A common charge against middleman minorities in countries around the world is that they operate illegally and often corrupt the authorities with bribes. What is often overlooked by those who make such charges is that discriminatory restrictions and prohibitions against middleman minorities make it virtually impossible for them to operate legally and still make a living. Sometimes they have been deprived of citizenship in the land of their birth, even when their families have lived there for generations, or the citizenship available to them does not include the same rights as those of indigenous citizens. Such discriminatory restrictions and prohibitions have applied to the Lebanese in West Africa, the Indians and Pakistanis in East Africa, the Chinese in Southeast Asia, and to Jews across much of Europe for centuries. That people who have had to struggle for survival against such discrimination have bent or broken laws is hardly surprising and the high levels of honesty and integrity that many middleman minorities have observed within their own circles suggest that they are not dishonest by nature. Similarly, the high levels of mutual help with family and within other close circles among middleman minorities often contrast with a cold-blooded attitude toward outsiders in societies that have been discriminatory and oppressive toward them.

The idea that middleman minorities are deceptive, unscrupulous and unreliable people is far more widespread in political and intellectual circles than among those in the business of extending credit to them. Professor P. T. Bauer of the London School of Economics found this to be true of Lebanese businessmen during his study of West African trade:

> The unfavourable attitude of many officials toward the Levantine communities contrasts notably with the financial support which European banks, manufacturers, export houses and merchants have given to many members of the Levantine communities in West Africa. Many of the Levantine enterprises enjoy the respect, confidence and financial backing of British banks and firms. In some instances the supporters are highly regarded old-established firms whose names are household words the world over. It would seem that personal and commercial contacts between members of the Levantine community and their supporters have not confirmed the suspicions and fears entertained in official circles.[37]

Economic Success

Armenians are among the middleman minorities who have worked their way up in various countries around the world. Armenians were very poor peasants for centuries in the Ottoman Empire. Over time, however, they evolved from rural entrepreneurs to urban entrepreneurs and financiers in Istanbul:

Previously they had directed the transit trade with Persia from Erzurum and eastern Armenia, but gradually they established themselves along the route from Persia to Istanbul. They were found in Sivas and Tokat, centers of agricultural production, in Ankara, center for sheep's wool and goat's wool *(tiftik)*, in Bursa, center for silk and tobacco, and in Uskudar, the Istanbul bridgehead in Asia and the destination of trade from Anatolia and Persia. Together with European merchants, they played an increasing role in this trade. Certain Armenians reached significant positions in commerce and finance, for their names appear in lists of money changers and bankers. In the eighteenth century they were the most important minority merchants in the capital.[38]

Both as peasants and as businessmen, Armenians were noted for "sobriety and thrift."[39] In the process of becoming the most important middleman minority in Istanbul, the Armenians displaced the Jews in that role.[40] Armenians were also prominent as traders in Iran:

> In Iran in the seventeenth century Armenians "dominated the Persian external trade and much of the internal commerce," their activity stretching from Europe to India.[41]

It has not been at all uncommon for groups whose background was in farming to go on to become middleman minorities, as the Armenians did. West African farmers, for example, have long engaged in trade as part of the marketing of their agricultural produce.[42] Indigenous middleman minorities, such as the Ibo in Nigeria, were thus not fundamentally different initially in skills or wealth from the farmers with whom they interacted, despite attempts to contrast the productive farmer and the unproductive middleman who "exploits" him. P.T. Bauer's landmark study of West African trade found this pattern:

> The rapacious and unproductive middleman in primary producing countries is often unfavourably contrasted with the allegedly more deserving farmer. This contrast is misleading. It neglects the fact that as long as entry is free the middleman is unlikely to secure an excessive income since this would quickly attract competitors. Perhaps more important, the dichotomy is a false

one. More often the real distinction is not between the producer and the middleman, but between unenterprising, indolent, unambitious and perhaps thriftless individuals, and others more venturesome, energetic, resourceful and frugal. The small-scale produce buyer or village trader is quite often the farmer who thinks the effort worth while to collect and market his neighbours' produce or to cater for their simple requirements. These intermediaries are generally members or former members of the agricultural community (or are at least closely connected with it), who have improved their position through their effort, enterprise and thrift. [43]

While such individuals might be of any ethnic background, in Nigeria they were often from the Ibo tribe, in whose culture "thrift, resourcefulness and foresight were the principal themes." [44] Some Ibos "began trading with a few shillings or even a few pence derived from the sale of agricultural or jungle produce." From there they proceeded to rise, step by step, as they "slightly enlarged their still very small scale of operations" until eventually they were able to become established in retailing. "In practically all cases they were members of farming families." [45]

In West Africa as elsewhere, the rise of middlemen from poverty to affluence has been widely seen as having taken place at the expense of others. This applies to both indigenous and immigrant middlemen, such as the Lebanese:

The opinion derives superficial plausibility from the fact that many traders began operations in West Africa with little or no capital, so that the increase in their capital and their prosperity have been obvious. However, this belief is fallacious because it ignores the productivity of trade. The wealth of the traders has not been taken or extorted from the Africans but has been created by their trading activities. It was not previously in existence.... [46]

As in the prisoner-of-war camp during World War II and in countries around the world, middleman activities have usually not been seen as producing wealth, but only as appropriating preexisting wealth, since the middleman does not visibly create a material thing. Neither does anyone else create or destroy matter, except for a few nuclear physicists. Turning iron ore into steel products is not creating a material thing but only changing its form to something that people want more. That is precisely what middlemen do when they make goods or money available earlier than otherwise through retailing, credit, or loans. They change the time when things become available. Consumers could, in theory, drive to factories to buy goods directly but retailers make this time-consuming activity unnecessary, for a price—a price whose legitimacy has often been questioned because the middleman did not change the physical nature of what was sold.

Resentments against both indigenous and expatriate middlemen in West Africa—with violence having erupted from time to time against both—underline the fact that it is the activity itself that is resented. The same has been true in other parts of the world and other periods of history. Moreover, moving into middleman occupations from other kinds of work has not been solely a characteristic of farmers. Korean shopkeepers in American black ghettos did not come from a farm or business background in Korea, but from an urban background. They had no special training in retailing, and the great majority had not even been salespeople before opening their own businesses.[47] Most relied on their own savings, rather than bank loans or government loans, and these savings came chiefly from working at low-paid jobs, including two jobs at a time for about one-fourth of the Korean businessmen in Atlanta. They worked an average of nearly four years before saving enough money to set up their own business.[48] In short, they worked their way up from the bottom, much like the Ibos in Nigeria and like other middleman minorities around the world.

When the very same ethnic group plays the middleman role in some countries but not in others, the hostility to them has been greatest where they have been middlemen. Japanese immigrants, for example, were long subjected to far greater hostility in Peru, where they worked in middleman occupations, than in Brazil, where they became agricultural producers—the latter partly as an organized and conscious effort to avoid the social and political problems associated with operating as middleman minorities.

The economic activity, rather than the ethnic group as such, was likewise crucial in determining public reaction in seventeenth-century Poland, where tens of thousands of Scots lived, most working as peddlers. Like most minorities who have taken on the role of peddlers and shopkeepers, the Scots faced local resentment and discriminatory laws designed to restrict their economic activities, not only in Poland but in Prussia as well.[49] Political attacks on Scots in Poland linked them with the classic middleman minority, the Jews.[50] Yet Scots seldom encountered such hostility in the many countries around the world where they worked as teachers, physicians, shipbuilders, and in many other occupations. Indeed, Scottish noblemen who immigrated to Poland were accepted into the Polish nobility, even while their fellow Scots who worked as middlemen faced much hostility.

Just as the same ethnic group can encounter very different amounts of social receptivity or resentments, depending on whether or not they play the role of middleman minorities, so different ethnic groups can encounter very similar hostility when they play the same role as middlemen. The hostility to Jews found in black ghettos, before Jews began pulling out in the wake of the ghetto riots of the 1960s, has been directed in later years at Korean and Vietnamese middleman minorities who succeeded the Jews in those roles. In even earlier times, before World War II, blacks in Harlem were resentful of fellow blacks from the Caribbean, who often played the role of middleman.[51]

Whatever the reasons for such widespread hostility to middleman minorities, it cannot be race, culture, religion, or nationality, since middleman minorities have differed from one another in all these respects. What they have had in common is performing a much misunderstood and much resented economic role—regardless of who performs that role. Even when the middleman role is played by people no different racially or ethnically from those around them, the resentment is still there. Thus, in centuries past, a Serb who charged interest on loans to fellow Serb peasants was called a "Greek," a term of condemnation, based on Serbian hostility to Greek money-lenders.[52]

Charging interest on loans was for centuries widely condemned as immoral, a condemnation often made with the sanction of religion. Jews played the role of money-lenders largely by default in medieval Christian Europe and in much of the Islamic world. Halfway around the world, Chettiars from India faced hostility, mob violence, and eventually expulsion as money-lenders in Burma, even though they generally charged lower interest rates than those indigenous Burmese who were money-lenders.[53]

The real measure of an economic function, however, is not its plausibility to observers but, rather, what happens to a society in its absence. Some countries have had disastrous famines, not from a lack of food, but from a lack of *distribution* of food. People have literally died of starvation in the interior while food supplies rotted on the docks in port cities. In other economies, both production and consumption suffer from a lack of credit. More to the point, mass expulsions of supposedly "parasitic" middleman minorities have created shortages, higher prices, and rising interest rates, in a number of countries and a number of periods of history.

Being a middleman involves more than retailing. There are also middlemen who buy up agricultural produce that is an ingredient in industrial production—cotton, for example—rather than simply something to be resold directly to consumers. Often, especially in Third World countries, this means buying small amounts from many farmers and combining all these small amounts in order to be able to sell in larger quantities to one or a few commercial or industrial firms. The money-lending function of middlemen can often be combined with both retailing, by selling to consumers on credit, or combined with buying raw produce, by advancing money to farmers to be repaid at harvest time. The Chinese in Southeast Asia, the Lebanese in West Africa and the Indians in East Africa have been involved in all these various middleman activities. Some middleman minorities, such as the Chettiars, specialize in money-lending as such, but many middleman minorities become involve in extending credit or loans as a part of their buying and selling of consumer goods or agricultural produce.

Middleman minorities have often been accused of "taking over" large portions of a country's economy, even in situations where it was they who largely—or solely—*created* particular businesses and industries. Many sectors of the local economy simply did not exist before the Chinese arrived in various countries in Southeast Asia, or the Lebanese in West Africa, or the Gujaratis from India in South Africa. But, whatever the historical origins of particular occupations or industries, middleman minorities have often been represented in them out of all proportion to their numbers in the general population—whether while they were still middleman minorities or in later generations when they moved into other professions, businesses and industries.

On the eve of the First World War, for example, Jews were 60 percent of all the merchants in Hungary, despite being only 6 percent of the population. By 1920, they were also half of all lawyers and three-fifths of all doctors. On the eve of Hitler's coming to power in Germany, Jews owned 60 percent of wholesale and retail clothing businesses in the country. In the late nineteenth century, Jews owned 80 percent of all retail clothing stores in New York City and 90 percent of the wholesale clothing trade.

The economic dominance of the overseas Chinese in various Southeast Asian countries has been even greater. Although less than 5 percent of the Indonesian population, the Chinese have controlled an estimated 70 percent of the country's private domestic capital and have run three-quarters of its 200 largest businesses. In Thailand, ethnic Chinese are about 10 percent of the population and have controlled all four of the country's largest private banks. Of the five billionaires in Indonesia and Thailand in the late twentieth century, all were ethnically Chinese. Although the overseas Chinese have long been known as "the Jews of Southeast Asia," perhaps Jews might more aptly be called the overseas Chinese of Europe.

Where middleman minorities have gone into manufacturing, clothing has been a favorite specialty. Like peddling, the manufacture of garments requires little initial capital and the main requirement for making a living at it is simply to work long hours. Much of this work can be done at home, so it is not necessary to invest in a shop or a factory, and sewing machines are relatively inexpensive, especially when bought on the second-hand market. When poverty-stricken Jewish immigrants were living packed into the tenements on the Lower East Side of Manhattan, the whirring of sewing machines could be heard behind the doors of their little apartments, as the whole family, including children, were making garments in their home "sweatshops."[54] As of 1908, 38 percent of the garment workers in New York City were teenage Jews.[55] Jews have been prominent, if not predominant, in clothing and textiles in medieval Spain, the Ottoman Empire, Argentina, and the United States.

It has been much the same story with Armenians. In the Russian province of Astrakhan in the eighteenth century, 209 of the 250 cotton cloth factories were owned by Armenians, who also owned 32 out of 38 silk-weaving enterprises.[56] Armenians were also prominent as dealers in silk in the Ottoman Empire.[57] A modern clothier has said, "Everyone you meet in Southeast Asia in apparel is Chinese."[58] Clothing and textiles were also occupations which attracted Lebanese immigrants in nineteenth-century São Paulo, Brazil:

> As Syrian and Lebanese pedlars accumulated capital, often by severely depressing their living standards, they opened textile and haberdashery stores along the major routes of communication and in the neighbourhood shopping areas.[59]

By the time of the First World War, "Syrian and Lebanese immigrants and their descendants dominated small-scale textile sales in both São Paulo and Rio de Janeiro," and "most members of the Syrian-Lebanese community were no longer pedlars."[60] In Colombia, as well, Lebanese immigrants were best known "for their retail trade in cloth."[61] Like the Jews, the individual Lebanese peddler or shopkeeper was part of a larger network of other members of their own ethnic group. The Lebanese formed "a world-wide network of textile traders," centered in Manchester, England.[62] As already noted, Lebanese-owned clothing manufacturing firms in the United States include companies that make Haggar and Farah trousers.

The manufacture of clothing is one of those industries that seems especially suited to those who begin with very little money, even if it is one in which a successful individual can later expand to become a large entrepreneur—in contrast to an industry like steel-making, where the initial capital has to be substantial, just to begin. Clothing and textiles are just two of many occupations, professions, and industries that middleman minorities have gone into, after they have achieved success in traditional retailing and money-lending enterprises. Often it is the later generations who go on to build upon the rise of their parents and grandparents from peddlers or small shopkeepers. While the earlier generations moved upward from peddlers to sedentary retail or wholesale merchants—as the Lebanese did in Sierra Leone, Brazil, Argentina, Colombia, Australia, the United States, and the Caribbean[63]—later generations have tended to move not only into manufacturing, transport, publishing, and other industries, but also into professions requiring advanced education, which those who went before them seldom had.

What was said of the Lebanese in Australia could be said of middleman minorities in other countries around the world: "Second- and third-generation Lebanese have been occupationally mobile and economically prosperous in comparison with their peddling and shop-owning predecessors."[64]

SOCIAL PATTERNS

Among the social patterns found among middleman minorities around the world have been close family ties and strong ties within the group, though these ties have seldom extended to the entire group, despite popular beliefs that Jews or other middleman minorities "all stick together." Another common pattern among middleman minorities has been an emphasis on education, even when living in the midst of others who were uneducated.

Family Ties

We have already noticed some of the social patterns of middleman minorities—the children working in the family business, for example. These businesses tended to remain family businesses, even when the peddler became a store owner and the store owner expanded into ownership of a chain of stores or the proprietor of a factory. This has been true of Jewish businesses, overseas Chinese businesses, Lebanese businesses, and businesses run by Gujaratis and Chettiars from India. Even when these enterprises became businesses of international scope, family ties spread across national boundaries. Among the reasons for the success of Jews and Lebanese, in particular, in the import-export business have been their family ties on both ends of many shipments and many international financial transactions. It was much the same story with the Armenians in earlier centuries.[65] Similarly today with the overseas Chinese in Southeast Asia, whose family financial links often reach from country to country in that region, with capital being shifted from place to place according to both economic and political developments in particular countries.

Intense family loyalties have led middleman minorities to take young relatives into their businesses, even when these might have to be brought from overseas in India or Lebanon or elsewhere. Among the Lebanese living in other countries, for example, "a successful emigrant would send back for others from his family and village," leading to "clusters of emigrants from the same district in some town or region of the country of settlement."[66] In Argentina or Sierra Leone, for example, established Lebanese would lend money to new arrivals or create business partnerships with them.[67] This has been just one aspect of strongly felt mutual obligations within families. Some middleman minorities have been noted for their remittances to family members in the countries from which they came or in other countries in which they have settled. Local populations have long resented this as exporting their countries' wealth—a charge often made against the Chinese in Southeast Asia and the Lebanese in many countries. Even in the early years of Jewish poverty in the United States, those in America managed to send money back to family members in Eastern Europe, not only for subsistence but also to pay for their passage to the United States. These international transfers of wealth, though large in the aggregate, were no net reduction of the wealth of the country from which they were sent because the middleman minorities had already added to the pre-existing wealth of the countries in which they settled and were sending abroad only a fraction of that net addition.

The central role of families—their cohesiveness, cooperation, and loyalties—has long been a common denominator among middleman minorities around the world. Their successes have not been simply the individual successes of "cream rising to the top" in isolation, though such groups have in fact turned out many remarkable individuals in many fields. Other groups, without the same strong and stable family backgrounds found among middleman minorities, have succeeded disproportionately in those few areas where purely individual talents are the over-riding factors, such as sports and entertainment. In the United States, the Irish in the nineteenth century and blacks in the twentieth century became spectacularly successful in boxing and baseball, as well as among singers and other entertainers, despite their lagging behind other groups in business, science, and other fields with more pre-requisites of cultural or social capital.

Both the nineteenth-century Irish and the twentieth-century blacks were noted for high rates of broken families, violence, alco-holism and crime. It is hardly surprising that both groups succeeded, not only as well as others, but far more so than most others, in fields where only the individual's abilities mattered. Such fields attracted a disproportionate share of their most able and ambitious young people, who often lacked the social prerequisites for widespread success in other fields. While intergroup compar-isons have been discouraged by the taboo against "blaming the victim," blame is in fact irrelevant. Certainly no individual or group has any control over the past from which their social and cultural legacy has come. What intergroup comparisons can tell us is which things have turned out to produce what results under what circumstances. If nothing else, that can warn us against blind alleys and counterproductive efforts—and against demagogues who would lead the young, especially, into those blind alleys and into self-destructive attitudes and behavior.

Patterns within Groups

Commercial, as well as family, ties have been strong within vari-ous middleman minorities. German Jewish businesses were among the main employers of Eastern European Jewish immigrants who arrived in the United States during the late nineteenth century. Even earlier, Jewish peddlers were able to get goods to sell on credit from more substantial Jewish businesses, not only in the United States but also in Latin America. Young men from commer-cial families in India and Lebanon were sent out to East and West Africa, respectively, to establish small businesses, often back in the interior hinterlands where European businesses seldom ven-tured. The international textile networks established by the Lebanese in Manchester supplied goods sold by Lebanese mer-chants and peddlers overseas. Cotton bought by Indian middlemen from East African farmers was shipped back to Bombay to be woven into cloth to be sold in international markets.

One of the many practical benefits of close ties within a middleman minority has been an ability to conduct business with one another at lower costs because of less need to resort to precautions before making transactions or to the formal legal system afterward, both of which can be costly and time-consuming. Thus Lebanese diamond dealers in Sierra Leone have handed over diamonds to one another without even getting receipts[68]—as Hasidic Jews have done in New York's diamond district.[69] Such mutual trust has also been common in commercial transactions in general among the overseas Chinese in Southeast Asia.[70] It was likewise the basis of international trade among the Armenians in earlier centuries:

> These widely spread but highly interrelated individual enterprises operated under the ethos of trust. Trust, and the shared moral and ethical norms underlying it, helped the Armenian trading houses to avoid the relatively rigid and costly operation of the hierarchic system of organization practiced by the English. Seen in this light, trust served as a human capital, but one that could not be acquired through a rational investment decision. It accrued to the Armenian merchant community as a result of their collective sociopolitical experiences over many generations. Based on family kinship and trusted fellow countrymen, the Armenian trading house did, indeed, rely on trust as its principal means of organization and control.[71]

These middleman minorities have thus been able to take advantage of business opportunities that others would either be reluctant to risk or could do so only with precautions that cost time and money. But such a mode of operation becomes practical only on the basis of strong social ties and enduring economic relationships that make cheating too costly to attempt.

Despite the frugal living common to middleman minorities around the world, they have also been notable for their donations to their own charitable institutions, such as hospitals and schools, and often to charitable institutions serving the larger society around them. At a minimum, they have avoided the social stigma of having the poorer individuals and families in their respective groups become public charges on the larger society.

The close ties within middleman minorities have led some to

imagine a wider web of loyalties than has actually existed. Such phrases as "Jews all stick together" confuse intense loyalties within particular subsets of Jews—or other middleman minorities—with a solidarity encompassing the whole population of the group. However, when Eastern European Jews began arriving in the United States in the late nineteenth and early twentieth centuries, the predominantly German Jewish community viewed their arrival with alarm. The Jewish press, which was largely controlled by German Jews at that time, characterized the new immigrants as "slovenly in dress, loud in manners, and vulgar in discourse," people speaking "a piggish jargon"[72]—that is, Yiddish.

The highly acculturated German Jews feared that the huge influx of Eastern European Jews with foreign ways would cause the larger society to raise barriers against all Jews—a fear that turned out to be well founded. Programs set up by German Jews to try to acculturate Eastern European Jews, in order to minimize the larger society's adverse reactions to Jews in general, included pointed lessons on the use of soap and water.[73]

When Eastern European Jews moved into German Jewish neighborhoods in Chicago, the German Jews moved out. Both in Chicago and New York at that time, most Eastern European Jews could not afford to live where German Jews lived, in the first place. German Jews were willing to employ Eastern European Jews but living near them was something else. Moreover, even within the poorer Eastern European Jewish neighborhoods on the lower east side of New York, Hungarian Jews had their own enclaves, separate from the enclaves of Russian or Polish Jews. There was a "low intermarriage rate" among these various subgroups of Eastern European Jews and a "mutual incomprehension and intolerance that kept Jews apart."[74]

Mutual aid societies among the Jews were likewise broken down by nationality groups, among other breakdowns. Even in the small Jewish communities back in colonial America, Sephardic Jews were known to disown children who married Ashkenazic Jews. Similar sectarian, national, and ideological divisions split Jewish communities throughout the Western Hemisphere and in Europe. In eighteenth-century France, Sephardic Jews expressed the same views as some Gentiles that Ashekenazic Jews were not yet ready for equal citizenship.[75] In some places, neither marriage nor burial crossed these lines of internal division.*

Similarly among the overseas Chinese in Southeast Asia and the Western Hemisphere, where people from different parts of China belonged to different formal and informal networks, and lived separate social lives, often speaking mutually unintelligible dialects and specializing in different sectors of the economy. As a scholarly study noted:

> Were the comprador of the Hongkong and Shanghai Bank in Singapore to be a Cantonese, it was less likely that a merchant who was Teochew could gain access to the Hongkong bank. Chinese banks themselves were dominated by these dialect and kin divisions. For example, the Chinese Commercial Bank (established 1912), the Ho Hong Bank (1917), and the Overseas Chinese Bank (1919) were all Hokkien banks. Lee Wah Bank (1920) was a Cantonese bank. The Overseas Union was a Toechew bank. Here not only the directors and officers but also the customers and depositors were drawn from a similar dialect background.[76]

Among the Lebanese, there was certainly no solidarity between Christian and Moslem Lebanese. Moreover, among the Moslems, there were divisions between the Sunni and the Shi'ites, and among the Christians there were divisions among the Catholics, Maronites, and Orthodox. These of course all had separate religious institutions, but they also had separate social and business networks. Among the Lebanese who settled in Australia, "their regional loyalties seldom extended beyond that of the village" in Lebanon from which they had come.[77] A history of bitter and lethal intergroup violence in Lebanon and Syria, taking thousands of lives at a time, was part of the legacy that Lebanese took to other countries in which they settled. Even in a small country like Sierra Leone, the many internal disputes among various Lebanese factions, which spilled over into the courts and involved political authorities, proved too baffling for either Europeans or

---

*When I was in Australia during my research on ethnic groups around the world, members of Jewish groups in Sydney and Melbourne both went to great lengths to tell me of the differences between the Jews who had settled in these cities. Both also repeated the same saying: "Melbourne is a cold city with warm Jews and Sydney is a warm city with cold Jews."

Africans to understand—much less settle—during the colonial era.
Indeed, one of the main tasks of diplomatic representatives from
Lebanon in Sierra Leone after independence was to arbitrate these
internal disputes among various Lebanese factions there.[78]
Conflicts among various Lebanese Shi'ite groups spread as far as
Australia and conflict among Lebanese political groups led to the
assassination of a refugee from Lebanon living in Brazil.[79]

The various Indian middleman minorities, such as the
Gujaratis and the Chettiars, have had separate social and economic
institutions, both in India and in the many countries where they
have settled overseas. As a study of Indian emigration pointed out,
"most Indians emigrate primarily as members of their subgroup—
as Gujeratis, Jains, Sikhs or Muslims," and most "still have arranged
marriages within their subgroup."[80] Another study, of Indians in
East Africa, notes that they have been "fragmented into so many lin-
guistic, religious, caste, and other sub-groups, as to constitute a
'community' almost exclusively in the minds of outsiders."[81] The
Armenian community in the Ottoman Empire was likewise "beset
by factionalism."[82]

The difference is not between atomistic independence and
group-wide ties. Subgroup ties and loyalties within middleman
minorities have often been intense, but have seldom encompassed
all the people lumped together by others.

Education

As communities determined to maintain their own values and
work ethic without allowing their children to be influenced by the
very different values they often found in the societies around
them, middleman minorities have often had their own social institutions, including their own private schools, after they reached an
economic level where they could afford them. Even when their
children went to public schools, as among Jews in the United
States, there were often supplementary schools, such as the
Hebrew schools. In other countries there were often full-time private schools for the children of middleman minorities, teaching in
the Chinese language, the Gujarati language, or whatever the particular language of the particular middleman minority might be.

Education has for centuries been a high priority among Jews, even in times and places where illiteracy was the norm among the people around them. A Russian official reported on the Jews in Russian-conquered Poland in 1818: "Almost every one of their families hires a tutor to teach its children" and "their entire population studies." He added:

> Girls too can read, even the girls of the poorest families. Every family, be it in the most modest circumstances, buys books because there will be at least ten books in every household. Most of those inhabiting the huts in [Gentile] villages have only recently heard of an alphabet book.[83]

Nearly two centuries later, when television host Brian Lamb asked author Abigail Thernstrom why Jews scored so well on the Scholastic Aptitude Test, she replied: "They have been preparing for it for a thousand years."

This is not to say that education was necessarily the factor that first lifted middleman minorities out of poverty. Among the immigrant Jews in America, for example, most worked in manual occupations during the last decades of the nineteenth century and no Jewish child in New York City graduated from a public high school then because the first graduating class from any public high school in New York was the class of 1902. A survey of City College students in 1951, when most of these students were Jewish, showed that only 17 percent of their fathers who were born before 1911 had completed the eighth grade.[84] But Jews were already beginning to rise economically. Their economic improvement meant that their children's labor was no longer necessary to enable the family to survive, so that these children could now go on to finish high school or college.

Higher education was the effect, rather than the cause, of their initial rise—and it would also become the vehicle by which later generations of Jews could move on into the professions. Even before that was possible, however, the intellectual *interest* was manifest. A survey of public libraries in New York's lower east side tenement neighborhoods where Russian Jews lived in 1912 showed that over half the books borrowed were non-fiction and that most of the fiction was by such authors as Tolstoy, Dumas, and Dickens, while light-weight best-sellers gathered dust on the shelves.[85] New York's free public libraries, free public lectures and—above all—free city colleges were a godsend to the Jews.

When the College of the City of New York, once known as the working man's Harvard, was a distinguished institution that admitted students strictly on their academic records, three-quarters of its students were Jewish. Some other colleges, notably Harvard, set upper limits on the number of Jewish students they would admit because of a fear that otherwise Jews would over-run the institution, because so many were so highly qualified. Similar limits were placed on the admissions of Jews to various universities in Eastern Europe between the two World Wars and in the Soviet Union after World War II for similar reasons.

Education was likewise not the basis for the initial rise of Lebanese immigrants in many societies. Although they came from a country with a tradition of education, 29 percent of the Lebanese immigrants who arrived in Brazil between 1908 and 1936 were illiterate, as were a majority of those who arrived in the first wave of Lebanese immigrants to nineteenth-century Australia, while most of those who immigrated to Mexico in the nineteenth century had not completed elementary school and those among them who were illiterate often kept letters from home for months until they could find someone to read them to them.[86] In Sierra Leone, the Europeanized Africans in Freetown initially "looked down on the Lebanese because they were uneducated and poor." Later this contempt "turned into dislike and even hatred when the Lebanese were successful in business."[87]

As with the Jews, the Lebanese first rose in occupations not requiring education but their tradition of respect for education then manifested itself in their later successful rise into the professions. The same pattern could be seen on the other side of the world, among the Chinese minority in Indonesia: "Everywhere they went the Chinese carried with them their reverence for learning," even though the earliest Chinese immigrants to Indonesia "were many of them illiterate."[88] In Burma, as late as 1931, there were more illiterate Chinese males than literate ones.[89] What the overseas Chinese had was not necessarily more education than others but more of an aspiration for education, which their economic rise through other means would allow them to fulfill. What was said of the Lebanese in the Dominican Republic—"Having achieved success in the commercial and industrial sphere, many Lebanese encouraged their sons to enter the professions"[90]—could be said of Lebanese in other countries, and of Jews and overseas Chinese as well. In nineteenth-century Germany and Austria, the Jewish intelligentsia was overwhelmingly from families that had succeeded in business.[91]

Jewish students, like students from other middleman minorities, tended to specialize in the more difficult and rewarding fields, such as science, medicine and law. In a later era, Chinese Americans would specialize disproportionately in engineering and science. Even during the era of anti-Chinese feeling in the United States before World War II, Chinese schoolchildren were among the favorites of teachers for their academic performance and their good behavior. At the college level, Asian American students have consistently scored higher than white American students on the mathematics portion of the Scholastic Aptitude Test. However, Asian Americans' success in academia and in later careers is not simply a reflection of higher test scores. A scholarly study found that white students had to have IQs 15 points higher to match either the educational or the economic performances of Asian Americans.[92]

When university admissions were based on academic performance in Malaysia, the Chinese minority there supplied an absolute majority of the students in higher education. During the decade of the 1960s, the Chinese students outnumbered students from the Malay majority by a hundred to one in the absolute number of degrees received in engineering. In Sri Lanka, children from the Tamil middleman minority outperformed members of the Sinhalese majority on admissions tests and in at least one year made an absolute majority of the A's on these tests. Here too the middleman minority students were particularly concentrated in science, medicine, and the law.

During the days of the Ottoman Empire, students in Armenian schools were found to perform not only better than students in Turkish schools but even wrote better in the Ottoman Turkish language than their Turkish counterparts.[93] During the era of the Soviet Union, Armenia did not require Russian experts to run its economic and other institutions, as some other Soviet republics did. As of 1960, 92 percent of the experts in Armenia were Armenians—and Armenia also exported about half of its experts to other Soviet republics.[94]

The Lebanese have long been among the more highly educated peoples of the Middle East, though in earlier times this did not mean universal literacy, as witnessed by the many illiterate Lebanese immigrants in the nineteenth and early twentieth century. Moreover, it was Christians in Lebanon who were especially likely to become educated. Partly this was because of Christian missionaries who established schools there for Lebanese Christians. Many of these educated Lebanese immigrated to other countries to live and work, and others went overseas to seek higher education. Before 1970, 40 percent of all Lebanese entering the United States did so as students.[95] Lebanese students in Brazil tended to specialize in courses that prepared them for careers in business and industry—and, later, law.[96] Yet even those students who went into law tended at first to become attorneys for their family businesses.

Political Activity

Various ethnic groups in countries around the world have differed greatly in the degree to which they participated in political activity and in the kind of political activity that they engaged in when they did. The Irish, for example, have heavily engaged in politics and have been highly successful at it. Irish political machines long dominated many American cities, even when Irish voters were a minority within those cities, and people of Irish ancestry have become presidents of the United States and prime ministers in Britain, Canada, and Australia. Middleman minorities have typically not been as involved in politics, nor as successful, and the kinds of politics they have pursued are usually different from the pragmatic, bring-home-the-bacon kinds of politics characteristic of the great Irish political machines.

For much of the history of Europe and the Islamic world, there was no place in positions of political authority for Jews, Armenians, or Lebanese, just as there was no place for the overseas Chinese in Southeast Asia or for Indians in Fiji or East Africa or

South Africa. Their whole orientation was usually in other directions, so that even the emergence of democratic societies did not attract as much participation among these groups as among some other ethnic groups. Even the belated emergence of individual politicians from middleman minority groups did not usually mean the development of ethnic-group politics. Rather, these political leaders usually rose to prominence as representatives of the larger society.

New York's Senator Jacob Javits and Governor Herbert Lehman were general politicians who were Jewish but not ethnic-group leaders. In Australia, where the Jews have never been as much as 1 percent of the population, Jewish politicians have been mayors of Melbourne, Adelaide and other communities, as well as serving in legislative and judicial posts, obviously not as a result of the Jewish vote, much less as standard-bearers of ethnic group politics. The overseas Chinese minorities in Southeast Asia or in the Western Hemisphere have typically avoided political careers, even where they were allowed to participate. Although there has been a Lebanese prime minister in Jamaica and a Peruvian president of Japanese ancestry, these posts were not achieved as a result of being ethnic politics leaders. Indeed, the virtual impossibility of middleman minority political power in these countries enabled these individuals to be viewed as national figures.

The exceptional cases where middleman minorities, as such, have played major political roles have involved countries where such minorities were a major portion of the total population—and their economic rise has generally *preceded* their political prominence, or even their political involvement on a large scale, rather than being a cause of it. Both in Fiji and in Guiana, people from India became at one time or another equal in number to the indigenous Fijian population, or to the population of African ancestry in the case of Guiana. In the latter country, Indian and black politicians formed a coalition to seek independence from Britain—a coalition which later split into polarized parties, each representing its own ethnic group, leading to internal disorder and political repression. In Fiji, the election of an Indian prime minister sparked a military coup led by indigenous Fijians. In Sri Lanka and Nigeria, both British former colonies like Fiji and Guiana, the emergence of independence and democratic government led to ethnic identity politics and to bloody civil wars.

The history of middleman minorities offers little support for those who see political power and ethnic identity politics as requirements for group economic advancement. Middleman minorities have typically advanced much more rapidly than other groups that have pursued political routes, even when those other groups have been successful in such pursuits. Nothing is easier than to name prominent political leaders of economically lagging racial and ethnic groups, but such leaders have usually not been as common among middleman minorities. Nor have the exceptional instances where middleman minorities have become heavily involved in politics led to better results for them.

SUMMARY AND IMPLICATIONS

Similarities in economic and social patterns among middleman minorities do not imply that any of these minorities copied others—that Parsees ever thought of themselves as "the Jews of India" or the Chinese as "the Jews of Southeast Asia." These patterns go back through centuries in which there was no such worldwide communication as the modern world takes for granted. Many of these groups had for centuries no way of knowing what middleman minorities elsewhere did or how. Yet, if these similarities do not imply emulation, what do they imply?

One of the implications of these similarities might be that the occupation of middleman minority itself has inherent requirements that must be met by those who successfully fulfill this role. The small capital needed for beginning in retailing at the bottom, perhaps as a peddler or as the owner of a tiny shop, means that many people can engage in this occupation, guaranteeing much competition and correspondingly low profit rates at the beginning of one's entrepreneurial career. Only those willing to endure such deprivations, and to put in long hours of work for the sake of the future, are likely to last long enough to begin to move up the economic ladder to the remarkable successes which middleman minorities have eventually achieved in many societies. Moreover, this may not be a process which can be completed, once and for all, for any given middleman minority. In many places and times, younger people have been brought in at the bottom, often in Third World countries, opening their own tiny businesses in remote hinterlands where few others have set up shop, whether in Africa or in Southeast Asia. Not everyone has either the temperament or the patience for this kind of life.

Various kinds of people are precluded from the outset. Brawling drunkards or live-for-the-moment individuals seldom even consider becoming middlemen, much less have any realistic chance of succeeding in such businesses. Given the long years that can pass between initial poverty and eventual prosperity, people with short time horizons are automatically precluded from this field. The utter dominance of particular minorities as middlemen amid vastly larger populations suggests that there are few members of the surrounding society who have all of the characteristics needed. Where differences between the whole lifestyle of the middleman minority and that of the majority population around them are so great, this means economic complementarity that benefits both—and social differences which alienate others and which can be exploited by demagogues to generate hostility and backlashes. The history of middleman minorities has been full of both.

Longer time horizons for middleman minorities influence their education and the kinds of careers their later generations pursue, as distinguished especially from the educational experiences of groups with shorter time horizons. Many years must elapse before any kind of education reaches a level where it pays off and this is of course particularly true where postgraduate education is a prerequisite for a professional career. People can become rock stars or professional athletes in a relatively few years, but it takes far longer to become a surgeon or scientist. There are correspondingly sharp differences in which groups become prominent or predominant in these different kinds of occupations. It is not only particular ethnic minorities, such as blacks or the Irish, who have at particular times dominated sports and entertainment in the United States, but also white Southerners.[97] All these groups have succeeded out of all proportion to their numbers in the general population, while all have been conspicuously rare among surgeons and scientists, where the descendants of middleman minorities have been over-represented.

Middleman minorities do not *happen* to be different. That differentness is central to their success and it carries over into other fields when they branch out into industry, commerce, and the professions. Middleman minorities must get used to long hours of work, for example. Consumers whose jobs leave them little time to shop, except early in the morning or later in the evening, can shop at stores run by people who work long hours. Consumers with low incomes can afford to buy in places where thin profit margins keep prices within reach, even when that restricts the standard of living of the peddlers or shopkeepers.

What all this implies is that middleman minorities must be very different from their customers. This differentness—and the social withdrawal needed to preserve this differentness in their children—then leave the middleman minorities vulnerable to charges of "clannishness" by political and other demagogues. Moreover, the lack of knowledge of either the business or the social imperatives of middlemen by outsiders leaves the majority population vulnerable to exploitation of their ignorance by politicians and activists who can spin plausible-sounding accusations against middleman minorities. These accusations can exploit racial, religious, or other differences, but this is not to say that such differences are the fundamental reasons for the hostility.

None of this need suggest that middleman minorities have done nothing to irritate the surrounding population or even to provoke their hostility. The many internal divisions within particular middleman minorities suggests that there are behaviors and attitudes that provoke negative reactions from other subgroups of Jews, overseas Chinese, Lebanese, and others. Against that background, it would hardly be surprising if members of the larger society were also irritated, repelled or made hostile by the behavior patterns or attitudes among middleman minorities. Moreover, there is independent evidence of illegal and other repellent behavior by members of middleman minorities, who have been no more free of sins than any other segment of the human race.

Illegal and often violent gang activities by overseas Chinese tongs in Southeast Asia go back for centuries and such activities have likewise followed Chinese immigrants to the Western Hemisphere. Jewish pimps made early twentieth-century Buenos Aires one of the world centers of prostitution, recruiting women as far away as Eastern Europe.[98] In the United States, there were many prominent Jewish gangsters during the immigrant era, including an organized group of killers for hire called "Murder, Incorporated." More widespread, if less violent, activities included corruption of public officials by the overseas Chinese in Southeast Asia and by Jews in Eastern Europe—both being places where such corruption was widespread in the general population and often especially necessary for middleman minorities, in order to escape discriminatory laws. Yet such habits did not end when middleman minorities settled elsewhere. A Yiddish-language newspaper in the United States complained of the corrupt behavior of Jews from Russia who got themselves in trouble offering bribes to American officials.[99]

In earlier centuries, middleman minorities and other merchants around the world included slaves among the merchandise they traded. These slave traders included Venetians, Greeks, and Jews in Europe,[100] the overseas Chinese in Southeast Asia,[101] and the Arabs who both captured and sold slaves in Africa.[102] Gujaratis from India often financed the African slave trade, though they did not usually conduct it.[103] In medieval Europe, Jews were major slave traders, often selling Slavs who had been enslaved by German conquerors.[104] Jews were also the principal suppliers of white eunuchs as slaves to the Ottoman Empire in the fifteenth century.[105] Later, as Italian merchants began displacing Jewish merchants in the eastern Mediterranean and the Black Sea during medieval times, they also began displacing Jews in the Black Sea slave trade.[106]

In ancient times, Jews were both slaves and slaveowners, as were many other peoples around the world.[107] By the time of the African slave trade to the United States, Jews played only a very minor role. During the antebellum era, Jews owned fewer slaves than free blacks owned and fewer even than American Indians owned.[108] Most Jewish immigrants arrived in the United States years after slavery had been abolished, and most arrived without enough money to buy a single slave, even had slavery still existed. The same was true of other groups that became middleman minorities in the United States. In short, during an era when slavery was an accepted and unquestioned institution around the world, neither middleman minorities nor any other group made a distinction between selling human beings and selling merchandise. The two things went together for centuries, whether among Europeans, Arabs, Asians or Africans. When the Yao, a Central African tribe, were the leading traders of ivory in their region, they were also the leading traders of slaves in that region.[109]

Too often the sources of irritation and hostility generated by the behavior and attitudes of middleman minorities themselves have been passed over in silence, lest one be accused of "blaming the victim." Yet explanation is not blame, much less an excuse for mass violence against the innocent or even for bigotry based on ignorance or arrogance. Hostility to middleman minorities has been widespread for centuries, though many have managed to live peacefully until some dramatic event or some talented demagogue managed to stir the population against them. For example, the plagues that decimated Europe in the Middle Ages were sometimes blamed on Jews, leading to mob violence against them.

Where has hostility to middleman minorities been greatest? There may not be any single predictor that covers all cases. Yet, in broad terms, it seems clear—painfully clear—that they have been most hated where they have been most essential. This has not always been the same as where they make their greatest economic or other contribution. Jews have made great contributions to the United States in a wide range of fields, but there are many other Americans who have also made great contributions in those same fields. Even if Jews' greatest contributions to the world have been in the United States, there have been other countries—in Eastern Europe, for example—where they were more essential because there were relatively few other people doing what they did.

Persecution and violence have driven many middleman minorities from many countries and some have been explicitly expelled by government authorities. The widespread belief that such groups have made no "productive" contribution to the economies in which they lived has often been belied by the decline or collapse of those economies after their departure. Yet even after such collapses, popular hostility has seldom abated. Twenty years after the expulsion of 50,000 Indians and Pakistanis from Uganda in the 1970s had wreaked havoc on that country's economy, economic desperation led the government to seek their return. But the Uganda Africa Trade Movement issued a statement declaring that its members "intend to wage an atrocious war everywhere in Uganda on any Asian returnee." More explicitly, they said:

> We intend to harm, maim, cause them a lot of suffering, even killing them in the most despicable way ever…if they don't leave our land and country immediately.[110]

What was threatened in Uganda has been carried out against middleman minorities in many places and times. For example, the Turkish persecutions and mass slaughters of the Armenians during the First World War included "bayoneting the men to death, raping the women, dashing their children against the rocks."[111] When the American ambassador protested to a Turkish official, the reply he received was: "The massacres! What of them! They merely amuse me!" On one death march in which thousands perished, "Ambassador Morgenthau reported that many of the women had been stripped stark naked by their guards and by brigands in league with them. The poor creatures could hardly walk for shame; they staggered into the city bent double."[112] These calculatingly sadistic tortures and humiliations were a foretaste of what would happen to the Jews in Nazi extermination camps a generation later.

Note that merely killing middleman minorities was not considered sufficient. Gratuitous infliction of both physical and psychic pain has marked violence against the Chinese in Southeast Asia, as well as against the Armenians in the Ottoman Empire, and the Jews in Europe. This suggests that what their enemies feel is not simply a need to be rid of them but also a need to rid themselves of feelings of inferiority by subjecting middleman minorities to humiliation and dehumanization. These middlemen—"their wealth inexplicable, their superiority intolerable"[113]—are basically an ego problem among those who have been so blatantly outperformed. This is also consistent with the history of the countries where middleman minorities have been either accepted or bitterly opposed.

It is in precisely those times and places where there are few others who can supply the skills of middleman minorities that they are most hated—whether it is the Koreans in today's American black ghettos, Jews in Eastern Poland in centuries past, Chinese in Southeast Asia, Armenians in regions of the Ottoman Empire where they were the predominant entrepreneurial group, Lebanese in West Africa, Ibos in northern Nigeria, Indians in East Africa or others in other places. Where middleman minorities have been more accepted have been places where others have had similar skills and entrepreneurial occupations, such as the United States, Australia, Britain, and the Scandinavian countries.

It has been precisely where middleman minorities have been most needed economically that they have been most hated, while places that have been not nearly as dependent on them have been places where they have found their greatest acceptance. This does not present a very reassuring picture of human reasonableness, but neither does the history of most middleman minorities.

Where members of middleman minorities have largely moved beyond their middleman occupations into other businesses and professions, and where they have also been accepted by the larger society, the "clannishness" of their earlier struggling times has tended to erode away as they became assimilated members of the larger society. This happened more often, for example, among Jews in Anglo-American societies, including Australia, than among those in Eastern Europe.

Notable examples in nineteenth-century Western Europe included Benjamin Disraeli, David Ricardo, and Karl Marx. While religious restrictions kept Jews out of the British Parliament during the first half of the nineteenth century, individuals of known Jewish ancestry were able to enter if they were Christians in religion. Thus David Ricardo sat in Parliament in 1819 and Benjamin Disraeli entered in 1837, eventually becoming Prime Minister. Although Karl Marx was descended from a long line of rabbis on both sides of his family, he was baptized and raised as a Christian living among other Christians in Germany. He never considered himself a Jew and always spoke of Jews in the third person.

Even religious Jews were so acculturated in pre-Hitler Germany that they referred to themselves as "Germans of the Mosaic faith." Even after emigrating overseas, they often settled among German immigrants in other countries and participated in German cultural organizations in those countries. But Polish Jews never considered themselves Poles, either in Poland or overseas, and did not settle in Polish immigrant neighborhoods. Much the same story could be told of the overseas Chinese, who continue to live in their own enclaves in countries where they encounter hostility but, in the United States, no longer live primarily in Chinatowns, which have been left to a minority of later arriving immigrants or others who have not assimilated.

It would be good to know what proportion of groups known as middleman minorities actually worked in middleman occupations at a given time but data are seldom available. Most Jews have been middleman minorities in some times and places but not in others. Apparently most Lebanese immigrants to Argentina were in such occupations, but most Armenians in the Ottoman Empire were not. Among the occupations declared by Middle Eastern arrivals in Argentina from 1876 to 1900, the overwhelming majority were merchants and more than a quarter were specifically peddlers as late as 1910.[114] However, it is known that more Armenians in the Ottoman Empire were peasants than were entrepreneurs or money-lenders.[115] But it was in the latter roles that they were more likely to come to the attention of members of the larger society, either through personal contact in the marketplace or through general notoriety. To a greater or lesser degree, that has been true of other middleman minorities. Moreover, the general attitudes of the surrounding society that were formed during the era when these various groups were prominent as middleman minorities have long outlasted that era and continued on as a majority in later generations of middleman minorities have gone into other businesses and professions. Moreover, the striking success of these later generations in education and in other occupations continues to fuel envy and resentment.

The role of middleman minorities in various countries around the world has attracted the attention of many scholars and produced many suggested explanations of their roles and experiences. One of the most often cited studies has been "A Theory of Middleman Minorities" by Edna Bonacich.[116] A crucial element in her theory is that of sojourning. Middleman minorities have often been sojourners rather than permanent settlers in the societies in which they live. Because "they begin as sojourners," according to Professor Bonacich, they have less reason to assimilate to the society around them. While sojourning "is not a sufficient condition of the middleman," Professor Bonacich says, "it is a necessary one." However, if the economic function performed by middlemen requires social separation from the surrounding society and its culture, then whether they plan to return somewhere else or not is no longer crucial.

The sojourning theory encounters serious problems that the economic explanation does not. One of the most prominent of middleman minorities has been American Jews who, as Professor Bonacich concedes, "had no plan to return to Eastern Europe."[117] American Jews in fact had far lower rates of return migration than did other contemporary immigrants to the United States or Mexican immigrants in a later era. Even less could Jews who settled in Australia or South America be likely to have had plans to return to their countries of origin.

Edna Bonacich attempts to salvage her sojourner thesis by saying that although American Jews did not see Eastern Europe as a place to which they would return, they retained "an unusual attachment to an ancestral homeland" in the Middle East. Yet Zionism was by no means common among Jews around the world during the period of mass migration to the United States, and in fact there was hostility to the idea among Orthodox Jews, as well as among Western European Jews in general. Moreover, emotional attachment to an ancestral homeland says nothing about any plans to return to it today. Irish Americans, like Jewish Americans, have maintained an emotional attachment to their ancestral homeland, but nevertheless there are more people of Irish ancestry living in the United States than in Ireland, just as there are more Jews living in the United States than in Israel.

By the time Zionism was rekindled after the Second World War by the establishment of Israel, American Jews were culturally assimilated and had rising rates of intermarriage with the general population, as well as moving out of middleman occupations and into the professions. In short, sojourning seems neither necessary nor sufficient, nor even plausible, to explain the cultural separation of Jews or other middleman minorities. While it is true that many middleman minorities began their careers abroad as sojourners—the Chinese in Southeast Asia or the Lebanese in West Africa, for example—so did other immigrant groups such as the Italians, an absolute majority of whom returned to Italy, not only from other European countries but also from the United States and even South America. That remains true today of immigrants from India and Pakistan working in the Middle East.

As Professor Bonacich concedes, the fact that many middleman minorities *began* as sojourners does not mean that most of them in fact returned home. There were growing permanent settlements of Chinese in Southeast Asia, for example, even as the Chinese continued to live wholly separate social lives from those of the surrounding Malay or Indonesian societies. Sojourning has been a phase in the immigration of many groups who never became middleman minorities, with their settlements abroad becoming permanent only after achieving a satisfactory modus vivendi with the surrounding population.

Another feature of middleman minorities cited by various scholars has been their tendency to invest in highly mobile capital—intellectual skills being the ultimate in portability—rather than in fixtures that could not move, such as the machinery of heavy industry, land, dams or transmission lines for electricity or conduits for water. No doubt centuries of a history of being victims of spoliation and confiscation, as well as being forced by mob violence or official expulsion to flee and leave much of their wealth behind, has made highly portable wealth particularly attractive to middleman minorities. Cash, gems, and intellectual skills are among these highly portable forms of wealth. Moreover, even forms of wealth that are not strictly portable, but which can be readily liquidated, such as inventories of groceries, textiles, clothing, or sewing machines, have been preferable to steel mills, railroads, or hydroelectric dams. None of this depends upon an "orientation toward a homeland," as Professor Bonacich contends.[118] Indians and Pakistanis fleeing Uganda fled to Britain more often than to India or Pakistan and, in an earlier era, Jews fleeing persecution in Eastern Europe fled to the United States far more often than to the Middle East.

While our focus has been on patterns among middleman minorities in general, what of the Jews specifically? To what extent are they generic and to what extent do they have their own separate and distinct patterns? Jews are, like every other individual and group, unique in some ways and very much like other people in other ways. Whatever has been unique, or thought to be unique, about them has been seized upon and used negatively by their enemies. Their supposed role in the crucifixion of Jesus—"Christ killers" in the bitter indictment of a bygone era of religious bigotry—can hardly have been the reason for that bigotry, for it was the Romans who actually crucified Jesus and no such guilt has been attached to the whole Italian people of later centuries. Moreover, wholly fictitious complaints have been invoked against the Jews—that they were responsible for medieval plagues, for example—when whoever made up these charges obviously had other reasons for hostility. It is these other reasons that have been common to numerous other groups who have faced similar hostility in countries around the world, despite differing from the Jews in religion, language and other social and cultural traits.

Some have regarded the Holocaust as making anti-Jewish feeling unique, at least in intensity. Yet what made the Holocaust possible were technological and organizational capabilities for mass murder that enemies of other middleman minorities simply did not have available. In view of what was actually done to some of these other groups, there is little reason to doubt that their persecutors would have used such technological and organizational capabilities if they had had them.

In Eric Hoffer's account of a mass movement's need for unifying elements, he classified hatred as one of those elements. He quoted Hitler as saying that if there were no such thing as a Jew, "We should then have to invent him. It is essential to have a tangible enemy, not merely an abstract one." Hoffer added:

F. A. Voigt tells of a Japanese mission that arrived in Berlin in 1932 to study the National Socialist movement. Voigt asked a member of the mission what he thought of the movement. He replied:"It is magnificent. I wish we could have something like it in Japan, only we can't, because we haven't got any Jews."[119]

The tragic history of middleman minorities around the world shows that often there are many substitutes for Jews in the role of scapegoats, as well as in their economic functions.

In terms of their achievements in the arts and sciences, Jews have been unique, not only among middleman minorities but also among the world's population at large. They have been particularly over-represented among the leading figures in such fields as mathematics, the sciences, and philosophy. In the second half of the twentieth century, Jews won 29 percent of all the Nobel Prizes in the sciences, medicine and literature combined, even though Jews were less than one-half of 1 percent of the world's population.[120] Such spectacular achievements have come only in relatively recent times, as history is measured. These have been largely the achievements of Ashkenazic Jews, who were excluded from civil society for many centuries in most of Europe where they lived, and their remarkable rise to prominence among the leading intellectual figures dates largely from the nineteenth century, when severe restrictions on them were relaxed in a growing number of European countries. It was in the new nation of the United States that Jews were first accorded civil equality and it was here that their greatest successes were achieved. Another way of looking at this is that much of the world for much of history lost the benefits of the talents of these people—and of similar people elsewhere— through suppression and persecution. While the intellectual achievements of Jews have been unique, the bigotry and persecution that they suffered has been the fate of middleman minorities around the world.

While there are characteristics and achievements which are uniquely Jewish, the history of middleman minorities around the world seems to suggest that it has not been these uniquely Jewish characteristics which called forth venomous hatreds but characteristics and achievements common to middleman minorities, both when they are in that occupational role and after they move beyond into a wide range of occupations. Whatever is unique to each of these groups may be seized upon by those promoting hatred of them but that does not mean that the promotion of hatred in the first place has been due to qualities unique to each group. However unique any of these groups may be, historically the kind of hostility and hatred they have faced has been generic.

The Real History of Slavery

S LAVERY WAS AN EVIL OF GREATER SCOPE and magnitude than most people imagine and, as a result, its place in history is radically different from the way it is usually portrayed. Mention slavery and immediately the image that arises is that of Africans and their descendants enslaved by Europeans and their descendants in the Southern United States—or, at most, Africans enslaved by Europeans in the Western Hemisphere. No other historic horror is so narrowly construed. No one thinks of war, famine, or decimating epidemics in such localized terms. These are afflictions that have been suffered by the entire human race, all over the planet—and so was slavery. Had slavery been limited to one race in one country during three centuries, its tragedies would not have been one-tenth the magnitude that they were in fact.

Why this provincial view of a worldwide evil? Often it is those who are most critical of a "Eurocentric" view of the world who are most Eurocentric when it comes to the evils and failings of the human race. Why would anyone wish to arbitrarily understate an evil that plagued mankind for thousands of years, unless it was not this evil itself that was the real concern, but rather the present-day uses of that historic evil? Clearly, the ability to score ideological points against American society or Western civilization, or to induce guilt and thereby extract benefits from the white population today, are greatly enhanced by making enslavement appear to be a peculiarly American, or a peculiarly white, crime.

This explanation is also consistent with the otherwise inexplicable contrast between the fiery rhetoric about past slavery in the United States used by those who pass over in utter silence the

111

traumas of slavery that still exist in Mauritania, the Sudan, and parts of Nigeria and Benin. Why so much more concern for dead people who are now beyond our help than for living human beings suffering the burdens and humiliations of slavery today? Why does a verbal picture of the abuses of slaves in centuries past arouse far more response than contemporary photographs of present-day slaves in *Time* magazine, the *New York Times* or the *National Geographic?*[1]

It takes no more research than a trip to almost any public library or college library to show the incredibly lopsided coverage of slavery in the United States or in the Western Hemisphere, as compared to the meager writings on the even *larger* number of Africans enslaved in the Islamic countries of the Middle East and North Africa, not to mention the vast numbers of Europeans also enslaved in centuries past in the Islamic world and within Europe itself. At least a million Europeans were enslaved by North African pirates alone from 1500 to 1800,[2] and some European slaves were still being sold on the auction block in Egypt, years after the Emancipation Proclamation freed blacks in the United States. Indeed, an Anglo-Egyptian treaty of August 4, 1877 prohibited the continued sale of white slaves after August 3, 1885, as well as prohibiting the import and export of Sudanese and Abyssinian slaves.[3]

During the Middle Ages, Slavs were so widely used as slaves in both Europe and the Islamic world that the very word "slave" derived from the word for Slav—not only in English, but also in other European languages, as well as in Arabic.[4] Nor have Asians or Polynesians been exempt from either being enslaved or enslaving others. China in centuries past has been described as "one of the largest and most comprehensive markets for the exchange of human beings in the world"[5] Slavery was also common in India, where it has been estimated that there were more slaves than in the entire Western Hemisphere—and where the original Thugs kidnapped children for the purpose of enslavement.[6] In some of the cities of Southeast Asia, slaves were a majority of the population.[7] Slavery was also an established institution in the Western Hemisphere before Columbus' ships ever appeared on the horizon. The Ottoman Empire regularly enslaved a percentage of the young boys from the Balkans, converted them to Islam and assigned them to various duties in the civil or military establishment.[8]

RACE AND SLAVERY

The instrumental use of the history of slavery today also underlies the claim that slavery grew out of racism. For most of its long history, which includes most of the history of the human race, slavery was largely *not* the enslavement of racially different people, for the simple reason that only in recent centuries has either the technology or the wealth existed to go to another continent to get slaves and transport them en masse across an ocean. People were enslaved because they were vulnerable, not because of how they looked. The peoples of the Balkans were enslaved by fellow Europeans, as well as by the peoples of the Middle East, for at least six centuries before the first African was brought to the Western Hemisphere.[9]

Before the modern era, by and large Europeans enslaved other Europeans, Asians enslaved other Asians, Africans enslaved other Africans, and the indigenous peoples of the Western Hemisphere enslaved other indigenous peoples of the Western Hemisphere. Slavery was not based on race, much less on theories about race. Only relatively late in history did enslavement across racial lines occur on such a scale as to promote an ideology of racism that outlasted the institution of slavery itself.

Wherever a separate people were enslaved, they were disdained or despised, whether they were different by country, religion, caste, race, or tribe. The Europeans who were enslaved in North Africa were despised and abused because they were Christians in a Moslem region of the world,[10] where they were called "Christian dogs." Race became the most visible difference between slaves and slaveowners in the Western Hemisphere. As distinguished historian Daniel J. Boorstin put it: "Now for the first time in Western history, the status of slave coincided with a difference of race."[11] To make racism the driving force behind slavery is to make a historically recent factor the cause of an institution which originated thousands of years earlier. This enshrinement of racism as an over-arching causal factor accords far more with current instrumental agendas than with history.

The form in which the story of slavery has reached most people today has been along the lines of the best-selling book and widely-watched television mini-series, *Roots* by Alex Haley. Challenged on the historical accuracy of *Roots,* Haley said: "I tried to give my people a myth to live by."[12] This instrumental use of history—or purported history—is open to the same objections as other instrumental myth-making. First is the objection to falsification itself, that the damage which this does to the general level of understanding and trust in a society is incalculable, and can easily outweigh, in its long-run consequences especially, any immediate good that might be expected from an expedient taking of liberties with the truth. Second, even the short-run benefits are by no means clear. Has a sense of special grievance helped advance any people—or has what happened in centuries past been a distraction and an incitement to counterproductive strife, much as territorial irredentism has been?

Rather than debate current ideological agendas, we can try to determine what we can about the actual history of slavery, including how it ended. No institution of comparable age and worldwide scope has ever disappeared, over almost the entire planet, leaving so little awareness of how and why it vanished or so little interest in that question. Volumes continue to be published about the decline and fall of the Roman Empire which, for all its greatness, did not encompass one-tenth as much of the world as the institution of slavery did. Archaeologists continue to excavate the ruins of ancient civilizations in Central America and the Middle East, while military historians pore through archives and examine ancient weapons to try to piece together the history of warfare. Yet remarkably little is written about one of the most momentous moral dramas in the history of the human species—the bitter worldwide struggle, which lasted for more than a century, to destroy the elaborate systems and institutions for the ownership and sale of human beings.

While there is a sizable literature on the American Civil War, for all its staggering carnage and historic legacy within the United States, in an international perspective it is only a small and highly atypical part of the story of the worldwide crusade against slavery. No other nation ended slavery in the same way as the United States did and few ended it after so short a struggle, as history is measured.

How and why did slavery end in most of the world?

There were two major processes. Over the centuries, as more and more territories around the world consolidated into nation states with their own armies and navies, raiding those territories to capture and enslave the people who lived within them became more hazardous in itself and also risked military retaliation against the countries from which the raiders came. Thus more and more peoples became off-limits to slave-raiders over time. Put differently, the areas which remained subject to slave raiding over the centuries were primarily those where the people lived in smaller or weaker societies. Such societies continued to exist where it was difficult, for geographic or other reasons, to consolidate large areas under one government. This was true of the Balkans, the backwaters of Asia, and much of sub-Saharan Africa. By the early modern era, sub-Saharan Africa with its numerous and severe geographic handicaps[13] was one of the last remaining areas from which vast numbers of people could be enslaved.

Far from being targeted by Europeans for racial reasons, as some have claimed, Africa was resorted to as a source of large supplies of slaves only after centuries of Europeans enslaving other Europeans had been brought to an end by the consolidation of nations and empires on the European continent, by internal shifts from slavery to serfdom in much of Europe, and by the Catholic Church's pressures against enslaving fellow Christians—which was by no means the same as the Church's saying that slavery, as such, was wrong.[14] Similar consolidations of political units in parts of Asia led to a decline of slavery in those realms.[15] While Africa became the main source of new slaves in later centuries, existing slaves continued to include peoples of many races living in many places around the world. Ending the slavery of all these peoples was a very difficult process and one requiring deliberate and sustained action for many generations.

Ironically, the anti-slavery ideology behind this process began to develop in eighteenth century Britain, at a time when the

British Empire led the world in slave trading, and when the economy of most of its overseas colonies in the Western Hemisphere
depended on slaves. Here again, the baffling present-day disregard
of an international saga of strife, full of individual dramas as well as
historic consequences, seems explicable only in terms of today's
ideological agendas. While slavery was common to all civilizations,
as well as to peoples considered uncivilized, only one civilization
developed a moral revulsion against it, very late in its history—
Western civilization. Today it seems so obvious that, as Abraham
Lincoln said, "If slavery is not wrong, nothing is wrong."[16] But the
hard fact is that, for thousands of years, slavery was simply not an
issue, even among the great religious thinkers or moral philosophers of civilizations around the world.

We may wonder why it took eighteen centuries after the Ser-
mon on the Mount for Christians to develop an anti-slavery
movement, but a more profound question is why not even the
leading moralists in other civilizations rejected slavery at all.
"There is no evidence," according to a scholarly study, "that slavery came under serious attack in any part of the world before the
eighteenth century."[17] That is when it first came under attack in
Europe.

Themselves the leading slave traders of the eighteenth century, Europeans nevertheless became, in the nineteenth century,
the destroyers of slavery around the world—not just in European
societies or European offshoot societies overseas, but in non-European societies as well, over the bitter opposition of Africans, Arabs,
Asians, and others. Moreover, within Western civilization, the principal impetus for the abolition of slavery came first from very
conservative religious activists—people who would today be
called "the religious right." Clearly, this story is not "politically cor-
rect" in today's terms. Hence it is ignored, as if it never happened.

WESTERN AND NON-WESTERN SOCIETIES

Slavery did not die out quietly of its own accord. It went down
fighting to the bitter end—and it lost only because Europeans had
gunpowder weapons first. The advance of European imperialism
around the world marked the retreat of the slave trade and then of

slavery itself. The British stamped out slavery, not only throughout the British Empire—which included one-fourth of the world, whether measured in land or people—but also by its pressures and its actions against other nations. For example, the British navy entered Brazilian waters in 1849 and destroyed Brazilian ships that had been used in the slave trade. The British government pressured the Ottoman Empire into banning the African slave trade and, later, threatened to start boarding Ottoman ships in the Mediterranean if that empire did not do a better job of policing the ban. Still later, Americans stamped out slavery in the Philippines, the Dutch stamped it out in Indonesia, the Russians in Central Asia, the French in their West African and Caribbean colonies. Germans, in their East Africa colonies, often hanged slave traders on the spot when they caught them in the act.[18]

No non-Western nation or civilization shared this animosity toward slavery that began to develop in the Western world in the late eighteenth century, reached its peak in the nineteenth century, and continued to fuel the anti-slavery efforts that were still necessary in much of Africa and the Middle East on into the first half of the twentieth century. This worldwide struggle went on for more than a century because the non-Western world in general resisted and evaded all efforts to get them to root out this institution that was an integral part of their economies and societies. When the British ambassador to the Ottoman Empire first raised the issue of abolishing slavery with the sultan in 1840, he reported this response:

> ...I have been heard with extreme astonishment accompanied with a smile at a proposition for destroying an institution closely inter-woven with the frame of society in this country, and intimately connected with the law and with the habits and even the religion of all classes, from the Sultan himself on down to the lowest peasant.[19]

Similarly, the Maoris of New Zealand responded to comments on their enslavement of some fellow Polynesians on other islands by saying:

> We took possession...in accordance with our customs and we caught all the people. Not one escaped. Some ran away from us,

these we killed, and others we killed—but what of that? It was in accordance with our customs.[20]

When British Foreign Secretary Palmerston sought in 1841 through his representative consul, Atkins Hamerton, to get the ruler of Zanzibar to end the flourishing slave trade there, this was the response:

> When Palmerston continued to press for an end to the slave trade, Said pleaded that if he acceded to British demands his subjects would withdraw their loyalty from him, and support another claimant to the throne. And was he not looked up to by all Arabs generally "as the person who should protect and guarantee for them their dearest interest—the right to carry on the slave trade?" He reminded Hamerton that Arabs were not 'like the English and other European people who were always reading and writing' and were unable to understand the anti-slavery viewpoint. The British obsession with it was quite inexplicable to them.[21]

In short, what was so patently wrong about slavery—in the eyes of Western civilization of the past two centuries—was almost incomprehensible to many non-Westerners. Eventually, some Westernized elites or intellectuals in non-Western societies also became embarrassed about slavery but these societies developed no such fervent anti-slavery movements as those which propelled successive European and European-offshoot societies to ban this practice for themselves and to stamp it out among others. In the Western world, hostility to slavery was by no means confined to elites. When a British ship stopped at Zanzibar in the nineteenth century, it was considered "dangerous" to let British sailors go ashore, for fear that they would riot if they saw the slave market there.[22] In the years leading up to the abolition of slavery in Brazil, soldiers and their officers "no longer believed in the legitimacy of slavery" and so dragged their feet when assigned the task of recapturing runaway slaves:

> Soldiers continued to be sent to places where slaves were on the loose, but were not afraid to express their unwillingness to capture fugitives. The commander of an army unit sent to a community in São Paulo early in 1888 agreed to maintain order but

openly declined to capture slaves.... In places runaways were loitering on the roads, refusing to work. Army units sent to control them did nothing.[23]

Not all Brazilian soldiers refused orders to control or recapture escaped slaves but there was enough opposition to this role that a formal request was made to the civil authorities by the military to relieve them of this distasteful duty.[24] With public opinion increasingly hostile to the continuation of slavery and many Brazilians keenly aware of, and painfully embarrassed by, the fact that their country was the last one in the Western world to still have slavery, the plantation owners were increasingly isolated and some began freeing their slaves themselves, in anticipation of official emancipation, and in some cases in hopes of retaining these workers as employees. Thus, when the official date of emancipation arrived in Brazil, most slaves were already free, either having been freed by plantation owners or having simply left the plantations on their own, secure in the knowledge that the surrounding population was not likely to cooperate in their recapture and return. Still, when the official day of emancipation arrived, it was a cause of national celebration:

> The novelist Machado de Assis recalled that the celebrations following the passage of the Golden Law were "the only instance of popular delirium that I can remember ever having seen." One São Paulo newspaper described the crowds that gathered to celebrate: "To try to describe the splendor of that festival of joy, to tell everything that happened, falls beyond our abilities.... Never has this capital seen such multitudinous and unanimous enthusiasm."[25]

Perhaps at no other period of history was the contrast between the Western and the non-Western world greater. Here was the scene when the Ottoman Empire announced the end of the slave trade:

> In 1855, when the Sultan's firman was read out in Mecca and Jedda, it caused a revolution. Turkish officials, including the kadi who read the firman, were murdered, the garrison shut, and Mecca was in a state of revolt until the Porte repealed the obnoxious order.... And when the Governor-General of the Hed-

jaz issued orders on 25 February 1860, forbidding the slave trade in all Turkish ports in the Red Sea, there was great excitement and fear of the recurrence of the 1855 violence. There was no Ottoman cruiser in the Red Sea capable of giving effect to this order, and Turkish officials were too frightened to enforce it.[26]

Although the slave *trade* was formally abolished in the Ottoman Empire, under pressure from the British government, slavery itself continued. As of 1891, the imperial palace purchased eleven slave girls for its harem, as others in the Ottoman Empire purchased women as concubines—typically white women from a region near the Caucasus and the Black Sea known as Circassia[27]— even though every nation in the Western world had by then outlawed slavery. Not only the Turks accepted such slavery, so did the Circassians. Mothers often groomed their daughters for this role and sold them into what was considered to be a desirable situation, at least by comparison with what was available in Circassia. British foreign secretary Palmerston said, "the only complaint we have ever heard from the Circassians has been against our attempts to stop the traffic."[28]

Contrary to the "myths to live by" created by Alex Haley and others, Africans were by no means the innocents portrayed in *Roots,* baffled as to why white men were coming in and taking their people away in chains.[29] On the contrary, the region of West Africa from which Kunte Kinte supposedly came was one of the great slave-trading regions of the continent—before, during, and after the white man arrived. It was the Africans who enslaved their fellow Africans, selling some of these slaves to Europeans or to Arabs and keeping others for themselves. Even at the peak of Atlantic slave trade, Africans retained more slaves for themselves than they sent to the Western Hemisphere.[30]

This pattern was not confined to West Africa, from which most slaves were sent to the Western Hemisphere. In East Africa, the Masai were feared slave raiders and other African tribes— either alone or in conjunction with Arabs—enslaved their more vulnerable neighbors. As late as 1891, it was reported that "Manyuema slavers had demoralized surrounding tribes, destroying crops, and famine reigned everywhere."[31] Even in the early twentieth century, Abyssinians were still raiding other Africans and carrying off slaves.[32] It was 1922 before the British had gained sufficient control in Tanganyika to stamp out slavery there.[33] Arabs were the leading slave raiders in East Africa, ranging over an area larger than all of Europe.[34] The total number of slaves exported from East Africa during the nineteenth century has been estimated to be at least two million.[35]

Despite the impression created by *Roots*, during the era of the massive slave trade from West Africa, a white man was more likely to catch malaria in Africa than to catch slaves himself. The average life expectancy of a white man in the interior of sub-Saharan Africa at that time was less than one year. By and large, men from Europe or the Western Hemisphere came to the coasts of Africa, bought their slaves, and left as soon as possible. Even so, the death rates among the white crews of the ships carrying slaves to the Western Hemisphere were as high as the death rates among the slaves themselves. It was only much later, after quinine and other medical measures enabled Europeans to survive where there were tropical diseases, was it possible for them to invade Africa in force and establish empires there. But, by then, the Atlantic slave trade had already been ended. During the era of that trade, Africa was largely ruled by Africans, who established the conditions under which slave sales took place. The crew of a slave ship was in no position to defy African rulers and their armies by going out across the land and capturing people willy-nilly. The stronger African peoples captured and enslaved the weaker peoples—the same pattern found over the centuries in Europe, Asia, the Western Hemisphere, and Polynesia:

> In Nyasaland, the Ngoni and Yao swaggered over and terrorized other tribes. In Uganda, the Baganda made life miserable for their neighbours; and the Nyoro and Hima of Ankole enslaved Toro women and children. The Tutsi dominated the Hutu in Ruanda; The Masai lorded it over the Kikuyu and Kamba, and the latter, in turn, held the Ndorobo in a kind of serfdom.[36]

It was precisely the fact that Europeans—except for the Portuguese—seldom participated in the raids that captured and enslaved Africans that enabled most people in Europe and the Americas to remain oblivious to the traumatic experience that this was, with some Africans committing suicide to avoid capture and wives being whipped as they tried to cling to their husbands or children. Historian David Brion Davis pointed out that "Europeans had little contact with the actual process of enslavement" and that "as late as 1721 the Royal African Company asked its agents to investigate the modes of enslavement in the interior."[37] Europeans typically saw only the end-results—enslaved people being offered for sale on the coast. It was much the same story in the Ottoman Empire, where those who bought slaves had no idea what these slaves had been through before.

Slavery was destroyed within the United States at staggering costs in blood and treasure, but the struggle was over within a few ghastly years of warfare. Nevertheless, the Civil War was the bloodiest war ever fought in the Western Hemisphere, and more Americans were killed in that war than in any other war in the country's history. But this was a highly atypical—indeed, unique—way to end slavery. In most of the rest of the world, unremitting efforts to destroy the institution of slavery went on for more than a century, on a thousand shifting fronts, and in the face of determined and ingenious efforts to continue the trade in human beings.

Within the British Empire, the abolition of slavery was accompanied by the payment of compensation to slave owners for what was legally the confiscation of their property. This cost the British government £20 million—a huge sum in the nineteenth century, about 5 percent of the nation's annual output.[38] A similar plan to have the federal government of the United States buy up the slaves and then set them free was proposed in Congress, but was never implemented. The costs of emancipating the millions of slaves in the United States would have been more than half the annual national output—but still less than the economic costs of the Civil War,[39] quite aside from the cost in blood and lives, and a legacy of lasting bitterness in the South, growing out of its defeat and the widespread destruction it suffered during that conflict.

While the British could simply abolish slavery in their Western Hemisphere colonies, they faced a more daunting and longer-lasting task of patrolling the Atlantic off the coast of Africa, in order to prevent slave ships of various nationalities from continuing to supply slaves illegally. Even during the Napoleonic wars, Britain continued to keep some of its warships on patrol off West Africa. Moreover, such patrols likewise tried to interdict the shipments of slaves from East Africa through the Indian Ocean, the Red Sea, and the Persian Gulf. Brazil capitulated to British demands that it end its slave trade, after being publicly humiliated by British warships that seized and destroyed slave ships within Brazil's own waters. In 1873, two British cruisers appeared off the coast of Zanzibar and threatened to blockade the island unless the slave market there shut down. It was shut down.

It would be hard to think of any other crusade pursued so relentlessly for so long by any nation, at such mounting costs, without any economic or other tangible benefit to itself. These costs included bribes paid to Spain and Portugal to get their cooperation with the effort to stop the international slave trade and the costs of maintaining naval patrols and of resettling freed slaves, not to mention dangerous frictions with France and the United States, among other countries.[40] Captains of British warships who detained vessels suspected of carrying slaves were legally liable if those vessels turned out to have no slaves on board. The human costs were also large:

> The heavy drain, physical and mental, in keeping squadrons on the East African coast was reflected in the loss of 282 officers and men in the ten years 1875-85; and this did not include these invalidated home. Naval personnel, wracked by fever, sunstroke and dysentery, were forced to retire prematurely and live on a small pittance. The cost of upkeep of the squadron over the twenty years prior to 1890 was estimated at four millions sterling, and this did not take into account the large amount of work imposed on consular and judicial staff at Zanzibar in trying cases and dealing with reports, etc.[41]

Even so, the results were slow in coming. More streamlined slave ships were designed, in hopes of being able to outrun the ships of the Royal Navy in the Atlantic.[42] Nevertheless, the dogged persistence of the British eventually reduced the shipment of slaves across the Atlantic and across the waters of the Islamic world. Although the French flag was for many years widely used as protection from the boarding of ships on the high seas by the

British navy, even by slave traders who were neither French nor authorized to fly the French flag, eventually France itself turned against slavery, outlawed the institution and sent some of its own warships to patrol the Atlantic off the coast of Africa to intercept and deter the shipment of slaves to the Western Hemisphere. The American flag was likewise so used[43] and the United States, like France, eventually turned against the slave trade and sent warships to join the Atlantic patrols to interdict slave shipments.

Although by 1860 the Atlantic slave trade had been effectively stopped, the slave trade from East Africa across the Indian Ocean, the Red Sea and the Persian Gulf took longer to be reduced significantly. Off the east coast of Africa, smaller Arab vessels called dhows hugged the coastlines, in waters too shallow for the British warships to enter.[44] One British commodore estimated that he captured one dhow for every eight that escaped.[45] Nevertheless, during the period from 1866 to 1869, 129 slave vessels were captured and 3,380 slaves were freed.[46] When the threat of being boarded seemed imminent, the Arabs would throw slaves overboard to drown, rather than have them be found on board, which could lead to British seizure of the vessel and punishment of those who manned it:

> The worst that could befall the slaves was when the slaver was overhauled by a British cruiser, and they might then be flung overboard to dispose of all evidence. Devereaux mentions a case where the Arabs, when pursued by an English cruiser, cut the throats of 24 slaves and threw them overboard. Cololm also states that Arabs would not hesitate to knock slaves on the head and throw them overboard to avoid capture.[47]

Because there were only a few naval ships available to cover a vast expanse of water in this region, British warships would often launch smaller boats to engage the Arab slave dhows. In these cases, as one study put it, "the slave traffickers frequently did not hesitate to attack boat crews in defence of their profits."[48] Battles between the Arabs' vessels and the smaller British craft were especially likely when the larger ships that launched them were too far away to reach the scene in time to join the battle. In other cases, the Arabs fled even from the smaller British vessels. An episode in 1866 was typical:

On 26 April 1866, the *Penguin* set out after a dhow and fired several shots in an effort to make the crew come to. When the dhow failed to lower its sail, Gartorth felt certain that she was a slaver and ceased firing for the sake of the slaves onboard. However, he managed to close with the dhow which then made for the rocks through a heavy surf. By the time the ship's boats could be lowered to follow, the Arab crew had fled but the pounding surf made any attempt by the slavers to salvage the human cargo too dangerous. To their horror, the boat crew found that they, too, could not reach the dhow which was rapidly filling with water drowning the slaves. The boat officer decided that he could not risk coming in close to the dhow but several of the crewmen of the cutter recklessly dived in and swam through the surf to the dhow. In a remarkable display of courage, the sailors managed to bring 28 of the slaves back to the boat. But the dhow appeared to have had more [than] 200 slaves on board and most died in the pounding waves.[49]

In another episode, the Arabs' ruthlessness toward the slaves was further revealed:

When the *Daphne's* cutter captured a dhow with 156 slaves on board many were found to be in the final stages of starvation and dysentery. One woman was brought out of the dhow with a month-old infant in her arms. The baby's forehead was crushed and when she was asked how the injury had happened she explained to the ship's interpreter that as the boat came alongside the baby began to cry. One of the dhowmen, fearing that the sailors would hear the cries, picked up a stone and crushed the child's head.[50]

This was not a unique act. British missionary and explorer David Livingstone related a similar incident on land: "One woman, who was unable to carry both her load and young child, had the child taken from her and saw its brains dashed out on a stone."[51] Dr. Livingstone also reported having nightmares for weeks after encountering Arab slave traders and their victims. Not only was this Christian missionary shocked by the brutality of the Arab slave traders, so was Mohammed Ali, the ruler of Egypt, who was a battle-hardened military commander.[52]

None of this means that the horrors of the transatlantic slave trade should be ignored, downplayed, or excused. Nor have they been. A vast literature has detailed the vile conditions under which slaves from Africa lived—and died—during their voyages to the Western Hemisphere. But the much less publicized slave trade to the Islamic countries had even higher mortality rates en route, as well as involving larger numbers of people over the centuries, even though the Atlantic slave trade had higher peaks while it lasted. By a variety of accounts, most of the slaves who were marched across the Sahara toward the Mediterranean died on the way.[53] While these were mostly women and girls, the males faced a special danger—castration to produce the eunuchs in demand as harem attendants in the Islamic world.

Because castration was forbidden by Islamic law, the operation tended to be performed—usually crudely—in the hinterlands, before the slave caravans reached places within the effective control of the Ottoman Empire. The great majority of those operated on died as a result,[54] but the price of eunuchs was so much higher than the prices of other slaves that the practice was still profitable on net balance.

The British governor-general of the Sudan, C.G. Gordon, estimated that, between 1875 and 1879, from 80,000 to 100,000 slaves were exported through his region.[55] General Gordon imposed the death penalty on those convicted of castrating slave men to market them as eunuchs.[56] His attempt to stamp out slave trading in the Sudan cost him his own life as an opposing army, raised and led by Mohammad Mahad, defeated his troops at Khartoum in 1885 and killed Gordon—after which the slave trade flourished again.[57] British control in the region was firmly re-established in 1898 by the crushing victory of troops led by Lord Kitchener at Omdurman and including a young officer named Winston Churchill.

On the issue of slavery, it was essentially Western civilization against the world. At the time, Western civilization had the power to prevail against all other civilizations. That is how and why slavery was destroyed as an institution in almost the whole world. But it did not happen all at once or even within a few decades. When the British finally stamped out slavery in Tanganyika in 1922 it was more than half a century after the Emancipation Proclamation in the United States, and vestiges of slavery still survived in parts of Africa into the twenty-first century.

The unique position of the Western world in the history—and especially the destruction—of slavery need not imply that there was unanimity within the West on this institution. In addition to whites who defended the enslavement of Africans on racial grounds, or who opposed general emancipation on social grounds, there were many whites—and even blacks—who defended slavery as a matter of self-interest as slaveowners. Although most black owners of slaves in the United States were only nominal owners of members of their own families, there were thousands of other blacks in the antebellum South who were commercial slaveowners, just like their white counterparts.[58] An estimated one-third of the "free persons of color" in New Orleans were slaveowners and thousands of these slaveowners volunteered to fight for the Confederacy during the Civil War.[59] Black slaveowners were even more common in the Caribbean.[60] In short, there were many defenders of slavery in the West, even in the nineteenth century—and, outside the West, slavery was too widely accepted to require defense.

THE MORAL DIMENSIONS OF SLAVERY

If slavery is not morally wrong, it is hard to imagine what else could possibly be wrong. Yet when Lincoln expressed this view, which was gaining currency in his time, it was a belief less than a century old in the West and still virtually non-existent outside the West.

In ancient times, Aristotle had attempted to justify slavery, but many other Western and non-Western philosophers alike took it so much for granted that they felt no need to explain or justify it at all. Some Moslems regarded attempts to abolish slavery as impious, since the Koran itself accepted slavery as an institution, while trying to ameliorate the lot of the slave. Only in the American South did a large apologetic literature develop, seeking to justify slavery, because only there was slavery under such large-scale and sustained attacks on moral grounds as to require a response. While slavery was referred to in antebellum America as a "peculiar institution," in an international perspective and in the long view of history it was not this institution that was peculiar but the principles of American freedom, with which slavery was in such obvious and irreconcilable conflict.

If all men were created equal, as the Declaration of Independence proclaimed, then the only way to justify slavery was by
depicting those enslaved as not fully men. A particularly virulent
form of racism thus arose from a particularly desperate need to
defend slavery against telling attacks that invoked the fundamental
principles of the American republic. Nowhere else in the world
was slavery in such dire straits ideologically and nowhere else did
racism reach such heights (or depths) in defense of the institution.
As a noted study of Brazil observed, "the defenders of slavery on
clearly racist grounds were as rare among public supporters of
slavery in Brazil as they were common in the United States."[61]
Brazil was not a democracy and so had no such ideological contradictions to overcome.

In short, racism was neither necessary nor sufficient for slavery, whose origins antedated racism by centuries. Racism was a
result, not a cause, of slavery and not all societies that enslaved
people of another race became pervaded with racism to the
extent that the American South did.

The stark contrast between the slave and the free which
made slavery a moral issue in the Western world in modern times
was simply not there for most societies and for most of history in
most of the world. In hierarchical societies, where people were
born into their stations in life, ranging through many gradations
from royalty to bondage, slavery was simply the bottom rung on a
ladder based on the accident of birth—one notch below the serf,
who was bought and sold with the land, instead of individually.

This is not to say that being a slave was a matter of indifference. A horror of becoming a slave has been widespread around
the world, but this is wholly different from a reluctance to enslave
others. Christians, Moslems, and Jews all forbad the enslavement of
their own respective fellow religionists—though they did not
always honor even this ban—but all considered it permissible to
enslave others. Clergy themselves had slaves and both Christian
monasteries in Europe and Buddhist monasteries in Asia owned
slaves.[62] Even Sir Thomas More's fictional ideal society, Utopia, had
slavery.

It was not until the late eighteenth century that there was
even an intellectual movement, much less a political movement,

for the abolition of slavery, and those in these movements were distinctly in the minority, even in the West—and had no counterparts outside the West. What was historically unusual was the emergence in the late eighteenth century of a strong moral sense that slavery was so wrong that Christians could not in good conscience enslave anyone or countenance the continuation of this institution among themselves or others. Nor was this view confined to religious leaders or congregations. Adam Smith in Britain and Montesquieu in France were among the secular intellectuals who wrote against slavery in the eighteenth century.

Slavery was one of a number of long-standing institutions and traditions which were being questioned in the eighteenth century in the West. Before then, both secular and religious philosophers going back to Plato had seen the mundane physical world as being far less important than the ideal or spiritual world, so that being right and free in one's mind was more important than one's fate in the physical world. Dissipating one's energies trying to reform the practices of a sinful world was considered less important than bringing one's own soul into line with spiritual imperatives. To the religious, the world of the here and now was a transient thing, a prelude and a testing ground for the world that really mattered, the world of eternity. However, as a humanistic philosophy began to affect both secular and religious thought, what happened in the mundane physical world began to assume greater importance than it had before in the eyes of intellectuals, philosophers, and religious leaders.

As the fate of human beings in the here and now loomed larger as a moral concern, the fate of slaves became part of the intellectual and moral agenda of the times. Over the centuries, established religious institutions in the West—notably the Catholic Church, but later including also established Protestant denominations—had made their peace with the institution of slavery as a fact of life and produced traditional rationales to reconcile it with the message of Christianity. Now these institutions, traditions, and rationales came under fire from within, as well as outside, the religious community across a broad front, of which slavery was just one battleground. Religious minorities, such as the Quakers or the Evangelicals within the Anglican Church, could not simply rely on religious tradition and authority because their very existence was based on a questioning of, and in some cases a break with, those traditions and authorities.

These insurgents had to think independently about slavery, as about other things, and derive their own conclusions—as most people do not have to think through things which have been accepted facts of life for centuries. The rising class of secular intellectuals in the West could even less rely on the authority of established religious institutions. This did not mean that either secular or religious insurgents were automatically anti-slavery. What it meant was that they both had to evolve some intellectually and morally defensible position because they could not simply base themselves on existing beliefs or practices. Different individuals resolved the issues differently but out of this process came some who began to see slavery as an intolerable evil.

Quakers were the first religious group to find slavery morally intolerable—a threat to their own eternal salvation, rather than simply a temporal misfortune of others. Yet even the Quakers did not arrive at this conclusion all at once. In the seventeenth and early eighteenth centuries, there were Quaker plantation owners in the West Indies and Quaker slave traders operating from London, Philadelphia, and Newport, Rhode Island.[63] As late as 1705, most of the leaders of the Philadelphia Quakers owned slaves. However, as anti-slavery sentiment grew among the Quakers, slave-ownership among these leaders declined to 10 percent by 1756. Then, just two years later, the Philadelphia Quakers banned the ownership of slaves by its members.[64]

In England as well, Quakers were the first to require members of their congregations to cease being slave owners. Evangelicals in the Anglican church—notably William Wilberforce in Parliament—joined the Quakers and took the issue to the general public with a decades-long political struggle to get the British government to ban the trading of slaves. Only optimists thought this possible at the time and even the leaders of the anti-slavery movement did not at first attempt the direct abolition of the institution of slavery itself, hoping instead that stopping the buying and selling of human beings would dry up the source and cause slavery as an institution to wither on the vine.

At this juncture in history, Britain was the world's largest slave trader and the powerful vested interests which this created were able to roundly defeat early attempts to get Parliament to ban the trade. In the long run, however, such powerful opposition to the proposed ban, combined with equal tenacity on the other side, simply dragged out the political struggle for decades, making ever wider circles of people aware of the issue. Something that had never been a public issue before now became a subject of inescapable and heated controversy for years on end. Slavery could no longer be accepted as simply one of those facts of life that most people do not bother to think about. The long, drawn-out political controversy meant that more and more people had to think about it—and many who began to think about slavery turned against it.

Eventually, such strong feelings were aroused among the British public that anti-slavery petitions with unprecedented numbers of signatures poured into Parliament from around the country, from people in all walks of life, until the mounting political pressures forced not only a banning of the international slave trade in 1808, but eventually swept the anti-slavery forces on beyond their original goals toward the direct abolition of the institution of slavery itself.

Nor was this a transient phenomenon. For more than a century, these political forces were so unremitting that no British government of any party could ignore them, and even British politicians and colonial officials with no personal sense of a need to ban slavery[65] were nevertheless forced further in that direction by political pressures. Not only were Britons forbidden to trade or hold slaves, the British navy intercepted slave ships from other nations on the high seas, set the slaves free and confiscated the ships.

Only Britain's overwhelming power made this possible—and even then not against a powerful nation like France—but only extraordinary political pressures at home made it necessary. Moreover, this was a moral crusade continually fanned by reports from British missionaries in Africa and elsewhere, as well as by anti-slavery sentiments from other sources. Queen Victoria told Harriet Beecher Stowe that she had wept when she read *Uncle Tom's*

Cabin. Yet one of the signs of our own times is that intellectuals have made desperate but futile efforts to depict the worldwide British anti-slavery crusade as somehow motivated by economic self-interest,[66] rather than by the kinds of moral imperatives activating the kinds of people that today's intellectuals find hard to understand. At the time, however, John Stuart Mill said that the British "for the last half-century have spent annual sums equal to the revenue of a small kingdom in blockading the Africa coast, for a cause in which we not only had no interest, but which was contrary to our pecuniary interest."[67]

While Britain spearheaded the anti-slavery movement in the world, the nineteenth century saw anti-slavery feelings spread until they became common throughout Western civilization—and only in Western civilization. By 1888, every country in the Western Hemisphere had abolished slavery, as had all European and European-offshoot nations around the world. Yet attempts to abolish slavery in the non-Western world provoked armed uprisings within the Ottoman Empire, and elsewhere peoples unable to directly mount challenges on the battlefield nevertheless engaged in massive evasions and concealments of their continued trade in human beings. After the open slave market in Istanbul was shut down, slaves continued to be smuggled in, often at night and in small groups, from the Caucasus and from around the Black Sea, among other places.[68] Suppressing the slave trade across the Persian Gulf and the Red Sea was much harder and took much longer than suppressing the Atlantic slave trade. While slaves were transported across the Atlantic in large ships packed with their human cargoes, slaves were carried in smaller and more numerous vessels, along with rice, fish, and other merchandise, from East Africa to the Islamic world.[69]

British naval patrols were overwhelmed by the task of sorting out which of the innumerable Arab vessels were carrying slaves at a given time and place, and these patrols were never able to intercept more than a fraction of the slaves being shipped out of East Africa to the Islamic world of the Middle East and North Africa.[70] Moreover, such success as the British had on the high seas led to a shifting of more of the slave trade to land, and especially to inland areas away from the ports and coastal outposts where British naval power could be exerted. With the passage of time, however, especially as other European powers began to adopt anti-slavery policies, not only for themselves, but for other nations that they conquered or influenced, the slave trade was forced to retreat further, though not to surrender. Moreover, the retreat of the slave trade did not mean the abolition of slavery itself.

A number of European nations, as well as the United States, officially banned the international slave trade in the early nineteenth century, and treaties among them decades later provided various means of making the ban more effective.[71] But, while nations could deter other nations from slave trading, it was much more difficult to deter free-lance pirates or free-lance marauders on land from capturing and selling people wherever a vulnerable source of supply might exist. Thus North African pirates raided the Mediterranean coast in the sixteenth and seventeenth centuries, while pirates in Asia raided islands in the Philippines and sold the people captured to buyers in Borneo, the Celebes, and other islands in the Pacific. The Spanish colonial authorities who controlled the Philippines organized resistance against these pirates but it was not until the United States took over the Philippines in 1898 that slave raiding was stopped.[72] In the French colony of Senegal, slavery itself was still thriving as late as 1904, though the slave trade had been reduced earlier.[73] The Portuguese did not put an end to the slave trade in their colony in Guinea until just before the First World War.[74]

Where European colonial military forces were spread thin and relied on "indirect rule" through indigenous authorities, as in much of Africa, local European colonial officials often found it expedient to turn a blind eye to the continued existence of slavery and the slave trade among the indigenous peoples, who saw nothing wrong with it and depended on it for a livelihood.[75] However, this simply provided more fuel for exposés by European missionaries and journalists, leading eventually to still more pressure from the home governments to stamp out slavery.[76] As one British historian put it, "public opinion would not tolerate even vestigial slave trading in an area controlled by Britain."[77]

One sign of the difference between the history of slavery in Western and non-Western societies is the very different language used to describe the very different processes by which slavery was ended in these societies. For the European offshoot societies of the Western Hemisphere, the term was the "abolition" of slavery, while for Africa and the Middle East the term was "the decline of slavery"—a much more uneven and protracted process in which local peoples continued the practice whenever and wherever they could escape the scrutiny or the power of European imperial authorities. In Asia as well, slavery continued to exist in backwaters and hinterlands, on into the early twentieth century. Writing in the last decade of the twentieth century, a scholar observed:

> Slavery in Southeast Asia is not a remote historical phenomenon. Laws certainly have prohibited private ownership of persons for a century or more, yet in more hills and islands of the region one still encounters people who admit to being slaves or the children of slaves.[78]

Even independent non-Western nations were pressured to end slavery, both directly and by a desire not to be embarrassed in the eyes of the world—meaning, during the nineteenth century, mostly the powerful European world. In short, where European and European-offshoot societies held direct and effective power in the nineteenth century, slavery was simply abolished. But where the Western world's power and influence were mediated, reduced or otherwise operated only indirectly, there non-Western peoples were able to fight a long war of attrition and evasion in defense of slavery—a war which they had, however, largely lost by the middle of the twentieth century, but which they had not yet wholly lost even at the beginning of the third millennium, when vestiges of slavery remained in parts of Africa.

Despite all this, those with an instrumental view of history have managed to turn things upside down and present slavery as an evil of "our society" or of the white race or of Western civilization. One could as well do the same with murder or cancer, simply by ignoring these evils in other societies and incessantly denouncing their presence in the West. Yet what was peculiar about the West was not that it participated in the worldwide evil of slavery, but that it later abolished that evil, not only in Western societies but also in other societies subject to Western control or influence.

This was possible only because the anti-slavery movement coincided with an era in which Western power and hegemony were at their zenith, so that it was essentially European imperialism which ended slavery. This idea might seem shocking, not because it does not fit the facts, but because it does not fit the prevailing vision of our time.

Selective Moral Indignation

Many who are selectively indignant about the immorality of slavery in American society or in Western civilization do not merely pass over in silence the larger-scale slavery in other parts of the world but sometimes even attempt to apologize for the latter. The argument often used by apologists for slavery in the antebellum American South, that slaves were treated "like members of the family," has often been uncritically accepted for African or Middle Eastern societies, though dismissed out of hand for slavery in the United States.[79] Some of the forms of involuntary servitude in non-Western societies have even been said not to have been "really" slavery, though scholars have differed among themselves on the definition of a slave.[80]

The treatment of slaves has varied enormously, usually according to the kinds of work that slaves did. Around the world, plantation slaves have been almost universally treated worse than slaves used as domestic servants, for example. Given that plantation slavery was more common in the Western Hemisphere than in the Ottoman Empire, where slaves were more likely to be domestic servants, an argument could be made that the treatment of slaves in some societies was in general worse than in others. However, the high mortality rates and low reproduction rates of slaves in the Islamic countries should caution against accepting self-serving arguments that slaves were treated "like members of the family" in that part of the world, any more than in the American South. The absence of a critical literature or an anti-slavery movement outside the West left the abuses of slaves in non-Western countries without the kind of exposure or denunciation that such abuses provoked in European and European-offshoot societies.

Even so, terrible mortality rates were known to exist among slaves in Egyptian salt mines or among slaves in Iraq. For all the

domestic slavery of Africa, there were also slave plantations in East
Africa and on the island of Zanzibar, and some African and Asian
slave owners used their slaves as human sacrifices in religious cer-
emonies, as did the Mayans in the Western Hemisphere.[81]
Europeans enslaved by North Africans were often used as galley
slaves, which could be killing work. But slaves or former slaves in
non-Western countries did not have an audience for stories of their
oppressions comparable to that of slaves or former slaves in the
United States, where the experiences of Frederick Douglass and
other former slaves were widely publicized outside the South. The
lone exception would be the narratives of European slaves in North
Africa, after they were ransomed or escaped back to Europe, or the
stories told by the smaller number of Americans who were
enslaved in North Africa and then rescued by the U.S. Navy in the
early nineteenth century.[82] But the audiences for their stories were
in the West, not in the Islamic countries where they had been
enslaved. Moreover, the stories of white slaves in the Islamic world
were of interest only in the West of their time, not in the West of
our time, when such experiences are largely passed over in silence,
like other historical facts that do not fit today's visions and agendas.

Direct observation of the treatment of slaves was less common with domestic slaves living behind walls, or galley slaves
hidden in the bowels of ships, as distinguished from plantation
slaves working out in open fields. However, what was directly
observable in the Islamic world were the slave caravans which
marched vast numbers of human beings from their homes where
they had been captured to the places where they would be sold,
hundreds of miles away, often after spending months crossing the
burning sands of the Sahara.

The death toll on these marches exceeded even the horrific
toll on packed slave ships crossing the Atlantic. Slaves who could
not keep up with the caravans were abandoned in the desert and
left to die a lingering death from heat, thirst and hunger. Thousands
of human skeletons were strewn along one Saharan slave route
alone—mostly the skeletons of young women and girls, who were
more in demand than men in much of the Islamic world. These
skeletons tended to cluster in the vicinity of wells, suggesting their
last desperate efforts to reach water. A letter from an Ottoman
official in 1849 referred to 1,600 black slaves dying of thirst on

their way to Libya. It has been estimated that, for every slave to reach Cairo alive, several died on the way. Whether or not the survivors were later treated better or worse than slaves in the Western Hemisphere, after reaching their final destinations, is by no means the whole story.

While much of the history of the treatment of slaves has been presented as a history of the treatment of African slaves, the treatment of European slaves in North Africa and elsewhere was by no means benign. For example, this was the scene in eighteenth-century Algiers as newly captured European slaves were paraded through town:

> Since the arrival of new slaves was a sign of prosperity and an occasion of civic pride for all the townsfolk, the resident Turks, Moors, Jews, and renegades all turned out to cheer and taunt the newcomers. Local children especially followed the slaves as they shuffled along, loudly humiliating them and sometimes threw refuse at them.[83]

The newly captured men's heads and beards were roughly shaved bare, as part of the demoralization process to break their spirit, and slaves of either sex could be stripped naked for sale at auction.[84] Most of the female slaves were used for domestic work but the men tended to be used for work requiring strength, including the brutal and degrading work of galley slaves:

> When the ship was idle, slaves who needed to relieve themselves could make their way to the opening at the hull side of their bench, known as the *borda,* dragging their part of the chain and presumably climbing over their sleeping companions—"The only liberty that is given us in the Galley," recalled Louis Marott, "is to go to this place when we have occasion." This, however, many slaves were apparently too exhausted or dispirited to do and often ended up simply fouling themselves where they sat. The resulting stench, as many observers agreed, was beyond belief, but besides the fumes in which they labored, the shackled *gaeotti* were also tormented by rats, fleas, bedbugs, and other parasites.[85]

In the middle of the sixteenth century, galleys propelled by the rowing of slaves were common in the Mediterranean, among both Europeans and their Islamic neighbors and enemies. In their epic naval battle of Lepanto in 1571, an estimated 80,000 rowers propelled the galleys of the warring powers, and these rowers were mostly slaves. The need for galley slaves later declined as Europeans first began to rely on sails for power, so that by the late 1600s, galley slaves were found primarily in vessels from North Africa and the Middle East.[86] Later, as sails became more common on Mediterranean vessels from the Islamic countries as well, the hideous work of galley slaves also declined.

While North African pirates enslaved Europeans primarily from the countries around the Mediterranean, they occasionally ranged much farther afield. Some of these pirates sailed into the English Channel and even into the Thames estuary. A seventeenth-century British Parliamentary report said: "The fishermen are afraid to put to sea, and we are forced to keep continual watch on all our coasts." Nevertheless, Algerians were estimated to have captured more than 350 British ships between 1672 and 1682, which would mean that they enslaved a few hundred Britons annually.[87] Earlier, in 1627, these pirates ranged even farther afield and raided Iceland, carrying off nearly 400 people into bondage.[88] As late as the early nineteenth century, Barbary pirates captured American ships on the high seas and enslaved their crews. The phrase "to the shores of Tripoli" is in the U.S. Marine Corps hymn because Marines were part of a naval expedition sent to rescue hundreds of Americans from bondage in North Africa and serve as a warning against further pirate attacks on American ships.[89]

Not all the captured Europeans became slaves. Some were ransomed, as were Americans. After a successful raid on a European coast, the pirates sometimes sailed out of sight and then returned a day or two later, under a white flag, to offer to sell some of their captives back to their families:

> This was especially effective when the captives were children or youths, who might be brought before their parents in the custody of a fearsome and leering Moor, to leave no doubt what awaited them in slavery, perhaps even before they arrived in Barbary.[90]

The story of how human beings treat other human beings when they have unbridled power over them is seldom a pretty story or even a decent story, regardless of the color of the people involved. When the roles were reversed, Africans did not treat Europeans any better than Europeans treated Africans. Neither can be exempted from moral condemnation applied to the other.

Anachronistic Morality

Moral principles may be timeless but moral choices can be made only among the options actually available at particular times and places. By the time the existence of slavery became an issue in the Western world of the late eighteenth century, the question was no longer whether such an institution should have been created in the first place, but what to do, now that both that institution and millions of people brought from Africa by that institution were already inside Western societies, such as the newly created United States. It was possible to abolish the institution but it was not possible to abolish the people. That simple, inescapable fact underlay the tangled and tortuous history of the issue of slavery in nineteenth-century America, where circumstances made the moral issue more acute than in most other Western nations, while it was no moral issue at all outside the West.

"Deep rooted prejudices entertained by the whites," Thomas Jefferson said, and "ten thousand recollections by the blacks, of the injuries they have sustained" made the peaceful co-existence of these two large populations in the South unlikely in his judgment. More likely, he thought, were "convulsions which will probably never end but in the extermination of the one or the other race."[91] James Madison likewise referred to the "repugnance of the whites" to blacks, which he saw as "founded on prejudices, themselves founded on physical distinctions, which are not likely soon, if ever, to be eradicated."[92] Therefore, like many other opponents of slavery in their day, Jefferson and Madison saw emancipation as something that needed to be combined with expatriation, in order to solve the problem of slavery without creating a bigger problem of a race war. The race war and bloodbath that erupted with the emancipation of blacks in Santo Domingo—today's Haiti—cast a long shadow over the South, and apprehensions were increased when Nat Turner's uprising in 1831 left a trail of death in Virginia before it was suppressed by lethal force.

Many Americans of that era who saw slavery as evil saw a

race war as a greater evil. Those who took this view had the most difficult moral choices to make and were most inclined to want to grope toward some plan that would ease slavery out of existence without consuming blacks and whites alike in mutually annihilating strife. The founders and early leaders of the American republic—including Southerners like George Washington, Thomas Jefferson, and James Madison—saw slavery as an evil that could be tolerated only in fear of greater evils, and even then not tolerated indefinitely. Among prominent Southerners of a later era, Robert E. Lee likewise declared in 1856 that he regarded slavery as an evil that he wished to see somehow gradually ended.[93]

Too often the reductionism of a later age has turned all such hesitation about immediate emancipation into either rationalizations for continued economic exploitation or sheer hypocrisy. These charges need to be examined carefully rather than being accepted or rejected *a priori.*

Few who actually lived in antebellum America thought that slavery could be ended in the South by simple fiat, even though it was abolished that way without incident in most Northern states. The situation was radically different in the two parts of the country. Slaves were only a relatively minor part of the Northern population and plantation slavery was virtually unknown, partly because the climate and soil did not lend themselves to the kinds of crops that could be grown efficiently on cotton plantations in the South or on sugar plantations in the Caribbean. Therefore in the North the question of abolishing slavery as an institution did not raise serious questions about what to do with the people who had been enslaved. Some affluent whites in the North lost their black household servants, or re-hired them as employees, or sold them to the South, where slavery was still prevalent. But the relatively small numbers of people involved meant that it was not a major problem for the North in any case.

Southerners faced a very different situation, with momentous economic and social implications. Blacks were a much higher percentage of the total Southern population than in the Northern states, and in some places were an absolute majority. From the first census of 1790 to the last census before the Civil War in 1860, slaves were approximately one-third of the total Southern population. As of 1860, slaves were more than 40 percent of the population of Alabama, Florida, Georgia, and Louisiana—and more than half the population of Mississippi and South Carolina.[94] Freeing in their midst millions of people of an alien race and unknown disposition, and with no history in either Africa or America that would prepare them to be citizens of a society such as the United States, was not an experiment that many were willing to risk in these states. Not when it could mean risking their lives.

Only those on opposite ends of a spectrum of opinion found the issue of slavery easy—those like Senator John C. Calhoun of South Carolina, who wished to keep blacks enslaved indefinitely, and those like Massachusetts' William Lloyd Garrison, who advocated immediate emancipation of blacks with the full rights of citizenship. Ironically, both men reasoned on the basis of abstract principles—legalistic principles in the case of Calhoun and moralistic principles in the case of Garrison.[95] In both cases, the relentless march of their syllogisms left the painful human realities and dilemmas fading into the dim background. For the majority of Americans in between, neither option was acceptable, nor was any other option able to command a general consensus.

The kind of strange cross-currents this situation generated were perhaps epitomized by the career of Congressman John Randolph of Virginia, a prominent and bitter opponent of the abolitionists, who nevertheless hated slavery. Slavery was to him "a cancer" but one which "must not be tampered with by quacks, who never saw the disease or the patient," for this could end in the race war that he too feared, threatening "the life's blood of the little ones, which are lying in their cradles, in happy ignorance of what is passing around them; and not the white ones only, for shall not we too kill?"[96]

Fears of a race war were not confined to Southerners, however, or even to Americans. Alexis de Tocqueville saw a race war in the South as a very real possibility in the wake of mass emancipation and one of many painful prospects created by the institution of slavery, especially a slavery in which the freed people and their descendants would be physically distinct and could not readily vanish by assimilation into the larger society, as in some earlier times and in other parts of the world. Moreover, slavery was a very poor preparation for freedom for blacks, economically, socially or otherwise. Free blacks were already very disproportionately represented in prison populations, creating fears of what would happen if the much larger slave population were suddenly freed.

Even a Northern opponent of slavery like Frederick Law Olmsted, having encountered and been appalled by slave field hands during his travels through the South, feared that their "presence in large numbers must be considered a dangerous circumstance to a civilized people."[97] He urged charitable efforts toward blacks after they were freed, lest "desperate want" make them dangerous to those around them. But he too saw the freeing of millions of people unprepared for freedom as creating a serious danger to the society as a whole. Nor was Olmsted alone. Abolitionists were hated in the North as well as the South: William Lloyd Garrison narrowly escaped being lynched by a mob in Boston, even though there were no slaveholders in Massachusetts, and another abolitionist leader was killed by a mob in Illinois. Abolitionists were also targets of mobs in New York and Philadelphia, and anti-abolitionist rallies were held in many Northern communities.[98]

None of this was based on any economic interest in the ownership of slaves in states where such ownership had been outlawed decades earlier. But, just as Southerners resented dangers to themselves created by distant abolitionists, so Northerners resented dangers to the Union, with the prospect of a bloody civil war. Even people who were openly opposed to slavery were often also opposed to the abolitionists. A leading historian of the Civil War era has called it "a moot question" whether even such leaders of the fight against slavery as Charles Sumner or Thaddeus Stevens could be called abolitionists in the sense in which the term was used at the time.[99] Quakers, who had spearheaded the anti-slavery movement on both sides of the Atlantic, nevertheless distanced themselves from the abolitionist movement exemplified by Garrison.[100]

Abraham Lincoln likewise was never an abolitionist in the sense in which that word was used at the time, even though he publicly argued for an end to slavery for decades before he was in a position to put an end to it himself. When he first ran for President, in 1860, abolitionists refused to support him, saying that the outcome of this election would make no difference "whether success be to the Democrats or the Republicans."[101] Accordingly, the abolitionists ran their own candidate for President, even though he had no realistic chance of being elected and in fact split the antislavery vote, so that Lincoln was elected with only a plurality. Even after Lincoln issued the Emancipation Proclamation, the abolitionist movement split on whether to support him for re-election.[102]

Some abolitionists even criticized Frederick Douglass for purchasing his legal freedom, rather than continue to be in danger as a fugitive slave, because paying compensation for one's freedom was taken as a legitimization of slavery.[103] It was the abolitionists' doctrinaire stances and heedless disregard of consequences, both of their policy and their rhetoric, which marginalized them, even in the North and even among those who were seeking to find ways to phase out the institution of slavery, so as to free those being held in bondage without unleashing a war between the states or a war between the races. Garrison could say "the question of expedience has nothing to do with that of right"[104]—which is true in the abstract, but irrelevant in a world where consequences matter. Too often the abolitionists were intolerant of those seeking the same goal of ending slavery when those others—including Lincoln—proceeded in ways that took account of the inescapable constraints of the times, instead of being oblivious to context and constraints.

While the dilemmas created by slavery were particularly acute in the United States, similar considerations applied in some other Western societies. In eighteenth-century Britain, Edmund Burke recognized the very same dilemmas for British colonies, such as those in the West Indies, and sought to devise ways around them. An opponent of the slave trade long before Parliament had been brought to that point by popular pressures, Burke put the problem, as he put so many other problems, in the context of the inherent constraints of circumstances. While seeing slavery as "an incurable evil,"[105] Burke was concerned with what would happen to the slaves themselves after they were freed, as well as the implications of their freedom for the society around them.

The "minds of men being crippled" by slavery, Burke said, "we must precede the donation of freedom" by developing in the enslaved people the capacity to function as responsible members of a free society. Therefore he proposed "the civilization and gradual manumission of negroes in the two hemispheres." [106] Later, he proposed "to give property to the Negroes" when they should become free. [107] But nowhere did Burke view this as an abstract question without considering the social context and the consequences and dangers of that context. He rejected the idea that one could simply free the slaves by fiat as a matter of abstract principle, since he abhorred abstract principles on political issues in general. Thomas Jefferson likewise regarded emancipation, all by itself, as being more like abandonment than liberation for people "whose habits have been formed in slavery." [108]

When Edmund Burke set forth his particular proposal to a colleague, he warned:

> Its whole value (if it has any) is the coherence and mutual dependency of parts in the scheme; separately they can be of little or no use. [109]

Burke's approach to slavery, as to other issues, was in terms of the actual context and the constraints implied by that context, not abstract principles. As he said on another issue:

> I do not enter into these metaphysical distinctions; I hate the very sound of them. [110]

In America, John Randolph of Roanoke took a similar position: "I am not going to discuss the abstract question of liberty, or slavery, or any other abstract question." [111]

Today, slavery is too often discussed as an abstract question with an easy answer, leading to sweeping condemnations of those who did not reach that easy answer in their own time. In nineteenth-century America, especially, there was no alternative that was not traumatic, including both the continuation of slavery and the ending of it in the manner in which it was in fact ended by the Civil War—at a cost of one life for every six slaves freed. [112] Many problems can be made simple, but only by leaving out the complications which those in the midst of these problems cannot so easily escape with a turn of a phrase, as those who look back on them in later centuries can.

Even at the individual level, it was not always legally possible for a slaveowner to simply set a slave free, for authorities had to approve in many states. When a motion was introduced into the Virginia House of Burgesses in 1769 to allow slaveowners to free their slaves unilaterally—a motion seconded by Thomas Jefferson—there was anger at such a suggestion and the motion was roundly defeated.[113] An unlimited power to release slaves into the larger society was considered too dangerous to leave in private hands.

Many who have dismissed the anti-slavery words of the founders of the American republic as just rhetoric have not bothered to check the facts of history. Washington, Jefferson, and other founders did not just talk. They acted. Even when they acted within the political and legal constraints of their times, they acted repeatedly, sometimes winning and sometimes losing. One of the early battles that was lost was Jefferson's first draft of the Declaration of Independence, which criticized King George III for having enslaved Africans and for over-riding colonial Virginia's attempt to ban slavery. The Continental Congress removed that phrase under pressure from representatives from the South.

When Jefferson drafted a state constitution for Virginia in 1776, his draft included a clause prohibiting any more importation of slaves and, in 1783, Jefferson included in a new draft of a Virginia constitution a proposal for gradual emancipation of slaves. He was defeated in both these efforts. On the national scene, Jefferson returned to the battle once again in 1784, proposing a law declaring slavery illegal in all western territories of the country as it existed at that time. Such a ban would have kept slavery out of Alabama and Mississippi. The bill lost by one vote, that of a legislator too sick to come and vote. Afterwards, Jefferson said that the fate "of millions unborn" was "hanging on the tongue of one man, and heaven was silent in that awful moment."[114]

Three years later, however, Congress compromised by passing the Northwest Ordinance, making slavery illegal in the upper western territories, while allowing it in the lower western territories. Congress was later authorized to ban the African slave trade and Jefferson, now President, urged that they use that authority to stop Americans "from all further participation in those violations of human rights which has been so long continued on the unoffending inhabitants of Africa."[115] Congress followed his urging. As a historian summarized the actions of these early leaders:

> If the Founding Fathers had done none of this—if slavery had continued in the North and expanded into the Northwest; if millions of Africans had been imported to strengthen slavery in the Deep South, to consolidate it in New York and Illinois, to spread it to Kansas, and to keep it in the border South; if no free black population had developed in Delaware and Maryland; if no apology for slavery had left Southerners on shaky moral grounds; if, in short, Jefferson and his contemporaries had lifted nary a finger—everything would have been different.[116]

In short, the ideology of the American revolution was not just words. Those ideas were not wholly without effect, even in the South, during the years immediately following creation of the United States, for a number of Southern states eased legal restrictions on private manumissions during that era and many blacks were freed voluntarily.[117] As a leading historian of slavery in the United States noted: "Manumissions were in fact so common in the deeds and wills of the men of '76 that the number of colored freemen in the South exceeded thirty-five thousand in 1790 and was nearly doubled in each of the next two decades."[118] Despite growing apprehensions in the South following the bloodbaths in Santo Domingo, even as late as 1832 the Virginia legislature considered a bill to abolish slavery, though it was defeated by a vote of just seventy-three to fifty-eight.[119]

Nevertheless, resistance to general emancipation was far stronger in the South than in the North. Moreover, that resistance grew more intransigent after the Nat Turner rebellion in 1831 and the rise of militant abolitionism in the North, exemplified by the founding of William Lloyd Garrison's fiery newspaper, *The Liberator,* that same year. Even the right of private manumission began to be severely restricted after the rise of the Northern abolitionist movement.[120] The free black population, which had been growing faster than the slave population in the decades of large-scale private manumissions immediately following the American Revolution, now grew much more slowly than the slave population in the decades leading up to the Civil War.[121] Southerners with a variety of views on the slavery issue were bitter against Northern abolitionists, who were seen as imposing dangers on the South that the distant abolitionists themselves would never have to face. Out of this bitterness came a sectionalism and intolerance in the South that led, especially from the 1830s on, to suppression of criticisms of slavery in the region, including restrictions on academic freedom and freedom of the press, state censorship of the U.S. mails, and a campaign to stop sending Southern young men to Northern colleges.[122]

Ultimately, such fears, bitterness, and sectionalism led to secession and the ensuing Civil War. Before things reached that point, however, there were many efforts, both individual and collective, in early nineteenth-century America to find some way out of the dilemma in which many felt themselves trapped by decisions made before they were born—indeed, decisions made before there was a United States. In colonial times, the colony of Georgia, for example, had tried to ban the introduction of slavery there, but was over-ruled in London. Quakers in colonial Pennsylvania had tried to put a high tax on the importation of slaves into that state but this too was over-ruled by the British government. The fact that nineteenth-century public opinion in both Britain and America was very different from what it had been two centuries earlier did not mean that either country could simply wipe the slate clean and escape the consequences of what had already been done in earlier times.

Some Americans—including Washington, Jefferson, Jackson and Lincoln[123]—sought a way out of the painful dilemma by sending freed slaves "back to Africa." However, by the time this idea became widespread, most of the slaves in the United States had never seen Africa and neither had their grandparents. They spoke no African languages and had no idea where their forebears had originated, on a continent more than twice the size of Europe, and one where local and tribal origins were—and still are—crucial to one's acceptance or even toleration by other Africans.

One concrete result of the back-to-Africa movement was the establishment of the colony of Liberia on the West African coast, to which freed American blacks were sent during the administration of James Monroe, for whom they named their capital Monrovia.

These first settlers were decimated by African diseases to which they no longer had biological resistance—which was just one of the problems of trying to undo the past. More fundamentally, the numbers that could realistically be transported to Africa for resettlement was less than the natural increase of the black population of the United States, so this was a foredoomed hope.[124] Nevertheless, the American Colonization Society and many others persisted in the hope that slavery could be ended as an institution, without releasing into American society millions of former slaves, by establishing colonies for them in Africa or Haiti.

Even when private manumissions of individual slaves was legally possible, it was not wholly without its dilemmas. Modern historian David Brion Davis denounced Congressman John Randolph for "hypocrisy" because Randolph publicly condemned the slave trade during a visit to England,[125] while he himself continued to hold slaves in the United States. However, Randolph was not just speaking for public consumption in England. He said similar things both in public and in private letters to friends in the United States.[126] Why, then, did Randolph not simply free his own slaves? This question reaches beyond one man and has implications for the whole set of contradictions which slavery presented in a free society.

At a personal level, the answer was clearest: Randolph could not simply free his own slaves legally, since he had inherited a mortgaged estate and the slaves were part of that estate.[127] Only after he had removed both financial and legal encumbrances was freeing his slaves possible, and only after he made some provision for their economic viability as free people did he consider it humane. During hard economic times, Randolph wrote to a friend of "more than two hundred mouths looking up to me for food" and though it would be "easy to rid myself of the burthen," morally it would be "more difficult to abandon them to the cruel fate to which our laws would consign them than to suffer with them."[128] Thomas Jefferson likewise owned a plantation encumbered by debt, as did many other Southerners, so emancipation of all of Jefferson's slaves was never a real possibility, though he did manage to free nine of them.

Like Burke and Randolph, Jefferson did not see slavery as an abstract issue. He saw the heavy moral stigma of slavery but also the social dangers to flesh and blood people. He wrote in a letter:

> I can say, with conscious truth, that there is not a man on earth who would sacrifice more than I would to relieve us from this heavy reproach, in any *practicable* way. The cession of that kind of property (for so it is misnamed) is a bagatelle, which would not cost me a second thought, if in that way a general emancipation and *expatriation* could be effected; and gradually, and with due sacrifices, I think it might be. But, as it is, we have the wolf by the ears, and we can neither hold him nor safely let him go. Justice is in one scale, and self-preservation in the other.[129]

Many other slaveowners of course saw their slaves as simply a source of wealth and were therefore determined to hold on to them for that reason. However, even those slaveholders with aversions to slavery in principle were constrained by a strong tradition of stewardship, in which the family inheritance was not theirs to dispose of in their own lifetime, but to pass on to others as it had been passed on to them. George Washington was one of those who had inherited slaves and, dying childless, freed his slaves in his will, effective on the death of his wife. His will also provided that slaves too old or too beset with "bodily infirmities" to take care of themselves should be taken care of by his estate, and that the children were to be "taught to read and write" and trained for "some useful occupation."[130] His estate in fact continued to pay for the support of some freed slaves for decades after his death, in accordance with his will.[131]

The part of Washington's will dealing with slaves filled almost three pages, and the tone as well as the length of it showed his concerns:

> The emancipation clause stands out from the rest of Washington's will in the unique forcefulness of its language. Elsewhere in it Washington used the standard legal expressions—"I give and bequeath," "it is my will and direction." In one instance he politely wrote, "by way of advice, I recommend to my Executors..." But the emancipation clause rings with the voice of command; it has the iron firmness of a field order: "I do hereby expressly forbid the sale...of any Slave I may die possessed of, under any pretext whatsoever."[132]

Long before reaching this point in his personal life, George Washington had said of slavery as a national issue: "There is not a man living who wishes more sincerely than I do to see a plan adopted for the abolition of it."[133] But, like Burke, he saw a need for a *plan* of some sort, rather than simply freeing millions of slaves in a newly emerging nation surrounded by threatening powers, just as the freed slaves themselves would be surrounded by a hostile population. In short, the moral principle was easy but figuring out how to apply it in practice was not. Moreover, in a country with an elected government, how the white population at large felt could not be ignored. When Washington congratulated Lafayette for the latter's purchase of a plantation where former slaves could live, he added: "Would to God a like spirit would diffuse itself generally into the minds of the people of this country; but I despair of seeing it." He saw legislation as the only way to end slavery and said that a legislator who did that would get his vote.[134]

Slaves that Washington took north with him when he entered public life he quietly left behind when he returned to Virginia after completing his terms as President—in effect freeing them "on the sly," as one biographer put it,[135] at a time when to free them officially could have set off controversies that neither he nor the new nation needed. George Washington was, after all, trying to hold together a fragile coalition of states bearing little resemblance to the world power that the United States would become in later centuries.

As a slaveowner in Virginia, Washington thought of ways he might sublet much of his estate, in which his current slaves "might be hired by the year, as labourers" by tenant farmers. He was clearly casting about for some way, as he put it in a letter, "to liberate a certain species of property which I possess very repugnantly to my own feelings."[136] But there were no takers. Washington's behavior as a slaveowner is also worth noting:

> Beginning in the early 1770s, he rarely bought a slave and he would not sell one, unless the slave consented, which never happened. Not selling slaves was an economic loss. Slave labor on a plantation with soil as poor as Mount Vernon brought in little or nothing....The only profit a man in his position would make was by selling slaves to states where agriculture was more flour-

ishing. Washington would not. "I am principled against selling negroes as you would do cattle at a market…." From 1775 until his death, the slave population at Mount Vernon more than doubled.[137]

As Southern states in the nineteenth century began to tighten restrictions on the right of slaveowners to free their slaves, in order to forestall the social problems that were widely feared, the laws made manumission increasingly difficult, legally complicated, and a costly process. Those slaveowners who were prepared to grant manumission found it less onerous to let those who were legally their slaves simply live as de facto free persons. In antebellum Savannah, for example, two of the churches in the free black community there were headed by ministers who were among the most prosperous members of that community, even though they were, legally speaking, still slaves.[138] Many blacks who had managed to gain freedom for themselves individually then legally owned members of their own families, because it was not financially or otherwise feasible to go through what it would take to free them all de jure. Quakers also held legal titles to many slaves in their Southern churches, while it was an open secret that these "slaves" lived free and independent lives.

In the case of John Randolph, the charge of hypocrisy is hard to sustain in view of the events surrounding his death. Never married, and so without heirs to his estate, he made provision in his will, years before his death, that his slaves were to be not only freed but provided with land in a free state, on which they might hope to live in peace and be self-supporting. In a will written a dozen years before his death, Randolph wrote: "I give and bequeath all my slaves their freedom, heartily regretting that I have ever been the owner of one."[139] An earlier will said: "I give my slaves their freedom to which my conscience tells me they are justly entitled."[140] That this was said by a conservative white Southerner—a bitter political opponent of the abolitionists and a man who asserted the right of secession long before the Civil War—suggests something of the complexity of the issue confronting those who faced it directly as a human reality, rather than as an abstract question.

Knowing the stringency of the laws of the South when it

came to the freeing of slaves, when Randolph felt that he was dying he summoned a doctor whom he wanted, ostensibly for medical treatment, but in fact as a white witness whose testimony would be accepted in a Southern court as to his dying wishes. Once the doctor was present, Randolph ordered his black servant not to let the doctor leave the room until he—Randolph—was dead, so that there would be no legal question about what he had done. This was the scene:

> Randolph was propped up in the bed with pillows at his back.... With his last remaining strength, eyes flashing, he pointed his long, bony index finger at the assembly: "I confirm all the directions in my will, respecting my slaves, and direct them to be enforced, particularly in regard to a provision for their support." Raising his arm as high as he could, he brought it down with his hand open on Johnny's shoulder. "Especially for this man." He then asked whether each of the witnesses understood him. Immediately, Randolph's keen, penetrating gaze clouded, his mind gave way, and he slumped down.[141]

Randolph's will provided money to purchase land for his freed slaves in a free state, in order to give them a chance to be self-supporting as free people. But, even in the free state of Ohio, the opposition of local whites made it impossible for them to live on the land he had provided. The racial animosity that he had feared from the beginning would blight their chances was rampant even in the North. Whatever the merits or demerits of Randolph's personal or public policy conclusions, "hypocrite" hardly seems the right word for him. Abstract moral decisions are much easier to make on paper or in a classroom in later centuries than in the midst of the dilemmas actually faced by those living in very different circumstances, including serious dangers.

One way to understand the constraints of the times and their effects on public attitudes is to examine the difference between the way that many in nineteenth-century America saw the slave trade, as distinguished from the way that they saw slavery itself. If the institution of slavery and the presence of millions of slaves were facts of life, within which many decision-makers felt trapped by having inherited the consequences of decisions made by others in generations before them, the continuing trade in slaves, whether from Africa or within the United States, was a contemporary problem that was within their control. Thus, decades before slavery was abolished, the United States joined in the outlawing of the international slave trade. Even many Americans not yet ready to support the abolition of slavery as an institution nevertheless made the bringing of more slaves from Africa a capital offense in the United States.

One of the few individuals whose appeal to President Abraham Lincoln for clemency was denied was a ship's captain named Nathaniel Gordon who was hanged in 1862 after having been caught bringing slaves out of Africa. His ship was bound for Cuba but was intercepted on the high seas by a warship of the American navy, because of the international ban on slave trading, even though slavery itself was still perfectly legal at that time in Africa, in Cuba, and in the United States. Clearly, the evil nature of slavery was recognized by the severe penalties imposed in America on those who continued to bring slaves from Africa, though there was not yet a consensus on what to do about the millions of enslaved people already in the country. "In the North, with all the hesitation in many matters, there existed unanimity in regard to the slave trade," according to W.E.B. Du Bois.[142] Gordon's trial and execution were not even controversial and received little attention in the press.[143]

Even in the antebellum South, Virginia Congressman John Randolph again exemplified the cross currents of the times in the dichotomy between the way that slave trading was seen and the way that slavery itself was seen. Although a fierce opponent of the abolitionists, Congressman Randolph was nevertheless adamant against slave trading, at home or abroad. Despite being a slaveowner, Randolph did not engage in the practice of buying or selling slaves himself,[144] and denounced on the floor of the House of Representatives those "hard-hearted masters" who broke up black families by selling their members. Randolph urged the federal government to act in an area where it had legal jurisdiction, to ban domestic slave-trading in the District of Columbia.[145]

The fact that there was no such general support for making domestic slave trading a criminal offense as for making the international slave trade a capital offense reflected the fact that the former did not increase the total number of slaves in the United

States nor take any more people out of Africa. However, being a domestic slave trader was not without social stigma, even in the antebellum South.[146] This moral distinction between slave trading and the continuation of slavery as an institution might be hard for some in later centuries to understand because, in the abstract, there is no moral difference. Only in the concrete circumstances faced by the people of the times was there a practical social difference.

The Civil War that grew out of tensions over slavery was the bloodiest war ever fought in the Western Hemisphere and cost more American lives than any other war in the country's history. Whether or not those fighting on either side thought of their battles as being over slavery, as distinguished from secession, without slavery there would have been no secession and no Civil War. The states that first seceded were states where slaves were the highest percentage of the population.[147] Contemporary words and deeds by the leaders of the Confederacy made unmistakably clear that slavery was at the heart of their secession and at the heart of the constitution that they established for their own new government.[148] In later times, as slavery became ever more repugnant to people throughout Western civilization and even beyond, apologists for the South would stress other factors.[149] But the real question is what factor moved Southern leaders when the fateful decision was made to secede—and that was "unashamedly," as a Civil War historian put it, slavery.[150]

As for the race war that so many had feared, the fact that it did not materialize after emancipation is hardly decisive evidence that the fear was unfounded. During the Civil War, blacks were freed only where Union troops were in occupation of Southern territory, and an army of occupation remained in the South for more than a decade after the Civil War. In the antebellum era, no one on either side of the issue of slavery and emancipation had anticipated that. Even so, the vigilante violence of the Ku Klux Klan and other white terrorists, even while under military occupation, suggests that the potential for a race war was quite real.

Among the other examples of anachronistic moral principles being applied in our own times to earlier times have been the many complaints that the Constitution of the United States did not abolish slavery. This was never a viable option because the South would not have remained united with the North if there had been such a clause. The clause would have been an empty symbolic gesture, leaving millions still enslaved in the South, but jeopardizing the existence of a vulnerable new country by splitting it in half at the outset. Even had both North and South survived as independent nations, slaves in the South were highly unlikely to have been freed by 1863, when Lincoln issued the Emancipation Proclamation. Would a meaningless clause have been worth the price of condemning even more generations of blacks to slavery? Moral principles cannot be separated from their consequences in a given context.

Those preoccupied today with the contemporary instrumental use of history have scored many talking points by referring to the Constitution's allowance of additional representation for the South in Congress by counting three-fifths of the slave population in determining the number of Congressmen to which the Southern states would be entitled. Like many political compromises, this one made no sense except as a means of obtaining agreement in a situation where a dangerous stalemate threatened. The talking point made today is that this political arrangement amounted to saying that a black man was only three-fifths as important as a white man. But would those who say this have preferred that the slave population had been counted as requiring the same representation in Congress as the free? What would have been the consequences? Or do consequences matter to those trying to score points?

Since slaves had no voice whatever in the selection of Southern Congressman, counting the slave population at full strength would only have given white Southerners a stronger pro-slavery contingent in Congress. Scoring points today and being serious are two very different things. It should also be noted that the Constitution's distinction in counting people for representation in Congress was between slave and free, not black and white. Free blacks were counted the same as whites—and free blacks existed before the Constitution existed.

Social Consequences in Different Societies

The situation in the Islamic world was very different from that in the West. Despite the larger total numbers of slaves sent from Africa to the Islamic world over the centuries,[151] the surviving African population in these countries was much less than the tens of millions in the Western Hemisphere. In addition to higher mortality rates of slaves en route to North African and Middle Eastern countries, the survival and reproduction rates of African slaves there were much less than in the United States. While slaves in the antebellum South lived in families, even though they lacked official legal sanction for their marriages, both marriage and casual sex among slaves were suppressed in the Islamic world and, among the relatively small numbers of children born to African slaves there, the mortality rate was so high that few lived to adulthood.[152] The sex imbalance among African slaves—far more women than men in the Islamic countries—and the fact that eunuchs were common among the relatively few African men likewise precluded a vast African slave population in the Moslem countries.

Among the European galley slaves in North Africa, there was even less chance for them to reproduce, and the European women who were domestic servants or concubines were in no position to leave behind European offspring raised in a European culture. The children born to them, fathered by North African or Middle Eastern slave owners, were absorbed both biologically and culturally into the Islamic world. By the late eighteenth century, visitors were commenting on the lighter complexions of the inhabitants of Algiers.[153]

What the United States had that the Islamic world did not have was a self-sustaining and racially distinct population of major proportions within the larger society. Non-Western countries in general faced neither the social nor the moral dilemmas that confronted nineteenth-century Americans. Moreover, the emancipation of slaves was not an issue faced by non-Western societies but rather was something imposed on them by the West. Even European powers with substantial slave populations in their Western Hemisphere colonies faced no major domestic social consequences from the freeing of those slaves, however much that might have economic repercussions, for their slaves were freed on the other side of the ocean. Both slavery and emancipation were peculiar in their consequences on American soil. It may be significant that the only other independent nation in the Western Hemisphere with a large slave population—Brazil—was the last Western nation to abolish the institution, a quarter of a century after the United States.

THE LEGACY OF SLAVERY

Slavery has left many legacies—some economic, some social, some psychological, some political—and most detrimental.

Economics

Those who think of slavery in economic terms often assume that it is a means by which a society, or at least its non-slave population, becomes richer. Some have even claimed that the industrial revolution in Western civilization was based on the profits extracted from the exploitation of slaves. Rather than rehash a large and controversial literature on this issue, we may instead look at the economic condition of countries or regions that used vast numbers of slaves in the past. Both in Brazil and in the United States—the countries with the two largest slave populations in the Western Hemisphere—the end of slavery found the regions in which slaves had been concentrated poorer than other regions of these same countries. For the United States, a case could be made that this was due to the Civil War, which did so much damage to the South, but no such explanation would apply to Brazil, which fought no civil war over this issue. Moreover, even in the United States, the South lagged behind the North in many ways even before the Civil War.

Although slavery in Europe died out before it was abolished in the Western Hemisphere, as late as 1776 slavery had not yet died out all across the continent when Adam Smith wrote in *The Wealth of Nations* that it still existed in some eastern regions. But, even then, Eastern Europe was much poorer than Western Europe. The slavery of North Africa and the Middle East, over the centuries, took more slaves from sub-Saharan Africa than the Western Hemisphere did (in addition to large imports of slaves from Eastern Europe and Southern Europe to the Moslem countries of North

Africa and the Middle East). But these remained largely poor countries until the discovery and extraction of their vast oil deposits.

In many parts of the non-Western world, slaves were sources of domestic amenities and means of displaying wealth with an impressive retinue, rather than sources of wealth. Often they were a drain on the wealth already possessed. According to a scholarly study of slavery in China, the slaves there "did not generate any surplus; they consumed it."[154] Another study concluded: "The Middle East and the Arab world rarely used slaves for productive activities."[155] Even though some slaveowners—those whose slaves produced commercial crops or other saleable products—received wealth from the fruits of the unpaid labor of these slaves, that is very different from saying that the society as a whole, or even its non-slave population as a whole, ended up wealthier than it would have been in the absence of slavery.

Not only in societies where slaves were more often consumers than producers of wealth, but even in societies where commercial slavery was predominant, this did not automatically translate into enduring wealth. Unlike a frugal capitalist class, such as created the industrial revolution, even commercial slaveowners in the American antebellum South tended to spend lavishly, often ending up in debt or even losing their plantations to foreclosures by creditors. However, even if British slaveowners had saved and invested all of their profits from slavery, it would have amounted to less than two percent of British domestic investment.[156]

In the United States, it is doubtful whether the profits of slavery would have covered the enormous costs of the Civil War—a war that was fought over the immediate issue of secession, but the reason for the secession was to safeguard slavery from the growing anti-slavery sentiment outside the South, symbolized by the election of Abraham Lincoln. Brazil, which had several times as many slaves as the United States, and perhaps consumed more slaves than any other nation in history, was nevertheless still a relatively undeveloped country when slavery ended there in 1888, and its subsequent economic development was largely the work of immigrants from Europe and Japan.

In short, even though some individual slaveowners grew rich and some family fortunes were founded on the exploitation of slaves, that is very different from saying that the whole society, or even its non-slave population as a whole, was more economically advanced than it would have been in the absence of slavery. What this means is that, whether employed as domestic servants or producing crops or other goods, millions suffered exploitation and dehumanization for no higher purpose than the transient aggrandizement of slaveowners.

Social and Psychological Legacies of Slavery

Just as enslaved peoples tend to be despised, so the work done by slaves tended to acquire social stigmas in countries around the world. In Java, for example, free people did not want to carry their own packages, since slaves carried packages, and therefore free people without slaves would hire a slave for such chores. Similarly in Egypt, work done by slaves was spurned by working class people, even after slavery was over. Sometimes it was not just particular kinds of work but hard work in general, or work under the direction of a foreman or overseer, that was stigmatized. Just as great conquerors like the Mongols or the Spaniards disdained commerce as beneath them, so ordinary people in slave societies disdained many kinds of work because it had been done by slaves.

One consequence of this was that immigrants with a work ethic, such as Italian immigrants to Brazil and Argentina, who often entered such societies much poorer than the existing white populations of these countries, began at the bottom by working at many tasks that local whites disdained, and ultimately rose to a higher economic plane than the whites who had been born there. Whatever their initial disadvantages, the immigrants were not burdened with the native-born whites' aversions to work. Former slaves and the descendants of slaves likewise developed aversions to tasks performed under slavery. In the British West Indies, for example, blacks after emancipation left the plantations in such numbers that a whole new plantation workforce had to be imported from India to replace them.

The economic costs of such attitudes, deriving from slavery and continuing for generations thereafter, cannot be quantified but also cannot be dismissed as negligible. Where slaves and slaveowners have been of visibly different races, then the racial animosities and distrust deriving from the era of slavery may also last for many generations after slavery itself is over, leading to economic and psychic costs to individuals, as well as social costs to nations. Although the negative economic consequences of slavery, including consequences among generations born long after slavery itself was ended, cannot be quantified, the patterns of lasting economic lags in regions where slavery was widespread may nevertheless be suggestive.

In the United States, and no doubt some other societies, one of the major psychological legacies of slavery has been a sense of shame and resentment among the black population and a sense of guilt among the white population. The reiterated depiction of enslavement as a peculiarly black experience falsely makes this seem to be a uniquely shameful fate to which a particular race submitted, requiring for some of their descendants compensatory bombast from themselves and, if possible, compensatory benefits to be extracted from others. To whites, the false depiction of the history of slavery makes some feel uniquely guilty and responsible for the current misfortunes of blacks. Such attitudes, and the many cross-currents they generate, are hardly the framework for a rational discussion or resolution of today's social issues.

The physical and psychic sufferings of slaves in the past are neither necessary nor sufficient to explain the economic and other differences between their present-day descendants and members of the general population. The economic and other disparities between Europeans and Africans living, respectively, in Europe and Africa are vastly greater than the disparities between the descendants of Europeans and Africans living in the United States. The latter have not lost but gained economically from living in the United States. That these gains derive from the tragic fate of their ancestors does not make them any less gains, over and above where these descendants would be today if their ancestors had been left alone in peace in their homeland. This cannot morally justify the seizing of their ancestors. It simply affects the cause-and-effect question of the reasons for black-white disparities today.

Often the economic lags or social pathology of American blacks have been blamed on "a legacy of slavery." Whether it is the dearth of marriages and families among contemporary blacks or their lower labor force participation than whites, or their high crime rates, slavery has often been invoked as an explanation. Yet the fact is that in the late nineteenth century, when blacks were just one generation out of slavery, there was nothing like today's levels of unwed births or failure to participate in the labor force. It has been from the 1960s onward that these social pathologies have escalated. Whatever the cause, it has arisen long after slavery had ended.

Two very different questions have been confused as regards the history of black families: (1) Why marriage rates differ between blacks and whites? and (2) Why marriage rates among blacks are much lower now than in the past? Official Census data show that blacks had slightly higher marriage rates than whites for every census from 1890 to 1940,[157] but far lower marriage rates than whites by 1960.[158] On the black-white difference, some have argued that the census data from the late nineteenth and early twentieth centuries are misleading, that black unmarried women with children in that era called themselves "widows" to avoid the embarrassment of being unwed mothers,[159] even though the mortality rate among black men was not enough to account for so many widows.

Interestingly enough, those who argued this way offered no explanation for the high rate of marriage among black men during that same era, since unmarried fathers were unlikely to have children living with them to require them to pretend to be married when they were not. As of 1940, for example, from 66 to 70 percent of non-white males in age brackets from 30 and up reported themselves in the census as married and living with a spouse. Adding those black males who were widowers, separated, or divorced, more than three-quarters of black males had been married,[160] despite being only the third generation after slavery.

However one resolves the question of the black-white differences in rates of married and unwed motherhood, the more fundamental question as regards the "legacy of slavery" argument is why black marriage rates began a precipitous decline in 1960— nearly a century after the end of slavery. While the percentage of first births that were premarital has long differed as between blacks and whites—as it differed between antebellum white

Southerners and white Northerners, and between other groups around the world in places where slavery cannot be invoked as an explanation—the sharp increase in premarital first births among blacks began in the 1960s. From 1930 to 1934, 31 percent of first births to black women were premarital, while from 1990 to 1994, 77 percent were. Moreover, whereas in 1930–34 premarital births plus the births of children conceived before marriage but born after marriage were together still a minority of all black births, by 1994 these two categories constituted 86 percent of all black births.[161] That such a "legacy of slavery" would take nearly a century to appear strains credulity.

SUMMARY AND IMPLICATIONS

The history of slavery can be looked at from several perspectives or for several purposes. Whether slavery is examined morally, causally, or politically is a matter of individual choice. But, once that choice is made, accuracy and consistency are crucial. Moral judgments must be made with the facts as they are or were, and applied consistently, regardless of the race, nationality, or religion of either the enslavers or the enslaved. These facts include the social context and the constraints and consequences implied by that context. We cannot assume twenty-first-century options, or even present-day knowledge, when judging decisions made in the nineteenth century. Nor can we assume that we have superior knowledge of the social realities of an earlier era that we never lived through, compared to the first-hand knowledge of those who confronted those realities daily and inescapably.

Moral questions about slavery have been, almost exclusively, *Western* moral questions. Non-Western societies had neither moral concerns about slavery nor, in most cases, the power to decide on the continuance or extinction of the institution for themselves during the era of European imperialism, when slavery was suppressed over most of the world by the West. Not only has the West's crucial role in the destruction of slavery around the world gone largely unnoticed, standards applied almost exclusively to the West have been used to condemn European and European offshoot societies for having once had slavery.

Even those Western leaders who sought to end slavery are condemned by critics today for not having done it sooner or faster. The dangers and constraints of their times have too often been either ignored or brushed aside as mere excuses, as if elected leaders operating under constitutional law could simply decree whatever they felt was right.

Even a sympathetic biography of George Washington, for example, said: "He had helped to create a new world but had allowed into it an infection that he feared would eventually destroy it."[162] This statement is breathtaking in its assumptions. Washington did not "allow" slavery, which existed on American soil and around the world before he was born, nor did he have the option to decree its end. Even to have made slavery a public issue at the time would have accomplished nothing except to jeopardize the survival of a fragile coalition of newly independent states. Yet this man who contributed more than anyone else to the introduction of free republican government in the modern world is widely seen as being under a moral cloud, as if he had chosen to introduce or abet slavery. Washington's actual behavior illustrated what Adam Smith had said, decades earlier, in his *Theory of Moral Sentiments,* that a man prompted "by humanity and benevolence," when he cannot establish the right, "will not disdain to ameliorate the wrong."[163]

Abraham Lincoln, who took advantage of a military conflict to stretch his powers as commander-in-chief to the point of issuing the Emancipation Proclamation, has been downgraded in the post-1960s world for not having done it sooner, more sweepingly, with more fervent moral rhetoric, and with affirmations of the equality of the races thrown in. The serious legal and political risks that Lincoln took when he emancipated Southern slaves are ignored. There was no groundswell of public opinion, even in the North, for freeing slaves. On the contrary, in a war-weary nation it was feared that the Emancipation Proclamation would stiffen Southern resistance and reduce the chances of an early negotiated settlement of a conflict that killed more Americans than any other war, before or since.

Lincoln himself was unsure what the net military effect of the proclamation would be.[164] Yet military necessity was the only rationale that had either a constitutional basis or a political chance of being accepted. Those in later times who judge only by words may be disappointed that Lincoln did not make a ringing moral case for emancipation. But seldom, if ever, do they ask whether that would have made the proclamation more likely or less likely to survive both constitutional and political challenges. Despite Lincoln's mastery of moral rhetoric—some consider his Gettysburg Address the finest speech in the English language—the Emancipation Proclamation was written in such dry and dull language that it has been likened to a bill of lading.[165] But Lincoln understood that ringing rhetoric can be as counterproductive in some situations as it is inspiring in others.

To have made the moral case for emancipation in the Proclamation would have undermined its acceptance as a matter of military necessity. The earlier emancipation of slaves in the British Empire likewise invoked military necessity and avoided ringing humanitarian rhetoric, in order to maximize the range of its political support.[166] As a distinguished scholar aptly put it, "we are so conditioned to expecting interest to masquerade as altruism that we may miss altruism when concealed beneath the cloak of interest."[167]

As it was, Lincoln was viciously attacked in the Democrats' press for issuing the Emancipation Proclamation. Nor was this simply a question of his own political career being in jeopardy. Lincoln warned Andrew Johnson "to remember that it can not be known who is next to occupy the position I now hold, nor what he will do"[168] at this critical moment in the history of the nation and of the fight against slavery. William Lloyd Garrison could indulge in ringing rhetoric without regard to the consequences but Abraham Lincoln had the heavy responsibility of consequences squarely on his shoulders as he faced his countrymen—and history. Lincoln had been elected to his first term by a plurality, rather than a majority, and it was by no means certain that he would be re-elected, especially with the controversy over the Emancipation Proclamation swirling around him.

Those who view slavery as an abstract moral issue are as disappointed with Lincoln today as William Lloyd Garrison was at the time. Garrison was dissatisfied with the language of the Emancipation Proclamation and with the fact that it did not decree "the total abolition of slavery," rather than just its abolition in the Southern states at war.[169] He seemed oblivious to the huge legal and political risks that Lincoln was taking—as many in later times would be when they criticized the limits of his actions and words. But had Lincoln's real concerns extended no further than the military effects of the Emancipation Proclamation, it would be hard to explain his many and strenuous behind-the-scenes efforts to get slave-holding border states and the Congress of the United States to extend the ban on slavery to the whole country.[170] Garrison's rhetoric may look better to a later generation but the cold fact is that William Lloyd Garrison did not free a single slave, while Abraham Lincoln freed millions.

Lack of awareness or concern for the context and constraints of the times is only part of the problem of those today assessing such historic figures as Washington, Jefferson, and Lincoln—or the American nation as a whole. No small part of the distortion and confusion about the history of slavery comes from attempts at scoring points about the past or using the past to try to extract concessions or largess in the present. Non-Western slave-holding countries, past and present, from whom no reparations or other concessions are even remotely to be expected, are passed over in silence by the most vocal critics of the West.

Scholars have long known that slavery was a worldwide institution, going back thousands of years, though that has not led them to provide comparable coverage to slavery outside Western civilization. One scholar whose study of slavery encompassed Islamic as well as Western countries observed: "Slavery has been a common feature of human history, appearing in nearly every part of the world"[171]—though his own study did not extend across the vast reaches of Asia or to the Polynesian islands. Another scholar distinguished for his studies of the Atlantic slave trade declared:

> Slavery until recently was universal in two senses. Most settled societies incorporated the institution into their social structures, and few peoples in the world have not constituted a major source of slaves at one time or another.[172]

Despite such common knowledge among scholars, the version of the history of slavery more commonly depicted to the general public, as well as to students in our schools and colleges, is more along the lines of *Roots* or other similar productions.

On the other end of the spectrum, one of the rationales for slavery used in both ancient times and in more recent centuries has been that consigning some people to perform the drudgery of the world freed others to pursue the higher things—education, invention, political leadership, the arts, etc.—and thus advance civilization as a whole. Plato and Socrates came out of a slaveholding society, as did many of the remarkable leaders who founded the American republic. But correlation is not causation—and even the correlation is not as clear as some apologists for slavery have assumed.

Although Brazil imported several times as many slaves as the United States, it would be difficult to find Brazilian equivalents of Plato or Socrates or other world leaders in the advancement of civilization in the arts or sciences. The remarkable number of early American leaders who came out of Virginia—including Washington, Jefferson, Madison, and Monroe—had no counterparts in other Southern states which collectively had vastly larger numbers of slaves than those of Virginia. The South as a whole lagged far behind the North in producing leaders in the arts and sciences.[173] Slavery has been too facile an explanation of both the positive and negative aspects of slaveholding societies.

The idea that slavery was based on race or racism is yet another popular notion that will not stand up to a scrutiny of history, as we have already seen. Yet beliefs about the innate ability of blacks in the United States by prominent American leaders of an earlier era have been invested with great moral implications by those seeking to score points. But beliefs are neither moral nor immoral. They may be accurate or inaccurate, founded or unfounded, but they acquire moral significance only when they are shaped to serve some ulterior purpose that is either moral or immoral. Belief in the innate equality of all people has been promoted in order to promote equal treatment of all people, and belief in innate inferiority has been promoted in order to justify discrimination against some people, but it is these goals which have moral significance. In the absence of such goals, the beliefs themselves are subject to the tests of evidence and logic, rather than the test of moral principles.

Abraham Lincoln, for example, said of blacks that their abilities were no measure of their rights.[174] Thomas Jefferson likewise said:

> Be assured that no person living wishes more sincerely than I do, to see a complete refutation of the doubts I have myself entertained and expressed on the grade of understanding allotted to them by nature, and to find that in this respect they are on a par with ourselves. My doubts were the result of personal observation on the limited sphere of my own State, where the opportunities for the development of their genius were not favorable, and those of exercising it still less so. I expressed them therefore with great hesitation; but whatever their degree of talent it is no measure of their rights. Because Sir Isaac Newton was superior to others in understanding, he was not therefore lord of the person or property of others.[175]

That took the question of Jefferson's beliefs about the innate ability of blacks out of the realm of morality. Elsewhere Jefferson pointed out how tentative any conclusion must be about the innate ability of blacks, given the lack of scientific precision possible on such questions.[176] Although Jefferson has been criticized for having expressed doubts—what he called "a suspicion only"[177]— about the innate ability of black people, his obvious pleasure at discovering the able work of Benjamin Banneker[178] suggests that his beliefs were not the servant of some ulterior purpose. The vast majority of blacks that Thomas Jefferson saw were illiterate people whose development had been stunted by slavery. He never in his entire life saw a black American who had a college degree because there were none. The first black man to receive a college degree in the United States did so two years after Jefferson's death and the first black woman more than a quarter of a century after that. As Jefferson himself realized, his observed sample of black people was inherently biased by time and place, which is an empirical deficiency of his circumstances, rather than a moral choice of his own.

Others, however, used their belief that blacks were innately lacking in ability to justify, for example, forbidding the teaching of blacks. Frederick Law Olmsted's response to the claim that blacks were no more capable of being educated than animals were was to ask why there were no laws forbidding animals from being educated.[179] The very need for such a law undermined the belief that was used to justify that law. Again, the moral significance of a belief derives from the purpose to which it is put. Otherwise, there is only a question of assessing the logic and evidence behind the belief.

While facts about slavery are essential, we need more than facts. Indeed, one of the principal uses of facts is to gain some sense of *causation,* some explanation of why history unfolded as it did. In the case of slavery, it has been too readily assumed that resistance to emancipation in nineteenth-century America was based simply on the economic interests of those who owned slaves, when in fact abolitionists were hated even in states that had outlawed slavery, and emancipation was feared even by white Southerners who owned no slaves—who were a majority of white Southerners. When slavery is viewed in worldwide perspective, still more common beliefs crumble when confronted with the facts of history.

The truth should need no apology but the truth about the history of slavery is urgently needed for reasons that go beyond historical accuracy. Both the present and the future are at stake when we look at the past. What lessons we draw from that past depend on whether it is viewed narrowly or against the broader background of world history.

From a narrow perspective, the lesson that some draw from the history of slavery, automatically conceived of as the enslavement of blacks by whites, is that white people were or are uniquely evil. Against the broader background of world history, however, a very different lesson might be that no people of any color can be trusted with unbridled power over any other people, for such power has been grossly abused by whatever race, class, or political authority has held that power, whether under ancient despotism or modern totalitarianism, as well as under serfdom, slavery, or other forms of oppression.

It was not because people thought slavery was right that it persisted for thousands of years. It persisted largely because people did not think about the rightness or wrongness of it at all. In very hierarchical societies, where most people were born into their predetermined niches in the social complex, slaves were simply at the bottom of a long continuum of varying levels of subordination based on birth. Even in colonial America, white indentured servants were a major part of the population and they were auctioned off just like black slaves. It was the rise of modern free societies and their accompanying ideologies in the West which made slavery stand out in stark contrast, and it was the emergence of a general questioning of institutions and beliefs in the eighteenth century—also in the West—that brought slavery into question.

Once that happened, slavery could not stand up under moral scrutiny. Outside the West, it did not have to, at least not until after the spread of Western ideas of individual freedom belatedly took hold in some other societies. That such an institution could last so long unchallenged, on every inhabited continent, is a chilling example of what can happen when people simply do not think.

Germans and History

ERMANS ARE AN OLD PEOPLE—THEIR LANGUAGE is centuries older than English, French, Spanish, or Italian[1]—but the history of a dozen years has cast a long shadow over the thousands of years of their existence as a people. The rule of Hitler and the Nazis from 1933 to 1945 not only sealed the fate of the Germans of that generation, it has colored the way Germans have been seen since then, as well as the way the previous history of Germans has been seen. German intellectual figures, social traditions, and political movements in centuries past that were once seen in the context of their own times are now often seen as precursors of Nazi totalitarianism or of the Holocaust. Was all of German history leading up to Hitler? Or were the Nazi years simply a tragic aberration on a monumental scale?

The collectivization of Germans in the minds of others has had major consequences in the real world, quite aside from its impact on intellectual conceptions of this people. At the end of the Second World War, millions of people of German ancestry living outside the Reich in various parts of Eastern Europe and the Balkans were sent "back" to Germany, even though many of these families had been living where they were for centuries and many of the individuals sent "back" to Germany had in fact never seen Germany. Winston Churchill protested these "mass expulsions of millions of Germans on a scale grievous and undreamed-of" and said, "we must banish revenge against an entire race from our minds."[2]

In order to assess the twelve fateful years of the Nazi regime and its relationship to German culture and history in general, we must first review that history and that culture. Germans as a people have extended well beyond the boundaries of present-day Germany, not only in Europe but in overseas settlements in the Western Hemisphere and as far away as Australia. The extent to which these far-flung settlements could be considered German, and for how long, depends of course on the extent to which German culture persisted among them and whether or not that culture was linked to the German nation-state. To assess that, we need to see, at least in outline, some of the prominent features of the culture and values historically associated with Germans. Moreover, the features of German culture stand out in sharper relief against the cultures of the surrounding peoples, such as the Slavs of Eastern Europe or the British and French to the west.

GERMANS BEFORE GERMANY

Germans were recognized as a distinct people as far back as Roman times, many centuries before there was a nation-state of Germany. Like other peoples, Germans evolved socially, culturally, and politically within the influence and constraints of geography and the imperatives of other peoples. The great cultural impact of the Roman Empire, which left enduring marks on the development of Western Europe, reached what is now France long before it reached what is now Germany, simply because the mountains that impeded movement into Central Europe and Eastern Europe were more formidable than the geographic obstacles to expansion into Western Europe. The great East-West divide that has split Europe culturally and economically for thousands of years since then goes back to the intractable facts of geography as the arena within which human achievements developed and spread—or failed to develop and failed to spread.

Eastern Europe has differed from Western Europe, not only in that the West was part of the Roman Empire for centuries and the East was not, but also that the many geographic advantages of Western Europe were lacking in much of Eastern Europe and the Balkans. Mineral deposits such as iron ore and coal, crucial to the industrial revolution, have been more abundant in Western Europe. The milder climate of Western Europe, warmed by the Gulf

Stream, has meant that its rivers have remained flowing when those of Eastern Europe are frozen for months at a time. Moreover, the navigable waterways of Western Europe empty into the open seas, providing access to the trade routes of the world, while many of the rivers of Eastern Europe, even when flowing, flow into lakes or inland seas.

Being part of the Roman Empire meant that Western Europe had not only a common language—Latin—but a literate language, centuries before there were written versions of the various Slavic languages of Eastern Europe. Written words have been essential to science, scholarship, and literature, as well as facilitating economic development—all of which flourished in Western Europe for centuries before they had a comparable impact in Eastern Europe. This meant that there was an accumulation of centuries of literature in philosophy, science, history and other fields in the languages of Western Europe and of Germany before any such literature began to be developed in Eastern Europe. One result of this was that for centuries whatever educated class existed in Eastern Europe read and wrote primarily in languages other than their own vernaculars, which had no comparable serious literature.

This association of class with language was so strong that, even when Czech nationalism developed within the Hapsburg Empire, those nationalists published their patriotic and anti-German tracts in German. When they wrote in Czech in the eighteenth century, they wrote such things as children's stories or light romantic novels or they wrote translations from German or other languages.[3] When the Ukrainian or Byelorussian languages began to be used in plays, they were used in dialogue for comic characters.[4] The rise of an indigenous intelligentsia was marked by their resentment of such cultural subordination, a resentment and a promotion of group identity that they spread to other members of their respective groups. This was as true among the Russians as among the Czechs or Latvians.

The historic lag of Eastern Europe and the Balkans behind the development of the rest of the European continent has had enduring consequences. At the beginning of the nineteenth century, the average real income per capita in Eastern Europe was only half of what it was in Britain—and that gap widened as

Britain developed more rapidly during that century.⁵ At the beginning of the twenty-first century, the nations of the European Union
as a whole, centered in the West, had double the per capita income
of most Eastern European countries.⁶ Western Europe also had a
longer tradition of free democracies and societies open to international cultural, technological, and economic influences.

Throughout the long centuries from Roman times to the
nineteenth century, the Germans, living concentrated in Central
Europe in what is today Germany and Austria, were economically
and technologically more advanced than the populations of Eastern Europe, but lagged behind those of Western Europe. In the
early nineteenth century, Britons came to Germany to create railroad systems and Germans went to Britain to study the advanced
technology of the times. Germans, however, were for centuries the
principal intermediaries through whom the advances of the West
moved eastward with a lag. German cultural influence pervaded
the urban centers of Eastern Europe from the Baltic to the Adriatic.

Over the centuries, the interactions of the Germans and the
Slavs have ranged from economic to military. In the Middle Ages,
the Mongol invaders from Central Asia forced Slavic populations
westward from the Ukrainian steppes and the Slavs in turn forced
the Germans westward. Later, the Germans forced the Slavs back
eastward, with the Oder River forming a boundary between them,
then as now.⁷ But Slavic-German interactions were not limited to
the interactions of whole societies. Enclaves of Germans were scattered throughout medieval Eastern Europe, bringing with them
craft, industrial, and agricultural skills more advanced than those of
the Slavic regions.

Many products of Western European societies, from coins to
castles, moved eastward in medieval times. So did more advanced
agricultural methods, such as improved plows, the horse collar,
and new systems of crop rotation.⁸ Germans living in Eastern
Europe became in effect enclaves of Western European culture
there. The landed nobility of Eastern Europe often deliberately
attracted German farmers by allowing them to settle in towns and
villages under German laws.⁹ Hundreds of villages in Silesia were
under German law at the end of the thirteenth century and more

than a thousand by the middle of the fourteenth century, when more than a hundred towns were also under German law.[10]

Germans were the predominant population in many Eastern European cities during the Middle Ages, while the Slavic populations predominated in the countryside. Until 1312, the official records of the city of Cracow were kept in German and that year they began to be kept in Latin. It was decades later when Poles became a majority of the population of the city.[11] For centuries, rural and urban populations differed in ethnicity throughout Eastern Europe and the Balkans. During the Middle Ages, most of the towns founded in Croatia and Transylvania were founded by Germans. Adriatic port cities such as Dubrovnik developed under Italian cultural influence and Sarajevo under the cultural influence of the Turks.[12] In Romania as well, Romanians were not only a minority in many of the towns and cities, they were a subordinate minority, working as servants and unskilled laborers, while Germans, Jews, and others predominated in higher-level occupations.[13] Even after Slavs and other Eastern European populations became, over a period of centuries, numerically predominant in the cities of the region, Germans remained the elite in such cities as Riga and Prague, and members of the local populations who wished to rise economically and socially had to learn to speak German and become part of the German culture in order to do so.

One reason for the German cultural predominance was simply that they were literate much more often than the indigenous populations of Eastern and Central Europe. Most Russians, for example, were illiterate in the late nineteenth century but 94 percent of the Germans in Riga could read and write.[14] In the Austrian Empire, even as late as the beginning of the twentieth century, the illiteracy rate of Polish adults was 40 percent and among Serbo-Croatians was 77 percent, but among Germans only 6 percent.[15] Education, however, was just one symptom of a vast difference in skills between the indigenous populations of Eastern Europe living overwhelmingly in the countrysides and the skills of the outsiders living in urban enclaves among them. Merchants from the indigenous populations in East Central Europe were usually unable to compete successfully with more experienced merchants who came from Western Europe and other places with a long history of commerce.[16] Even in agriculture, places with rich soil such as Romania and Russia had lower crop yields than those in Western Europe, where agricultural practices were more advanced. The difference was in the people rather than the soil. German farming communities in Eastern Europe likewise had higher crop yields than those of the surrounding populations.

During the Middle Ages, the mining skills for which Germans became widely known led to the establishment of predominantly German mining communities in the Balkans.[17] German priests converted the Czechs to Christianity[18] and the University of Prague—the first university in Eastern Europe—was founded in 1348 with a predominantly German faculty. Dorpat University in Riga, established by the czar in 1802, was likewise in effect a German university on Russian soil, with nearly half its faculty coming from Germany itself.[19] Although Germans were only about one percent of the population of the Russian Empire, they lived clustered in enclaves—both urban and rural—that remained culturally German for centuries.[20] In the 1880s, more than half the Russian foreign ministry was German, as were nearly all members of the St. Petersburg Academy of Sciences.[21] Polish authorities imposed German agricultural practices on Polish peasants.[22] German words crept into the languages of Eastern Europe, and Slavic rulers in medieval Mecklenburg gave their children German names.[23] In Russia, there were such phrases as "as punctual as a German" and "as honest as a German."[24]

The transfer of skills and cultures into Eastern Europe was by no means always socially harmonious, however. Those who had cultural advantages resisted having their cultures diluted by the culture of the indigenous people around them and the indigenous people resented those advantages and the foreigners who had them. During the Middle Ages, Slavs were barred from membership in some German guilds in Eastern Europe and members of those guilds who married Slavs were subject to expulsion. Conversely, Germans were barred from employment in a Polish hospital founded in the fourteenth century and an organization founded among Czechs in that same century required that those admitted must be "born from two Czech-speaking parents."[25] Mob violence was unleashed against Germans in Cracow in this same era.

With the eventual rise of an indigenous educated class, resentments were fanned as these newly educated people led in the promotion of group identity movements, intolerant of outsiders, and insisting on preferential treatment and the imposition of the group's language and symbols on others. In 1892, for example, street signs in Prague, which had been written in both German and Czech, were changed to become exclusively Czech.[26] Group identity movements were not confined to Czechs by any means but were led by the intelligentsia, including students and lawyers, among a number of groups in the Hapsburg Empire.[27] It was much the same story in the Russian Empire, where an emerging Latvian educated class, educated at culturally German Dorpat University, promoted group identity agitation in the Baltic.[28]

Among Germans of this later era, whether in the Hapsburg or the Russian Empire, a cosmopolitan attitude long prevailed, rejecting arguments or policies based on ethnic origins, and welcoming into the German culture the educated classes of Latvian, Czech, Jewish, or other origins who chose to share in that culture and had achieved mastery of it.[29] German was the language of Prague's educated classes, whether in business, the clergy, or the military—regardless of the ancestry of the individuals involved.[30] However, the unrelenting promotion of group identity politics by others, directed against people of German ancestry, eventually led to a defensive solidarity among the Germans and thus to ethnic polarization.

The full and fatal fruition of these group antagonisms would come only in the twentieth century, when discrimination and violence against Germans in Czechoslovakia, for example, made them ripe for Nazi propaganda and willing accomplices of Hitler's takeover of that country. Elsewhere in Eastern Europe, including the Soviet Union, abused German minorities likewise collaborated with the German invaders during the Second World War and many of them accompanied Hitler's armies on their retreat back into Germany. After the war, millions of Germans—whether collaborators or not—were forced to go "back" to Germany from Eastern Europe, many of them dying either from mob violence against them or from the brutal conditions in which they were suddenly seized and transported. The Potsdam agreement among the victo-

rious Soviet, American, and British governments facilitated these
mass expulsions but the expulsions and the hatred behind them
were visible even before that agreement:

> In early May, 1945, Czech nationalists in conjunction with Com-
> munists began to treat the Germans of the Sudetenland like the
> Nazis had treated the Jews: murders, atrocities of all kinds, thefts,
> expropriation, became the order of the day. Even before Pots-
> dam, Germans were required to wear white badges, were
> allowed on the streets only at certain times, and were forbidden
> to ride on public transportation or even walk on the pavements.
> Certain types of German property were confiscated and special
> ration cards were issued to Germans, denying them goods the
> Czechs could obtain.[31]

More than three million Germans were expelled from
Czechoslovakia. Millions more were expelled from Poland, Hungary, Romania, and Yugoslavia, often under brutal conditions that
lead to deaths on a large scale.[32]

GERMAN CULTURE

In an era when all general characterizations about peoples are
likely to be met with cries of "stereotypes," it is especially useful to
note the consistency of these characterizations of the same group
living in lands separated by thousands of miles of land and water—
even in times before modern communications, when people in
South America had no way of knowing what beliefs existed in Russia about the Germans living there or how similar those beliefs
were to their own observations about Germans living in South
America. The ease with which charges of "stereotypes" are made
suggests that those with flesh-and-blood people before their eyes
have been mistaken more often than observers far distant in space
and time, and relying on general presumptions—a proposition that
lacks even plausibility, much less evidence or proof.

Craft Skills

Long before German societies became industrialized, Germans
were skilled craftsmen in many fields. Germans were known for
brewing beer in Roman times[33] and Germany today produces more

beer than any other country in Europe. People of German ancestry have set up breweries as far away as Australia and China—the famous Tsingtao beer of China having been created by Germans there. The leading American brands of beer—Budweiser, Coors, and Miller—were likewise all created by people of German ancestry. German breweries in Buenos Aires drove English beer out of the market there.[34] In the Brazilian state of São Paulo, the only producers of beer in the early twentieth century were Germans. Beer-brewing Germans are not simply a stereotype.

German craftsmen also pioneered in making pianos and took this skill with them to other countries. The first pianos in colonial America were built by Germans, who also led the way in building pianos in Australia, Russia, France, and England.[35] German craftsmanship also created optical products that made such firms as Zeiss, Schneider, Rodenstock, and Voigtländer world leaders in high-quality lens production. The leading lens-making firm in the United States was founded by two German immigrants named Bausch and Lomb. Printing was another area in which Germans led the way. Gutenberg introduced printing with movable type in Europe and, centuries later, Germans set up the first printing press in the Western Hemisphere. When printing presses began to spread from Western Europe into Eastern Europe, they spread first into German enclaves in the east, because here were concentrated people who could read.

Germans also pioneered in map-making.[36] The name "America" was given to the Western Hemisphere by a German map-maker.[37]

Mining was another area in which Germans became renowned as far back as the sixteenth century. Copper mines in Britain were opened up by Germans, as were silver mines in Mexico, Spain, and Norway,[38] in addition to the German mining communities in the Balkans already noted. German craftsmanship in metal created the first armor and swords manufactured in Mexico, as well as the renowned "Kentucky rifle," which was in fact made by Germans in Pennsylvania.[39]

For thousands of years, Germans excelled in military operations. German generals held positions of high command in the Roman legions, as they would in later centuries command armies in czarist Russia,[40] in South America,[41] and in the United States from the Revolutionary War of 1776 to the two world wars of the twentieth century,[42] in both of which the U.S. Army was commanded by generals of German ancestry—Pershing and Eisenhower, respectively. German commanders of American military forces in the Second World War also included Admiral Chester Nimitz who commanded the Pacific fleet and General Carl Spaatz, whose bombers reduced much of Germany to rubble. In both World Wars, the armies of Germany inflicted far more casualties on opposing forces than the Germans sustained themselves.[43]

During the Middle Ages, the Teutonic Knights conquered Prussia, which became the heartland of German military prowess for centuries to come. German fighting men were in demand by rulers in Eastern Europe and in the Ottoman Empire, and were used by the British in their attempt to suppress the rebellious American colonies—as well as by the Americans in order to bring their citizen army up to the military standards required to fight the British. Ironically, Germans produced not only leading military men but also leading pacifist groups, such as the Mennonites, who also spread to other countries.

Whether in agriculture, industry, commerce, or the military, Germans became known for thoroughness, organization, punctuality and hard work, as well as for specific skills. Other countries not only welcomed German immigrants but some actively recruited them and, in some cases, subsidized their travel. Not only in Eastern Europe but also in developing nations in the Western Hemisphere and in Australia, Germans were recruited to pioneer in opening up undeveloped wilderness.[44]

Cultural Persistence

Wherever Germans settled around the world, there were newspapers printed in German. In Russia, the *St. Petersburger Zeitung* was founded in 1727, followed in later years by the *Saratov Deutsche Zeitung* in the German agricultural settlements on the Volga and the *Odessaer Zeitung* among Germans who settled by the Black Sea. In the United States, during the immigrant era, most of the foreign language newspapers in the country were German.[45] St. Louis had two daily newspapers in German as early as 1845[46] and, out on the plains, there was an *Odessa Zeitung,* set up by German immigrants from Russia, who had kept their language and culture intact after settling in Russia for generations and then re-settling in the United States.[47] German language newspapers were published daily in 15 American cities, with such names as *Die New Yorker Staats-Zeitung,* the *Cincinnati Volksblatt,* the *Chicago Abendpost,* the *Louisville Anzeiger* and the *Deutsche Zeitung* in New Orleans.[48] In Brazil, there were the *Santa Cruz Anzeiger,* the *Deutsche Zeitung* and the *Brasil Post.*[49] Elsewhere in South America there were the *Argentinisches Tageblatt* and the *Deutsche Zeitung für Paraguay,* among others.[50] In the Australian city of Adelaide, the *Australische Zeitung* was still being published in the late twentieth century.[51]

These German language newspapers in countries around the world were just one indication of the persistence of German culture among people settled for generations, or even centuries, in other countries. German settlers in Australia built houses and communities in the style that they had been used to in their homeland.[52] A German traveler in nineteenth century Australia wrote of an immigrant settlement there:

> There are German public houses, a German drug store, German doctors, stores, blacksmith, carpenter, school, church, in fact everything is German. The traveller would believe himself in some little village of the old country between the Rhine and the Oder.[53]

A rural village in Argentina was described this way by a visitor in 1967:

> I entered the church and heard something I did not remotely expect in this distant place—traditional German hymns of Holy Week, sung in typical Volga German style in which each voice remains distinct. I looked around; men, women and children were in their Sunday dress. Some of the women wore scarves. Beneath them were faces like those of the country people in Germany. In front of the nave the minister was preaching in common German to the parishioners.
>
> It was difficult to believe that I was in Latin America, that the ancestors of these people had left Germany for Russia 200 years ago.[54]

This cultural persistence among Germans around the world represented a loyalty to the particular subculture of the locality from which they had come, not a political loyalty to the German nation. Many had in fact immigrated before there was a German nation created in 1871. A nineteenth-century German community in Australia was described as the re-creation of a Silesian village. In the United States as well, Germans from particular localities settled together and maintained the culture of that area. Frankfort, Kentucky, was founded by Germans from Frankfurt, Germany, and Grand Island, Nebraska, by Schlesweig-Holsteiners.[55] Lomira, Wisconsin, was settled almost exclusively by Prussians from Brandenburg, while the nearby towns of Hermann and Theresa were settled by Pomeranians.[56]

Even among Germans who immigrated from Russia to the United States, those who came from the Volga settlements established their own communities in the plains states distinct from the communities in those states established by those Germans who came from the Black Sea settlements. Even when they resettled again in California, the Volga Germans and the Black Sea Germans settled separately—the former around Lodi and the latter around Fresno.[57]

How long and to what extent the Germans remained culturally separate varied with circumstances. Rural enclaves tended to remain culturally insular longer and more completely than was the case where Germans settled in urban communities that included people of other nationalities and cultures. Where the Germans were the numerically predominant urban group, as they were for centuries in much of Eastern Europe, they could assimilate the local population—or at least its upwardly mobile elements—to the German culture. But where the Germans were greatly outnumbered, and especially where the great majority of the German immigrants were male, then interactions among groups, including intermarriage, eroded the German culture. This was the case in much of nineteenth-century Australia, but not in South Australia, where whole families of Germans tended to settle together and there were as many women as men, so that these communities could maintain their separate social and cultural identities for generations.

It was much the same story in Brazil, where there was very little intermarriage with members of the local population living near German agricultural communities, well into the twentieth century, while in cities and in some rural areas where there were more diverse populations, acculturation and assimilation became more common.[58] Yet even living in cities with large numbers of people from other backgrounds did not automatically lead to rapid assimilation. In New York City, where 90 percent of the population was non-German, in the early twentieth century most people of German ancestry nevertheless married other people of German ancestry. That changed over the years, but not immediately or rapidly.[59]

This cultural cohesiveness was seldom accompanied by political cohesiveness or group-identity politics. Germans were usually not very politically active in any case and they tended to be underrepresented among career politicians. Where German political leaders arose in other countries, it was seldom as representatives of ethnic Germans in those countries. In the United States, for example, those people of German ancestry who did achieve prominence in politics—the Muhlenbergs in the eighteenth century, Carl Schurz and John Peter Altgeld in the nineteenth, and Herbert Hoover and Dwight D. Eisenhower in the twentieth century—did so as representatives of the American people at large, rather than as spokesmen for ethnic German interests.

There were similar patterns in other countries. In Australia, Germans tended to be under-represented in politics and those Germans who achieved political office were elected from constituencies where there were few Germans, as well as from constituencies where Germans were the predominant population.[60] In Russia, the presence of Baltic Germans in high positions in the czarist government was of no benefit to the Volga Germans or the Black Sea Germans, in whom these German officials took no interest and whom they looked down on as peasants. In Brazil, Germans long remained politically apathetic until after the Second World War, when they began to elect more deputies.[61] However, in places where the German minority was under sustained political attack, such as by the Latvians or the Czechs, Germans were provoked into political activity.

The persistence of German culture did not in most cases mean making public dramatizations of a separate identity—exceptions again being in places like Czechoslovakia. More commonly, Germans maintained their culture without making a public issue of it. In the United States, such American sports icons as Babe Ruth and Lou Gehrig grew up speaking German and so did Nobel-Prizewinning economist George Stigler.

Education

Among the things that Germans had in common, wherever they were from and wherever they settled, was making education a high priority. Even among German farmers pioneering in the wilderness of nineteenth-century Brazil, German schools appeared in the first clearings in the woods,[62] while most native-born Brazilians remained illiterate on into the twentieth century.[63] This reflected the high priority of education among Germans in Europe, where the term *kindergarten* originated and where the German research-oriented and doctorate-granting university became the model for modern American universities. Education was not just for intellectuals or academics, however. German farmers and craftsmen learned to read and write, even in times and places where the surrounding population was illiterate, as in most of Eastern Europe and in Brazil.

Education became the foundation for German prominence in the professions and in science and technology, both at home and abroad. In nineteenth-century America, one-third of all the physicians in New York State were of German ancestry.[64] As already noted, in czarist Russia Germans predominated in the St. Petersburg Academy of Sciences. In Argentina, German academics predominated in the Institute of Physics, Astronomical Laboratory, Natural History Museum, National Bureau of Mines and Geology, and in its Institute of Military Geography.[65]

THE GERMAN NATION

With the passing generations, the kinds of Germans who immigrated from their homeland changed, as that homeland itself changed. In the early nineteenth century, the small German states and principalities which existed prior to their being consolidated into a nation in 1871 were a largely agrarian world in which three-quarters of the population lived in small villages and towns. Its manufactured goods, such as textiles and metal products, were produced largely by artisans and craftsmen, rather than by large-scale industrial enterprises, such as were developing in Britain.[66] While Germans were economically more advanced than the peoples of Eastern Europe, they lagged behind other countries in Western Europe in technology and in sophisticated commercial and financial institutions. But all of that changed during the course of the nineteenth century.

At first, the Germans simply borrowed the more advanced methods of the British in industry and agriculture.[67] Britons installed industrial equipment and built railroads in Germany, and taught Germans how to operate both.[68] British capital financed the industrial production of wool and helped create the German steel industry, with Belgians and the French also contributing technology to German economic development.[69] Yet, once launched into the industrial age, the Germans surpassed their mentors before the end of the nineteenth century. The number of German steam engines tripled between 1834 and 1850 and, between 1815 and 1850, coal production increased more than tenfold.[70] Germans had nearly double the railroad mileage of the French by the middle of the nineteenth century.[71] In the crucial area of steel production, Germany overtook Britain by the last decade of the nineteenth century and, on the eve of the First World War, German steel production was double that of the British.[72]

Political developments were equally dramatic. When the German states and principalities were consolidated into a nation in 1871, it was the most economically advanced nation in Europe and militarily the most powerful, as demonstrated in its crushing victory over France that same year and its seizing of the iron and coal deposits of Alsace-Lorraine. Strong nationalistic fervor accompanied these dramatic economic, political, and military developments, not only among Germans in Europe but also as far away as Australia. German immigrants from the new era when Germany reached the forefront of industrial development brought with them more industrial skills, more science and technology.

Others took abroad artisan skills as before. While artisans and craftsmen were being superseded by modern industry in Germany, their skills were still in demand in other countries that had not yet reached that same level of technology.

Germany's belated but dramatic emergence among the great powers of the world, like that of Japan in the same era, led to an aggressive nationalism that provoked armed conflicts with its neighbors. Although the First World War began with the Hapsburg Empire's military action against Serbia, in response to a Serb's assassination of the heir to the imperial throne, it was Germany's military backing and urging that led the Hapsburg Empire to take that fatal step, with the full knowledge that existing alliances and alignments risked bringing Russia, France, and Britain into the war. The same nationalistic overconfidence which led to Germany's willingness to challenge these powers later led to the sinking of American ships bound for Britain, bringing the United States into the war, thereby tipping the military balance toward the defeat of Germany and the dismemberment of its allies, the Hapsburg and Ottoman Empires.

The rise of Adolf Hitler to power in 1933 and his swift transformation of Germany into a militaristic and totalitarian dictatorship set the stage for a new and more bloody World War and, in the end, a more catastrophic defeat that now led to the dismemberment of Germany. While Germany rose from the rubble of wartime destruction to recover economically and eventually was reunited politically, the unprecedented horrors inflicted by the Nazis at home and abroad raised questions about the whole German culture and character that have not yet been put to rest in the twenty-first century.

What the Nazis had done went far beyond launching a war. Their conscienceless persecutions at home and abroad, their racial fanaticism, and the murders of millions of unresisting civilians of both sexes and all ages reached unprecedented depths of depravity. As *Time* magazine commented after the collapse of that regime:

> This war was a revolution against the moral basis of civilization. It was conceived by the Nazis in conscious contempt for the life, dignity and freedom of individual man and deliberately prosecuted by means of slavery, starvation and the mass destruction

of noncombatants' lives. It was a revolution against the human soul.[73]

What did the Nazi era say about the German people who, after all, gave Hitler the electoral plurality that put him in power? How much of what the Nazis did reflected the culture and history of the German people?

Political Developments

The political freedom and individual rights which are loosely characterized as democracy had existed for less than a generation in Germany when Hitler came to power. Germany itself had existed for less than a century at that point, though there were Germanic states before, such as Prussia and the Holy Roman Empire, not to mention contemporary Austria, the remnant of the Hapsburg Empire that had been ruled politically and dominated economically by people of German ancestry. Autocratic and authoritarian governments had long been the norm among Germans, as they had been across much of the world for most of history. Yet Hitler was more than just an autocratic ruler in a country with a militaristic tradition.

What did putting Hitler in power say about the German people? Strictly speaking, it could reflect only on those Germans who voted Hitler into office in a democratic election, after which he seized dictatorial powers. Hitler never received a vote of a majority of the citizens of Germany, even to be put into office as chancellor, much less to become dictator. The millions of Germans outside of Germany of course had no part in any of this. Yet, when all is said and done, there can be little question that Hitler's massive support in Germany reached levels of adoration seldom seen in any country before or since. How much of that was support for the Nazi ideology or its known agenda, much less for its hidden agenda that unfolded later to shock and outrage the world?

While Hitler himself was even more ruthless and reckless than the Kaiser who led Germany into the First World War, there was among the German people no such exaltation at the launching of the Second World War as had existed in countries across Europe when the First World War began with both sides full of confidence of quick and easy victories. William L. Shirer's monumental eye-witness history of Nazi Germany described the scene in Berlin on the first day of World War II this way:

> The people in the streets, I noticed, were apathetic despite the immensity of the news which had greeted them from their radios and from the extra editions of the morning newspapers. Across the street from the Adlon Hotel the morning shift of laborers had gone to work on the new I.G. Farben building just as if nothing had happened, and when newsboys came by shouting their extras no one laid down his tools to buy one. Perhaps, it occurred to me, the German people were simply dazed at waking up on this first morning of September to find themselves in a war which they had been sure the Fuehrer somehow would avoid. They could not quite believe it, now that it had come.
>
> What a contrast, one could not help thinking, between this gray apathy and the way the Germans had gone to war in 1914. Then there had been a wild enthusiasm. The crowds in the streets had staged delirious demonstrations, tossed flowers at the marching troops and frantically cheered the Kaiser and Supreme Warlord, Wilhelm II.[74]

Hitler counted on no enthusiasm for war on the part of the German people. On the contrary, he preceded his invasion of Poland with elaborate charades of seeking peace. In order to make it appear that the Poles had attacked Germany, he even staged border incidents, using Germans in Polish uniforms to fire weapons and leaving concentration camp inmates dying as "casualties" of the purported Polish attacks.[75] None of this was expected to fool the outside world. That it was considered necessary to fool the German people, insulated by a government-controlled press, suggests a serious difference between the aims and values of the Nazis and the aims and values of the people whom they were leading and misleading. Differences between the goals and imperatives of the Nazis and those of the millions of Germans living outside the Reich were even clearer.

The Volksdeutsche

As of 1935, there were an estimated 95 million Germans living in various countries around the world—65 million in Germany itself, 6.5 million in Austria, 3.3 million in Czechoslovakia, and 1.2 million in the Soviet Union, as well as sizeable numbers of Germans scattered through other European countries to the east and south of Germany.[76] Many of these became involved politically with the German nation before and during the Nazi era in a way very different from that of people of German ancestry living in the Western Hemisphere or Australia.

In addition to those Germans who had settled in Eastern and Southern Europe in centuries past, Germans living outside Germany—ethnic Germans (*Volksdeutsche*), as distinguished from German citizens living at home or abroad (*Reichsdeutsche*)—included Germans who suddenly found themselves minorities in new nations created by the breakup of the Hapsburg Empire and Germans stranded across new national boundary lines created by the Treaty of Versailles that ended the First World War. While the Germans living in Czechoslovakia's Sudetenland were the largest and best known of these, others included Germans living in the South Tyrol that had been transferred from Austria to Italy and Germans living in the newly reconstituted nation of Poland. These *Volksdeutsche* faced varying degrees of discrimination from country to country and from time to time, with that discrimination becoming more severe during the Great Depression of the 1930s, when economic opportunities became more scarce for everyone.

Years before the Nazis came to power in Germany, these *Volksdeutsche* in other countries organized themselves for various forms of protest and political activity in self-defense. Not only did the Nazis have little interest initially in these *Volksdeutsche* organizations and movements, the *Volksdeutsche* had little interest in Germany's Nazis, and even those Germans abroad who established relationships with organizations within Germany usually did so with non-Nazi organizations.[77] Only as the Nazis saw a possible usefulness of Volkdeutsche organizations in furthering Hitler's international ambitions did they take an interest in them, championing their cause when its suited Germany's national purposes and abandoning them to their fate when *Volksdeutsche* interests conflicted with Hitler's national ambitions. Thus, while Nazi Germany championed the cause of the Sudeten Germans as part of Hitler's plan to take over Czechoslovakia, and encouraged Sudeten German militancy, extremism, and violence there, German officials

were exerting pressure against *Volksdeutsche* in the South Tyrol
to restrain themselves and accept Italian rule, since Hitler valued
his alliance with Mussolini more than he cared about the fate of
South Tyroleans.[78]

Similarly, *Volksdeutsche* leaders in Lithuania were pressured
to restrain the hotheads in their ranks, in order to avoid creating
international problems that would distract from Hitler's current
international strategies. The *Volksdeutsche* in the Slovak protec-
torate were likewise sacrificed to Germany's international designs
and *Volksdeutsche* from the Soviet-occupied eastern region of
Poland were relocated to Germany for the same reason.[79] Perhaps
the biggest clue to the Nazi strategy was that, during the years of
Hitler's complaints about the treatment of Germans in other countries during the 1930s, emigration of those *Volksdeutsche* to
Germany was discouraged.[80] As disaffected minorities they were
useful where they were, both as fifth columns within countries targeted for conquest and as propaganda justifications for Nazi
invasions.

Prior to the achievement of power by the Nazis in Germany
in 1933, the various *Volksdeutsche* organizations and movements
were not Nazi movements or movements sharing the racial or
national fanaticism of the Nazis. Only after Hitler came to power in
Germany were they gradually won over to cooperation with the
Nazis in their own self-interest as beleaguered minorities seeking
allies and to varying degrees imbued with the Nazi ideology, especially after Germany's conquests cast them in the role of a "master
race" collaborating with *Reichsdeutsche* in the subjugation of the
peoples who had formerly oppressed them. Among overseas Germans, things never reached that stage and the ability of the Nazis
to infiltrate and co-opt German communities and cultural organizations was far more limited. As early as 1938, authorities in
Germany were aware of how little they were accomplishing with
people of German ancestry in the United States and cut back their
activities there as a result.[81]

In short, among *Volksdeutsche* as among *Reichsdeutsche*,
there was little to suggest a predisposition toward Nazi aims or
ideology before Hitler took power. Their role in, and their responsibility for, the tragedies of the Nazi era are an entirely different

question from that of whether the prior history of the German people was one uniquely leading toward the Nazi catastrophes.

Nationalism and Nazism

Fanatical nationalism was at the heart of the Nazi creed. To what extent did most Germans share that creed during the Nazi era? Was it a creed going back into history or continuing on past the Second World War?

Patriotism has been common to peoples around the world, particularly in wartime and especially when people have been led to believe that their country has been attacked. There is no reason to doubt the patriotism of the Germans during the Nazi era. But gauging public opinion in a totalitarian state can hardly be done with any precision. The euphoria with which the beginning of the First World War was greeted in Germany was all too common across Europe at the time. What of Germans outside of Germany— and across a wider stretch of history than a few decades of the twentieth century?

Despite the tenacity with which Germans clung to their own culture in the farthest reaches of the world, there was no such political loyalty to the German nation or its antecedents. Germans in Russia fought loyally against Germany in the First World War, as German Americans did in both World Wars. No one found it noteworthy during the Second World War that so many top American military leaders were of German ancestry, nor was any question of conflicts of national loyalties raised. In Australia, those Lutheran churches that were subsidized from Germany tended to be sympathetic toward Germany, while those subsidized from the United States were not. Yet, once Australia went to war, even the Lutheran churches that had been sympathetic to Germany before now urged their members to fight for Australia and otherwise cooperate with Australian authorities.[82] The Nazis worked hard to infiltrate German organizations in the United States, Brazil and Australia during the years leading up to World War II, but with only limited success, despite tactics that sometimes included threats of reprisals against family members in Germany if their overseas relatives did not cooperate.[83]

Where German minorities had been badly treated, as in

Czechoslovakia and the Soviet Union, it was a different story. Germans in the Sudeten region of Czechoslovakia helped create the crisis that was resolved at the infamous Munich conference of 1938, where Britain and France agreed that Nazi Germany should take over that whole region of Czechoslovakia. Later, when the German army invaded the Soviet Union in 1941, Black Sea Germans welcomed them as liberators—as did some non-German minorities—and then, after the Soviet army counter-attacked, more than a quarter of a million ethnic Germans followed the Nazi army as it retreated back to Germany.[84] During the postwar Red Army occupation of East Germany, tens of thousands of former Soviet Germans were forced to return to the USSR, though tens of thousands of others used false identities to avoid this fate and still others avoided it by committing suicide.[85]

During the war, many Germans in the conquered lands, suddenly elevated to privileged positions as members of the "master race" by the Nazi occupiers, collaborated actively, leading to a postwar backlash that led to the expulsion of millions of Germans as mass punishment, irrespective of individual guilt or innocence.

The question here, however, is not the balance of justifiable or reprehensible behavior on the part of Germans in Europe during a period of several years but the larger historical question of whether the Nazi ideology and its horrifying consequences represented an enduring set of distinctive characteristics of Germans as a people. Those Germans living overseas in lands where they had no special grievances and were free to express themselves showed no such loyalty to Germany as a nation, much less to Nazi ideology, as to sustain a conclusion of indelible cultural characteristics favorable to the values of Hitler and the Nazis.

Racial Fanaticism

The Nazi amalgamation of nation and race under totalitarian rule—"one people, one country, one leader"—led to the horror most unforgettably burned into the history of Germany and of Germans, the murder of millions of Jews and others deemed to be of inferior races. Was this the culmination of long-standing beliefs and actions of the German people or a monstrous new creation of the Nazis?

In Germany, as in other countries, there were people hostile to the Jews on religious, racial, or other grounds. Nor were these isolated anti-Jewish individuals. There were institutions, movements, and political parties hostile to Jews, sometimes bitterly and venomously so, and these included historic figures from Martin Luther to Richard Wagner. But the ultimate question is how all this affected the behavior of the German people as a whole, as compared to other peoples in Europe and elsewhere.

Self-aggrandizement and bias against others has been too tragically pervasive throughout human history and among peoples around the world to make it a distinctive characteristic of a particular people or a particular era. However, racism in its modern sense of belief in innate genetic inferiority and superiority of particular races has had a shorter history, dating from the last half of the nineteenth century, when some regarded this doctrine as a logical corollary of Darwin's theory of evolution by natural selection. Hostility to Jews, for example, had existed for thousands of years, but anti-Semitism in the strict sense of believing in the biological inferiority of Jews as a Semitic people was one of the offshoots of what was regarded as "scientific" racism.

This new racism that wrapped itself in the mantle of science was neither peculiar to Germany nor limited in its application to Jews. In the United States, some referred to the immigrants from Eastern and Southern Europe as "the beaten men of beaten races," who would be incapable of being able to be absorbed into American society. The eugenics movement sought to limit the reproduction of "inferior" individuals and races, so as to prevent the lowering of the national intelligence in future generations. Planned Parenthood was founded not simply as an organization for limiting the size of families in general but more particularly to reduce the reproduction of the black population in the United States, as Planned Parenthood founder Margaret Sanger herself noted. Such ideas were common among intellectuals who considered themselves "progressive" at the beginning of the twentieth century.

Ironically, although the logical corollary of this genetic determinism was that national IQs would fall over time, as less successful people with generally lower IQs tended to reproduce at a higher rate than more successful people with higher IQs, research in the last years of the twentieth century showed that scores on IQ tests had in fact risen substantially in more than a dozen nations during the course of a generation or two.[86] The question here, however, is not the validity of genetic determinism but how widespread and how openly avowed it was during a particular era. Germans were neither exempt from nor unique in their susceptibility to this doctrine. Hitler's racism represented the gutter-level application of an idea discussed in more lofty tones at higher intellectual levels.

Racism in our narrow modern sense has been a significant force for little more than a century, while violent and lethal hatred of other groups goes back thousands of years. There were pogroms against Jews in Europe, and similar mass slaughters of Chinese minorities in Southeast Asia, centuries before most people had ever heard of genetics. What, then, has been the record of Germans in this longer and broader history of intergroup hostility, discrimination, and violence?

Comparing Germans with other Europeans for the sake of convenience, it seems clear that whatever differences there were historically tended to show the Germans not as intolerant as most Eastern Europeans, for example, toward the Jews. Jews fleeing from Eastern Europe to Germany constituted about one-fifth of the Jewish population in Germany when Hitler came to power.[87] However tragic that was in the light of later events, it was a very reasonable move in light of the differences between Germany and Eastern Europe at that time. Jews were so widely accepted in Germany that nearly half of all Jewish marriages there between 1921 and 1927 were marriages to people who were not Jews.[88] German Jews were noted for being far more assimilated to the larger Western society than were Jews from Eastern Europe, and this was true not only in Germany but in the United States and as far away as Australia.

German American immigrant communities welcomed German Jewish immigrants as members of their *Turnvereine*, singing groups, and other cultural organizations.[89] Nineteenth-century German Jews living in Chile and Czechoslovakia likewise took part in the general cultural life of German communities in those countries.[90] Jewish views of pre-Hitler Germany were very favorable, not only in Germany itself but overseas. During the First World War, American Jewish publications were so favorably disposed toward Germany that they were investigated and prosecuted for favoring an enemy nation in wartime, leading to the famous "clear and present danger" doctrine in favor of free speech by Justice Oliver Wendell Holmes in cases involving Jewish writers, *Abrams v. United States* and *Schenk v. United States.* Even some Zionists in Palestine returned to Germany during the First World War to fight for the Fatherland.[91]

Jews were of course not the only targets of racial hostility nor Germany the only place where such hostility was expressed and acted out. What has been the record of Germans with regard to other racial or ethnic groups in other countries and in other times?

We have already noted the cosmopolitan tone that Germans sought to maintain in the face of group-identity extremism among Latvians and Czechs, though in both cases the Germans eventually decided that they had to defend themselves as Germans. In the Western Hemisphere, the first anti-slavery meeting in North America was held by Germans in 1688 and Germans in Brazil were likewise opposed to slavery there.[92] A history of the antebellum South referred to a "colony of antislavery Germans" who settled in Texas, as well as Germans in Virginia who were "antagonistic to slavery" and Germans in St. Louis who were "strongly antislavery."[93]

When whites in early nineteenth-century North Carolina voted to deny the franchise to free blacks, this disenfranchisement was opposed by voters in almost all of the western counties of the Piedmont region[94]—where the Germans and the Scotch-Irish were concentrated. While Germans were split on many of the complex issues revolving around race and slavery, no prominent German American leader was pro-slavery and, when the Civil War came, the large German population in Missouri was credited with keeping that state in the Union, despite many Confederate sympathizers among other Missourians.[95]

As for relations with the indigenous population of the Western Hemisphere, Germans were noted for getting along with the Indians better than other Europeans did,[96] though all had clashes with the indigenous peoples at some point or other. Germans in Paraguay likewise treated the indigenous people in a more conciliatory manner than other Europeans had.[97] In Australia, Germans established missions to help the aborigines.[98] As noted in an earlier essay, in the German colonies in East Africa slave traders were hanged on the spot when they were caught in the act.[99]

The history of pre-Hitler Germans, whether at home or abroad, can readily stand comparison with that of most Europeans, just as the record of Europeans can stand comparison with that of most other races around the world. That is what makes what happened under Hitler and the Nazis even more chilling. If this could happen with Germans, it could happen with any other people. There were anti-Semites in Germany, as in other countries, and their words can now be read as alarming warnings in light of our knowledge of what lay ahead. But there was little at the time to serve as a credible warning of such a monstrous and almost inconceivable event as the Holocaust.

Even if we confine the question to those Germans living in Germany during the fatal dozen years of the Nazi regime, the issue is whether the Germans of that era, or even those particular Germans whose votes put Hitler in power, were attracted to him for his racist agenda. In elections held from 1871 through 1928, German political parties explicitly devoted to anti-Jewish principles reached a high of 7 percent of the vote and a low below one percent.[100] These parties included, but were not limited to, the Nazis. A study of anti-Semitism in Germany concluded, "by 1914 the anti-Semitic parties were practically defunct and their press was in ruins."[101]

Hitler's speeches during the election campaigns of 1928, 1930, and 1932 made no specific proposals on what he intended to do about Jews.[102] He apparently did not see German public opinion as ready for any of the actions that he would in fact later take against the Jews. When the desperation of Germans in the face of severe economic and social crises created by the worldwide Great Depression of the 1930s elevated Hitler from a fanatic in the streets to a dictatorial ruler, the die was cast, fatally. From that point on, it no longer mattered what most other Germans thought, whether about race or war or anything else. But, before then, when voters in Germany had their last free choice, what were Hitler's supporters supporting? What did they know and when did they know it? A study that attempted to answer these questions concluded:

> Middle-class and other voters did not vote for Hitler because he promised to exterminate European Jewry. Neither did they vote for him because he promised to tear up the constitution, impose a police state, destroy labor unions, eradicate rival political parties, or cripple the churches. Even Hitler's *Mein Kampf* did not forecast these events.[103]

During the years leading up to the Second World War, Hitler moved against the Jews in orchestrated stages, allowing him to gauge the extent to which German public opinion supported his actions. A Nazi-sponsored boycott of Jewish stores in 1933 failed so badly that it was called off after four days, rather than have it be an ongoing fiasco.[104] Even after five years of anti-Jewish propaganda in Germany, when the Nazis in November 1938 unleashed Kristallnacht—the night of broken glass, featuring violence against Jews, their homes and their businesses—the negative reactions of Germans, including some Nazi party members, led Hitler to proceed against the Jews thereafter with as much secrecy as possible.[105] Even when Jews were rounded up and sent off to concentration camps, there was nothing at that point to indicate the grisly fate awaiting them and it was a crime punishable by death to reveal the extermination program.[106]

Rumors circulated and some undoubtedly knew more than rumors but rumors and speculations always abound in wartime. Moreover, even those who were certain of what was happening had no ability to stop it in a totalitarian state and they and their families could pay with their lives for publicly protesting. Even a prominent German Jewish leader like Leo Baeck said that he did not know about Auschwitz and the systematic killing of Jews until 1943, even though millions of Jews had already been killed by then.[107]

Genocide against the Jews was a government program, not the lethal mob violence unleashed against the Jews in earlier pogroms in Eastern Europe or against the Armenians in Turkey during the First World War or against the Ibos in Nigeria in the 1960s or against the Chinese in a number of Southeast Asian countries on a number of occasions over the centuries. Given the fact that Jews had been stripped of legal protections early in the Nazi regime, any of these things might have been done by the German people. Indeed, Hitler tried to represent Kristallnacht as a spontaneous burst of public outrage, rather than as the staged event that it was. But what the German people did not do in these circumstances may be more revealing about their own attitudes. None of this denies that there were anti-Semitic fanatics in Germany, both in the Nazi party and among the German public. It simply makes the dimensions and duration of anti-Semitism among Germans at large subject to question.

What must also be noted is that Jews were a very small minority in pre-Hitler Germany—never as much as two percent of the population,[108] despite their prominence or even predomi- nance in particular fields such as medicine, journalism, or banking. The average German had no compelling reason to be thinking about Jews, one way or another, and indications are that most were apathetic about anti-Semitism, both before and during the Nazi era.[109]

Nevertheless, the egregious behavior of the Nazis toward the Jews prompted some Germans to come to their aid, even during wartime, when that meant risking death for themselves and their families. Estimates of the number of Jews hidden in Berlin alone during the Second World War run into the thousands.[110]

As for post-Hitler Germany, perhaps the following capsule account from *Commentary* magazine—published by the Ameri- can Jewish Committee—is as revealing as any:

> All told, Germany's voluntary payments for past wrongs amount thus far to more than $55 billion over a period of six decades, and are unparalleled in history.[111]

These were not like the reparations after the First World War, imposed on Germany by the victorious powers; these were repa- rations voluntarily paid by a democratically elected German government. This did not of course mean that all hostility to Jews had been obliterated in Germany. It does suggest that such hostility was not pervasive nor necessarily greater than in other European countries. It is hard even to imagine such reparations being paid to persecuted groups by democratically elected governments in places like Rwanda, Uganda, Fiji, or other countries where minorities have been expelled or slaughtered.

SUMMARY AND IMPLICATIONS

The role of the Germans as bearers of more advanced skills to other countries in Europe and the Western Hemisphere has by no means endeared them to all these peoples. Farmers in Honduras complained about having to compete with German farmers there who worked too hard.[112] Latvians and Czechs complained that to become educated, they had to learn the German language—this at a time when there was little serious literature in their own native languages. Russian farmers resented the greater success of German farmers there and the rise of Communism, with its theories of "exploitation," enabled them to unleash an orgy of violence and destruction on German farm communities. In short, productivity does not imply popularity, whether for Germans or for any other race or class. The history of middleman minorities around the world underscores that point as well. Moreover, it is not usually the masses of the people who most resent the more productive people in their midst. More commonly, it is the intelligentsia, who may with sufficiently sustained effort spread their own resentments to others.

When considering the question of the extent to which the Nazi era in Germany reflected the culture or history of Germans as a people, two very different questions must be distinguished from one another: (1) the culpability of that generation of Germans who enabled, abetted, or promoted the cause of the Nazis and its catastrophic human consequences, and (2) the extent to which the prior cultural, political, or social history of Germans as a people made Hitler and the Nazis inevitable, likely, or an aberration. The first question is harder but the second question has wider and more enduring implications.

The issue is not whether there have been anti-Jewish individuals, institutions, writings, movements, or political parties in

Germany—there were in fact all of these, for centuries before the rise of the Nazis—but the ultimate question is: What was the net effect on the actual behavior of Germans toward Jews, not compared to an ideal, but compared to the behavior of others toward Jews or toward other minority groups around the world? Here the pre-Hitler behavior of Germans toward Jews compares favorably with that of most other peoples in most other places, not only in behavior toward the Jews but toward minorities in general. This is no exoneration of anti-Semites, either before or after Hitler. Each generation and each individual bears the heavy burden of guilt for what they did—but not for what others did in other places and other times.

Hitler's accession to power, followed by his coup of converting the constitutional power of a chancellor into the totalitarian dictatorship of a *führer,* was of course made possible by the German voters who gave him a plurality in a democratic election in 1933, setting in motion this whole tragic chain of events. Yet the dictatorship, war, and Holocaust that we associate with the Nazi regime in retrospect was not on the ballot, or even on the horizon, of those who voted for Hitler in 1933. They were seeking a political savior in a chaotic and economically depressed time. The relative political apathy of Germans and their historic law-abiding habits enabled Hitler to seize far more power than he was elected to, with perhaps less resistance than such an action might have provoked in some other societies, and the German military tradition and military prowess made him more dangerous than he might have been as the leader of some other nation.

Looking back through German history, one can find examples of anti-Jewish words and actions by both elites and masses. Tragically, that does not distinguish Germans from Europeans in general—or from human beings in general, when it comes to vile or vicious things being said or done to any number of ethnic or other minorities in countries around the world. But the Holocaust was unique. The question then is whether there was anything correspondingly unique in the breadth or depth of German antipathies toward minorities in general, or Jews in particular, in their pre-Hitler history. No such uniqueness stands out prior to the era of Nazi rule, either in Germany itself or among German communities around the world.

The racial fanaticism of Hitler and the Nazi movement, which spread to the German generation of their day and led ultimately to the Holocaust, were not historically distinct characteristics of Germans as a people. On the contrary, the rise of such a man as the leader of such a people should serve as a permanent warning to all people everywhere who are charmed by charisma or aroused by rhetoric.

Black Education

Achievements, Myths and Tragedies

ILL ROGERS ONCE SAID THAT IT WAS not ignorance that was so bad but, as he put it, "all the things we know that ain't so." Nowhere is that more true than in American education today, where fashions prevail and evidence is seldom asked for or given. Nowhere does this do more harm than in the education of black children.

The quest for esoteric methods of trying to educate black children proceeds as if such children had never been successfully educated before, when in fact there are concrete examples, both from history and from our own times, of schools that have been successful in educating black children, including those from low-income families. Yet the prevailing educational dogma is that you simply cannot expect children who are not middle class to do well on standardized tests, for all sorts of sociological and psychological reasons.

This dogma is not even true for the children for whom it is most often invoked—black American children—much less for minority children in general, whether in the United States or in other countries.

SCHOOLS: PAST ACHIEVEMENTS

Contrary to prevailing educational dogmas, there are schools in America today where low-income black and other minority students do in fact score well on standardized tests—both public schools and private schools, secular and religious—even as the vast majority of ghetto schools have abysmal performances on such tests. Moreover, there has been successful black education as far back as the nineteenth century.

High-Performance Schools

In 1899, there were four academic public high schools in Washington, D.C.—one black and three white.[1] In standardized tests given that year, students in the black high school averaged higher test scores than students in two of the three white high schools.[2] Today, more than a century later, it would be considered Utopian even to set that as a goal, much less expect it to actually happen. Yet what happened back in 1899 was no isolated fluke. That same school repeatedly equaled or exceeded national norms on standardized tests in the 1930s, 1940s, and early 1950s.[3] Back in the 1890s, it was called the M Street School and in 1916 it was renamed Dunbar High School.

When this information on Dunbar High School was first published in the 1970s, those few educators who responded at all dismissed the relevance of these findings by saying that these were "middle class" children and therefore their experience was not "relevant" to the education of low-income minority children. Those who said this had no factual data on the incomes or occupations of the parents of these children—and the data that existed said just the opposite. The problem, however, was not that these dismissive educators did not have evidence. The more fundamental problem was that they saw no *need* for evidence. According to their doctrines, children who did well on standardized tests were middle class. These children did well on such tests, so therefore they must be middle class.

It so happens that there was evidence on the occupations of the parents of the children at this school as far back as the early 1890s. As of academic year 1892–93, of the known occupations of these parents, there were 51 laborers, 25 messengers, 12 janitors, and *one* doctor.[4] That hardly seems middle class. Over the years, a significant black middle class did develop in Washington and most of them may well have sent their children to the M Street School or to Dunbar High School, as it was later called. But that is wholly different from saying that most of the children at that school came from middle-class homes.

More detailed data on parental occupations are available for a later period, from the late 1930s through the mid 1950s. These data reveal that there were far more children whose mothers were maids than there were whose fathers were doctors.[5] Mary Gibson Hundley, who taught at Dunbar for many years, wrote:

> A large segment of the homes of the students had one or more government employees for support. Before the 1940s these employees were messengers and clerks, with few exceptions."[6]

It is possible, of course, to redefine "middle class" in relative terms for the black community as it existed at that time, but such verbal dexterity serves only to salvage words at the expense of reality. The parents of Dunbar students may or may not have been a random sample of the black parents of their time, either occupationally or in terms of their aspirations for their children, but neither were most of them people with professional careers or levels of income that would be considered middle class by the standards of American society as a whole. Intellectual or academic achievements for blacks, as for everyone else, no doubt have pre-conditions but the crucial question is whether these are *economic* preconditions, as so widely asserted—and so widely assumed to be insuperable barriers to good education for minority children from low-income families.

A related stereotype is that the children who went to Dunbar High School were the light-skinned descendants of the black elite that derived from miscegenation during the era of slavery. Here again, the facts have been readily available—and widely ignored. Photographs in old yearbooks from the era of Dunbar's academic success show no such preponderance of light-skinned blacks. Here again, there is a fundamental difference between saying that certain types of people were more likely to send their children to Dunbar, or that such children were over-represented, and saying that most of the children who went to Dunbar came from such families.

Whether in economic or other terms, the families from which the students of Dunbar High School came cannot be nearly so atypical as suggested by those who say that they were mostly "Washington's growing black bourgeoisie."[7] For many years, there was only one academic high school for blacks in the District of Columbia and, as late as 1948, one-third of all black youngsters attending high school in Washington attended Dunbar High School. "If we took only the children of doctors and lawyers," a former Dunbar principal asked, "how could we have had 1400 black students at one time?" This was not a "selective" school in the sense in which we normally use that term—it was not necessary to take tests to get in, for example—even though there was undoubtedly *self-selection* in the sense that students who were serious went to Dunbar and those who were not had other places where they could while away their time, without having to meet high academic standards.

A spot check of attendance records and tardiness records showed that the M Street School at the turn of the century and Dunbar High School at mid-century had less absenteeism and less tardiness than the white high schools in the District of Columbia at those times. In the nineteenth century, tardiness had at first been a problem,[8] but it was a problem that was apparently not tolerated. The school had a tradition of being serious, going back to its founders and early principals, who reflected the influence of the New England culture which contrasted so much with that of the culture of most blacks.

Among those early principals was the first black woman to receive a college degree in the United States—Mary Jane Patterson from Oberlin College, class of 1862. At that time, Oberlin had different academic curriculum requirements for women and men. Latin, Greek and mathematics were required in "the gentlemen's course," as it was called, but not in the curriculum for ladies. Miss Patterson, however, insisted on taking Latin, Greek, and mathematics anyway.[9] We can only imagine what fortitude and sense of purpose that must have taken, at a time when no black woman had ever gotten a college degree in the entire history of the country, and when most members of her race were still slaves in the South. Not surprisingly, in her later 12 years as principal of the black high school in Washington during its formative period, Mary Jane Patterson was noted for "a strong, forceful personality," for thoroughness, and for being an "indefatigable worker."[10] Having this kind of person shaping the standards and traditions of the school in its early years undoubtedly had something to do with its later success. Other early principals included the first black man to graduate from Harvard, class of 1870. Three of the school's first ten principals had graduated from Oberlin, two from Harvard, and one each from Amherst and Dartmouth.[11] Because of restricted academic opportunities for blacks, Dunbar could get teachers with very high qualifications, and even had Ph.D.s among its teachers in the 1920s. Mary Gibson Hundley pointed out, in her history of Dunbar High School: "Federal standards providing equal salaries for all teachers, regardless of sex or race, attracted to Washington the best trained colored college graduates from Northern and Western colleges in the early days, and later from local colleges as well."[12]

One of the other educational dogmas of our times is the notion that standardized tests do not predict future performances for minority children, either in academic institutions or in life. Innumerable scholarly studies have devastated this claim intellectually,[13] though it still survives and flourishes politically. But the history of this black high school in Washington likewise shows a pay-off for solid academic preparation and the test scores that result from it.

Over the entire 85-year history of academic success in this school, from 1870 to 1955, most of its graduates went on to higher education.[14] This was very unusual for either black or white high-school graduates during that era. Because these were usually low-income students, most went to a local free teachers college or to relatively inexpensive Howard University, but significant numbers won scholarships to leading colleges and universities elsewhere.[15]

Early in the twentieth century, some M Street School graduates began going to Harvard—the first in 1903[16]—and other academically elite colleges. A French educator who visited the M Street School that year described its students as "pursuing the same studies as our average college student."[17] During the period from 1918 to 1923, graduates of this school went on to earn 25 degrees from Ivy League colleges, Amherst, Williams, and Wellesley.[18] At one time during this era, there were nine black students at Amherst—six from Dunbar High School.[19] Over the period from 1892 to 1954, Amherst admitted 34 graduates of the M Street School and Dunbar. Of these, 74 percent graduated from Amherst and 28 percent of these graduates were Phi Beta Kappas.[20] Nor was Amherst unique; Dunbar graduates also became Phi Beta Kappas at Harvard, Yale, Williams, Cornell, Dartmouth, and other elite institutions.[21]

At one time, the reputation of Dunbar graduates was such that they did not have to take entrance examinations to be admitted to Dartmouth, Harvard, and some other selective colleges.[22] When Robert N. Mattingly graduated from the M Street School in 1902, he entered Amherst College, receiving credit for freshman mathematics and first-year college physics—and he graduated in three years, Phi Beta Kappa. Yet, far from being one of the elite, Mattingly was, in his own words, "at Amherst on a shoestring."[23]

No systematic study has been made of the later careers of the graduates of M Street and Dunbar High School. However, when black educator Horace Mann Bond studied the backgrounds of blacks with Ph.D.s in 1970, he discovered that more of them had graduated from M Street-Dunbar than from any other black high school in the country. "The first black who" pioneered in a number of fields also came from this school.

The first black man to graduate from Annapolis came from Dunbar.[24] The first black enlisted man in the army to rise to become a commissioned officer also came from this same institution.[25] So did the first black woman to receive a Ph.D. from an American university.[26] So did the first black full professor at a major American university (Allison Davis at the University of Chicago). So did the first black federal judge, the first black general, the first black Cabinet member, the first black senator elected since Reconstruction and, among other notables, the doctor who pioneered the use of blood plasma, historian Carter G. Woodson, author and poet Sterling Brown, and Duke Ellington, who studied music at Dunbar.[27] During World War II, when black military officers were rare, there were among this school's graduates "many captains and lieutenants, nearly a score of majors, nine colonels and lieutenant colonels, and one brigadier general"[28]

All this contradicts another widely believed notion—that schools do not make much difference in children's academic or career success because income and family background are much larger influences. If the schools do not differ very much from one another, then of course it will not make much difference which one a child attends. But, when they differ dramatically, the results can also differ dramatically.

This was not the only school to achieve success with minority children. But, before turning to other examples, it may be useful to consider why and how this 85-year history of dramatic success was abruptly turned into all too typical failure, virtually overnight, by the politics of education.

The landmark racial desegregation case of *Brown v. Board of Education* initially led to a strong resistance to school desegregation in many white communities, including that in Washington, D.C. Ultimately a political compromise was worked out in the District of Columbia: In order to comply with the Supreme Court decision, without having a massive shift of students, the D.C. school officials decided to turn all public schools into neighborhood schools. By this time, the neighborhood around Dunbar High School was rundown and there was a local saying that children who lived near Dunbar didn't go to Dunbar. This had not affected the school's academic standards, however, because black students from all the rest of the city went to Dunbar.

When Dunbar became a neighborhood school, however, the whole character of its student body changed radically—as did the character of its teaching staff. In the past, many Dunbar teachers continued to teach for years after they were eligible for retirement because it was such a fulfilling experience. Now, as inadequately educated, inadequately motivated, and disruptive students flooded into the school, teachers began retiring, some as early as 55 years of age. Dunbar quickly became just another failing ghetto school, with all the problems that such schools have, all across the country. Eighty-five years of achievement simply vanished into thin air.

It is a very revealing fact about the politics of education that no one tried to stop this from happening. When I first began to study the history of this school, back in the 1970s, it seemed to me inconceivable that this could have been allowed to happen without a protest. The Washington school board in the 1950s had included a very militant and distinguished black woman named Margaret Just Butcher, who was also a graduate of Dunbar High School. Surely Dr. Butcher had not let all this happen without exercising her well-known gifts of withering criticism.

Yet I looked in vain through the minutes of the school board meetings for even a single sentence by anybody expressing any concern whatever about the fate of Dunbar High School under the new reorganization plan. Finally, in complete frustration and bewilderment, I phoned Dr. Butcher herself and asked: Was there anything that was said off the record about Dunbar that did not find its way into the minutes that I had read? "No," she replied. Then she reminded me that racial "integration" was the battle cry of the hour in the 1950s. No one thought about what would happen to black schools, not even Dunbar.

Now, decades later, we still do not have racial integration in many of the urban schools around the country—and we also do not have Dunbar High School. Such are the ways of politics, where the crusade of the hour often blocks out everything else, at least until another crusade comes along and takes over the same monopoly of our minds.

Ironically, black high schools in Washington today have many of the so-called "prerequisites" for good education that never existed during the heyday of Dunbar High School—and yet the educational results are abysmal. "Adequate funding" is always included among these "prerequisites" and today the per pupil expenditure in the District of Columbia is among the highest in the nation, while its test scores are among the lowest. During the years of Dunbar's success, it was starved for funds and some of its classes had more than 40 students.[29] As a failing ghetto school today, Dunbar has a finer physical plant than it ever had when it was an academic success. Politics is also part of this picture. Immediate, tangible symbols are what matter within the limited time horizon of elected politicians. Throwing money at public schools produces such symbolic results, even if it cannot produce quality education.

The aftermath of the decline and academic collapse of Dunbar High School is also revealing. With a new school building, the question arose as to the disposition of the original building. Dunbar alumni wanted that building preserved as some sort of memorial to an historic achievement, but Washington's political leaders—representing the kind of people who had not gone to Dunbar—were bitterly opposed.[30] This became a heated legal issue, fought all the way up to the federal Circuit Court of Appeals. After the political leaders won in court, one of them spoke for those "who say that the school represents a symbol of an elitism among blacks that should never happen again. I say we should raze it."[31] They did. The dog in the manger triumphed once more.

Washington Post columnist William Raspberry summarized the conflicting feelings about Dunbar High School in the black community when he wrote:

> Fill a room with middle-aged blacks who grew up in Washington, mention the word "Dunbar," and then take cover. That one word will divide the room into two emotion-charged, outraged, warring factions: those who did and those who didn't attend Dunbar High School "when it was Dunbar."[32]

Despite the Supreme Court's pronouncement in the historic 1954 case of *Brown v. Board of Education* that racially separate schools "are inherently unequal,"[33] there have been many predominantly or wholly minority schools whose test scores were at or above the national average. The average IQ at Dunbar High School was 111 in 1939 and again in 1950.[34] Ironically, Dunbar was within walking distance of the Supreme Court which in effect declared its existence impossible. However, it was not the only black school of which this was true, much less the only minority school, for there have also been all-Chinese American schools and at least one all-American-Indian school which have done the same.[35]

Many, if not most, predominantly minority schools have performed very poorly, but enough others have not that this cannot be blamed simply on their being racially segregated schools. Not only did M Street-Dunbar High School have a racially segregated student body throughout the 85 years of its academic success, so did St. Augustine School, a Catholic high school in New Orleans, which also met national standards in its early history. The first black student from the South to win a National Merit Scholarship came from St. Augustine. So did the first Presidential Scholar of any race from the state of Louisiana. When St. Augustine was studied back in the 1970s, 20 percent of all Presidential Scholars in the history of the state had come from this one school with about 600 black students.

Test scores were never used as a rigid cutoff for admission to St. Augustine. There were students there with IQs in the 60s, as well as others with IQs more than twice that high. Moreover, the average IQ of the school as a whole rose over the years—being in the 80s and 90s in the 1950s and then reaching the national average of 100 in the 1960s. To put that in perspective, both blacks and whites in the South during this era tended to score below the national average on IQ and other standardized tests.

By contrast with a private Catholic high school like St. Augustine, P.S. 91 in Brooklyn, New York, was a public elementary school, located in a rundown ghetto and housed in an even older building than the original Dunbar High School. Yet the students in most of the grades in this predominantly black school scored at or above the national norms on standardized tests when I studied it back in the 1970s. It was the only school in its district whose students were reading at or above the national average. The next best school in that district had fewer than 40 percent of its students reading at or above national norms and a number of other schools in the district had fewer than 30 percent who reached that level.[36]

This was not in any sense a middle-class school or a magnet school. It was just an ordinary ghetto school run by an extraordinary principal. What was more extraordinary to me than even the test scores of the students was the openness with which I was welcomed and allowed to see whatever I wanted to see.

Educators often like to give guided tours to selected (and often atypical) places, much like the Potemkin village tours in Czarist Russia. But, in P.S. 91, I was allowed to wander down the halls and arbitrarily pick out which classrooms I wanted to go into. I did this on every floor of the school. Inside those classrooms were black children much like children you can find in any ghetto across the country. Many came from broken homes and were on welfare. Yet, inside this school, they spoke in grammatical English, in complete sentences, and to the point. Many of the materials they were studying were a year or more ahead of their respective grade levels.

None of these successful schools had a curriculum especially designed for blacks. Most had some passing recognition of the children's backgrounds. Dunbar High School, for example, was named for black poet Paul Laurence Dunbar and it set aside one day a year to commemorate Frederick Douglass, but its curriculum could hardly be called Afrocentric. As Senator Edward Brooke, a Dunbar alumnus, put it:

> Negro History Week was observed, and in American history they taught about the emancipation of slaves and the struggle for equality and civil rights. But there was no demand by students for more, no real interest in Africa and its heritage. We knew about Africa as we knew about Finland.[37]

Throughout the 85 years of its academic success, Dunbar High School taught Latin. In some of the early years, it taught Greek as well. Its whole focus was on expanding the students' cultural horizons, not turning their minds inward. Still less was its focus on giving students a sense of victimhood or of doors closed, though in fact many doors were closed to them throughout the history of Dunbar's academic success. On the other hand, many Dunbar alumni were the first to open some of those doors. Instead of today's fashionable focus on grievances, the tone was set by a poem on the assembly wall, written by Paul Laurence Dunbar, for whom the school was named. Its first stanza said:

> Keep a-pluggin' away.
> Perseverance still is king;
> Time its sure reward will bring;
> Work and wait unwearying—
> Keep a-pluggin' away.

This was written at a time when racial segregation and discrimination were pervasive across the South and were spreading into the North, when blacks were being lynched, and when the very school in which these words were posted received less money than white schools in the same city. Many today might disdain this message of self-improvement as naive at best. But the fact is that it worked—and much that is considered more sophisticated today has a dismal record of failure.

A particularly painful example of contemporary failure is this account of Dunbar High School in 1993:

Rodney McDaniel is a senior at Dunbar High School in Washington, D.C. He is the captain of its football team, which is the best in the city.... Rodney McDaniel evidently has the ability to take harder courses than he does. But he, like other students at Dunbar, has been held to low standards by teachers unwilling or unable to demand more....A smaller percentage of Dunbar students go to college now than did 60 years ago.[38]

Sixty years earlier would have been in the depths of the Great Depression of the 1930s.

Harlem and the Lower East Side

Important as the history of outstanding schools for black students has been, there is also much to learn from the history of very ordinary urban ghetto schools, which often did far better in the past—both absolutely and relative to their white contemporaries—than is the case today. The test scores in ordinary Harlem schools in the 1940s were quite comparable to the test scores in white working-class neighborhoods on New York's lower east side at that same time.

Sometimes the Harlem schools scored a little higher and sometimes the lower east side schools scored a little higher but there were no such glaring racial disparities as we have become used to in urban schools in recent years. In April 1941, for example, some lower east side schools scored slightly higher on tests of word meaning and paragraph meaning than some schools in Harlem but, in tests given in December of that same year, several Harlem schools scored higher than the lower east side schools. Neither set of schools scored as high as the city-wide average, though neither was hopelessly below it.[39]

While the lower east side of New York is justly known for the many people who were born in poverty there and rose to middle-class levels—and some to national prominence—very little attention is paid to a very similar history in Harlem during that era. Some years ago, a national magazine ran a flattering profile of me, expressing wonder that I had come out of Harlem and gone on to elite colleges and an academic career. Shortly thereafter, I received a letter from a black lawyer of my generation, pointing out that my experience was by no means so unusual in those days. He had grown up in Harlem during those same years, just a few blocks from me. From the tenement building in which he lived came children who grew up to become a doctor, a lawyer, a priest, and a college president. Indeed, where did today's black middle class come from, if not from such places and such schools?

Parents have been an important ingredient in the success of schools, whatever the racial or social backgrounds of the students. But the specific nature of parental involvement can vary greatly— and has often been very different from what is believed among some educational theorists. In some of the most successful schools, especially of the past, the parents' role has been that of giving moral support to the school by letting their children know that they were expected to learn and to behave themselves.

Current educational fashions see parents' roles as more active, both on site in the schools and in such things as helping with their children's homework. Whatever the merits or demerits of these notions, historically that was certainly *not* the role played by parents of children at successful schools in the past. Nor were parents necessarily equipped to play such a role. As of 1940, for example, the average black adult in the United States had only an elementary school education, usually in inferior Southern schools.

During that era, parents of children going to school on the lower east side of New York were similarly ill-equipped to be participants in the educational process. Immigrant children who grew up there have expressed painful memories of how their parents, with their meager education and broken English, hated to have to go see a teacher—and how embarrassed their children were when their parents showed up at school. Among immigrant Japanese parents on the West Coast, what they had to offer their children was the value of education and discipline, "even when the parents themselves were poorly educated."[40] American parents today may be more educated and more sophisticated but it is not clear that their involvement in schools has been a net benefit. At the very least, history shows that it has never been essential.

Successful minority schools are not confined to history, however. They still exist in the third millennium—and they are still largely ignored by educators, politicians, community activists, and intellectuals.

SCHOOLS: CONTEMPORARY ACHIEVEMENTS

While schools for low-income and minority students that succeeded in the past often had to do so despite the indifference of boards of education run by white officials, those which have succeeded in our own time have often had to do so in the face of active hostility by education officials of whatever race.

The principal of Bennett-Kew Elementary School in Inglewood, California, whose student body is 52 percent Hispanic and 45 percent black, raised these children's reading levels from the third percentile to the fiftieth percentile in just four years. But she was threatened with loss of money because she used phonics instead of the mandated "whole-language" teaching methods and taught exclusively in English, instead of using the "bilingual" approach required by education authorities. The fact that she was succeeding where others were failing carried no weight with state education officials. Fortunately, it carried enough weight with the parents of her students that they bombarded these officials with protests that caused them to relent and let this principal continue to succeed in her own way, instead of failing in their way.[41]

In Houston, Texas, students in Wesley Elementary School—92 percent black and 7 percent Hispanic—were reading "several years below grade level" before a new principal installed a new curriculum and raised their reading and math scores above the national average. But, again, the methods he used were not those favored by the education establishment, which tried to stop him. Fortunately, a new district superintendent—Rod Paige, later U. S. Secretary of Education—was more supportive, so that the success of this school and these methods continued under a new principal, who said bluntly, "The teachers' colleges are to blame for so much school failure."[42]

Educational success usually provides no protection from the wrath of those who impose their educational dogmas on the schools and will not tolerate seeing those dogmas ignored. High school math teacher Jaime Escalante, whose successes in teaching Mexican American students was celebrated in the movie *Stand and Deliver,* was eventually hounded out of Garfield High School in Los Angeles. Yet, while he was there, about one-fourth of all Mexican American students—in the entire country—who passed Advanced Placement Calculus came from Garfield High School.

Documented results are not allowed to override the prevailing educational dogmas—which pervade the schools of education, the teachers' unions, and state and federal education bureaucracies—none of whom pays the price for the failure of these dogmas.[43] Neither do their children, who are typically enrolled in private schools. What they would have to pay a price for would be widespread demonstrations that the methods to which they are committed produce educational results that are grossly inferior to those produced by the methods they oppose. Should such revelations become widely known among parents and voters, this would threaten not only their careers but also their agendas, which include the use of public schools to promote fashionable beliefs and attitudes—political correctness—rather than to equip students' minds with knowledge and develop their capacity for independent use of logic and evidence.

None of this says that there is just one best way of teaching all students. That would be repeating the dogmatic approach of the education establishment. What the record of successful minority schools shows, both in history and among contemporary schools, is that educational achievement is not foredoomed by economic or social circumstances beyond the school grounds, as the education establishment constantly strives to prove. Poverty, broken homes, and unruly environments are not to be ignored, downplayed or apologized for. But neither are the failings of others proof that the education establishment is doing its job right. Perfect students with perfect parents in a perfect society cannot learn things that they are not being taught—and that includes an increasing number of basic things in our public schools.

While successful minority schools do not use any single formula or ideology, they do make sure to teach those basic things that get neglected by more typical or more trendy schools, beginning with reading.

Portland Elementary School, in Portland, Arkansas, has multiple violations of prevailing educational dogmas—and such academic success that it is besieged with requests from parents who want to transfer their students in. Ironically, white students were once transferring out, back in 1970, in response to racial desegregation. Until recent years, declining educational standards were painfully visible in the fact that half the students in the fourth through sixth grades were scoring two or more years below grade level. Then came a new principal with old-fashioned ideas about education who began to get old-fashioned results. Now 100 percent of the students are reading at grade level or higher and a majority of the students are above the national average on both reading and math tests.

One of these old-fashioned ideas is called "Directed Instruction"—what used to be called just plain teaching, as distinguished from the more trendy notion that teachers are to be "facilitators" on the sidelines, letting students "discover" and "create" knowledge themselves. In Portland Elementary, Directed Instruction has proven to be especially effective with "at risk" students. In other words, kids who have nobody to teach them at home improve greatly when there is somebody to teach them at school, instead of using them as guinea pigs for experiments.

Not satisfied with violating educational dogma by plain old teaching, Principal Ernest Smith also groups students by ability and gives them tests every ten lessons or about every seven or eight days—all of which is taboo in educational establishment circles. So successful has this approach turned out to be that whites have been transferring back in and now constitute a majority of the students.[44]

Another successful minority school—99 percent black with 80 percent of its students coming from low-income families—is Cascade Elementary School in Atlanta. Although its demographics would be considered to be a formula for automatic failure by those in the education establishment, in fact these students have scored at the 74th percentile on reading tests and at the 83rd percentile on math tests. Principal Alfonso L. Jessie is so old-fashioned that he will not tolerate misbehavior:

> ...Jessie explains to parents at the beginning of the year that if their children misbehave in school, they will be personally escorted to the parents' place of work. Not surprisingly, Cascade has almost no discipline problems.[45]

Such a principal might well be accused of stereotyping or

racism by civil rights groups, community activists, or white liberals—if he were not black.

Like other schools for minority children, the Marva Collins Preparatory School in Chicago has its founder's "no-nonsense, back-to-basics curriculum that is centered on phonics and memorization for the younger students, and higher-level reasoning and literary analysis for the older ones." It also features "weekly tests in all subjects every Friday."[46] It is not hard to understand why Marva Collins was unpopular with education authorities when she taught in the public schools, and had to go set up her own private school in order to teach the way that she wanted to.

Chicago public schools were declared to be the worst in the nation back in the 1980s by William J. Bennett, then U.S. Secretary of Education. Despite some improvements, even as late as 1996 half of all the children in the Chicago schools were performing below grade level in four-fifths of the city's schools. Yet even here there has been an exception, using methods that are an exception to the prevailing educational dogmas. Children in Earhart Elementary School, in Chicago's south side ghetto, score at the 70th percentile in reading and the 80th percentile in math. Ninety nine percent of these children are black and more than four-fifths of them qualify for the free lunch or reduced-price lunch program.

Taking advantage of a 1988 law that allowed individual schools more leeway to escape rigid educational dogmas, a new principal began teaching reading based on phonics and memorization of sight-words, devoting an hour and a half each morning exclusively to reading. During this reading period, all physical education, music, art, and library activities were brought to a halt so that the entire support staff could help the children with their reading. The school taught things like grammar and composition, which are considered passé in educational circles. But it achieved success—which is also passé in too many public schools today.

The KIPP Academy in Houston, Texas—its name derived from the Knowledge Is Power Program—has achieved such success on both math and reading tests than it has spawned a spinoff with the same name in the Bronx. The first KIPP school began with a "campus" that consisted of twelve trailers parked near a baseball field at Houston Baptist University.

Like many other successful schools for low-income minority students, its emphasis is on work. "If you're off the bus, you're working," said its principal and co-founder Michael Feinberg. KIPP students spend 67 percent more time in the classroom than the average public school student:

> Each morning students receive a worksheet of math, logic, and word problems for them to solve in the free minutes that appear throughout the day.

KIPP co-founders Michael Feinberg and David Levin (who later headed the Bronx school of the same name) did not begin with theories, such as teachers' colleges do. Instead, they studied what worked in various schools around the country and made that the basis for their program. Not only is this the opposite of the approach used by education "experts," so is the KIPP rejection of any single magic formula for teaching. KIPP teachers are free to teach as they see fit—so long as they get results. These teachers also visit parents in their homes to explain what they are doing and what the parents need to do—and they carry cell phones with toll-free numbers so that they can be reached after school hours.[47] They mean business.

Many other successful minority schools—too numerous to mention—are operating in various communities around the country. Twenty-one of them were studied by the Heritage Foundation under its "No Excuses" program. To be eligible for this program, a school must score at or above the 65th percentile on national achievement tests and 75 percent of their students must qualify for the subsidized or free lunch program. Most schools where such a high percentage of students come from homes with low enough incomes to qualify for this lunch program score below the 35th percentile.[48] Yet the 21 schools that met the "No Excuses" program criteria and whose results were published were by no means the only such schools—just the ones that happened to be found in the survey that was conducted.

What are the "secrets" of such successful schools?

The biggest secret is that there are no secrets, unless work is a secret. Work seems to be the only four-letter word that cannot be used in public today.

Aside from work and discipline, the various successful schools for minority children have had little in common with one another—and even less in common with the fashionable educational theories of our times. Some of these schools have been public, some private. Some have been secular and some have been religious. Dunbar High School had an all-black teaching staff but St. Augustine in New Orleans began with an all-white teaching staff. Some of these schools were housed in old rundown buildings and others in new, modern facilities. Some of their principals were finely attuned to the social and political nuances, while others were blunt people who could not have cared less about such things and would have failed Public Relations One.

MYTHS AND TRAGEDIES

Some of the myths surrounding the education of black students have already been noted in passing—that only middle-class youngsters can do well on standardized tests, that racially separate schools are inherently inferior, and that standardized tests are too culturally biased to predict the academic or later success of black students. There are many other myths and they all contribute to the tragedies that afflict the education of most black students. More than isolated false beliefs are involved, however. Most of these beliefs reflect an over-all vision and an agenda that need to be scrutinized.

The Racial Mix

Perhaps the most widespread and most consequential of these myths, promulgated by the Supreme Court of the United States, is that racially separate schools cannot achieve quality education. In addition to all the black schools that have belied that assumption, there have been successful all-Chinese schools in the United States, all-Tamil schools in Sri Lanka, and all-Armenian schools in the Ottoman Empire, among others.

Sometimes the unspoken assumption is that a racial mix of students is helpful, or even necessary, because students from one group need to acquire better educational habits and attitudes from another group. That attitude has been found among those Malay parents in Singapore who want their children to emulate the more serious and hard-working attitudes of the Chinese students there.[49] But that same assumption cannot be openly avowed about black students in the United States, in the skittish atmosphere surrounding racial issues. Yet the long, bitterly divisive, and ultimately futile campaign of busing students to schools far from home for the sake of racial "balance" is hard to understand without the underlying assumption that black students need to be with white students in order to learn. Thus "the white man's burden" doctrine of nineteenth-century imperialism became in effect the white child's burden doctrine of twentieth-century education.

A later variation on this theme has been a "diversity" rationale that all students learn more in an environment where there are children from other racial, cultural, or other social backgrounds. While more politically palatable than the separate-is-inferior doctrine, this diversity rationale has had no more empirical evidence to support it, unless endlessly repeating the word "diversity" and rhapsodizing over its presumed virtues is considered to be evidence. If one seriously wished to test this doctrine, it would be hard to explain how a racially homogeneous nation like Japan could have its students better educated than those in the United States, especially since Japan is one of the most culturally insular contemporary nations, with nothing like the interest in multiculturalism found in Britain and in British-offshoot societies like the United States and Australia. But neither this nor any of innumerable other possible empirical tests has been applied to the diversity doctrine. It has simply become dogma, like so much else in education circles.

The opposite dogma, that black children require a separate, racially oriented or "Afrocentric" education, has seized the imagination of many, with no more empirical evidence to support it than its Eurocentric counterpart. This vision has spawned such subsidiary notions as a need for racial "role models" for inspiration and a "critical mass" of black students, in order for these students to feel socially comfortable enough to do their best. Hard evidence for any of these beliefs has been neither asked for nor given. Moreover, such evidence as exists points in the opposite direction.

One of the few attempts to examine the facts, a study titled

Increasing Faculty Diversity, found no empirical evidence to support the belief that same-sex, same-ethnicity role models are any more effective than white male role models at the college level.[50] This is consistent with the experiences of successful black schools examined here, some of these schools having all-black, others all-white, and still others a racially mixed assortment of teachers. If role models of the same race are so important for successful education, then it is virtually impossible to explain the spectacular rise of second-generation Japanese Americans after World War II. The great majority of the previous generation of Japanese Americans were farmers and it is doubtful whether most of the second generation children ever saw a Japanese-American teacher or professor, much less Japanese Americans who were successful in the fields in which the Nisei generation would rise, such as science and engineering.

What of the "critical mass" theory that has been used to support preferential college admissions for black students? Do black students do better educationally where there are enough other black students to create a socially comfortable subculture in schools or on college campuses? As with so many other educational doctrines, the issue is not even posed in such empirical terms. It is simply stated as an imperative and those who question it are scorned as having uncomprehending minds or unworthy motives. But what do the facts show?

Again, there have been remarkably few systematic studies of this or many other educational doctrines, especially those involving racial issues. Certainly the remarkable educational success of Dunbar High School graduates who went on to Amherst College from the late nineteenth century to the middle of the twentieth century cannot be attributed to either a critical mass of black students on that campus, or to black role models on the faculty, because they had neither. Studies from more recent times have shown that the education of black students has been negatively affected by the presence of large numbers of other black students.

An empirical study published by the National Bureau of Economic Research found that "a higher percentage of Black schoolmates has a strong adverse effect on achievements of Blacks and, moreover, that the effects are highly concentrated in the upper half of the ability distribution."[51] Another study, focusing on the effect of ability-grouping on the performances of students in general, mentioned among its conclusions: "Schooling in a homogeneous group of students appears to have a positive effect on the achievements of high-ability students' achievements, and even stronger effects on the achievements of high-ability minority youth."[52] In other words, a "critical mass" of black students seems to drag down the academic performance of high-ability black students.

Yet another study, this one about black students in the affluent suburb of Shaker Heights, Ohio, showed a pervasive pattern of not only neglecting school work, but even of disdaining it to the point of resenting those black students who applied themselves, or who spoke standard English, denouncing them for "acting white."[53] Similar social patterns among black students have been found around the country and are much more consistent with Berkeley Professor John McWhorter's thesis that there is an anti-intellectual black subculture which keeps many black students from doing their best. No wonder that a "critical mass" of black students has the opposite effect on education from what its advocates claim.

History

There is a particularly painful irony in the notion that blacks who are seeking to become educated are "acting white." During Frederick Law Olmsted's celebrated journeys through the antebellum South, he was appalled to learn that a free black man had been publicly whipped in Washington, D.C., for conducting a clandestine school for black children. Not only was it illegal to teach slaves to read and write, it was illegal in many places for free blacks to go to school. Yet clandestine schools for black children existed all over the South, some of which were ignored by the local authorities, though not by all, as this courageous black man discovered in Washington. What a mockery of him and of other courageous black pioneers to say that seeking an education is "acting white"!

Despite bans on education for blacks in the antebellum South, and by no means universal access of blacks to public schools in the North, the census of 1850 showed that most of the approximately half-million free blacks could read and write. After emancipation, the achievement of literacy by a majority of black Americans within two generations has been called "an accomplishment seldom witnessed in human history,"[54] by a noted economic historian.

Literacy may be something that we take for granted today, but most of the people in Albania were still illiterate in the 1920s and most of the people in India were still illiterate half a century after that. But how and why literacy was achieved among black Americans as rapidly as it was is a matter of little or no interest to those who treat the history of blacks as the history of white people's treatment of blacks. Thus the history of the education of blacks in the United States is presented largely as a history of segregated schools, starved for funds, and of biases against black students by white teachers, or by white students in racially integrated settings, or other such things which transform the history of black people into a history of white people in their treatment of blacks.

History is too often the handmaiden of contemporary visions or agendas. Accomplishments among blacks are often either magnified or downplayed, or glided over entirely, according to whether these accomplishments do or do not advance the agenda of portraying victimhood or struggles against victimhood. In this context, it is explicable, though hardly justified, that the history of successful black schools has attracted virtually no interest from either historians or educators. That history does not advance any contemporary political agenda, though it might help advance the education of a whole generation of black students.

Things that do advance contemporary agendas include demands for money to promote the teaching of "black English" or "ebonics."[55] Here there is much appeal to history, though largely a fictitious history. The peculiarities of ghetto speech, often imitated even among contemporary black middle-class youth, are said to derive from African speech patterns, when in fact most of those very same words and phrases were part of the speech patterns in those parts of Britain from which white Southerners came, centuries ago.

False history is not unique to black Americans. As Daniel Patrick Moynihan said of his fellow Irish Americans:

> The cruel part of this history is that by 1916 Irish nationalism in America had little to do with Ireland. It was a hodgepodge of fine feeling and bad history with which the immigrants filled a cultural void.[56]

Much of what calls itself "Afrocentric" education is similarly remote from Africa and is similarly filling a cultural void. But now there is huge political support for such things and that has brought forth large amounts of money to subsidize these escapisms. Moreover, these are now regarded as sacrosanct parts of black culture, which insulates them from inquiries into either their authenticity or their educational consequences.

Cultural Handicaps

The consequences of deficiencies in the education of black students are grave—and getting worse, in the sense that an increasingly demanding technology and an increasingly complex world economy have few places for those who without skills of the mind. Black students, by and large, lag appallingly behind whites, and still more so behind Asian Americans, in those skills. In 2001, for example, there were more than 16,000 Asian American students who scored above 700 on the mathematics SAT, while fewer than 700 black students scored that high—even though blacks outnumbered Asian Americans several times over.[57]

This cannot be explained away by poverty, racism, or innate inferiority. Even Arthur Jensen, the leading proponent of the theory of genetic racial differences in IQ, has said that among "the disadvantaged" there are "high school students who have failed to learn basic skills that they could easily have learned many years earlier" if taught in different ways.[58] Far from justifying the schools' failures to educate black children or regarding these children as uneducable, Professor Jensen concluded: "One of the great and relatively untapped reservoirs of mental ability in the disadvantaged, it appears from our research, is the basic ability to learn. We can do more to marshal this strength for educational purposes."[59] In short, even the leading proponent of the belief in innate differences in intelligence does not believe that this could explain the educational deficiencies actually found among disadvantaged youngsters, who could "easily" have mastered the academic skills in which they are lacking.

As for income, Asian American students from low-income families score higher on the SAT than black students from upper-income families.[60] But Asian Americans are not self-handicapped by the counterproductive attitudes toward education found even in middle-class black communities. As for the racism of whites as an explanation of black educational deficiencies, there are enough black-run schools, colleges and universities where there would be dramatically better results than in white-run institutions, if racism were the explanation. But no such dramatic differences are visible.

The segregated schools in which most blacks were educated for most of their history have provided a tempting explanation of racial differences in test scores and other indices of academic achievement—especially since the "separate but equal" rationale for segregation was a mockery in practice. Yet the fact that a neat combination of moral and causal arguments can be made does not mean that those arguments should escape empirical scrutiny. Not only have segregated schools not proven to be inferior in many cases, even ethnic groups who sat side-by-side in the same schools have had as large IQ differences as those between blacks and whites attending segregated schools in the Jim Crow South. Back in the 1950s, Japanese American and Mexican American youngsters in the same school system, and whose parents at that time and place had very similar occupational status, had an average IQ difference of 20 points, slightly more than black-white IQ differences nationwide and the same as black-white IQ differences in the Jim Crow South. There was an even larger disparity—an average of 26 IQ points' difference—between Jewish and Puerto Rican students attending the same school from the early 1930s to the mid 1950s. Even earlier in the twentieth century, German American children graduated from high school at a rate many times that of Irish American children.[61] Vast differences in educational performances between groups have been common, not only in America but in other countries as well, whether they attended the same or different schools.

One of the most obvious reasons for the deficient educational performances of blacks is also one of the most overlooked or suppressed: By and large, black students do not work as hard as white students, much less Asian students. The Shaker Heights study is just one that has found this to be so, though many have been reluctant even to investigate this factor that will be very unsurprising to anyone who has taught black students, white students, and Asian students.[62] The remarkable exceptions in schools where substandard work has not been tolerated only reinforce this point. If the fundamental problem were income, segregation, or even innate inferiority, there would be no such dramatic contrasts among black schools. Although each of these explanations has been common at various times and places, none of them stands up to empirical scrutiny.

If successful education of blacks were just a matter of isolated individuals—of "cream rising to the top"—then it would be hard to explain such concentrations of educational success at such schools as Dunbar and its counterparts today. Such success has been disproportionately concentrated not only in particular schools but also in particular families. Of 4.3 million black families in the United States in 1966, a mere 5.2 *thousand* produced *all* the black physicians, dentists, lawyers, and academic doctorates in the country.[63] As rare as people at this level were among blacks, the average black family that included someone in one of these categories averaged 2.2 such individuals.[64] While family concentrations alone might suggest heredity, similar institutional concentrations suggest that it is the culture which promotes or impedes educational achievement.

In a sense, it is misleading to single out blacks for not sharing cultural values that are in fact by no means universal among other groups in the United States or in other countries around the world. Certainly the dedicated work of Chinese American or Japanese American students is not the norm among most ethnic groups or in most countries. In white, lower-class communities in Britain, the same counterproductive attitudes toward education found among blacks in the United States are just as prevalent and just as self-defeating.[65]

HIGHER EDUCATION

One sign of the sharp social contrasts within the black population, past and present, is that there were blacks going to college in the United States, even during the era of slavery, and some of the more affluent free blacks sent their children abroad to be educated. Meanwhile, the vast majority of blacks, held in bondage, could neither read nor write.

As with other groups, historic differences had enduring consequences. Well into the twentieth century, much of the black leadership and blacks prominent in the professions were descendants of the antebellum "free persons of color." An exception was Booker T. Washington, who was born in bondage during the last years of slavery and who in adulthood was preoccupied with the education of others like himself from the black masses, rather than the education of the offspring of the more cultured black elite, such as W. E. B. Du Bois. It would be hard to understand these two men's real differences—as distinguished from the caricatures about them produced in later generations—without understanding the very different constituencies they served.

Colleges specifically for blacks were established after the Civil War, but most were essentially white institutions for black students, given the scarcity of blacks with the educational qualifications to become professors. Indeed, the scarcity of black students qualified to be in college often meant, in the nineteenth century, that many of these colleges were essentially elementary and secondary schools by another name. For example, of the 251 students attending Atlanta University in academic year 1872–73, only 12 were taking college courses, while 128 were taking elementary school courses.[66] Over the first quarter-century of its existence, fewer than 5 percent of Atlanta University's students took college-level courses.[67] Nor was Atlanta University unique.

In order to understand this early era of black higher education, it is necessary to understand the extreme scarcity of black students who had received the preparatory education required for real college education. The first public high school for black children in America was established in 1870—the Washington school that later became known as Dunbar High School. Twenty-two years

later, the first public high school for blacks in Baltimore was
founded. As late as school year 1915–16, there were just 64 public
high schools for black children in all 18 Southern states put
together—with more than half of these high schools being in just
four states: West Virginia, Kentucky, Tennessee, and Texas.[68] A survey
of 16 Southern and border states, plus the District of Columbia,
showed a grand total of fewer than 9,000 black students enrolled
in public secondary schools in 1916.[69]

A federal government report on black students noted at that
time: "While only a fourth of the secondary pupils in the border
States are educated at private expense, almost two-thirds of those
in the other Southern States are in private institutions."[70] The states
of the deep South were the most reluctant to build public high
schools for black children. During the 1920s, behind-the-scenes
pressure was necessary to get a public high school for blacks built
in Atlanta[71] and, as late as the 1930s, only 7 percent of black youngsters of high school age were attending high school in
Mississippi.[72] Writing in 1944, Gunnar Myrdal noted: "High schools
for Negroes in the South have existed in significant numbers for
only about twenty years and are still inadequate."[73]

The situation would have been even more bleak than it was
except for the existence of private schools where black young
people could get elementary or secondary education. All schools
for blacks in the antebellum South were of course private, as well
as clandestine. In the first decades after the Civil War, the American
Missionary Association, established thousands of schools for blacks
in the South. Most of the teachers in these schools were young,
unmarried women from New England, bringing with them not
only academic education but also a whole culture very different
from that of Southern society. Many black children thus acquired
advantages that they would take with them into the adult world in
later life. As a noted historian observed: "It was no accident that so
many black leaders of twentieth century civil rights movements
came from missionary schools."[74]

During the half-century following the Civil War, an estimated
$57 million was contributed from the North to educate black stu-
dents in the South and blacks themselves contributed an
additional $24 million.[75] But the Southern states dragged their feet

on creating schools—and especially high schools—for black children. This was an era not just of slow progress but of actual retrogression in some respects. As a scholarly study of this period noted: "The disparity between black and white public schools in per capita expenditures was greater in 1910 than in 1900 in every southern state."[76] It was 1916 before as many black children were attending public high schools as were attending private high schools.[77]

A federal agency, the Freedman's Bureau, also contributed to the education of blacks in the years following the Civil War, spending about $3.5 million in the years from 1865 to 1870. Its most enduring legacy was the creation of Howard University in Washington, which became the most prominent of the institutions of higher education for black students. During the decades after the Civil War, it was much easier to create institutions for black students and call them colleges than to supply them with students actually prepared to do college work. Moreover, in this postbellum era, it was hard to find blacks with the qualifications to become professors, deans, and college presidents. There was a reason why many of what were called colleges and universities for black students were doing largely pre-college work and why those who ran these institutions and taught the courses were usually white.

The Du Bois–Washington Controversy

The contemporary habit of reducing serious issues and historic figures to the dimensions of cartoon characters has led to widespread depiction of the rivalry between W. E. B. Du Bois and Booker T. Washington as a clash between a black militant and an Uncle Tom. Despite very real differences between the two men, Du Bois himself refused to make any such characterization of Washington. Du Bois was among the many people around the country—black and white, North and South—who sent congratulations to Booker T. Washington on his historic 1895 speech at the Atlanta Exposition that set forth Washington's philosophy and marked his emergence as a black educator and leader. More than half a century later, even as a self-exiled Communist living in Ghana, Du Bois corrected a student who spoke disparagingly of Booker T. Washington.[78]

Du Bois and Washington had overlapping goals in education and in society, but different emphases. Both recognized the very low standards of education, skills, behavior, and hygiene among most blacks at the end of the nineteenth century, just one generation removed from the world of the slave plantation. During this era, Du Bois not only criticized the extravagant spending habits he found among blacks in his study *The Philadelphia Negro,* he spoke more generally of "the Great Lack which faces our race in the modern world, Lack of Energy," which he attributed to "indolence" which had now become a kind of "social heredity."[79]

Even if whites were to lose their racial prejudices overnight, it would make little difference in the economic position of most blacks, according to Du Bois. Although "some few would be promoted, some few would get new places" as a result of an end of discrimination, nevertheless "the mass would remain as they are" until the younger generation began to "try harder" as the race "lost the omnipresent excuse for failure: prejudice."[80] Du Bois saw many of the blacks as sunk into "listless indifference, or shiftlessness, or reckless bravado."[81] In short, Du Bois, like Washington, saw an enormous need for self-improvement among blacks at this juncture in history. The big difference was that Washington made self-improvement the principal and over-riding goal of the kind of education he established at the Tuskegee Institute, which he founded.

Students at Tuskegee were taught job skills, including the skills that enabled them to build many of the buildings at the institute itself. They were taught deportment, hygiene, and other mundane but important things needed to take control of their own lives and advance in the world. Contrary to legend, Washington never renounced equal rights. "It is important and right that all privileges of the law be ours, but it is vastly more important that we be prepared for the exercises of these privileges," he said in his historic Atlanta Exposition speech.[82] By linking rights and responsibilities, Washington was able to address both the blacks and the whites in the audience on common ground. And by linking the fates of the two races, he was able to enlist the support of some whites by arguing that blacks would either help lift up the South or help to drag it down.[83] W. E. B. Du Bois likewise said to Southern whites: "If you do not lift them up, they will pull you down."[84]

Although the two men said many things that were very similar at that time, their differing emphases were clear as well, beginning with education. Du Bois emphasized academic education for those whom he called "the talented tenth" of the race—largely people like Du Bois himself, educated and cultured descendants of the antebellum "free persons of color," for whom vocational education would have been a step backward. The very phrase "talented tenth" implicitly acknowledged that this was not what was most needed by most blacks at that time. Although Du Bois acknowledged the necessity and the achievements of vocational education—"accomplishments of which it has a right to be proud"[85]—he was promoting a very different kind of education for a very different class of people. Moreover, this education and this class of people were intended to spearhead political agitation for civil rights, as exemplified in the National Association for the Advancement of Colored People, which Du Bois helped found.

Just as Du Bois acknowledged the need for vocational education for many blacks, so Washington acknowledged the need for academic education for other blacks. He served on the board of trustees for Howard University and Fisk University, whose educational missions were very different from that of Tuskegee Institute, and he used his influence to get financial support for Howard and other black academic institutions such as Talladega College and Atlanta University.[86] He declared: "I would say to the black boy what I would say to the white boy, Get all the mental development that your time and pocket-book will allow of," though he saw most blacks of his time as needing to acquire practical work skills first. Still, he said, "I would not have the standard of mental development lowered one whit for, with the Negro, as with all races, mental strength is the basis of all progress."[87] Kelly Miller saw the controversy over differences in educational philosophy to be the work of "one-eyed enthusiasts,"[88] rather than of men like Du Bois and Washington, who saw the need for both.

Booker T. Washington saw his own primary task as "the promotion of progress among the many, and not the special culture of the few."[89] He saw his work as an educator in his times as preparatory, as "laying a foundation for the masses,"[90] but not to confine the whole race to the work for which Tuskegee Institute would immediately prepare its students. After speaking proudly of a Tuskegee graduate whose knowledge of chemistry had increased the acreage yield of sweet potatoes several-fold, he said, "my theory of education for the Negro would not, for example, confine him for all time to farm work—to the production of the best and most sweet potatoes—but that, if he succeeded in this line of industry, he could lay the foundations upon which his children and grand-children could grow to higher and more important things in life."[91] Even in the present, he said, "we need professional men and women"[92] and he looked forward to a time when there would be more successful black "lawyers, Congressmen, and music teach-ers."[93]

As regards civil rights, although Booker T. Washington wrote in 1899, "I do not favour the Negro's giving up anything which is fundamental and which has been guaranteed to him by the Con-stitution of the United States,"[94] his general public posture was that he was too busy with the self-improvement of blacks to become involved in political controversies. Yet, when his papers were examined after his death, it became clear that he had privately goaded other blacks to crusade for civil rights, and had even secretly financed legal challenges to the Jim Crow laws in the South.[95]

Washington was fully aware that to have done these things publicly would have jeopardized the white financial support on which Tuskegee Institute depended. Nor was this simply a matter of protecting his own interests. He understood the repercussions for others if he made explosive statements in the volatile racial atmosphere of the times. "I could stir up a race war in Alabama in six weeks if I chose," he said, but to do so "would wipe out the achievements of decades of labor."[96] Yet he also understood that open challenges to racial discrimination had to be made. As he wrote to Oswald Garrison Villard, one of the founders of the N.A.A.C.P., "there is work to be done which no one placed in my position can do."[97]

Although Du Bois could not have known of all the things that Washington was doing secretly, he had an insight into the man himself and knew where his loyalties were. Du Bois said of Wash-ington: "He had no faith in white people, not the slightest."[98]

Booker T. Washington practiced what a later generation of black militants would only preach, to advance the cause of blacks "by all means necessary."[99] A leading black educator of his time, Dean Kelly Miller of Howard University, said of Washington that the advancement of the black race "is the chief burden of his soul."[100]

Despite differences between Du Bois and Washington, and rivalries between their respective followers, this did not prevent civility between the two men themselves. In Booker T. Washington's autobiography, *Up from Slavery,* he wrote of a meeting arranged by some "good ladies in Boston" in 1899 where, in addition to "an address by myself, Mr. Paul Lawrence Dunbar read from his poems, and Dr. W. E. B. Du Bois read an original sketch."[101]

In 1903, Du Bois wrote a critical essay about Washington that has since been widely quoted. What has not been so widely known is that Du Bois's aunt chided him for that essay, explaining how his role and constraints were very different from those of Booker T. Washington, and expressing her hope that he would never write about the Tuskegee educator that way again. Decades later, recalling this conversation, Du Bois added, "And I never did."[102]

Black Colleges

Although most black colleges began as institutions run by white administrators and staffed by white professors, pressures to change that began in the nineteenth century. There were at that point relatively few blacks with the education needed to take on these roles, but there were even fewer opportunities for such people to find employment elsewhere. Moreover, there was a concern for the effect on the black students of being educated by whites. As one of the more militant black leaders said in 1885, "the intellects of our young people are being educated at the expense of their manhood," because in their classrooms "they see only white professors," thereby reinforcing the superiority-inferiority stereotypes.[103]

Others, however, cautioned that "our youth have the right to the best possible training, and we should not allow a mistaken race pride to cause us to impose upon them inferior teachers."[104] Significantly, the *parents* of these students usually preferred the skills of white teachers to the symbolism of black representation.[105] The pool of qualified black scholars was small: Prior to the First World

War, only fourteen black Americans had ever received a Ph.D. from a recognized American or European university.[106] Nevertheless, with the passing years the political pressures eventually won out and colleges for black students began to be staffed increasingly by black professors and run by black administrators—whether or not these professors and administrators had sufficient training or ability. In 1926, half a century after its founding, Howard University had its first black president. A leading black scholar of a later era, E. Franklin Frazier, wrote of this transition period as an educational setback and Dean Kelly Miller, who lived through that era at Howard University, called it "a misfortune barely short of a calamity."[107]

This was not just a misfortune for that era. Putting under-qualified people in charge of black colleges and universities meant that the whole development of these institutions would be shaped or warped by department chairmen, deans, and college presidents whose priorities—including holding on to their jobs—made better qualified blacks who would emerge over time be seen as rivals to be repressed, rather than assets to be treasured, and the latter's more intellectual orientation as nothing to be encouraged. The first black president of Howard University, Mordecai W. Johnson, has been cited as a major obstacle to the research of internationally renowned black scientist Ernest Just, whose research grants from prestigious outside institutions were interfered with by Johnson.[108] As late as 1971—decades after the transition to black academic leadership—a study of black colleges concluded: "The administration is usually not interested in scholarly performance, though this kind of activity is tolerated, and the spoon-feeding method of teaching certainly does not call for it." The result was that, with a relative handful of exceptions among black institutions, "the writing pens of members of these institutions have been virtually silent."[109]

The years in office of administrators at black colleges and universities tended to be some multiple of that of administrators in white institutions, given the black administrators' lack of viable alternatives in the larger society. Mordecai Johnson, for example, remained president of Howard University for 34 years. The net result was that the influence of the initial generation of under-qualified people lasted longer and shaped the enduring values and priorities that prevailed on black campuses. These values and priorities in turn shaped the kinds of people who would be groomed and selected to become their successors, perpetuating low academic standards, frivolous social activities among students, and indifference, incompetence, and corruption among the administration and faculty.[110]

The transition from white to black leadership in black colleges was much more than a racial change. It was a major cultural change from a missionary generation of academic leaders, bent on supplanting the existing black redneck culture with a transplanted culture representing very different values, to new leaders more accommodating to the black redneck culture in all its aspects, from academic laxity to sexual laxity, showiness, and corruption. In the words of E. Franklin Frazier: "The entire orientation and aim of higher education of Negroes was changing."[111] Among these changes was that "traditional standards of morals and manners" gave way among both students and their teachers. Students became far less interested in academic study than in such things as fraternities, sororities, and parties.

Partly this reflected a changing mix of students, as colleges black and white drew on a broader social range after the Second World War, partly as a result of the availability of financial support from the G.I. Bill. Writing in the middle of the twentieth century, Frazier said:

> The average Negro who enters the Negro college has had little contact with books and has not developed reading habits. Moreover, when he enters college he does not find an atmosphere where educational values and scholarship are highly respected.[112]

Frazier described the new black college students as "listless" and "less concerned with the history or understanding of the world around them than with their appearance at the next social affair." Moreover, such concerns were supported by the new generation of administrators:

> The girl with a peasant or working-class background may be irritated by her mother's inability to buy an expensive "party" dress.

> But what can be expected when the dean of women has instructed her to tell her mother that she must have the dress at any sacrifice?[113]

As for the faculty, Professor Frazier described them this way in the middle of the twentieth century:

> Unlike the missionary teachers, the present teachers have little interest in "making men," but are concerned primarily with teaching as a source of income which will enable them to maintain middle-class standards and participate in Negro "society." It appears that the majority of them have no knowledge of books nor any real love of literature. Today many of the teachers of English and literature never read a book as a source of pleasure or recreation.[114]

In short, the black colleges retrogressed toward the black redneck culture. The stultifying and anti-intellectual atmosphere on many black college campuses has been described with painful frankness in Professor Frazier's 1958 book *Black Bourgeoisie,* by black novelist Ralph Ellison in *The Invisible Man,* and by white scholars Christopher Jencks and David Riesman in a comprehensive 1967 article in the *Harvard Educational Review,* which may well have been the last honest study of black colleges, given the rising racial militancy and the automatic labeling of white critics as racists.

There have been no black college equivalents of Dunbar High School or other high-achieving black elementary and secondary schools. One major historic difference between black colleges and Dunbar High School was the highly qualified, if not over-qualified, early leadership of Dunbar and the under-qualified first generation of black leadership of the black colleges, the latter put in place for purposes of symbolic racial representation. There were enduring consequences to the different calibers of people who shaped these different institutions in their formative stages and set in motion values and priorities which shaped and selected their successors in the generations ahead.

In a much later era, beginning in the 1960s, a similar setting up of black studies departments at predominantly white colleges across the country—with little or no regard to the wholly inadequate numbers of academically qualified people to staff so many departments established simultaneously—likewise put in place a first generation of black academics who would lead such departments in non-academic or even anti-intellectual directions. Even though there was no inherent reason why the scholarly study of the history, economics, politics, or sociology of black Americans could not be a serious enterprise, in practice black studies programs by and large became noted for shoddy standards for both students and faculty. It is doubtful whether so many academic departments could be set up simultaneously in any academic field without exhausting the pool of qualified faculty members but no one attempted such a thing in traditional academic departments.

As with many of the black colleges, the inadequacies of the black pioneers in black studies warped the future, even after those pioneers passed from the scene and better qualified people became available. By the same token, the kinds of highly qualified people who shaped the future Dunbar High School in its formative years left an enduring legacy of high standards and performances.

White Colleges

Although black students were admitted to some white colleges—notably Oberlin, Bowdoin, Hillsdale, and Western Reserve[115]—even before the Civil War, most post-bellum black students pursued their higher education at the black colleges until the 1960s. In the decades that followed, up to the present, the majority of black students have attended predominantly white colleges. Given the scarcity of black students with the educational background and academic achievements common among other students at the predominantly white colleges, these institutions' desires to secure a demographically representative student body made lower standards of admissions for blacks virtually inevitable.[116]

This problem was not confined to colleges with very high academic standards. When top-tier colleges and universities accepted black students who met the normal qualifications for second-tier institutions, similar pressures led second-tier institutions to accept black students who would normally qualify for third-tier colleges and universities—and so on down the line. With black students systematically mismatched with academic institutions across the spectrum, it can hardly be surprising that most black students nationwide failed to graduate.

Such negative educational results repeated a pattern of bad educational results from making educational decisions on non-educational grounds that began with the creation of black colleges that were colleges in name only in the nineteenth century, for the sake of denominational rivalry, and later putting under-qualified people in charge of these black colleges for the sake of racial representation.

Very similar corrupting and anti-intellectual consequences have followed latter-day educational policies based on demographic representation.[117] Moreover, these consequences have endured, even through turnovers of students and faculty over the years. The admission of black students with qualifications markedly lower than those of the other students at the same institutions was soon followed by hiring black faculty members with qualifications likewise lower than those of their white and Asian faculty colleagues. This was done for the same reason, namely, that there were simply not enough blacks with the usual academic qualifications to achieve demographic representation any other way.

Not only are there far fewer black students than Asian American students who reach the usual test score levels found at selective colleges, this shortfall is even more drastic at the postgraduate level, where future faculty members are produced. In some years, the absolute numbers of blacks receiving Ph.D.s in mathematics did not reach double digits.

SUMMARY AND IMPLICATIONS

Education has played a crucial role in the advancement of blacks over the generations—and in the lags of blacks behind others in the American economy. In order to understand both the lags and the advancement, it is necessary to understand the extremely low level from which the education of most black Americans began and the very long time before the great majority of blacks had the kind of education that would qualify them for many of the occupations in which education was essential.

Racial discrimination barriers kept educated blacks out of some of these occupations but, until perhaps the middle of the twentieth century, there were relatively few blacks to be kept out by such barriers. Looked at differently, the dramatic increases in the numbers of blacks in many professional occupations in the last half of the twentieth century cannot be attributed solely—or even primarily—to the removal of these barriers by civil rights legislation. The rise of blacks into professional and other high-level occupations was greater in the years *preceding* passage of the Civil Rights Act of 1964 than in the years following passage of that act.[118]

What had happened was a dramatic increase in the numbers of blacks with college and postgraduate education. Prior to the First World War, fewer than 5,000 college degrees had been granted to black students in the entire history of the United States but, by 1935, that had increased five-fold—and by 1947 the black colleges alone granted in one year more degrees than blacks had ever received in all the years prior to the First World War. Increases in the numbers of doctorates received by blacks were also dramatic.[119]

Similarly, despite a widespread tendency to see the rise of blacks out of poverty as due to the civil rights movement and government social programs of the 1960s, in reality the rise of blacks out of poverty was greater in the two decades *preceding* 1960 than in the decades that followed. Education was a major factor in this as well. As of 1940, non-white males averaged just 5.4 years of schooling, compared to 8.7 for white males. Over the next two decades, the absolute amount of education increased for both— and the gap between them narrowed. In 1940, the difference in schooling between black and white young adult males, aged 25 to 29, was four years but, by 1960, that had shrunk to less than two years.[120] Because this was an era of massive black migration out of the South, this quantitative narrowing of the gap in schooling may well have been accompanied by a qualitative improvement, as many blacks left behind the low-quality schools in the Jim Crow South.

How did this translate into economic change? As of 1940, more than four-fifths of black families—87 percent, in fact—lived below the official poverty level. By 1960, this had fallen to 47 percent.[121] In other words, the poverty rate among blacks had been nearly cut in half before either the civil rights revolution or the Great Society social programs began in the 1960s. The continuation of this trend can hardly be automatically credited to these political developments, though such claims are often made, usually ignoring the pre-existing trends whose momentum could hardly have been expected to stop in the absence of such legislation. By 1970, the poverty rate among blacks had fallen to 30 percent—a welcome development, but by no means unprecedented. A decade after that, with the rise of affirmative action in the intervening years, the poverty rate among black families had fallen to 29 percent.[122] Even if one attributes all of this one percent decline to government policy, it does not compare to the dramatic declines in poverty among blacks when the only major change was the rise in their education.

Whatever the merits of various movements and programs on other grounds, the claim that they were the primary factor in the *economic* advancement of blacks cannot be squared with the facts. Yet a whole generation of black leaders, intellectuals, and activists have become committed to such movements and programs and their accompanying rhetoric. However, Frederick Douglass warned, as far back as the 1870s, that blacks should "cultivate their brains more and their lungs less."[123]

While no one can deny the existence of racial discrimination in employment, housing, and other areas, the assumption that the magnitude of employment discrimination can be measured by relative numbers of blacks in particular occupations ignores the huge quantitative and qualitative differences in education between blacks and whites which existed in past generations—often as a result of government discrimination in the provision of educational resources. Without an understanding of the reasons for both the lags and the progress of blacks in the past, policy prescriptions for future advancement risk misplaced emphases. More specifically, it risks under-estimating the importance of the quantity and quality of education, which depends upon both students and teachers, and much less on the amount of money fed into education bureaucracies or on the fads and panaceas that come and go in the schools and colleges. While the New England culture that was transplanted into various Southern enclaves after the Civil War had remarkable successes, later successful black schools a century later usually had no New England origins but, like New England, they represented a culture very unlike the black redneck culture. Ralph Ellison has pointed out that such stellar black singers as Paul Robeson and Marian Anderson "received their development from an extensive personal contact with European culture, free from the influences which shape Southern Negro personality in the United States."[124]

For those who are interested in schools that produce academic success for minority students, there is no lack of examples, past and present. Tragically, there has been an utter lack of interest in academically successful black schools by most educators. Among the few who have even bothered to take notice, too many have been as dogmatic as Kenneth B. Clark, who said that "excellence at Dunbar represented the few," that Dunbar "is the only example in our history of a separate black school that was able, somehow, to be equal," a result of unique circumstances "that could scarcely have existed in any other part of the country."[125] Every one of these unsubstantiated claims was demonstrably untrue. One-third of all the black high school students in Washington were not "the few"; there were and are other black schools that met or exceeded national norms, as examples discussed here have shown—and, far from being confined to Washington, they have been found from New England to California.

Why this ignoring or dismissal of examples of black educational success? Sometimes the reason is ideological: Some, like Professor Clark, have a vested interest in the doctrine that separate is inferior, which underpinned the historic *Brown v. Board of Education* Supreme Court decision, in which his research was cited. To say that mixing and matching racial groups is not a prerequisite for quality education would call into question the decades-long school busing struggle, which might then be seen in retrospect as a costly and divisive wild goose chase, and questions might be raised about the current mantra of "diversity."

Other reasons for ignoring or downplaying successful black schools include the fact that there is no political mileage or financial benefits to be gotten from focussing on such schools, despite how much of an educational gold mine their experience might be for black children. Put bluntly, failure attracts more money than success. Politically, failure becomes a reason to demand more money, smaller classes, and more trendy courses and programs, ranging from "black English" to bilingualism and "self-esteem." Politicians who want to look compassionate and concerned know that voting money for such projects accomplishes that purpose for them and voting against such programs risks charges of mean-spiritedness, if not implications of racism.

Ironically, many of the bitter-end defenders of the current public school system and its educational dogmas are also in favor of preferential admissions of minority students to colleges and universities. In other words, having denied minority children an opportunity to develop the kinds of intellectual skills that would make lower admissions standards for them unnecessary, they then send minority students on to institutions where they are less likely to meet course standards designed for better prepared students—and where most minority students do not last long enough to graduate. During their time on campus, such students help present a photogenic picture of "diversity" on many campuses but their roles are much like those of movie extras, who simply provide a background for others.

Despite many pious expressions of goodwill and hope for improvements in the education of minority students, few are prepared to do what it takes, including taking on entrenched vested interests in the schools of education, the teachers' unions, and state, local, and national educational bureaucracies. Even fewer are prepared to challenge black students to work harder and abandon the counterproductive notion that seeking educational excellence is "acting white."

Despite the heartening achievements of some black schools, which have repeatedly demonstrated what is possible even with children from low-income backgrounds, the general picture of the education of black students is bleak. Much of what is said—and not said—about the education of black students reflects the political context, rather than the educational facts. Whites walk on eggshells for fear of being called racists, while many blacks are preoccupied with protecting the image of black students, rather than protecting their future by telling the blunt truth. It is understandable that some people are concerned about image, about what in private life might be expressed as: "What will the neighbors think?" But, when your children are dying, you don't worry about what the neighbors think.

History versus Visions

It requires courage to cast the accumulated myths of a lifetime to the wind. Our natural desire for simplicity, certitude, and the approval of others occasionally causes us to defend even our most flawed worldviews as if our very lives depended on them. Dead belief systems are difficult to bury, for in doing so we enter a world we do not recognize; we watch the carefully crafted towers of our understanding crash down in ruins; and we lose an integral piece of the only reality we have known, reinforced and imprinted on our minds by a thousand voices, internal and external.

—John Perazzo[1]

NOWHERE HAS HISTORY BEEN MORE IN thrall to belief systems—visions—than in the history of racial and ethnic groups. Too often the past has been twisted to fit the visions and the agendas of the present. Much of the history written about minority groups has in fact been a history of how others treated these groups, more so than a history of the groups themselves. This bias has distorted both the histories of racial and ethnic groups and the histories of the societies in which they have lived.

Black Americans are just one of the groups whose history has been seen in this strange and twisted way as a commentary on American society and an opportunity to score ideological points or promote guilt or gain some contemporary political advantage. Mention Japanese Americans and "internment camps" come up.

Mention Mexican Americans and the things suffered by them or by Mexico are sure to become the focus of discussion. Injustices should not be swept under the rug, but whole peoples are more than the sum of the injustices they have suffered. At least they should be seen as more, if history is truly to be history and not just the projection into the past of contemporary visions and agendas.

Where world history is concerned, the same skewed approach has too often prevailed. Few things attract less attention than the achievements of the West, which have improved the lives of peoples around the world through medical science, technology, and economic organizations more effective at producing the material output on which people depend for food, shelter and the comforts and amenities of life. Those who warn against being Eurocentric are themselves often the most Eurocentric of all when it comes to assigning blame for slavery, imperialism, wars, and other human tragedies that have originated on every inhabited continent, at one period of history or another.

"Multiculturalism" has not meant warts-and-all portraits of different societies around the world. For many, it has meant virtually a warts-only portrait of the West and a no-warts portrait of non-Western peoples. More is involved than a simple bias, however. The central doctrine of multiculturalism—the equality of cultures—cannot be sustained when that means equality of concrete achievements—educationally, economically, or otherwise.

It is not only the West whose achievements must be brushed aside or glided over in silence. Particularly dangerous to contemporary visions and agendas are achievements by groups that began in poverty and rose to prosperity, such as emigrants from Japan, Italy, China, or India who settled in various countries around the world. It is not just their achievements, but the very concept of achievement, which is antithetical to the multicultural vision—and which is therefore often evaded or denied. Much verbal ingenuity has been used circumventing the concept of achievements by calling them "advantages" or "privileges," even when this does violence to the meanings of words and the facts of history. Often discussions of the supposedly impenetrable social barriers of poverty and skin-color prejudice pass over in utter silence the history of various emigrants from Asia whose eco-

nomic levels have in fact often begun in poverty and later surpassed that of the white majorities in countries of the Western
Hemisphere.

When visions and agendas suppress history, that not only distorts the achievements of groups, nations, or civilizations, it for-
feits valuable knowledge as to the things that have led to past
progress and can lead to progress for others who are still lagging
today. In short, it sacrifices the material interests of millions for the
ideological or other parochial interests of a few.

HISTORY AND CAUSATION

History offers not simply a chronicle of events but, more importantly, opportunities to gain insights about the human condition
from the experiences of other times and places. That is, it offers
not merely facts but explanations. When it comes to the history of
different racial, ethnic, or other social groups, nothing calls more
obviously for explanation than the great differences in rewards
and performances among them. Here causal explanations impinge
on prevailing visions. Where the prevailing vision is one of external causation, verbal ingenuity often seeks to banish internal
explanations

External versus Internal Explanations

One of the ways of sealing off a vision from the intrusion of discordant facts is with an ideological vocabulary that neutralizes
such facts. One of the most important facts to be neutralized and
excluded *a priori* from the prevailing vision of our times is the fact
of differences in capabilities among individuals, groups, nations,
and civilizations. When achievements are described as advantages
or privileges, differences in outcomes *ex post* are treated as evidence or proof of differences in opportunities *ex ante*. What these
verbal fashions accomplish, in a wide range of circumstances, is to
preclude internal explanations of intergroup differences in favor of
external explanations. Thus the success of Lebanese businessmen
in competing with their European counterparts in colonial Africa
has been attributed to various Lebanese "advantages":

Firstly, the Lebanese had lower personal consumption levels

than the Europeans. Besides, they had the advantage of having members of the family work in their shops and thus be an economic asset instead of a liability as was the case with the Europeans. In a situation where Lebanese skill was at least as good as their rivals, they could win over a gradually increasing share of the business by price competition. In addition, the Lebanese skill was in some respects superior to that of the Europeans. The former had many more contacts with the African clients, were willing to talk and bargain with them at length, and therefore had closer knowledge of them. As a result, they could grant credit to the Africans with less risk than the Europeans, could have earlier indication of shifts in consumer demand or crop prospects, and could manage the repayment relationship more skillfully. Another advantage of the Lebanese, in the early days at least, was that little of his profit had to be diverted to the amortization of fixed capital because there was little fixed capital. Thus, successful price competition by the Lebanese merchant was based on the advantages of both lower business and personal costs.[2]

Not one of these *internal* achievements of the Lebanese was due to any external benefits being made available to them that were not equally available to Europeans. On the contrary, the Lebanese typically began with less money than their European rivals, though even their "little fixed capital" is described as if it were an asset. But such a situation would not have been confined to "the early days" before the Lebanese achieved prosperity if in fact it were an asset. Here again, the vocabulary of the prevailing vision must neutralize or evade the plain fact that some people *achieve* better than others by describing the means of their achievements as "advantages." If the very concept of achievement is a threat to the vision, then overcoming adversity is even more of a threat. Both must be verbally transformed into privileges and advantages, in order to protect the vision.

Conversely, the failure of particular people to achieve is often transformed verbally into a denial of "access" or "opportunity" to them by others. Those who do not meet the same standards for college admissions or mortgage loans as often as others do are said to be denied an "opportunity" for a higher education or "access" to loans to buy a home. Any adverse information on such groups must be verbally transformed into "stereotypes" or "myths." There simply cannot be any facts contrary to the vision.

This vision has become part of the law of the land, so that an American employer can be found guilty of discrimination without a speck of evidence of discrimination against any specific individual, if the demographic make-up of his workforce differs from what prevailing preconceptions say it would be in the absence of discrimination. The absurd limit to which this vocabulary can go is illustrated by scholarly—or at least academic—studies of Malaysia that describe the Malays as a "deprived"[3] group there and non-Malay minorities as having "privilege"[4] because the latter have had greater economic success than the Malay majority which controls the government—and which is guaranteed various benefits that are denied to non-Malays.

"Prejudice" is another word that has been distorted beyond recognition in order to sustain a vision. The straightforward meaning of prejudice—prejudgment—is, in an ethnic or racial context, stretched and twisted to mean any adverse opinion about a minority group. This implicitly assumes that any unfavorable judgment about the behavior or performance of any minorities cannot have any factual basis and so can only be explained as being a result of a prejudgment. But when German Jews in America were socially accepted into many elite circles from which all Jews were later barred, after an influx of Eastern European Jews, the origins of these barriers cannot have been anti-Jewish prejudice, as such, though the persistence of such barriers long after Eastern European Jews had become acculturated to American society shows the weight of inertia.

Similarly, blacks lived in white neighborhoods in many Northern cities in the late nineteenth century, and their children went to racially integrated schools, before the massive influx of blacks from the South at the beginning of the twentieth century. Can the change to racial segregation in both housing and schools be attributed to prejudice—or to experience? To say that it must have been prejudice is itself a prejudgment. Again, inertia would cause these adverse reactions to outlast the circumstances which gave rise to them and to apply to individuals quite different from those whose behavior provoked racial barriers in the first place.

Blacks are by no means the only ethnic group whose advancement has been promoted by its own internal transformations, with greater acceptance by the surrounding population being an effect more so than a cause of the group's advancement. Acculturated German Jews who had achieved respectability and social acceptance in nineteenth-century America lamented the arrival of masses of Eastern European Jews who were far less acculturated, less educated, and were often poverty-stricken. The German Jews' fear, which proved to be well founded, was that the arrival of huge numbers of such people, foreign in appearance and repellent in behavior to American society at large, would lead to hostility and barriers against all Jews. This understanding led, among other things, to organized attempts by German Jews to assimilate the Eastern European Jews to American standards of behavior, cleanliness, and lifestyle. This internal transformation of the Jewish population led over the years to lessening hostility and greater acceptance by the American population as a whole. Again, this did not mean that there were no inveterate anti-Semites who would be hostile to Jews in spite of anything that the latter could do. But neither can hostility to Jews, after the arrival of vast numbers from Eastern Europe, be explained as simply an arbitrary prejudice, especially coming after German Jews had already been accepted, even in the higher reaches of society.

In the case of immigrants from Ireland, the massive efforts of the Catholic Church in the nineteenth century to Americanize Irish immigrants are seldom mentioned among the reasons why the "No Irish Need Apply" signs faded away during the twentieth century. The picture too often presented might lead one to believe that it was all just a matter of prejudice and bigotry in American society that lead to such signs in the first place, leaving their disappearance in later times unexplained, except by some such generality as "progress" or by the efforts of the enlightened to dispel such prejudices and bigotry. The very possibility that the Irish themselves were different in the twentieth century from what they had been in the nineteenth century is too often passed over in silence. The long social struggle that led to this result virtually disappears from history, as seen by those who make "prejudice" an all-purpose explanation. This not only deprives these and other minorities of credit for past improvements; more importantly, it deprives others today of a potentially valuable example of ways of improving their own futures.

Strained terminology such as "prejudice" is just one aspect of the power of a vision. A prevailing vision can become the default setting for thought and action. Assertions consistent with the vision can be made without meeting the additional requirement that they be consistent with the facts. Indeed, facts themselves may be viewed suspiciously, or subjected to higher standards of proof, when they are inconsistent with the vision.

Achievements have preconditions and those preconditions—whether internal to those seeking achievement or external aspects of the surrounding world—would need to be considered. Redefining achievements out of existence avoids all these complications that distract from ideological visions and political agendas. But neither internal nor external preconditions can be ignored if we are serious about history and its integrity as a record that can be relied on when weighing present-day alternatives.

The history of groups and whole nations that rose from poverty to prosperity is especially valuable for those who would like to see today's lagging groups advance. But the experiences of such groups are an especially dangerous threat to those with a vision of external causation. Immigrants from Asia to various countries around the world have been prominent among groups that have risen from poverty to prosperity, often in the face of racial discrimination.

One of the remarkable things about people from China and India has long been that they have prospered in countries around the world—except in their own homelands. Even with all due allowance for selective migration—the emigrants including more than their share of able and ambitious people—there has still been a striking contrast between the ethnic Chinese economic domination of the economies of a number of Southeast Asian countries and the poverty of the Chinese in China. As late as 1994, the 36 million "overseas Chinese" produced as much wealth as the billion people living in China itself.[5] Immigrants from India living in the United States averaged higher incomes than the American population. People of Japanese ancestry have likewise had higher

incomes than the average American in the United States and higher than the average Canadian in Canada, while in Brazil they have
owned three-quarters as much land as there is in Japan.[6]

In all these cases, economic success stories began in poverty. At the beginning of the twentieth century, Japanese immigrants
to the United States were domestic servants and agricultural field
hands to an even greater extent than black Americans.[7] As late as
1920, a majority of all the Chinese living in the United States were
either laundry workers or restaurant workers.[8] Most overseas
Indians began their careers in the nineteenth century in East
Africa, Fiji, Trinidad and Guiana as indentured laborers. In more
recent times, Korean immigrants to the United States have likewise begun at the bottom and progressed upward into small businesses and their children into the professions.

While some may regard such experiences as inspiring and a
heartening example of what can be done to overcome poverty, to
those with a vested interest in the prevailing vision in the media
and in academic "social science," including history, these stories
undermine their fundamental beliefs and the general thrust of
welfare state government. To the political representatives of other
groups that are still lagging behind the general economic and
social levels of their societies at large, the success of Asian immigrants is resented. Whether to Maoris in New Zealand or blacks in
the United States, Asian immigrant success stories are bitter medicine. The stirring up of animosity and even violence toward Asian
"blood suckers" by racial activists is just one consequence of this.

At higher intellectual levels, the rise of Asian immigrants
from poverty is often glided over in silence when portraying less
successful groups as victims of arbitrary barriers based on race or
when depicting external circumstances in general as decisive factors in group advancement. Still less does the success of Asian
immigrants support the view that protests and politics are key
requirements for raising lagging groups out of poverty. Any rea-
sonably informed American, for example, can far more easily name
five prominent black leaders than can name even one prominent
Chinese American or Japanese American leader.

The fact that the Chinese have long prospered better outside
of China, and Indians outside of India, undermines the multicul-

tural view that Western prosperity in general is not due to any superior features of Western institutions. The fact that both China and India have had sharp upturns in their economic growth rates after they began transforming their economies in the direction of Western capitalism toward the end of the twentieth century provides further evidence against current efforts at promoting a neutral agnosticism about differences among societies.

It is not just ethnic minorities whose fates tend to be explained—or explained away—by external circumstances in keeping with the prevailing vision among intellectuals. So have behavior patterns among Southern whites:

> Cotton has created another culture pattern for the south. The seasonal and cyclical nature of his money not only serves to give the cotton grower a shifting standard of living but throws him back upon credit and prevents his acquiring habits of thrift. After a season of deprivation and close living on niggardly credit comes the sale of the crop and cash income to be husbanded if possible until the sale of next year's crop. The income of the cotton grower has its peaks of high prices but these peaks are not planned for and they do not serve to level up the general standard of living. In the Cotton Belt luxuries are likely to be bought on the spur of the moment during a good season in cotton and to be paid for in the poverty of next year's living. One can neither exercise a systematic thrift, budget expenses, nor indulge in installment buying on irregular returns from cotton.[9]

This ignores the fact that the ancestors of these people lived in the same spur-of-the-moment way on the other side of the Atlantic, in places where cotton did not grow. But, once an external explanation of behavior is available, internal explanations are seldom sought—and weighing the two against one another is rarer still. That is what is meant by saying that the prevailing vision is the default setting for many.

Poverty is one of the most widely used external explanations of intergroup differences but, like other external explanations, it is seldom tested empirically against alternative internal explanations. Many poorer groups lag in intellectual development but others do not. As noted in an earlier essay, poor Jewish immigrants in the early twentieth century made use of free public libraries in

New York and the books they checked out were primarily serious works, while lighter and more popular books were left gathering dust on the library shelves.[10] Among their ancestors in Eastern Europe a century earlier, even the poorest somehow managed to have books in their homes, while the larger population around them were overwhelmingly illiterate. A similar pattern was found among the people in eighteenth-century Scotland:

> Even a person of relatively modest means had his own collection of books, and what he couldn't afford he could get at the local lending library, which by 1750 virtually every town of any size enjoyed.[11]

At about that same time, on the other side of the Atlantic, Thomas Jefferson was complaining that there was not a single bookstore in his vicinity and a century later Frederick Law Olmsted commented on how seldom he saw books, even in the homes of Southerners who could have afforded them. Still later, in the twentieth century, E. Franklin Frazier commented on how seldom even black college faculty read books.[12]

Nothing better illustrates the dominance of unsubstantiated dogma over empirical evidence than the pervasive belief that the advancement of economically or socially lagging groups requires a sense of group pride, identity, and self-esteem, and that "self-hate" must be exterminated as a barrier to such advance. The plausibility of this belief is not in question. What is open to very serious question is whether or not it is supported by any hard evidence. Yet such evidence is seldom asked for or given.

Putting aside for the moment the emotionally loaded terms of such discussions, is it in fact the case that groups which exhibit pride and identity advance faster or further than groups which see themselves as inferior in achievements, knowledge, and sophistication to some other groups whose progress they wish to emulate? Ultimately, this is an empirical question and does not depend on anyone's philosophical or ideological orientation, though such orientations may make some more willing or less willing to investigate the empirical evidence.

Any serious investigation must begin with an understanding that we cannot see directly into the hearts and minds of other human beings. All that we can see are the outward manifestations. This simple fact must be confronted at the outset, as equally applicable to those who hold one belief rather than another, rather than have it surface at the end, when one set of beliefs has failed the empirical tests and seeks escape by saying that we have not discussed "real" pride or "real" self-hate, as they exist in the recesses of other people's minds.

Judging by what we can see and by what history has recorded, what is in fact the track record of breast-beating versus the "cultural cringe"? A definitive answer would require an encyclopedic survey of history that would take longer than anyone's lifetime. However, we get along with less than definitive answers to most of life's questions, so this is not an insuperable barrier to learning what we can and reaching tentative conclusions, subject to later revision. Modest as this goal may be, it is better than a blind refusal to look at the facts, for fear that they will undermine some cherished beliefs.

Two of the most remarkable examples of dramatic advancement by whole peoples have been the Scots in the eighteenth century and the Japanese in the late nineteenth and early twentieth centuries. Both provide evidence on the issue of "pride" versus "self-hate."

Scotland

As far back as Roman times, Scotland lagged behind England and, as late as the fourteenth century, there was said to be no Scottish baron who could write his own name. Scottish agriculture was primitive and its industry virtually non-existent. The people were illiterate and there was no law and order, except for the arbitrary edicts of local clan chiefs. The largest city in Scotland in the seventeenth century—Edinburgh—had a population of just 16,000. Part of the reason for Scotland's lag behind England was geographic isolation. Scotland was on the outer fringes of European civilization. England was closer to continental Europe, which was for centuries more advanced than the British Isles, so that cultural artifacts of a more advanced civilization found their way across the channel to the English. But, whatever the reasons, the Scots lagged behind the English—and were painfully aware of that fact.

After centuries of conflict, the English invaded Scotland—first the lowlands and then the highlands. They conquered Scotland both militarily and culturally. Scots "were conscious to a painful degree of their backwardness, their poverty, their lack of polish, their provinciality."[13] Scots began to speak English, usually with a heavy accent. A society "for promoting the reading and speaking of the English language" was formed, and lectures on the subject drew hundreds, including James Boswell. Even such an intellectual giant as David Hume took lessons in English pronunciation and he warned fellow Scots against using peculiarly Scottish expressions, a warning repeated both in his letters and in *Scots Magazine.*[14]

James Mill deliberately purged his speech of Scottish pronunciation and expressions. He moved to England and raised John Stuart Mill and his other children as Englishmen who never heard him speak of Scotland. Nor was he unique:

> Demeaning or not, the overwhelming desire to pass as English and to transcend Scottish origins was symbolic of the more pervasive fertilization of Scottish life with external influences. It eventually facilitated the universalization of Scottish scholarship, which was the hallmark of the Enlightenment and the outreach of its own culture.[15]

Back in Scotland, lowland Scots copied the English and highland Scots copied the lowland Scots. Scottish farmers even used an English plow that was completely unsuitable for the soil of Scotland.[16] In short, eighteenth-century Scots represented a clear example of the "cultural cringe." What was the result?

First of all, the spread of the English language, beginning in the Scottish lowlands, opened a whole new world of literature in numerous fields to the Scots—fields in which there was little or no literature in the indigenous Gaelic language. Education caught on so widely in the Scottish lowlands that they had compulsory education before England did and developed the most extensive system of schools in Europe. Not only an educated class but an intellectual class developed in Scotland. As a distinguished historian put it, "in every branch of knowledge this once poor and ignorant people produced original and successful thinkers."

From the middle of the eighteenth century to the middle of the nineteenth century, most of the leading British intellectual figures were either from Scotland or of Scottish ancestry. These included David Hume in philosophy, Adam Smith in economics, Joseph Black in chemistry, Robert Adam in architecture, James Watt in engineering, Sir Walter Scott in literature, and John Stuart Mill in economics, philosophy, and political science.

In medicine, Scots likewise moved to the forefront, not only in Britain but also in Russia, where Catherine the Great had a Scottish physician, and in America, where Scots established some of the earliest medical schools. Scots also set the world standard in engineering in general and shipbuilding in particular. By 1871, nearly half the ships built in Great Britain were built in Scotland. Scottish universities surged ahead of English universities in science and engineering. In short, the Scots eventually surpassed those from whom they had once learned.

Japan

The isolation which has often kept some societies lagging far behind others was a self-imposed isolation for Japan. From 1638 to 1868, emigration from Japan was forbidden, on pain of death, and foreigners and foreign trade and foreign cultures were kept out. In short, Japan was one of the most self-insulated countries in history—and was also very poor and backward.

This era ended dramatically when American warships under the command of Commodore Matthew Perry entered Japanese waters in 1854 and demanded that Japan open its ports to the outside world. Helpless in the face of such overwhelming modern force, Japan had no choice but to submit to this demand. It was a turning point in the country's history. This painful demonstration of Japan's weakness and backwardness, before its own people and before the world, set in motion internal reforms and an agenda for national development that dominated the country's history for the next century.

Japan's leaders in that era held up the West in general, and the United States in particular, as examples to be emulated. Western technology was imported and Japanese students were sent to study in the West. The English language began to be taught in Japanese schools and there was even a suggestion at one point that English be made the national language of Japan. Textbooks issued by the Japanese government held up Abraham Lincoln and Benjamin Franklin as models for the young to imitate, even more so than Japanese heroes. There were euphoric descriptions of the United States as "an earthly paradise." It would be hard to find a more striking example of the "cultural cringe" than nineteenth-century Japan.

An episode shortly after Americans forced Japan to open up to the outside world illustrates the situation at that time. Commodore Perry presented a train as a gift and the Americans proceeded to demonstrate it:

> At first the Japanese watched the train fearfully from a safe dis-
> tance, and when the engine began to move they uttered cries
> of astonishment and drew in their breath. Before long they were
> inspecting it closely, stroking it, and riding on it, and they kept
> this up throughout the day.[17]

No one could have predicted then that, a century later, Japan would produce its own "bullet train" that surpassed anything available in the United States. But it happened only because the Japanese recognized their own initial backwardness and were determined to overcome it. They began by learning all that they could from the West and emulating the West until they reached the point when they had amassed the knowledge, skill, and experience to take their own independent direction. In the first half of the twentieth century, Japanese products were widely known as cheap, inferior imitations of European or American products. Even after Japan later began to produce higher quality products, such as cameras, the first Canon was an imitation of the German Leica and the first Nikon was an imitation of its German rival, the Contax. Over time, however, these and other Japanese cameras evolved into the leading cameras in the world, both technologically and in terms of sales. Similarly spectacular developments occurred when the Japanese entered the electronics, automotive, and other fields.

Black Americans

Against the background of the history of Scotland and Japan, today's assumptions about the effects of "pride" and "self-hate" as factors in progress are hard to sustain. Against the history of blacks in the United States, many other assumptions are equally hard to sustain.

The history of the black population of the United States might be summed up in broad outlines as follows: Sold into slavery by African leaders, at a time when slavery was widely accepted in all civilizations, blacks entered a particular segment of American society and culture at the bottom, acquiring only the rudiments of Western civilization—not including literacy, in most cases—and a way of life influenced by a peculiar redneck culture.

Freed after the Civil War but poverty-stricken, illiterate, unskilled and unacculturated to the demanding way of life in a free republic with a market economy, blacks began their history as a free people at the bottom of American society. One sign of their lack of preparation for life as a free people was a rate of mortality among blacks in the aftermath of emancipation that was greater than it had been under slavery.[18] This was just one sign of a more general lag in adjusting to the norms of the society around them.

The small enclaves of New England culture transplanted among blacks—via Oberlin College and Dunbar High School, as well as in black colleges established in the South by New Englanders—did *not* promote pride in the existing black redneck culture. On the contrary, the clear message in these enclaves was that the way most blacks talked, the way they behaved, and the whole set of redneck values they inherited, were all wrong and were things to be overcome. The wholly disproportionate number of black leaders and high achievers who came out of these small enclaves is further evidence in the case of "pride" versus "self-hate."

Among both blacks and white liberals, there were those who thought that cultural changes among blacks were unnecessary, that there could be progress without internal cultural change, effects without causes. In the post-1960s world, such views gained the ascendancy—and those who held these views often wondered why it was so hard to raise ghetto blacks out of poverty and social disintegration. Their answer was usually a call for more welfare state programs, more "pride" and "self-esteem," more steeping in the history of black achievement or white injustice. The actual track record of this approach, compared to the opposite approach in the New England enclaves, received virtually no attention.

Fortunately, in the decades before this mindset became fixed, most blacks had become better educated and had lifted themselves out of poverty at a rate *higher* than that after the civil rights revolution of the 1960s. For example, more blacks rose into professional and other higher level occupations in the years preceding the Civil Rights Act of 1964 than in the years following its enactment.[19] This factual history served no one's political agenda and has since been replaced by a fictional history that does.

The economic advancement of blacks has been widely portrayed as due to the civil rights movement, and to political leaders—black and white—who have proclaimed themselves champions of black Americans. Since no one has as large a vested interest in opposing this view as its proponents have in perpetuating it, the politically more convenient view has prevailed, along with attributing the continuing economic and social gaps between blacks and whites to the sins and shortcomings of the latter.

Nothing is easier to find than sins and shortcomings among human beings, regardless of their race. The question is: How much of a *causal* factor these moral failings have been in history and to what extent have they been effects rather than causes? For example, the decline in whites' hostility and discrimination toward blacks in Northern cities during the nineteenth century, followed by a resurgence of hostility at the turn of the century, were not just inexplicable swings of the pendulum in white public opinion. The masses of blacks arriving in the North at the end of the nineteenth and the beginning of the twentieth century were denounced in the *black* newspapers of the time for their crudeness, violence, and crime.[20] It was not just a question of "perceptions" or "stereotypes" among whites, though undoubtedly some whites reacted in ways wholly unjustified by the situation, as elements of other racial groups do.

Contemporary preoccupation with the evils of "society" distorts the history of many groups, passing over internal improvements that took decades or generations of effort, because those improvements—whether modest or dramatic—imply that there was something that needed to be improved within these groups, that not all their problems were due to the "perceptions" or "stereotypes" of others.

Clinging to a counterproductive culture in the name of group pride and avoiding changes because they could be labeled "self-hate" are patterns that have no track record that would justify optimism. The evidence is all on the other side—but that matters only to those who value evidence over ideology, history over visions.

COSMIC JUSTICE AND INJUSTICE

Few things are more common or more painful than sharp contrasts between the prosperity of some racial or ethnic groups and the poverty of others in the same society. At one time, such things were accepted as either Divinely ordained or as being a consequence of innate racial characteristics. However, as both these explanations were discarded over time, a new notion arose—that these economic contrasts were consequences of injustices visited upon minorities by majorities. Yet that explanation is not without its own serious problems, as great as the problems of earlier explanations that did not stand the test of time.

One of the strongest arguments against the injustice explanation of intergroup differences is that, in many countries around the world, minorities with virtually no political power or other means of discriminating against the majority population have nevertheless been far more successful—economically, educationally, or otherwise—than those who constitute the bulk of the nation's people. This has long been true of the Chinese in Malaysia, Indonesia, and the Philippines, Germans in Russia and Brazil, Jews in Eastern Europe and the United States, Lebanese in West Africa, Scots in North America and Australia, and the Japanese in Brazil, Canada, the United States, and Peru. Clearly, in these and other cases, the minority has simply outperformed the majority population, often in both the educational system and the economic system.

Even when it is clear that some groups have excelled without any power to suppress or oppress other groups, there is often still a rankling sense of the injustice of it all—that a child born into one group has so much greater prospects of success in life than a child of no greater innate ability born into another group. Sometimes this is blamed on a lack of "social justice," though the causes of such differences extend well beyond things controlled by any society and which could therefore legitimately be called "social." Each group trails the long shadow of its own history and culture, which influence its habits, priorities, and social patterns, which in turn affect its fate. If there is an injustice, it is an injustice which extends beyond the control of any existing government, institution, or society, because it involves the confluences of history, demography, culture, geography, and other factors, including luck. If there is an injustice, it is at this cosmic level in the vagaries of fate.

Lamenting the vagaries of fate may leave us with a galling sense of helpless frustration, which many escape by transforming the tragedy of the human condition into the specific sins of specific societies. This turns an insoluble problem of cosmic justice into an apparently more manageable issue of social justice. Since the sins of human beings are virtually inexhaustible, there is seldom a lack of examples of wrongdoing to which intergroup differences can be attributed, rightly or wrongly. Where the quest for injustice is over-riding, among the things it over-rides are logic and evidence. For example, various kinds of differences between white and aboriginal Australians were lumped together by a white Australian woman as examples of social injustice:

> The fact that I wake up each morning in a warm, safe, comfortable home, secure in the knowledge that the schools I send my children off to are organised to enhance their life chances and choices, and that good health, employment opportunities and respect are the norm not the goal in our lives has been made possible through the 208-year exploitation of land that belonged to indigenous Australians since the beginning of time.[21]

Here differences in life chances are attributed to the seizure of land by the transplanted Europeans who settled Australia. If this were meant seriously as an empirical proposition, rather than as an ideological indictment, then the most obvious question would be: Were there no differences in life chances between the Europeans and the aborigines before they met, when they were each living in their own respective homelands? Are differences today greater than they were then?

None of this provides a *moral* justification for the invasion of Australia, but it raises a question about the *causal* claim that differences in life chances today are due to expropriations of land in the past or exploitation of the indigenous people then or now.

Had no invasion of Australia ever occurred, and this white Australian woman had been born in the land of her ancestors—probably England—would she not have awakened each morning to better circumstances and prospects than aborigines in a distant and undisturbed Australia? Nor would she have been any more deserving of this windfall gain in England than in Australia. Yet her sense of guilt for her personal advantages and her ancestors' sins is greater because she lives in Australia. More important, it leads her to a conclusion all too characteristic of the quest for cosmic justice—that the aborigines should not have to change in order to achieve equality of results with whites in Australia. Clearly, the aborigines would have had to change in order to achieve equality of economic results with Englishmen, had both remained alone in their respective homelands. Yet those with the vision of cosmic justice want both groups to have the same effects without having the same causes, when both are living in the same country.

Such reasoning is by no means peculiar to Australia, much less to this particular Australian. Very much the same kind of reasoning—or lack of reasoning—has been used by a well-known American professor of history:

> I was born into a middle-class family of WASP ancestry. My parents prized education and sent all of their children to college.... The cultural environment that encouraged white males to hope for careers at the top of the professional and business pyramid but discouraged, inhibited, or prohibited women and minorities from doing the same was a more powerful form of affirmative action than anything we have more recently experienced in the other direction.[22]

He and others like him were also "beneficiaries of a sort of demographic affirmative action," since they were "born during the trough of the Depression-era birth rate," so that they entered the job market just as "the baby-boom expansion in college enrollments" created a great demand for professors from the smaller preceding generation.[23] What this professor chooses to call "demographic affirmative action" is an injustice only in some cosmic sense, rather than an injustice growing out of some chosen policy, like affirmative action. Since all things are the same except for the differences, and different except for the similarities, strained analogies like this may pass muster among those who are determined to ignore all differences internal to different groups of people.

Despite vast differences in income and wealth between Europeans and Africans in their respective homelands, much smaller differences between the descendants of Europeans and the descendants of Africans in the United States are widely attributed to the sins of the former against the latter. Had both groups migrated voluntarily to America and both been treated fairly, there would still have been no reason whatever to expect their economic levels to be the same, especially since people who did migrate voluntarily from different parts of Europe had income and wealth differences that were at one time greater than those between black and white Americans today.

None of this denies that there were in fact sins committed by whites against blacks in the United States or by the British against the aborigines in Australia. *Those sins are not in dispute.* The point here is that statistical disparities are not evidence of either the existence or the magnitude of those sins, for which there is ample other evidence. Such disparities are all too common around the world—with and without discrimination, with and without invasion, with and without slavery. This does not mean that these disparities are all due to individual merit. Inherited cultural advantages and disadvantages are windfall gains and windfall losses. More fundamentally, merit is a moral category and confusing morality with causation is a fatal weakness in trying to understand history.

Huge, unmerited, and unintentional differences in life

chances have been common among Europeans in Europe. As an insightful scholar has aptly pointed out, "a European child will have a very different life depending on whether that baby was born east or west of a line that starts at the Baltic and stretches southward along Poland's eastern border, down Slovakia's western border and along the middle of Hungary, then continues down through the middle of Bosnia to the Adriatic Sea."[24]

There are historic, geographic, social and other reasons for the large economic and other disparities between the life chances of people living in Eastern and Western Europe.[25] These differences existed at least as far back as the Roman Empire and, as late as 2003, the average per capita income in most Eastern European countries was less than half that of the Western European countries.[26] Neither in Europe nor elsewhere do all the innumerable influences on people's fate balance out to produce the equality of outcome that is taken as a baseline from which to measure social injustices that are used to explain inequalities of results. Nor have the various *causal* factors involved implied any such *moral* notion as "blaming the victim."

Morality is not causation and confusing the two does not advance either understanding or social improvement.

In a sense, it is healthy that more prosperous individuals or societies recognize that their prosperity is not all due to what they themselves have done in their own lifetimes, but is in fact the fruit of the efforts and contributions made by many other people before they were born. However, gratitude for whatever has made their prosperity possible has for many been replaced by guilt for having been more fortunate than others. Thus their forebears are seen not as having bequeathed a valuable heritage but as having perpetrated great injustices.

THE WEST IN HISTORY

Some who assume the posture of citizens of the world view the survival of their own particular society as a matter of no great moment, viewing it as simply a matter of choosing among alternative political and social arrangements. But history shows that more than transformation is involved. A society or a civilization

may be destroyed and its successor improvised from the ruins—
not just the physical ruins, but from anarchy as the ruins of law
and order and ignorance as the ruins of systems of education and
other instruments of cultural transmission. After the decline and
fall of the Roman Empire, it was centuries—some estimate a millennium —before the standard of living in Western Europe rose
again to the level it had reached in Roman times. The survival of a
society or a civilization is not just a question of a preference for
one particular set of political or social arrangements over another.
It is easy to discuss alternative arrangements around a seminar
table, as if transformations were no problem, but the painful alternatives amid the ruins can be very different.

Europeans lived for centuries with the presence of ruins
more magnificent than anything they were capable of creating or
even restoring. It is hardly surprising that they looked back at the
ancients with awe, long before they developed the modern
Western tendency to look forward to greater accomplishments in
the future than those of the past or the present. Another modern
Western tendency, at least among the intelligentsia, is to be anti-
Western—to apply double standards that ignore or excuse behavior in non-Western societies that would be excoriated in the West
or to picture the sins of the human race as if they were peculiarities of "our society." Specific examples include the history of conquest, slavery, and war.

Conquest

While European imperialism has been dominant in the past 500
years, in the preceding centuries Europe was itself subjected to
foreign conquests. It was invaded from Asia by the Mongols, to
whom the Russians paid tribute. It was invaded from the Middle
East by the Ottoman Empire, whose armies reached the gates of
Vienna in the sixteenth century. Europe was invaded from North
Africa and the whole Iberian peninsula was subjugated for centuries by the Moors. There was nothing peculiarly European about
either conquering or being conquered—or about changing from
one of these roles to the other in the course of history. The year in
which the last of the North African conquerors was driven out of
Spain—1492—was the same year that marked the beginning of
Europeans' creation of worldwide empires.

Conquest, like slavery, existed on every inhabited continent and involved all the races of mankind as both conquerors and subjugated peoples. Slavery and conquest existed in the Western Hemisphere before the first white man set foot on the shores of the Americas. The Zulus were conquering other African peoples when the British arrived in Southern Africa and conquered them all. Europeans also displaced other conquerors in Asia and among the Polynesians. What was different about European imperialism was how widely scattered its empires were, which was possible only because of revolutions in naval technology and a pre-existing base of wealth available to finance overseas expansion. But, morally, what the Europeans did was the same as what non-Europeans had been doing for thousands of years. This is not a moral justification for either. But it is an argument against the selective localization of evil.

Against that background, it is possible to see what a gross distortion of history it is for schools to be asking American school children such questions as how they would feel if they were the indigenous American Indians being forced from their land by the westward movement of invaders from Europe. These children, with no historical background, and coming from a society which condemns conquest, cannot possibly re-create the attitudes and beliefs which prevailed among either the Indians or the Europeans of earlier centuries.

While today's American children would of course think it wrong to take other people's lands by force, the American Indians had no such conception and took one another's lands by force long before they ever laid eyes on a white man. Indeed, Indians often joined with the European invaders to attack other Indians, in order to share in the spoils or to exact revenge for these other Indians' prior spoliation of them, including the taking of their lands and the enslavement of their people. When Cortés marched against the Aztec capital of Tenochtitlán, he led an army of 900 Spaniards and thousands of Indians.

No doubt those Indians forced off their lands in the United States or Brazil were bitter at being on the losing end of so many battles, but that is wholly different from a belief that battles were not the way to settle such things. No one wants to be conquered or enslaved. But that is wholly different from not wanting to be a conqueror or enslaver, or thinking that either or both are morally wrong. This is not a question of moral relativism or situational ethics. We may today condemn all conquests at all periods of history but that is wholly different from imagining that such feelings were those of Indians in centuries past. Clearly, such "how would you feel" questions are put to American children—and adults—to advance a contemporary vision and a contemporary agenda, rather than to provide a realistic understanding of history. It is a betrayal of the trust of those who send their children to school to be educated, not manipulated.

Studying Western imperialism in isolation from other, non-Western, imperialism—such as that of Genghis Khan or the Ottoman Turks—makes all the injustices, oppressions, and horrors incident to imperialism itself seem like depravities peculiar to the West. The tendentiousness of such a view of history stands out particularly when efforts are made to depict the United States as especially guilty of sins common to the human race around the world. One such history, after mentioning the Americans' "wresting the island remnants of Spain's empire in the Pacific and Caribbean" during the Spanish-America war, declared that "Russians were not comparably aggressive overseas."[27] This was said, not by a street-corner demagogue but by an academic scholar at a prestigious university.

Russians in reality conquered vastly more area than the United States ever did and continued to conquer after the United States began to withdraw from its few colonies. The difference was not in how "aggressive" Americans were but in the fact that the United States had a powerful navy and the Russians did not, so that the Russian empire expanded through land conquests of contiguous territory. The word "overseas" allows the author an escape hatch but the word "aggressive" describes an attitude, not a capability.

The prevalence of European imperialism in general since the sixteenth century is likewise due to special capabilities rather than special attitudes. Whatever their attitudes may have been in the Middle Ages, Europeans lacked the military and economic capabilities required to become imperial powers on the world stage, just as most non-European countries have lacked that capability since then. The history of which peoples, nations, or civilizations have conquered or enslaved which other peoples, nations, or civilizations has been largely a history of who has been in a position to do so.

Western Cultural Values

The misuse of history to condemn evils common around the world as if they were peculiarities of the West has serious practical implications. Two wrongs do not make a right but undermining the society which has the smaller evil only makes it more vulnerable to the greater evils in other societies and in international terrorist networks.

Far more is involved than questions of objectivity or honesty, important as such questions are. Without understanding the features of one's own society that have provided a prosperity, a freedom, and a security rare to non-existent over much of the rest of the world, one risks losing by default all these things for oneself and posterity. American society is one whose underlying bases are always under attack by both internal opportunists and external enemies. Those who have no conception of the Constitution of the United States, except as an object for nit-picking, cannot be expected to defend its integrity against the inevitable encroachments of political opportunists and judicial power-seekers. Those who have no conception of the unique heritage of Western civilization have no idea of what losing that heritage would mean—to them and to generations yet unborn—and why it must be defended against passing fads at home and lethal threats from abroad.

Freedom is one of those values of Western civilization whose uniqueness has been aptly highlighted by Professor Orlando Patterson of Harvard:

> For most of human history, and for nearly all of the non-Western world prior to Western contact, freedom was, and for many still remains, anything but an obvious or desirable goal. Other values and ideals were, or are, of far greater importance to them—values such as the pursuit of glory, honor, and power for oneself or one's family and clan, nationalism and imperial grandeur, militarism and valor in warfare, filial piety, the harmony of heaven and earth, the spreading of the "true faith,"

nirvana, hedonism, altruism, justice, equality, material progress—
the list is endless. But almost never, outside the context of
Western culture and its influence, has it included freedom.

Indeed, non-Western peoples have thought so little about
freedom that most human languages did not even possess a
word for the concept before contact with the West.[28]

It would take a vast study to elaborate the benefits that the
West has created for itself—and for the world. Advances in science, technology, and medicine are some of the more obvious. But
Western advances in the realm of ideas and institutions have been
fundamental as well, though these have not always traveled as
well when transplanted into cultures very different from the cultures in which these ideas and institutions evolved over the centuries. Here it may be useful to sketch just two fundamental
Western mental products, a universalistic conception of human
beings and the rule of law.

Perhaps the most important, and certainly the most distinctive, characteristic of Western civilization since at least the eighteenth century has been a growing universalism. Nothing has
been more common among human beings around the world, and
for thousands of years of history, than to disregard the troubles
inflicted on other people outside the group to which they happened to belong. Some have taken positive pleasure in their ability to dominate, oppress, humiliate, or kill others, as for example
Genghis Khan did. The Mayans developed to a high art form both
the prolonged tortures and humiliations they heaped upon those
they had conquered and the commemoration of such acts in their
art. Nor had such things died out in the twentieth century, when
the Japanese in World War II delighted in savaging and humiliating
American and other prisoners of war, as well as civilians in their
conquered territories, and when their Nazi allies found mass
slaughter not enough unless it was accomplished by soul-searing
degradations inflicted on inmates of their concentration camps.

No society thus far has entirely escaped this older tendency.
In other words, universalism has not yet become universal in any
society. Nor did universalism in terms of having regard for other
people's feeling or well-being imply any sense of equality in ability or even likeability. It simply meant that all people deserved to

be treated decently and fairly, whomever they might be and whatever the state of their ability or their culture.

Nothing epitomized this universalism more than Queen Victoria's concern about the fate of slaves in other lands. When *Uncle Tom's Cabin* author Harriet Beecher Stowe was granted an audience with Her Majesty during a trip to England, she found the queen able to discuss the *Dred Scott* case "in great detail," as well as saying that she had wept over some of the passages in the novel.[29] There could hardly be a greater social distance than that between the ruler of the largest empire the world had ever known and a slave being whipped in another country on the other side of an ocean. Yet this universalism was more than an incidental phenomenon in Western civilization. It fueled a worldwide crusade against slavery for more than a century—and the fact that it took more than a century to destroy slavery over most of the world clearly indicates that this universalism did not prevail outside of Western civilization.

One of the implications of universalism is that those who are more fortunate need not be any more deserving than those in misery. For some, this suggests an imperative for redistribution of wealth, while for some others it may suggest a sharing of the knowledge and the development of the habits, priorities, and values that would enable others to create wealth for themselves. For those who believe the latter, simply giving people things is counterproductive from the standpoint of getting them to become productive themselves. Nor is what is given likely to equal what the recipients could have created for themselves if the *sources* of productivity had been shared, rather than the fruits.

Like anything human, universalism can take foolish forms, as with the Australian woman who confused morality and causation, as so many others have done when seeking historical redress for historical abstractions at the expense of creating new problems for flesh-and-blood human beings.

Another great Western advance has been the rule of law—again, as with universalism, not everywhere or at all times but sufficiently to become a characteristic distinguishing Western from non-Western societies. Every society has its rules or its laws, but the rule of law implies far more than this. When the English beheaded King Charles I, this made unmistakably clear—to all at the time and to the generations that followed, throughout the English-speaking world—that no one was above the law. Decades later, when Charles II learned that his subjects were reacting adversely to his expansive conception of his role as king, he found it prudent to sneak out of London in the middle of the night, cross the channel to France, and never return to the British Isles. In many other societies, especially non-Western societies, the notion that the supreme ruler was subject to the law would be foreign, if not incomprehensible. In many of these societies, the ruler's word was itself law.

The rule of law implies more than the principle that no one is above the law. It implies also that those with power cannot take action against individuals without some prior evidence of violations of existing laws and some prior determination through institutionally established "due process" that the individual in question is in fact guilty of transgressing specific prohibitions. What this means for individual freedom and dignity can be illustrated by seeing what can happen in the absence of such safeguards. When Sultan Mehmed of the Ottoman empire ordered one of his subjects to bring his adolescent son to him for his own sexual pleasure and the subject declined, they were both decapitated and their heads displayed before the sultan at his banquet table.[30]

Western conceptions of the rule of law in general, and the Constitution of the United States in particular, reflect a vivid awareness of the dangers of power—and the need to divide that power among different institutions that can counterbalance one another. The principles implicit in the Constitution were made explicit in *The Federalist,* the collection of popular essays designed to explain to eighteenth-century Americans why the Constitution was written as it was, in order to persuade them to ratify this new document on which a new nation would be built.

While the rule of law is distinctive to Western civilization, it has not been pervasive at all times and places within that civilization. Even in England, its evolution took centuries. Although the kinds of free societies which emerged in the West were often called "democracies" in the twentieth century, they were societies with the rule of law, long before they were societies in which democratic majorities chose political leaders. More than seven hundred years elapsed between Magna Carta and universal adult suffrage in England or the United States.

While some non-Western societies have selectively adopted varying aspects of Western civilization, that is very different from saying that Western nations can directly "export democracy" to non-Western lands, even those that they have conquered militarily.

While they can bring the outward forms of Western culture—an independent judiciary, elections, markets, technology—what they cannot export are the centuries of evolution that led up to these things and the resulting ingrained traditions and attitudes which enable Western institutions to function.

A far more urgent challenge faces the West than spreading its culture to other lands. The real culture war is within Western civilization itself, and history is one of its crucial battlegrounds. In addition to the usual disputes over particular facts or their interpretation, there is a more fundamental and more pervasive attempt to make the sins of the human race look like peculiar depravities of Western civilization. Thus Uganda's brutal expulsions of 50,000 Asians in the 1970s, and Britain's acceptance of some of them as refugees, was described this way by an American scholar:

> The crowning disgrace in the treatment of East African Asians came when the United Kingdom refused entry to Asian holders of British passports who had been booted out of Kenya. At least South Africa does not prevent its own citizens from entering its borders. If the Mother of Parliaments and the cradle of Western democracy behaved more badly towards them than the most racist tyranny in the world, what do Asians have to look forward to?[31]

Britain's sense of not having an unlimited capacity to absorb refugees was denounced more strongly than Africans' arbitrary expulsions, which is what created the problem in the first place. Most of these Asians had lived in Africa for generations and had never lived in Britain. The fact that those expelled held British passports from the days of the British empire did not mean that they had ever been part of the society of the British Isles or could be readily absorbed there in unlimited numbers. None of this, however, was allowed to inhibit the seizing of an opportunity to condemn the West—again, by a respected academic scholar, not a street-corner demagogue.

SUMMARY AND IMPLICATIONS

We do not have a choice whether or not to discuss history. History has always been invoked in contemporary controversies. The only choice is between discussing what actually happened in the past and discussing notions projected into the past for present purposes. History is the memory of the human race. For an individual to wake up some morning with no memory would be devastating. In addition to the emotional trauma of suddenly finding everything and everybody unknown and unfathomable, there would be no way to carry out the practical necessities of work or managing a home, much less maintaining or establishing relations with other human beings. It would not be much better to wake up some morning with a false memory, induced in you by some means by some other person—to serve that other person's purposes, with all memories expunged that do not serve that end and other memories twisted or created out of thin air to make you the willing instrument of some ulterior design.

Much has been written about the sheer neglect of history in our educational institutions, with students able to graduate from some of the most prestigious colleges in the land without having had a single course in the history of their own country or of the world. Far more insidious and dangerous, however, is the promotion of a history created as a projection into the past of current notions and agendas.

History, with its integrity as a record of the past intact, is a gold mine of experience from many times and peoples under a wider range of circumstances than any given generation can find in its own time. Contemporary plans, theories, beliefs, and hopes can be checked against the record of what has happened in the past when similar notions were put into practice. Merely to discover how often the same ideas have occurred to others, centuries ago, can be a sobering experience for those inclined to become carried away by supposedly new and brilliant insights about an unprecedented situation. But history cannot be a reality check for visions when history is itself shaped by visions.

There has been much hand-wringing about the difficulty or impossibility of achieving objectivity in writing history. If there is anyone who is objective, it is hard to imagine how others who are not objective would know that. The unattainability of objectivity is too often a distraction from something more mundane that is quite attainable but is often absent—honesty. When facts about racial or ethnic groups that are both known and relevant are deliberately suppressed because they would undermine a particular vision, doctrine, or agenda, then history is prostituted and cannot serve as a check against visions, because facts have been subordinated to visions.

Objectivity is too often a red herring. No one makes the impossible demand that mathematicians be objective but that does not mean that the logic of geometry or equations depends on how each individual chooses to look at it. Nor can a mathematician who gets his geometry or equations wrong take refuge in the truism that no one is objective. Neither should historians be able to find refuge in such truisms. None of this denies that there are honest differences in interpreting history. But that in turn cannot deny that there are also dishonest differences. The pretense of looking at history from someone else's point of view—that of the downtrodden or the dispossessed, for example—is just one example, for neither today's author nor reader can achieve such a feat when discussing the past.

Taking Sides

From the undeniable fact that an individual's personal leanings for or against particular groups, nations, or civilizations can influence the way that individual sees history, some have concluded that it is just a matter of choosing sides when writing history and looking at history from the viewpoint of those whose side one is taking. As the author of a widely read history text says: "I prefer to try to tell the story of the discovery of America from the viewpoint of the Arawaks, of the Constitution from the standpoint of the slaves, of Andrew Jackson as seen by the Cherokees, of the Civil War as seen by the New York Irish."[32]

One need only ask how many slaves—the vast majority of whom were illiterate—contemplated the Constitution of the United States at all to see the absurdity of such posturing. As for the Arawaks, the first people Columbus encountered in the Western Hemisphere, none has survived and none left any writings. How Columbus or Andrew Jackson or any other historic figure looked to any Western Hemisphere Indians is knowledge vouchsafed only to those Indians at that time—certainly not to others centuries removed from the scene, living in a very different cultural universe, and possessing not even isolated written statements from the indigenous peoples, much less any scientifically conducted polls among them.

We may, from our own viewpoint today, lament that bloody and brutal conquests took place at all, but that is by no means to say that the Indians themselves rejected bloody and brutal conquests, or that they lamented anything about the battles that took place other than the fact that they lost most of them. What their true feelings were we can only speculate about.

To look at history as a matter of taking sides is to turn the human failing of bias, which mars what we do to a greater or lesser extent, into a principle that is to permeate—and pollute—our whole endeavor. It is an all-or-nothing argument, that if we cannot completely eliminate bias, then we should give it free rein, perhaps even congratulating ourselves for having admitted our biases. Perfection is not attainable in any aspect of human life but does that mean we should turn imperfections into virtues? Does the fact that we cannot eliminate 100 percent of the impurities in air or water mean that we should celebrate smog or polluted water and boast of our realism?

Making a case for or against an individual, group, or society is fundamentally different from seeking the facts and analyzing the context and constraints which explain those facts. Making an indictment may be easier and more emotionally satisfying than following the ancient admonition, "With all your getting, get understanding." Neither indictments nor apologies are the same as understanding. Nor is a preconceived neutrality. The truth does not necessarily "lie somewhere in between." Like anything else, only after you find it can you know where it is.

Taking sides too easily degenerates into being morally one-up and imagining that we would have handled the problems of the past so much better than those who were there. Nothing is easier than creating higher standards for judging other people. Intellectuals whose whole careers are built around words are especially vulnerable to the temptation to judge historic figures by their words. Thus the wording of Lincoln's Emancipation Proclamation has been a disappointment to many, then as now. Without a sense of context, and of the constraints and dangers inherent in that context, it may be hard to understand that ringing words of moral passion could have aroused far more legal challenge and political backlash than a mundane assertion of military necessity in wartime. It was by no means a foregone conclusion that the Emancipation Proclamation would have survived such challenges—and its purpose was to survive, to free millions of human beings, not to seek a place in the anthologies.

Some historic figures—Winston Churchill for example—are renowned for both their words and their deeds. But a historic figure such as George Washington contributed little to the anthologies, while making landmark contributions to the creation of a new kind of nation and, by example, to the development of free societies in the modern world. The issue, however, is not simply one of assigning the proper stature to individuals. More fundamentally, the task is to assess causation. But those seeking moral indictments too often condemn past leaders for not having made such futile gestures as putting a clause banning slavery in the Constitution, when such a clause would have banned the Constitution itself from the South, making that section a separate nation in which slavery is unlikely to have been ended as early as Lincoln ended it.

Among the many other distortions of history growing out of a posture of taking sides is casting particular groups or societies in the role of victims, while overlooking their victimization of others. Peoples subjugated and oppressed by others have often been the objects of solicitude by intellectuals, as well as by political movements seeking their liberation. Yet, time and again, that liberation has been followed almost immediately by the liberated peoples oppressing the minorities now subject to their power. The grandly proclaimed "right of self-determination of peoples," used by the victors in the First World War as a rationale for breaking up the defeated Hapsburg and Ottoman empires, led to waves of intolerance and oppression against the minorities within the newly freed or newly created nations of Eastern Europe and the Middle East—oppressions that have not yet ceased even in the twenty-first century.

It was much the same story after the Second World War. When the Malays gained their independence from the British and the Indonesians from the Dutch, both immediately began discriminating against their Chinese minorities. Nor was newly liberated Europe exempt from such persecutions of minorities, beginning with the expulsions of millions of Germans, including people from families that had settled in Eastern Europe or the Balkans centuries earlier. When the nations of Africa began achieving independence during the 1960s, those in East Africa likewise began discriminating against their Asian minorities and the nations of West Africa began discriminating against their Lebanese minorities. In many cases, mob violence punctuated this discrimination. Even indigenous minorities were targeted in some newly independent African nations—the Ibos in Nigeria, for example. Nor were newly freed colonies in the Caribbean exempt from these patterns, with Indians and Pakistanis being targeted in Trinidad and Guiana.

In all these cases, Western intellectuals who had taken sides against European imperial powers and in favor of liberating these nations, tended to pass over in silence outrages more severe than those they had protested vigorously against when committed by Europeans against indigenous peoples. On a smaller scale, this pattern recurred in the United States, when blacks freed from various legal and social oppressions by the civil rights revolution of the 1960s in many cases turned anti-Jewish and anti-Asian in both words and deeds, including murders of store owners during ghetto riots. The very word "racism" was then redefined to exclude groups without "power" so that the most anti-Semitic rantings or anti-Asian violence committed by blacks was exempted from the term, even though power had never been a prerequisite for defining racism before the need to exempt black racism arose.

Reaching conclusions after the fact is not the same as taking sides before the facts, even if those conclusions reflect credit or discredit on different individuals or groups to differing degrees. The historian is the agent of the reader. That is whose side is supposed to be served and it is a conflict of interest to set out to serve some other cause while pretending to be informing the reader.

A hyper-critical view of one's own society or civilization may express a sense of personal guilt for the undeserved good fortune of being a member of a society whose economic, political, and social benefits far exceed those available to other people of no less merit who happen to live in other kinds of societies or in a different social setting within the same society. Wanting to line up on the side of such people may be a generous impulse, but it can also be a dangerous self-indulgence. Such moral partisanship is unlikely to do much good to those unfortunate enough to be born without the social and cultural prerequisites for prosperity or freedom.

Whatever chances such people have of acquiring the missing ingredients for their own advancement are reduced to the extent that their problems are misdiagnosed as the sins of other people rather than things that they themselves lack—even if they lack those things for reasons beyond their control. Often the things they lack can be acquired sooner and more extensively than they can either reform other people or get the society as a whole to provide for them through a redistribution of existing wealth what they are capable of producing for themselves through an upgrading of their own productivity. Moreover, rising productivity adds to the net wealth of the society and the world, which is more likely to gain the respect of others, as well as self-respect, than are reiterated pleas or demands for a share of what others have created.

Looking at history as a matter of taking sides encourages the collectivization of people, not only as of a given time, but also over time, so that "Germans" or "Czechs," for example, become intertemporal abstractions. This creates not only intellectual problems but even more painful and sometimes catastrophic practical problems in the real world. For example, the confiscation of the lands of Czech nobles who revolted against the Hapsburg Empire in 1620 meant a transfer of vast amounts of land to people of German ancestry—a process which leaders of the newly created nation of Czechoslovakia after the First World War sought to reverse in the name of "social justice" so as to "put right the historic wrongs of the seventeenth century."[33]

Obviously, no one from the seventeenth century was still alive to be either punished or rewarded, so Germans and Czechs were being conceived of as intertemporal abstractions, and the reversal of historic wrongs was to be done with flesh-and-blood people alive in the twentieth century. Both Germans and Czechs went through horrible and murderous traumas over the next several decades as a result of events set in motion to reverse what had happened three centuries earlier. These traumas included the dismemberment of the country as a result of the Munich crisis of 1938, provoked by the embittered German minority that had been discriminated against within Czechoslovakia, in the name of "social justice," and then, after the Second World War, massive and brutal expulsions of Germans from Czechoslovakia, with losses of lives by the tens of thousands. Both Germans and Czechs in the twentieth century ended up far worse off than if seventeenth-century issues had been left in the seventeenth century.

The confusion of intertemporal abstractions with living flesh-and-blood human beings has by no means been confined to Czechs and Germans, or even to people under the hypnotic sway of demagogues. A very thoughtful book about various Asian countries, for example, noted the lack of remorse among those Japanese who committed hideous atrocities against defenseless people in the lands they conquered during the Second World War, but added: "The United States, after all, has never formally apologized for enslaving Africans, invading Mexico and Canada, stealing Texas, colonizing the Philippines or Guam, or carpet-bombing Vietnam."[34] The distinction between living, flesh-and-blood Japanese military veterans who personally committed atrocities and an intertemporal abstraction of Americans committing various acts over a period of centuries was simply ignored.

Intertemporal abstractions not only facilitate taking sides, such abstractions can also facilitate moral equivalence, such as that between people who committed atrocities against the defenseless and those whose only offense is being born descended from people who committed evil acts in the past. There is a slippery versatility to intertemporal abstractions. These abstractions can, among other things, promote invidious comparisons, stretching across centuries, and also create a zero-sum concept of the world, in which gains of one group or nation mean losses for other groups or nations. It can also promote a dog-in-the-manger mentality, in which the good fortune of others is a grievance to be prevented or avenged, whether or not that good fortune can be shown to have produced any ill effects on others. Thus, when Nigeria became independent in 1960, a high priority on the agenda of the political authorities in northern Nigeria was getting rid of southern Nigerians, who held many desirable positions in the civil administration and in the economy of the northern region, even though there were not nearly enough educated or experienced northern Nigerians to replace them. The southern Nigerians were nevertheless forced out, even when this left vacancies that had to be filled with European expatriates.

Resentment of better educated or more entrepreneurial groups has been by no means peculiar to Nigeria. Such groups have been targeted, expelled or forced to flee for their lives from countries in Europe, Asia, Africa, the Caribbean and the South Pacific, not to mention black ghettoes in the United States. In many cases, those who forced them out have suffered economic devastation afterwards from the loss of the skills, talents, experience and businesses of those who departed. After the expulsion of the Moriscoes from sixteenth-century Spain, a bishop who had favored that expulsion nevertheless asked: "Who will make our shoes now?" It was a question that might well have been asked *before* the expulsions—and the kind of question that might well be asked by others with a dog-in-the-manger view.

One of the consequences of looking at the study of history as an occasion for taking sides, rather than seeking the truth, is that this taking sides has often lead to a twisting of events to produce the desired condemnation of the other side. More fundamental than a twisting of particular events, however, has been a general forcing of historical episodes into a preconceived pattern based on an ideological vision, even when that requires turning historical figures and the complex circumstances in which they acted into editorial cartoon characters in a cartoon world.

Another consequence of the taking-sides perspective is that many then see strong group solidarity as a prerequisite for the victory of the side they have chosen. But, where the advancement of one group is not seen as axiomatically taking the form of victory over some other oppressing group, it cannot be assumed *a priori* that the benefits of solidarity exceed their costs. Groupthink does not always lead to wiser decisions than what emerges from a clash of differing individual ideas from within and beyond the group. More dangerously, group solidarity often means letting the lowest common denominator shape the culture and life within the group and determine the direction of its future. This can range from black students' being accused of "acting white" for being conscientious about their studies to automatic criticisms of police actions against rioters or criminals. These are self-inflicted wounds that can jeopardize the whole future of a people.

Repudiating criminals whose principal victims are members of their own group is imperative and casting aside counterproductive aspects of the group culture can be essential for advancement. Contrary to popular belief, highly successful groups do not "all stick together." The history of such groups as the Jews, the Lebanese, the overseas Chinese, and others clearly belies this belief. Chinese American leaders, for example, at one time urged San Francisco policemen—mostly white—to crack down on young Chinese hoodlums and gangsters, including administering "curbstone justice" with vigorous use of billy clubs. Moreover, some elements within the Chinese American community apparently took their own actions, for the bound and gagged bodies of some of these criminals were found floating in San Francisco Bay.[35]

Groupwide solidarity that includes hoodlums and criminals means absorbing enormous costs imposed on the rest of the ethnic community, not only directly as victims of crime, but also indirectly when businesses and jobs flee the community, leaving an economic wasteland. Chinese American leaders were particularly sensitive to this possibility because much of the prosperity of the

Chinatown area in San Francisco depended on its remaining a place attracting large numbers of tourists. By contrast, it has long been the practice of black Americans to "protect any Negro from the whites, even when they happen not to like that individual Negro," as Gunnar Myrdal put it more than half a century ago.[36] Such tendencies have only increased since then. Such automatic group solidarity ties the fate of the community as a whole to the fate of its most unsavory elements in many ways. It not only identifies the community with the acts of these individuals in the eyes of the larger society, it puts great leverage in the hands of irresponsible and criminal elements, whose actions can cause backlashes against blacks in general—whether in the form of political reactions, social isolation, violence, or simply the withdrawal of businesses from black neighborhoods, taking jobs and a tax base with them.

Where a particular group culture is itself a handicap impeding the acquisition of the education, skills, and experience required for economic and other advancement, group solidarity can have huge and lifelong consequences with staggering costs. Even with such mundane things as the prices charged in local stores, group solidarity can obscure the causes of the higher prices which often confront lower income people. The costs created by crime and violence are often blamed on outsiders who charge these high prices rather than on the local delinquent and criminal elements that create the costs which these prices reflect. Group solidarity may not only seal a group off from the larger surrounding society, it may seal them off from the truth about the internal causes of their own problems, making a solution more remote.

The prevailing vision is one of a solidified minority in a stance of defiance against the larger society, with minority leaders and activists ever ready to protest police actions against any members of the community. Outside intellectuals, celebrities, politicians, judges, and others who see racial and ethnic issues as a matter of taking sides may also adopt this posture, in order to be on the side of the minority community, perhaps in order to atone for their own good fortune. But such a stance and such a vision impose great costs on the community that they intend to help, though these outsiders pay no part of any of those costs—and so have little or no incentive to scrutinize their social vision and its assumptions to discover their actual effects.

One of the subsidiary notions growing out of group solidarity is that of "role models." Efforts to find, praise or exaggerate the numbers and achievements of these role models can be counterproductive by insinuating the idea that people can be inspired only by others who physically resemble themselves. But history has repeatedly demonstrated the falsity of that notion. Japan went from being a backward feudal society to becoming a modern industrial nation by learning from Europeans and Americans, both by sending their students to study in Europe and the United States and by bringing Europeans and Americans to Japan to teach the needed skills or to provide the industrial experience required to launch Japanese industries. In the United States, the immigrant generation of Jewish children in late nineteenth and early twentieth-century New York City were taught largely by Irish Catholic teachers, while the generation of black children arriving in Harlem in the 1930s and 1940s were far more often taught by Jewish teachers than by black teachers.

In both cases, these were the generations that rose into positions that their parents had seldom achieved. The second generation of Japanese American children likewise rose to positions that their parents—overwhelmingly farmers—had never achieved. Moreover, Japanese American youngsters of that generation were unlikely ever to have had a Japanese American teacher or to have seen a Japanese American working in any professional or scientific field, even though these became fields in which Japanese Americans later excelled. The notion of "role models" is not merely false but pernicious when it becomes part of the straightjacket of groupthink.

Lessons of History

History whose integrity has not been compromised by contemporary agendas is not "irrelevant" to our times. On the contrary, it can often be of great value, not only in correcting factual errors but also in dispelling feelings and attitudes that needlessly encumber our lives today. For example, Shelby Steele has aptly pointed out that much that is said and done today that makes no sense in itself is a result of a desperate desire of whites to avoid being considered racists and a desperate desire of blacks to avoid being considered inferior. For blacks, there is also a desire to escape the stigma of being a race which shamefully submitted to the degradation of slavery. Honest history deflates such distractions from the task of dealing with today's problems today.

While racism has sometimes been a major factor in history, it has often been a result—of slavery, for example—instead of an autonomous cause, and in any event its waxing and waning in the history of white reactions to black Americans shows that its effects are neither immutable nor inevitable. It is futile for people who are not racists to try endlessly to prove a negative. Nor should people who are in fact racists be exempt from the charge because of verbal sleight-of-hand, such as adding a proviso of "power" to the definition. It is equally futile, and equally unnecessary, for blacks to try to prove a negative, that they are not genetically inferior or not less manly than other races in having submitted to slavery.

The notion that blacks were unusual in submitting to slavery is one that cannot survive any serious study of the history of slavery around the world. Every race was enslaved and few were in any position to revolt, much less to succeed in their uprisings. Slavery could not have lasted for thousands of years around the world if it could be readily overthrown by rebellion. The most famous slave revolt—that of Spartacus in ancient Rome—ended in a devastating defeat of the slaves and mass agonizing deaths publicly inflicted on them. Neither Europeans, Asians, or Africans escaped the fate of being slaves or the guilt of being enslavers. Only in unusual circumstances—where the slave population greatly outnumbered the enslaving race, for example—were slave uprisings likely to succeed, even locally, or communities of escaped slaves likely to survive, as among blacks in some Caribbean islands.

One of the painful consequences of a history constrained by contemporary agendas and contemporary attitudes has been a taboo against researching and discussing the history of IQ and other mental test results among various groups. This social taboo

has in recent times been backed up by legal restrictions on giving
IQ tests to black school children and, in too many cases, by campus disruptions and violence against speakers attempting to discuss research and conclusions on this subject that others disagree
with. But only research and analysis by those who have defied the
taboos has brought out the fact that people of a variety of ances-
tries, in countries around the world, have had average IQ scores at
the same level as that of blacks in the United States. In India, for
example, mental test score differences among various groups are
even greater than those between black and white Americans.

Only historical research has brought out regional differences
in mental test results that cut across racial lines, so that white soldiers in various Southern states scored lower on mental tests than
black soldiers from various Northern states during the First World
War. Only historical research has brought out the fact that black
children attending Dunbar High School in Washington consistently equaled or exceeded the national average on IQ tests for
decades, even though they were a substantial proportion of all
black high school students in the city and were not pre-selected
for admission by mental tests. Indeed, there were some students at
Dunbar with subnormal IQs but they were offset by others whose
IQs considerably exceeded the national average.[37]

The weightiest evidence of all has been the historical
research of James R. Flynn, showing what has been called "the
Flynn effect," that contrary to both the logic and the predictions
of believers in genetic determination of IQs, national performances on IQ tests have risen substantially over the years in more than
a dozen countries, with black Americans at the end of the twentieth century answering as many IQ test questions correctly as
whites answered in the middle of that century. This does not
change the racial gap but it undermines genetic determinism as an
explanation for that gap. None of this would have been known if
the taboo on IQ research had not been defied, and much of this
research would not have been done without the previous
research of those who concluded that IQ differences were largely
due to genetic differences. In other areas as well, history shows
that initially mistaken beliefs have provided the impetus for study
and research which advanced human understanding beyond

where it was before the mistaken beliefs arose. Chemistry, for example, developed out of discredited alchemy and astronomy out of astrology.

In an age of clashing civilizations and of hatreds so fierce as to provoke suicide terrorism, history is both a treasure chest of experience and a powder keg. As Edmund Burke aptly put it, more than two centuries ago:

> In history a great volume is unrolled for our instruction, drawing the materials of future wisdom from the past errors and infirmities of mankind. It may, in the perversion, serve for a magazine, furnishing offensive and defensive weapons...and supplying the means of keeping alive, or reviving, dissensions and animosities, and adding fuel to civil fury.[38]

While the lessons of history can be valuable, the twisting of history and the mining of the past for grievances can tear a society apart. Past grievances, real or imaginary, are equally irremediable in the present, for nothing that is done among living contemporaries can change in the slightest the sins and the sufferings of generations who took those sins and sufferings to the grave with them in centuries past. Galling as it may be to be helpless to redress the crying injustices of the past, symbolic expiation in the present can only create new injustices among the living and new problems for the future, when newborn babies enter the world with pre-packaged grievances against other babies born the same day. Both have their futures jeopardized, not only by their internal strife but also by the increased vulnerability of a disunited society to external dangers from other nations and from international terrorist networks.

To be relevant to our times, history must not be controlled by our times. Its integrity as a record of the past is what allows us to draw lessons from it.

One of the most chilling lessons of the history of the twentieth century is how deceptive domestic tranquility can be in a multi-ethnic society, when it takes only the right circumstances and the right demagogue to turn neighbor murderously against neighbor. There was not a single race riot between the Sinhalese majority and the Tamil minority in Sri Lanka during the first half of

the twentieth century and the relations between the two groups
at mid-century were regarded by many observers as a model for
how different ethnic groups could co-exist in harmony. Yet the
second half of the century saw not only massive and lethal riots
between these two groups, but also unspeakable atrocities inflicted on individuals from one group who just happened to fall into
the hands of the other group. Moreover, all this fomented hatred
and violence escalated into a full-scale civil war, in which this
small country suffered more deaths than the United States suffered during all the long years of the Vietnam War. Both "sides"
lost—and they lost because they became sides, instead of remaining fellow countrymen with different cultures.

Sri Lanka was not unique. Neighbors who had lived in peace
for years, or even generations, turned on one another murderously in Indonesia, in the Balkans, and in sub-Saharan Africa, as ethnic
polarization and strife were stirred up by either fanatics or opportunists. In Germany in the 1920s, Jews were so widely accepted
socially that nearly half of all Jewish marriages in Germany during
that decade were marriages with non-Jews. But that did not prevent the Holocaust.

While history is an explicit legacy of the past, cultural patterns and traditions are its inarticulate legacy in the differential
survival of varying practices. Many who seek to subordinate history to current visions and agendas likewise seek to replace this
cultural legacy. Those who regard the accumulated experiences of
successive generations, distilled in social traditions, as mere "constructions"—on the same plane as alternative "constructions" that
they excogitate—are ignoring the consequential processes
through which those traditions have been filtered and from which
they have emerged. The viability of these traditions is attested to
by the mere fact that they are still here to be criticized, while the
viability of alternative "constructions" has yet to be proved and
they may be able to survive only in the minds of those who put
them together. Notions and knowledge are different precisely
because the former have not passed through the verification
process, while the latter has.

Although our misunderstanding of the past cannot affect the
past, it can affect the future, sometimes catastrophically. Human

beings have survived too many mistakes and misjudgments to make mere inaccuracy fatal by itself. Yet the fact that nations and whole civilizations have also collapsed, with tragic repercussions lasting for centuries, is a sobering reminder that there is not an unlimited latitude for error or misconception. Sealing ourselves off from reality within a vision risks the kinds of catastrophes that blind rulers have brought down upon themselves and their countries, from the days of the Roman Empire to the cataclysm into which Hitler led Germany. The key factor in these calamities has often been a blocking of feedback from reality, epitomized by the figurative or literal killing of messengers bringing bad news.

Where beliefs are not checked against facts, but instead facts must meet the test of consonance with the prevailing vision, we are in the process of sealing ourselves off from feedback from reality. Heedless of the past, we are flying blind into the future.

Notes

Black Rednecks and White Liberals

1. Lewis M. Killian, *White Southerners*, revised edition (Amherst: University of Massachusetts Press, 1985), pp. 98, 99, 109.

2. David Hackett Fischer, *Albion's Seed: Four British Folkways in America* (New York: Oxford University Press, 1989), p. 57.

3. Glenn G. Gilbert, "Introduction," *The German Language in America: A Symposium*, edited by Glenn G. Gilbert (Austin: University of Texas Press, 1971), p. xi. Moreover, even after later generations of people in these enclaves began to speak English, their English also often contained archaic words and expressions once peculiar to the local region of the United States where they first learned English. Carroll E. Reed, "The Dialectology of American Colonial German," Ibid., pp. 7-8.

4. Frank L. Owsley, *Plain Folk of the Old South* (Baton Rouge: Louisiana State University Press, 1982), p. 92.

5. Lewis M. Killian, *White Southerners*, p. 100.

6. Alexis de Tocqueville, *Democracy in America* (New York: Alfred A. Knopf, 1966), Vol. I, p. 365.

7. Frederick Law Olmsted, *The Cotton Kingdom: A Traveller's Observations on Cotton and Slavery in the American Slave States*, edited by Arthur M. Schlesinger, (New York: Modern Library, 1969), pp. 476n, 614-622.

8. Hinton Rowan Helper, *The Impending Crisis of the South:*

How to Meet It, enlarged edition (New York: A. B. Burdick, 1860), p. 34.

9. David Hackett Fischer, *Albion's Seed*, pp. 634-635. See also Grady McWhiney, *Cracker Culture: Celtic Ways in the Old South* (Tuscaloosa: University of Alabama Press, 1988), pp. 16-18.

10. T. C. Smout, *A History of the Scottish People: 1560-1830* (London: Collins, 1969), p. 367. See also Grady McWhiney, *Cracker Culture*, p. 231. G. M. Trevelyan, *English Social History: A Survey of Six Centuries* (New York: Viking Penguin, Inc., 1986), p. 451.

11. Henry Thomas Buckle, *On Scotland and the Scotch Intellect* (Chicago: The University of Chicago Press, 1970), p. 38; James G. Leyburn, *The Scotch-Irish: A Social History* (Chapel Hill: University of North Carolina Press, 1962), p. 18.

12. Grady McWhiney, *Cracker Culture*, pp. 84, 93-94, 231-232.

13. Clement Eaton, *The Freedom-of-Thought Struggle in the Old South* (New York: Harper & Row, 1964), p. 81.

14. Grady McWhiney, *Cracker Culture*, pp. 55-56. Even after Scottish schools became strong, "they were not strong in areas of the southwest which contributed much to the American migration." David Hackett Fischer, *Albion's Seed*, p. 722.

15. David Hackett Fischer, *Albion's Seed*, p. 630.

16. Grady McWhiney, *Cracker Culture*, pp 45-47, 49; David Hackett Fischer, *Albion's Seed*, pp. 365-366, 740-743; Lewis C. Gray, *History of Agriculture in the Southern United States to 1860* (Gloucester, Mass: Peter Smith, 1958), Vol. I, p. 484; Frederick Law Olmstead, *The Cotton Kingdom*, pp. 12, 65, 147, 527; Alexis de Tocqueville, *Democracy in America* (New York: Alfred A. Knopf, 1966), Vol. I, pp. 363, 369; Forrest McDonald, "Cultural Continuity and the Shaping of the American South," *Geographic Perspectives in History*, edited by Eugene D. Genovese and Leonard Hochberg (London: Basil Blackwell, Ltd., 1989), pp. 231-232; Lewis M. Killian, *White Southerners*, pp. 108-109.

17. Grady McWhiney, *Cracker Culture*, Chapter VI; David Hackett Fischer, *Albion's Seed*, pp. 622, 624, 626, 628, 629,

736-738, 766-771; Lewis C. Gray, *History of Agriculture in the Southern United States to 1860*, Vol. I, p. 484. See also Frederick Law Olmsted, *The Cotton Kingdom*, pp. 334, 341, 554, 555.

18. Grady McWhiney, *Cracker Culture*, Chapter VIII. See also David Hackett Fischer, *Albion's Seed*, pp. 718, 721-723, 755-756; Frederick Law Olmsted, *The Cotton Kingdom*, pp. 301, 415, 426, 558-560, 592; Lewis C. Gray, *History of Agriculture in the Southern United States to 1860*, Vol. I, pp. 484, 488; Forrest McDonald, "Cultural Continuity and the Shaping of the American South," *Geographic Perspectives in History*, edited by Eugene D. Genovese and Leonard Hochberg (Oxford: Basil Blackwell, Ltd., 1989), p. 233; Lewis M. Killian, *White Southerners*, p. 100.

19. Grady McWhiney, *Cracker Culture*, pp. 172-173; David Hackett Fischer, *Albion's Seed*, pp. 298-306, 345-346, 680-682.

20. Grady McWhiney, *Cracker Culture*, pp. 246-247; David Hackett Fischer, *Albion's Seed*, pp. 367-368; Lewis C. Gray, *History of Agriculture in the Southern United States to 1860*, Vol. I, pp. 460, 496; Forrest McDonald, "Cultural Continuity and the Shaping of the American South," *Geographic Perspectives in History*, edited by Eugene D. Genovese and Leonard Hochberg, p. 233.

21. Grady McWhiney, *Cracker Culture*, pp. 90-92, 128-132.

22. Ibid., pp. 258-259.

23. Ibid., pp. 146-147; Frederick Law Olmsted, *The Cotton Kingdom*, edited by Arthur M. Schlesinger, p. 414.

24. Grady McWhiney, *Cracker Culture*, pp. 118-122.

25. See, for example, David Hackett Fischer, *Albion's Seed*, pp. 705-708; Frederick Law Olmsted, *The Cotton Kingdom*, edited by Arthur M. Schlesinger, pp. 207-211.

26. See, for example, David Hackett Fischer, *Albion's Seed*, pp. 606, 615, 668, 736, 755, 756; Frederick Law Olmsted, *The Cotton Kingdom*, edited by Arthur M. Schlesinger, p. 555.

27. David Hackett Fischer, *Albion's Seed*, p. 621.

28. Frederick Law Olmsted, *The Cotton Kingdom*, p. 12.

29. David Hackett Fischer, *Albion's Seed*, p. 615.

30. Grady McWhiney, *Cracker Culture*, p. 257.

31. David Hackett Fischer, *Albion's Seed*, pp. 737-738.
32. Philip E. Vernon, *Intelligence and Cultural Environment* (London: Metheun & Co., 1970), p. 154.
33. Grady McWhiney, *Cracker Culture*, p. 163.
34. Samuel C. Hyde, Jr., "Backcountry Justice in the Piney-Woods South," *Plain Folk of the South Revisited*, edited by Samuel C. Hyde, Jr. (Baton Rouge: Louisiana State University Press), pp. 229-230.
35. Frederick Law Olmsted, *The Cotton Kingdom*, p. 555,
36. Ibid., 476n.
37. Daniel J. Boorstin, *The Americans*, Vol. II: *The National Experience* (New York: Random House, 1965), p. 208.
38. Clement Eaton, *The Freedom-of-Thought Struggle in the Old South*, p. 163.
39. Daniel J. Boorstin, *The Americans*, Vol. II, p. 210.
40. David Hackett Fischer, *Albion's Seed*, p. 756.
41. Forrest McDonald, "Prologue," Grady McWhiney, *Cracker Culture*, p. xxi.
42. Ibid., p. 30.
43. David Hackett Fischer, *Albion's Seed*, p. 633.
44. Lewis C. Gray, *History of Agriculture in the United States to 1860*, Vol. I, p. 484.
45. David Hackett Fischer, *Albion's Seed*, pp. 607, 684.
46. J. C. Furnas, *The Americans: A Social History of the United States 1587-1914* (New York: G. P. Putnam's Sons, 1969), p. 29.
47. Grady McWhiney, *Cracker Culture*. p. 147.
48. Daniel J. Boorstin, *The Americans*, Vol. II: *The National Experience*, pp. 100-101.
49. J. C. Furnas, *The Americans: A Social History of the United States 1587-1914*, p. 295.
50. Grady McWhiney, *Cracker Culture*, pp. 146-147, 148-149, 151.
51. Ibid., p. 149-150.
52. Grady McWhiney, *Cracker Culture*, p. vii. See also pp. xiv-xv; David Hackett Fischer, *Albion's Seed*, p. 758.
53. Forrest McDonald, "Prologue," Grady McWhiney, *Cracker Culture*, p. xxiv.

54. Gunnar Myrdal, *An American Dilemma: The Negro Problem and Modern Democracy* (New York: Harper & Brothers, Publishers, 1944), p. 560.

55. David Hackett Fischer, *Albion's Seed*, pp. 766-767.

56. Ibid., pp. 765, 767.

57. George Shepperson, "Scotland: The World Perspective," *The Diaspora of the British*, Collected Seminar Papers No. 31, Institute of Commonwealth Studies (London: University of London, 1982), p. 52n. See also Arthur Herman, *How the Scots Invented the Modern World* (New York: Crown Publishers, 2001), p. 108.

58. J. E. Cairnes, *The Slave Power* (New York: Harper & Row, 1969), p. 81.

59. Lewis Cecil Gray, *History of Agriculture in the Southern United States to 1860*, Vol. I, pp. 483-484.

60. Ibid., pp. 81-82, 143, 144; Frederick Law Olmsted, *The Cotton Kingdom*, pp. 64, 85, 87, 90, 147, 257, 290, 327, 391, 397, 421, 448, 527.

61. Frederick Law Olmsted, *The Cotton Kingdom*, pp. 103, 305.

62. Ibid., p. 12.

63. Frederick Law Olmsted, *The Cotton Kingdom*, pp. 168, 177, 212, 214, 220, 317, 423.

64. Grady McWhiney, *Cracker Culture*, pp. 258-259, including footnotes.

65. Lewis C. Gray, *History of Agriculture in the Southern United States to 1860*, Vol. 1, p. 47.

66. Frederick Law Olmsted, *The Cotton Kingdom*, pp. 295, 302, 540.

67. Ibid., p. 540.

68. Lewis C. Gray, *History of Agriculture in the Southern United States to 1860*, Vol. II, p. 831.

69. Ibid., p. 839.

70. Hinton Rowan Helper, *The Impending Crisis of the South*, p. 48.

71. Lewis C. Gray, *History of Agriculture in the Southern United States to 1860*, Vol. II, p. 838.

72. Ibid.

73. Ibid., pp. 838-839.

74. Robert B. Vance, *Human Geography of the South: A Study in Regional Resources and Human Agency* (Chapel Hill: University of North Carolina Press, 1932), p. 148.

75. Grady McWhiney, *Cracker Culture*, Chapter III; Rory Fitzpatrick, *God's Frontiersmen: The Scots-Irish Epic* (London: George Weidenfeld & Nicolson, Ltd. 1989), pp. 71-72.

76. Daniel J. Boorstin, *The Americans: The Colonial Experience* (New York: Random House, 1958), p. 261.

77. Rupert B. Vance, *Human Geography of the South: A Study in Regional Resources and Human Adequacy* (Chapel Hill: University of North Carolina Press, 1932), p. 148.

78. Ibid., p. 168.

79. Ibid., pp. 168, 175.

80. Grady McWhiney, *Cracker Culture*, p. 19; Virginia Brainard Kunz, *The Germans in America* (Minneapolis: Lerner Publication Co., 1966), pp. 11-12.

81. Rupert B. Vance, *Human Geography of the South*, p. 106.

82. Alexis de Tocqueville, *Democracy in America* (New York: Alfred A. Knopf, 1945), Vol. I, pp. 362-363.

83. Robert E. Lee, *Lee's Dispatches: Unpublished letters of General Robert E. Lee, C.S.A. to Jefferson Davis and the War Department of the Confederate States of America*, edited by Douglas Southall Freeman, New Edition (New York: G. P. Putnam's Sons, 1957), p. 8.

84. Ulrich Bonnell Phillips, *The Slave Economy of the Old South: Selected Essays in Economic and Social History*, edited by Eugene D. Genovese (Baton Rouge: Louisiana State University Press, 1968), p. 107.

85. See Ibid., Chapter II, *passim*.

86. Grady McWhiney, *Cracker Culture*, pp. 256-258.

87. Ibid., p. 256.

88. Clement Eaton, *The Freedom-of-Thought Struggle in the Old South*, p.259.

89. Grady McWhiney, *Cracker Culture*, pp. 253-258.

90. David Hackett Fischer, *Albion's Seed*, pp. 367-368.

91. Ibid., p. 360.

92. Grady McWhiney, *Cracker Culture*, p. 256.

93. Frederick Law Olmstead, *The Cotton Kingdom*, p. 8.
94. Rupert B. Vance, *Human Geography of the South*, p. 301.
95. Ibid., p. 304
96. Ibid., p. 304.
97. Lewis C. Gray, *History of Agriculture in the Southern United States to 1860*, Vol. I, p. 5.
98. Ibid., p. 23.
99. Ibid., Vol., I, pp. 188-190; Ibid., Vol. II,, p. 825.
100. Ibid., Vol. II, p. 826.
101. Rupert D. Vance, *Human Geography of the South*, p. 127.
102. Grady McWhiney, *Cracker Culture*, p. 258.
103. Ibid., p. 254.
104. David Hackett Fischer, *Albion's Seed*, p. 624.
105. Ibid., p. 663.
106. William Cabell Bruce, *John Randolph of Roanoke: 1773-1833* (New York: Octagon Books, 1970), Vol. I, p. 136.
107. Rupert B. Vance, *Human Geography of the South*, p. 451.
108. Grady McWhiney, *Cracker Culture*, p. 49.
109. Daniel J. Boorstin, *The Americans*, Vol. I: *The Colonial Experience* (New York: Random House, 1958), pp. 302, 303, 344.
110. Grady McWhiney, *Cracker Culture*, p. 196.
111. David Hackett Fischer, *Albion's Seed*, pp. 722, 723.
112. Hinton Rowan Helper, *The Impending Crisis of the South*, p. 338.
113. Clement Eaton, *The Freedom-of-Thought Struggle in the Old South*, p. 261.
114. Hinton Rowan Helper, *The Impending Crisis of the South*, p. 337.
115. David Hackett Fischer, *Albion's Seed*, p. 133.
116. Grady McWhiney, *Cracker Culture*, p. 253. As of 1860, the total population of the South was 39 percent of the total population of the United States. Since slaves were about one-third of the population of the South, and were usually in no position to invent, that leaves white Southerners as 26 percent of the total population of the country and approximately one-third of the white population. For population statistics, see Lewis Cecil Gray, *History of Agriculture in the Southern United States to 1860*, pp. 656, 811.

117. Grady McWhiney, *Cracker Culture*, p. 253.

118. Frederick Law Olmsted, *The Cotton Kingdom*, p. 615.

119. H.J. Butcher, *Human Intelligence: Its Nature and Assessment* (New York: Harper & Row, 1968), p. 252. In 1968, blacks from Rhode Island and Wisconsin scored higher on the Armed Forces Qualifications Test than whites from Tennessee and Kentucky. Arthur R. Jensen, *Educability and Group Differences* (New York: Harper & Row, 1973), pp. 63-64. For a critique of the World War I data, see Audrey M. Shuey, *The Testing of Negro Intelligence* 2nd edition (New York: Social Science Press, 1966), pp. 310-311.

120. Charles Murray, *Human Accomplishment: The Pursuit of Excellence in the Arts and Sciences, 800 B.C. to 1950* (New York: HarperCollins, 2003), p. 306.

121. Arthur Jensen has suggested that particular regional subgroups of Southern whites might be biologically less capable mentally as a result of in-breeding, especially "relatively isolated groups in the 'hollows' of Appalachia." Arthur R. Jensen, *Educability and Group Differences*, p. 61. But this seems hardly likely to account for lower mental test scores for whites in whole Southern states.

122. Grady McWhiney, *Cracker Culture*, pp. 175-177; David Hackett Fischer, *Albion's Seed*, p. 682.

123. David Hackett Fischer, *Albion's Seed*, p. 89.

124. Ibid., pp. 681-682

125. Ibid., pp. 90-91.

126. Ibid., pp. 75, 284.

127. Ibid., p. 304.

128. Ibid., p. 304.

129. Grady McWhiney, *Cracker Culture*, p. 191.

130. David Hackett Fischer, *Albion's Seed*, p. 705.

131. Frederick Law Olmsted, *The Cotton Kingdom*, pp. 207-208.

132. For the description of such preachers in eighteenth century Virginia see Daniel J. Boorstin, *The Americans*, Vol I: *The Colonial Experience*, p. 135. For a very similar description of preaching in eighteenth century Scotland, see David Hackett Fischer, *Albion's Seed*, p. 706.

133. David Hackett Fischer, *Albion's Seed*, pp. 121-122.

134. Ibid., pp. 125-126.

135. Ibid., p. 127.

136. Grady McWhiney, *Cracker Culture*, p. 186.

137. Ibid., p. 191; Frank L. Owsley, *Plain Folk of the Old South* (Baton Rouge: Louisiana State University Press, 1982), p. 97.

138. David Hackett Fischer, *Albion's Seed*, p. 706.

139. Grady McWhiney, *Cracker Culture*, p. 179.

140. Ibid., p. 188.

141. Ibid., p. 183.

142. Ibid., p. 85.

143. *Ibid.*, pp. 256-264, 653-654. See also Lewis M. Killian, *White Southerners*, revised edition (Amherst: University of Massachusetts, 1985), p. 100.

144. David Hackett Fischer, *Albion's Seed*, p. 257. "The speech of the plain folk and that of the more cultivated Southern people was basically the same," according to another historian. Frank L. Owsley, *Plain Folk of the Old South*, p. 93.

145. David Hackett Fischer, *Albion's Seed*, 256-258; Frank L. Owsley, *Plain Folk of the Old South*, p. 92.

146. David Crystal, *The Cambridge Encyclopedia of the English Language* (Cambridge: Cambridge University Press, 1995), p. 319.

147. Lawrence Otis Graham, *Our Kind of People: Inside America's Black Upper Class* (New York: Harper Collins, 1999), pp. 215-216.

148. David Hackett Fischer, *Albion's Seed*, p. 282.

149. W. E. B. Du Bois, *The Philadelphia Negro: A Social Study* (New York: Schocken Books, 1970), p. 178.

150. Jacob Riis, *How the Other Half Lives* (Cambridge, Massachusetts: Harvard University Press, 1970), p. 102.

151. Gunnar Myrdal, *An American Dilemma:*, pp. 701, 763.

152. Ibid., p. 208.

153. Ibid., p. 959.

154. Ibid., p. 976.

155. Ibid., p. 965.

156. Ibid., p. 938.

157. Ibid., p. 962.

158. Frank L. Owsley, *Plain Folk of the Old South*, p. 92.

159. George Brown Tindall, *The Ethnic Southerners* (Baton Rouge: Louisiana State University Press, 1976), p. 20

160. Dinesh D'Souza, *The End of Racism: Principles for a Multicultural Society* (New York: The Free Press, 1995), p. 261.

161. Ibid., p. 503.

162. Ibid., p. 16.

163. John Perazzo, *The Myths That Divide Us: How Lies Have Poisoned American Race Relations*, second edition (Briarcliff Manor, N.Y.: World Studies Books, 1999), pp. 401-402.

164. Shelby Steele, *The Content of Our Character: A New Vision of Race in America* (New York: St. Martin's Press, 1990), p. 51.

165. Ibid., pp. 26-27.

166. See, for example, Robert Klitgaard, *Choosing Elites: Selecting the"Best and the Brightest" at Top Universities and Elsewhere* (New York: Basic Books, 1985), pp. 104-115; Richard J. Herrnstein and Charles Murray, *The Bell Curve: Intelligence and Class Structure in American Life* (New York: The Free Press, 1994), pp. 280-281; Arthur R. Jensen, "Selection of Minority Students in Higher Education," *University of Toledo Law Review,* Spring-Summer 1970, pp. 440, 443; Donald A. Rock, "Motivation, Moderators, and Test Bias," ibid., pp. 536, 537; Ronald L. Flaugher, *Testing Practices, Minority Groups and Higher Education: A Review and Discussion of the Research* (Princeton: Educational Testing Service, 1970), p. 11; Arthur A. Jensen, *Bias in Mental Testing* (New York: The Free Press, 1980), pp. 479-490.

167. James R. Flynn, *Asian Americans: Achievement Beyond IQ* (Hillsdale, New Jersey: Lawrence Erlbaum, 1991).

168. Audrey M. Shuey, *The Testing of Negro Intelligence*, 2nd edition, pp. 468, 499; H.J. Eysenck, *The I.Q. Argument* (New York: The Library Press, 1971), pp. 23, 84. Some have explained this difference culturally and others have explained it genetically by the selective migration of more intelligent blacks from the South to the North. There is some evidence that those blacks who migrated from the South to the North had higher test scores even before they migrated but there is also evidence that the I.Q.s of South-

ern blacks rose after they moved to the North. See H. J. Butcher, *Human Intelligence: Its Nature and Assessment* (New York: Harper & Row, Publishers, 1968), p. 252; Alice S. McAlpin, "Changing in the Intelligence Quotients of Negro Children," *Journal of Negro Education*, April 1932, pp. 44-48.

169. E. Franklin Frazier, *The Negro in the United States,* revised edition (New York: The Macmillan Co., 1971), p. 484.

170. Clifford Kirkpatrick, *Intelligence and Immigration* (Baltimore: The Williams and Wilkins Co., 1926), p. 24; Rudolf Pintner and Ruth Keller, "Intelligence Tests of Foreign Children," *Journal of Educational Psychology*, Vol. 13, p. 215; Nathaniel D. Mittron Hirsch, "A Study of Natio-Racial Mental Differences," *Genetic Psychology Monographs*, Vol. 1, Nos. 3 and 4 (May and July, 1926), pp. 287, 320.

171. Rudolf Pintner and Ruth Keller, "Intelligence Tests of Foreign Children," *Journal of Educational Psychology*, Vol. 13, p. 215; Nathaniel D. Mittron Hirsch, "A Study of Natio-Racial Mental Differences," *Genetic Psychology Monographs*, Vol. 1, Nos. 3 and 4 (May and July, 1926), pp. 287, 320.

172. Philip E. Vernon, *Intelligence and Cultural Environment* (London: Metheun and Co., Ltd., 1970), p. 155; Lester R. Wheeler, "A Comparative Study of the Intelligence of East Tennessee Mountain Children," *Journal of Educational Psychology*, Vol. 33, No. 5 (May 1942), pp. 322, 324; H. Gordon, *Mental and Scholastic Tests Among Retarded Children* (London: Board of Education pamphlet No. 44), p. 38.

173. In principle, heredity and environment together exhaust all possible explanations of test score differences, but in practice much depends on how these two words are defined. For example, the era of mass immigration from southern Italy to the United States coincided almost exactly with the era of mass immigration of Jews from Eastern Europe to America. Both groups arrived poor and often lived in the same neighborhoods, with their children sitting side by side in the same schools. Yet for centuries even the poorest Jews had struggled to find money to buy books while in southern Italy the introduction of compulsory education set off

riots in which some school houses were burned. When the
children from these two radically different cultural backgrounds lived in the same physical surroundings and
attended the same schools, did they have the same environment? If so, then their very different performances in school
would have to be attributed to heredity. But, if environment
includes their cultural heritages, an entirely different conclusion emerges. For a record of the IQs of Jewish and
Italian children attending the same school over a period of
more than 20 years, see page 24 of my article "Assumptions
versus History in Ethnic Education" in the Fall 1981 issue
of *Teachers College Record*, published at the Teachers College, Columbia University.

174. Ivan Light, *Ethnic Enterprise in America: Business and Wel-
fare Among Chinese, Japanese and Blacks* (Berkeley:
University of California Press, 1972), pp. 33-35; Nathan
Glazer and Daniel Patrick Moynihan, *Beyond the Melting
Pot*, second edition (Cambridge, Massachusetts: The M.I.T.
Press, 1970), p. 35; Gilbert Osofsky, *Harlem: The Making of
a Ghetto: Negro New York, 1890-1930* (New York: Harper &
Row, 1966), p. 133; Claude McKay, *Harlem: Negro Metropo-
lis* (New York: Harcourt, Brace, Jovanovich, 1968), p. 93.

175. Ira De A. Reid, *The Negro Immigrant: His Background,
Characteristics and Social Adjustment, 1899-1937* (New
York: AMS Press, 1970), p. 248.

176. Ibid., p. 226.

177. Ibid., pp. 138-139.

178. Ibid., p. 120.

179. Ibid., p. 35.

180. Nancy Foner, "West Indians in New York City and London: A
Comparative Analysis," *International Migration Review*,
Summer 1979, p. 285.

181. Computed from data in Thomas Sowell, "Three Black Histories," *Essays and Data on American Ethnic Groups*, edited
by Thomas Sowell (Washington: The Urban Institute, 1978),
p. 43.

182. Ibid., p. 44.

183. An argument has been made that "data from the 1980 cen-

sus are unambiguous in reporting that foreign-born blacks
earned just about as much as native blacks and that both
groups earned about 20 percent less than comparable
whites" and that this is evidence for "the hypothesis that
racial discrimination accounts for the current economic status of blacks." Reynolds Farley and Walter R. Allen, *The Color
Line and the Quality of Life in America* (New York: Russell Sage Foundation, 1987), p. 403. But the 1980 census data
do not distinguish between new arrivals from the
Caribbean and those who have been in the country for
many years, including those West Indians who were born
in the United States. However, the later censuses on which
these critics have relied have not distinguished new West
Indian immigrants from those born in the United States—
and immigration from the Caribbean increased greatly in
later years, as a result of changes in American immigration
laws. As of 1980, the majority of immigrants from the
Caribbean had arrived in the United States within the previous 15 years. Philip Kasintz, *Caribbean New York: Black
Immigrants and the Politics of Race* (Ithaca: Cornell University Press, 1992), p. 54. Other research has shown that
immigrants from a wide variety of groups begin with below-
average incomes and then rise over a period of years above
the incomes of native-born people of the same ethnicity.
Barry Chiswick, "The Economic Progress of Immigrants:
Some Apparently Universal Patterns," in *Contemporary Economic Problems*, ed. William Fellner (Washington, D.C.:
American Enterprise Institute, 1979), p. 374. Comparing
immigrants in transition with long settled natives is comparing apples and oranges.

184. Sara Rimer and Karen W. Arenson, "Top Colleges Take More
Blacks, But Which Ones?" *New York Times*, June 24, 2004,
pp. A1, A18.

185. Charles Murray, *Losing Ground: American Social Policy
1950-1980* (New York: Basic Books, 1994), pp. 116-117.

186. Stephan Thernstrom and Abigail Thernstrom, *America in
Black and White: One Nation, Indivisible* (New York:
Simon & Schuster, 1997), p. 239.

187. Ibid., p. 138.
188. Ibid., p. 240.
189. Much has been made of the fact that information given to the census by black women in the past is inconsistent with demographic facts which suggest that many of these women may have been unwed mothers while reporting themselves to the census as "widows." While this would bias census data on unwed mothers, no comparable data or motive can explain why far more black *men* would have reported themselves as married in the past as compared to the present.
190. U.S. Bureau of the Census, *Changing Characteristics of the Negro Population* by Daniel O. Price, pp. 224, 225. See also Herbert G. Gutman, *The Black Family in Slavery and Freedom 1750-1925* (New York: Vintage Books, 1976), pp. 445, 452.
191. *Ibid.*, p. 305.
192. E. Franklin Frazier, *The Negro in the United States*, p. 314; Herbert Gutman, *The Black Family in Slavery and Freedom, 1750-1925* (New York: Vintage Books, 1976), pp. 204-207.
193. James M. McPherson, *The Abolitionist Legacy: From Reconstruction to the NAACP* (Princeton: Princeton University Press, 1975), p. 198.
194. Johnetta Cross Brazzell, "Bricks without Straw: Missionary-Sponsored Higher Education in the Post-Emancipation Era," *Journal of Higher Education*, January-February 1992, p. 30.
195. James M. McPherson, *The Abolitionist Legacy*, Chapter 10.
196. E. Franklin Frazier, *Black Bourgeoisie: The Rise of a New Middle Class in the United States* (New York: Collier Books, 1962), p. 65.
197. Ibid., p. 56.
198. Ibid., pp. 70, 71.
199. Ibid, p. 71.
200. President Wm. W. Patton, "Change of Environment," *The American Missionary*, August 1882, p. 229.
201. Ibid., p. 230.
202. James D. Anderson, *The Education of Blacks in the South,*

1860-1935 (Chapel Hill: University of North Carolina Press, 1988), p. 46.

203. "Principal of the Hampton Institute at the Anniversary Meeting of the American Missionary Association at Syracuse, N.Y., October 24, 1877," *Southern Workman*, Vol. VI, December 1977, pp. 94-95.

204. James M. McPherson, *The Abolitionist Legacy*, p. 168.

205. E. Franklin Frazier, *The Negro in the United States*, pp. 422, 458.

206. James M. McPherson, *The Abolitionist Legacy*, p. 198.

207. Ibid., p. 161.

208. Ibid., p. 178. Greek seems to have been given great importance in those days and South Carolina's antebellum Senator John C. Calhoun opined that he would be willing to concede the humanity of black people if he could find one who could parse Greek. How diligently he looked is not known but it was after the Civil War—and after Calhoun's death—before there were enough educated blacks to make this a real possibility. Ironically, the first black man to graduate from Harvard, in 1870, taught Greek at the University of South Carolina. Another black man, a graduate of Dartmouth, taught Greek at the University of Mississippi. See Allison Blackely, "Richard T. Greener and the 'Talented Tenth's' Dilemma," *Journal of Negro History*, October 1974, p. 307; Horace Mann Bond, *The Education of the Negro in the American Social Order* (New York: Octagon Books, 1966) p. 146.

209. Ibid., p. 162. See also James H. Fairchild, *Oberlin: The Colony and the College 1833-1883* (Oberlin: E. J. Goodrich, 1883), pp. 9-10.

210. See The Atlanta University Publications, No. 15, *The College-Bred Negro American*, edited by W. E. Burghardt Du Bois and Augustus Granville Dill (Atlanta: The Atlanta University Press, 1910), pp. 48-49.

211. James M. McPherson, *The Abolitionist Legacy*, pp. 196-198.

212. Maldwyn Allen Jones, *American Immigration* (Chicago: University of Chicago Press, 1970), pp. 13, 32; John Hope Franklin, *From Slavery to Freedom: A History of Negro Americans* (New York: Vintage Books, 1967), p. 71.

213. John Hope Franklin, *From Slavery to Freedom*, pp. 71-72.

214. Ibid., p. 217.

215. Ulrich Bonnell Phillips, *American Negro Slavery: A Survey of the Supply, Employment and Control of Negro Labor As Determined by the Slave Regime* (Baton Rouge: Louisiana State University Press, 1969), p. 426. In addition, laws in many places became more protective of the slave and less restrictive of "free persons of color" in the years following the American revolution. See, for example, Lewis C. Gray, *History of Agriculture in the Southern United States to 1860*, Vol. I., pp. 514, 526.

216. Bureau of the Census, *Negro Population: 1790-1915* (Washington, D.C.: U.S. Government Printing Office, 1918), p. 41.

217. Ibid., p. 55. In Mississippi, for example, the number of slaves more than doubled between 1840 and 1860, while the number of "free persons" of color" was nearly halved during those same years. In Arkansas, the number of slaves increased fivefold during those same years while the number of free Negroes fell by more than two-thirds. Ibid., p. 57.

218. E. Franklin Frazier, *The Negro in the United States*, p. 65.

219. Wilbur Zelinsky, "The Population Geography of the Free Negro in Anti-Bellum America," *Population Studies*, March 1950, p. 287.

220. Carter G. Woodson, *The Education of the Negro Prior to 1861* (New York: Arno Press, 1968), pp. 227-228; U.S. Bureau of the Census, *Historical Statistics of the United States, Colonial Times to 1970* (Washington, D.C.: U.S. Government Printing Office, 1975), Part I, p. 382; *The Seventh Census of the United States: 1850*, pp. xliii, lxi.

221. Wilbur Zelinsky, "The Population Geography of the Free Negro in Anti-Bellum America," *Population Studies*, March 1950, p. 387; Reynolds Farley, "The Urbanization of Negroes in the United States," *Journal of Social History*, Spring 1968, p. 255.

222. See Thomas Sowell, "Three Black Histories," in *Essays and Data on American Ethnic Groups*, ed. Thomas Sowell (Washington, D.C.: The Urban Institute, 1978), pp. 12-13.

223. See, for example, Edward Byron Reuter, *The Mulatto in the*

United States: Including a Study of the Rôle of Mixed-Blood Races Throughout the World (Boston: Richard G. Badger, 1918) *passim*; Willard B. Gatewood, *Aristocrats of Color: The Black Elite, 1880-1920* (Bloomington: Indiana University Press, 1990), pp. 13, 20, 88, 100-101, 108, 127.

224. See, for example, Willard B. Gatewood, *Aristocrats of Color*, p. 116.

225. Ibid., p. 4.

226. Ibid., p. 18; E. Delorus Preston, Jr., "William Syphax: A Pioneer in Negro Education in the District of Columbia," *Journal of Negro History*, October 1935, pp. 448-450.

227. Robert Samuel Fletcher, *A History of Oberlin College: From Its Foundation Through the Civil War* (Oberlin: Oberlin College, 1943), pp. 528-529.

228. See Willard B. Gatewood, *Aristocrats of Color*, *passim*; Theodore Hershberg and Henry Williams, "Mulattoes and Blacks: Intra-group Color Differences and Social Stratification in Nineteenth-Century Philadelphia," *Philadelphia: Work, Space, Family, and Group Experience in the Nineteenth Century*, edited by Theodore Hershberg (Oxford: Oxford University Press, 1981), pp. 392-394; Adele Logan Alexander, *Ambiguous Lives: Free Women of Color in Rural Georgia* (Fayetteville: University of Arkansas Press, 1991), pp. 173-175, 197-200.

229. Theodore Hershberg and Henry Williams, "Mulattoes and Blacks: Intra-group Color Differences and Social Stratification in Nineteenth-Century Philadelphia," *Philadelphia*, edited by Theodore Hershberg, pp. 494-495.

230. *Ibid.*, p. 407.

231. *Ibid.*, p. 416.

232. See, for example, William B. Gatewood, *Aristocrats of Color: The Black Elite, 1880-1920*, especially pp. 149-181. See also Gunnar Myrdal, *An American Dilemma*, pp. 695-700; E. Franklin Frazier, *The Negro in the United States*, revised edition (New York: The Macmillan Co., 1971), pp. 283n, 289-291; Bernard E. Powers, Jr. *Black Charlestonians: A Social History, 1822-1885* (Fayetteville: University of Arkansas Press 1994), pp. 185-186; Stephen Birmingham,

Certain People: America's Black Elite (Boston: Little, Brown, and Co., 1977), pp. 70-71, 130-131.

233. Willard B. Gatewood, *Aristocrats of Color*, p. 190.

234. Ibid., pp. 153, 157, 169, 171, 181, 345.

235. Carter G. Woodson *The Education of the Negro Prior to 1861*, p. 239.

236. Ibid., Chapter X.

237. Jacob Riis, *How the Other Half Lives*, p. 99; David Katzman, *Before the Ghetto* (Urbana: University of Illinois Press, 1975), pp. 35,37, 102, 138, 139, 160; St. Clair Drake and Horace B. Cayton, *Black Metropolis* (New York: Harcourt, Brace and World, 1970), Vol. I, pp. 44-45 ; Willard B. Gatewood, *Aristocrats of Color*, p. 125.

238. E. Franklin Frazier, *The Negro in the United States*, p. 192.

239. Ibid., p. 230.

240. Carter G. Woodson, *A Century of Negro Migration* (New York: AMS Press, 1970), p. 180.

241. Willard B. Gatewood, *Aristocrats of Color*, pp. 186-187, 332; Allan H. Spear, *Black Chicago* (Chicago: University of Chicago Press, 1967), p. 168; E. Franklin Frazier, *The Negro in the United States*, pp. 284-285; Florette Henri, *Black Migration: Movement North, 1900-1920* (New York: Anchor Books, 1976), pp. 96-97; Gilbert Osofsky, *Harlem: The Making of a Ghetto*, pp. 43-44; Ivan H. Light, *Ethnic Enterprise in America* (Berkeley: University of California Press, 1972), Figure 1 (after p. 100); W.E.B. BuBois, *The Black North in 1901:A Social Study* (New York: Arno Press, 1969), p.25.

242. E. Franklin Frazier, *The Negro in the United States*, p. 643.

243. Ibid., p. 630.

244. David M. Katzman, *Before the Ghetto*, p. 26. See also pp. 55, 69, 73.

245. St. Clair Drake and Horace R. Cayton, *Black Metropolis*, Vol. I, p. 176n. See also Allan H. Spear, *Black Chicago* (Chicago: University of Chicago Press, 1970), Chapter 1.

246. Gilbert Osofsky, *Harlem: The Making of a Ghetto*, p. 12; W.E.B. Du Bois, *The Philadelphia Negro*, p. 7; Constance Green, *The Secret City: A History of Race Relations in the*

Nation's Capital (Princeton: Princeton University Press, 1967), p. 127.

247. Stephen Birmingham, *Certain People:America's Black Elite* (Boston: Little, Brown and Company, 1977), p. 186. See also Jeffrey S. Gurock, *When Harlem was Jewish 1870-1930* (New York: Columbia University Press, 1979).

248. Florette Henri, *Black Migration: Movement North, 1900-1920* (Garden City, N.Y.:Anchor Books, 1976), pp. 17, 86.

249. Willard B. Gatewood,*Aristocrats of Color*, p. 250; E. Franklin Frazier, *The Negro in the United States*, p. 441.

250. Willard B. Gatewood, *Aristocrats of Color* (Bloomington: Indiana University Press,1990), p. 65; E. Franklin Frazier, *The Negro in the United States*, pp. 250-251.

251. W. E. B. Du Bois, *The Black North in 1901*, p. 39.

252. Ibid., pp. 39, 40.

253. Ibid., p. 168.

254. Ibid., pp. 171, 173.

255. Ibid., p. 174.

256. Ibid., p. 173.

257. E. Franklin Frazier, *The Negro in the United States*, p. 270.

258. Stephan Thernstrom and Abigail Thernstrom,*America in Black and White: One Nation, Indivisible* (New York: Simon & Schuster, 1997), p. 233.

259. Orley Ashenfelter,"Changes in Labor Market Discrimination Over Time," *Journal of Human Resources*, Fall 1970), p. 405.

260. James P. Smith and Finis Welch, *Race Differences in Earnings* (Santa Monica, California:The Rand Corporation, 1978), p. 15.

261. Arnold Rampersad,*Jackie Robinson:A Biography* (New York:Alfred A. Knopf, 1977), p. 188.

262. See Thomas Sowell, *Civil Rights: Rhetoric or Reality?* (New York:William Morrow and Co., 1984), p.49.

263. U.S. Bureau of the Census, *Changing Characteristics of the Negro Population* by Daniel O. Price, pp. 117, 118, 133.

264. U. S. Bureau of the Census, *Historical Statistics of the United States: Colonial Times to 1970* (Washington: U.S. Government Printing Office, 1975), p. 381.

265. W. E. B. Du Bois, *The Black North in 1901*, p. 26.

266. Quoted by Dinesh D'Souza, *The End of Racism: Principles for a Multicultural Society* (New York: The Free Press, 1995), p.339.

267. Jonathan D. Glater, "Law Firms Are Slow in Promoting Minority Lawyers to Partner Role," *New York Times*, August 7, 2001, pp. 1 ff.

268. Dinesh D'Souza, *The End of Racism*, p. 250.

269. Ibid., pp. 250-252.

270. See, for example, Heather Mac Donald, *Are Cops Racist? How the War Against the Police Harms Black Americans* (Chicago: Ivan R. Dee, 2003), pp. 27, 30-31, 61, 90-91, 122.

271. Jim Sleeper, *Liberal Racism: How Fixating on Race Subverts the American Dream* (Lanham, Md.: Rowman & Littlefield, 2001), p. 73.

272. Dinesh D'Souza, *The End of Racism*, p. 414.

273. Ibid., pp. 414-415.

274. John H. McWhorter, "How Hip-Hop Holds Blacks Back," *City Journal*, Summer 2003, p. 72.

275. James Sullivan, "Tupac's Messages are Given New Life," *San Francisco Chronicle*, November 14, 2003, p. 15.

276. "Rappers' Violent Link Stretches into Society," *USA Today*, March 11, 1997, p. 10A.

277. Michael Lewis, "Common Ground," *The New Republic*, September 30, 1996, p. 26.

278. Mikal Gilmore, "Easy Target," *Rolling Stone*, October 28, 1999, p. 49.

279. Mike Barnicle, "Lyrics Reflect a Bleak Reality," *Boston Globe*, June 6, 1995, p. 17.

280. Jon Pareles, "Pop Culture Views; Rapping and Politicking: Show Time on the Stump," *New York Times*, June 11, 1995, Section 2, p. 32.

281. U.S. Bureau of the Census, *Changing Characteristics of the Negro Population* by Daniel O. Price (Washington: U.S. Government Printing Office, 1969), p. 44.

282. Ralph Ellison called this using blacks as a "receptacle" for "one's own infantile rebellions." Ralph Ellison, *Shadow and Act* (New York: Vintage International, 1964), p. 124.

283. See Ibid., pp. 107-143.
284. Best-selling black author John H. McWhorter, for example, refers to the "cocky, confrontational cadence" of hip-hop or gangsta rap. John H. McWhorter, "How Hip-Hop Holds Blacks Back," *City Journal*, Summer 2003, p.73.
285. Daniel J. Boorstin, *The Americans,* Vol. II: *The National Experience* (New York: Random House, 1965), p. 213.
286. Peter Kolchin, *A Sphinx on the American Land:The Nineteenth Century South in Comparative Perspective* (Baton Rouge: Louisiana State University Press, 2003), p. 39.
287. Ibid., p. 27.
288. Eric Hoffer, *The Passionate State of Mind* (Cutchogue, NY: Buccaneer Books, 1955), p. 111.
289. Eric Hoffer, *Before the Sabbath* (New York: Harper & Row, 1979), p. 137.

Are Jews Generic?
1. Victor Purcell, *The Chinese in Southeast Asia*, second edition, (Kuala Lumpur: Oxford University Press, 1980), p. 184.
2. See U.S. Bureau of the Census, *Historical Statistics of the United States: Colonial Times to 1970* (Washington: U.S. Government Printing Office, 1975), p. 422.
3. Victor Purcell, *The Chinese in Southeast Asia*, p. 184.
4. Solomon Grayzel, *A History of the Jews: From the Babylonian Exile to the Present, 5728-1968* (New York: Mentor Books,1968), pp. 306, 440-442; Jonathan I. Israel, *European Jewry in the Age of Mercantilism 1550-1750* (Oxford:The Clarendon Press, 1985), pp. 120-121.
5. David Marshall Lang, *The Armenians: A People in Exile* (London: George Allen & Unwin, 1981), pp. 10, 12.
6. Howard Becker, *Man in Reciprocity: Introductory Lectures on Culture, Society and Personality* (New York: Frederick A. Praeger, 1956), p. 227.
7. Ibid., p. 230.
8. David Marshall Lang, *The Armenians*, p. 79.
9. H. L. van der Laan, *The Lebanese Traders in Sierra Leone* (The Hague: Mouton & Co., 1975), pp. 40-46, 230-231.
10. Victor Purcell, *The Chinese in Southeast Asia*, pp. 195, 204, 431, 433.

11. Ibid., p. 433.

12. F. A. Hayek, *The Collected Works of F. A. Hayek*, Vol. I: *The Fatal Conceit: The Errors of Socialism*, edited by W. W. Bartley III (Chicago: University of Chicago Press, 1988), p. 91.

13. R. A. Radford, "The Economic Organization of a P.O.W. Camp," *Economica*, November 1945, p. 185.

14. Ibid., p. 199.

15. Hasia R. Diner, *The Jews of the United States 1654 to 2000* (Berkeley: University of California Press, 2004), pp. 81, 102.

16. Irving Howe, *World of Our Fathers* (New York: Harcourt Brace Jovanovich, 1976), p. 148.

17. Victor Purcell, *The Chinese in Southeast Asia*, p. 433.

18. "Indeed, if we were translating the milder Hindu epithet in as inoffensive a way as possible, we might call the Parsees clannish." Howard Becker, *Man in Reciprocity*, p. 232.

19. Gurcharan Das, *India Unbound* (New York: Alfred A. Knopf, 2001), p. 45.

20. Hasia R. Diner, *The Jews of the United States 1654 to 2000*, p. 100.

21. Ibid.

22. Ibid., p. 99.

23. Ibid., pp. 101-102.

24. Milton & Rose D. Friedman, *Two Lucky People: Memoirs* (Chicago: University of Chicago, 1998), p. 21.

25. H. L. van der Laan, *The Lebanese Traders in Sierra Leone*, p. 11.

26. Victor Purcell, *The Chinese in Southeast Asia*, p. 546.

27. Alixa Naff, "Lebanese Immigration into the United States: 1880 to the Present," *The Lebanese in the World: A Century of Emigration*, edited by Albert Hourani and Nadim Shehadi (London: I. B. Tauris & Co., Ltd., 1992), p. 157.

28. H. L. van der Laan, *The Lebanese Traders in Sierra Leone*, p. 229.

29. Ilsoo Kim, *New Urban Immigrants: The Korean Community in New York* (Princeton: Princeton University Press, 1981), p. 114.

30. Ibid., pp. 115-116, 120.

31. Pyong Gap Min, *Ethnic Business Enterprise: Korean Small*

Business in Atlanta (New York: Center for Migration Studies, 1988).

32. Alixa Naff, "Lebanese Immigration into the United States: 1880 to the Present," p. 148.

33. Antonio S. Tan, "The Changing Identity of the Philippine Chinese, 1946-1984," *Changing Identities of the Southeast Asian Chinese since World War II,* edited by Jennifer Cushman and Wang Gungwu (Hong Kong: Hong Kong University Press, 1988), p. 192.

34. Haraprasad Chattopadhyaya, *Indians in Africa: A Socio-Economic Study* (Calcutta: Bookland Pvt., Ltd., 1970), pp. 66, 263-264.

35. Robert P. Bartlett, *Human Capital: The Settlement of Foreigners in Russia 1762-1804* (Cambridge: Cambridge University Press, 1979), p. 150.

36. Victor Purcell, *The Chinese in Southeast Asia,* p. 546.

37. P.T. Bauer, *West African Trade: A Study of Competition, Oligopoly and Monopoly in a Changing Economy* (Cambridge: Cambridge University Press, 1954), p. 149. Professor Bauer defined the term "Levantine" as members of various groups from the Levant, of whom "Lebanese are numerically the most important in West Africa." Ibid., p. 9n.

38. Robert Mantran, "Foreign Merchants and the Minorities in Istanbul during the Sixteenth and Seventeenth Centuries," *Christians and Jews in the Ottoman Empire: The Functioning of a Plural Society,* edited by Benjamin Braude and Bernard Lewis, Vol. I: *The Central Lands* (New York: Holmes & Meier, 1982), p. 134.

39. Lord Kinross, *The Ottoman Centuries: The Rise and Fall of the Turkish Empire* (New York: William Morrow, 1977), p. 554.

40. Benjamin Braude and Bernard Lewis, "Introduction," *Christians and Jews in the Ottoman Empire,* Vol. I: *The Central Lands,* pp. 21, 25.

41. Charles Issawi, "The Transformation of the Economic Position of the *Millets* in the Nineteenth Century," Ibid., p. 262.

42. Ibid., pp. 11-12.

43. Ibid., p. 30.

44. Ibid.

45. Ibid., p. 31.

46. Ibid., p. 32.

47. Pyong Gap Min, *Ethnic Business Enterprise*, pp. 2, 19, 57.

48. Ibid., p. 82.

49. Th. A. Fischer, *The Scots in Germany: Being A Contribution Towards A History of the Scots Abroad* (Edinburgh: John Donald Publishers, Ltd., no date), pp. 35-36.

50. *Ibid.*, pp. 38-39, 55.

51. See, for example, Ivan Light, *Ethnic Enterprise in America: Business and Welfare Among Chinese, Japanese and Blacks* (Berkeley: University of California Press, 1972), p. 33.

52. Traian Stoianovich, "The Conquering Balkan Orthodox Merchant," *Journal of Economic History*, Vol. 20, No. 2 (June 1960), p. 304.

53. Usha Mahajani, *The Role of Indian Minorities in Burma and Malaya* (Bombay: Vora & Co., 1960), p. 29; John William Henderson, et al, *Area Handbook for Burma* (Washington: U.S. Government Printing Office, 1971), p. 238.

54. Jacob Riis, *How the Other Half Lives* (Cambridge: Harvard University Press, 1970), p. 82.

55. Selma C. Berrol, "Education and Economic Mobility: The Jewish Experience in New York City, 1880-1920," *American Jewish Historical Quarterly*, March 1976, p. 262.

56. Robert P. Bartlett, *Human Capital*, p. 151.

57. Robert Mantran, "Foreign Merchants and the Minorities in Istanbul during the Sixteenth and Seventeenth Centuries," *Christians and Jews in the Ottoman Empire*, Vol. I: *The Central Lands*, p. 130; Charles Issawi, "The Transformation of the Economic Position of the *Millets* in the Nineteenth Century," Ibid., p. 263; Vahé Baladouni, "Introduction," *Armenian Merchants of the Seventeenth and Early Eighteenth Centuries: English East India Company Sources*, edited by Vahé Baladouni and Margaret Makepeace (Philadelphia: American Philosophical Society, 1998), pp. xxxiii-xxiv.

58. Joel Kotkin, *Tribes: How Race, Religion and Identity Determine Success in the New Global Economy* (New York: Random House, 1993), p. 192.

59. Clark S. Knowlton, "The Social and Spatial Mobility of the Syrian and Lebanese Community in São Paulo, Brazil" *The Lebanese in the World*, p. 300.

60. Jeff H. Lesser, "From Pedlars to Proprietors: Lebanese, Syrian and Jewish Immigrants in Brazil," *The Lebanese in the World,* p. 403.

61. Ibid., p. 370.

62. Albert Hourani, "Introduction," *The Lebanese in the World*, p. 8.

63. H. L. van der Laan, *The Lebanese Traders in Sierra Leone*, pp. 41, 105-106; Neil O. Leighton, "Lebanese Emigration: Its Effect on the Political Economy of Sierra Leone," *The Lebanese in the World*, p. 586; Estela Valverde, "Integration and Identity in Argentina: The Lebanese of Tucuman," Ibid., p. 318; Louise L'Estragne Fawcett, "Lebanese, Palestinians and Syrians in Colombia," Ibid., p. 369; Alixa Naff, "Lebanese Immigration to the United States: 1880 to the Present," Ibid., pp. 145-148; Clark S. Knowlton, "The Social and Spatial Mobility of the Syrian and Lebanese Community in Sào Paulo, Brazil," Ibid., p. 293; David Nicholls, "Lebanese of the Antilles: Haiti, Dominican Republic, Jamaica and Trinidad," Ibid., pp. 345, 352, 355; Andrew Batrouney and Tevor Batrouney, *The Lebanese in Australia* (Melbourne: Australasian Educa Press, 1985), p. 42.

64. Trevor Batrouney, "The Lebanese in Australia, 1880-1989," *The Lebanese in the World*, p. 426.

65. Vahé Baladouni, "Introduction," *Armenian Merchants in the Seventeenth and Early Eighteenth Centuries*, pp. xxvii-xxix.

66. Albert Hourani, "Introduction," *The Lebanese in the World*, p. 7.

67. Estela Valverde, "Integration in Argentina: The Lebanese of Tucuman," *The Lebanese in the World*, p. 317; H. L. van der Laan, *The Lebanese Traders in Sierra Leone*, pp. 242, 276.

68. H. L. van der Laan, *The Lebanese Traders in Sierra Leone*, pp. 191-192. See also p. 43.

69. Renée Rose Shield, *Diamond Stories: Enduring Change on 47th Street* (Ithaca, N.Y.: Cornell University Press, 2002), p. 102.

70. Janet T. Landa, "The Political Economy of the Ethnically Homogeneous Chinese Middleman Group in Southeast Asia: Ethnicity and Entrepreneurship in a Plural Society," *The Chinese in Southeast Asia,* edited by Linda Y. C. Lim and L. A. Peter Gosling (Singapore: Maruzen Asis Pte. Ltd., 1983), Vol. I, pp. 90–93.

71. Vahé Baladouni, "Introduction," *Armenian Merchants of the Seventeenth and Early Eighteenth Centuries,* p. xxiv.

72. Irving Howe, *World of Our Fathers,* p. 230.

73. Ibid., p. 229.

74. Ibid., pp. 110, 111.

75. Albert S. Lindemann, *Esau's Tears: Modern anti-Semitism and the Rise of the Jews* (Cambridge: Cambridge University Press, 1997), p. 45.

76. Rajeswary Brown, "Chettiar Capital and Southeast Asian Credit Networks in the Interwar Period," *Local Suppliers of Credit in the Third World, 1750-1960* (New York: St. Martin's Press, 1993), p. 274.

77. Trevor Batrouney, "The Lebanese in Australia, 1880-1989," p. 424.

78. H. L. van der Laan, *The Lebanese Traders in Sierra Leone,* p. 245. See also p. 310.

79. Albert Hourani, "Introduction," *The Lebanese in the World,* p. 9; Michael Humphrey, "Sectarianism and the politics of Identity: The Lebanese in Sydney," Ibid., p. 444.

80. Joel Kotkin, *Tribes: How Race, Religion, and Identity Determine Success in the New Global Economy,* pp. 227-228.

81. Pierre L. van den Berghe, "Asian Africans before and after Independence," *Kroniek Van Afrika* (Netherlands), New Series, Vol. III, No. 6 (1975), p. 198.

82. Kemal H. Karpat, "*Millets* and Nationality: The Roots of the Incongruity of Nation and State in the Post-Ottoman Era, *Christians and Jews in the Ottoman Empire,* Vol. I, p. 164.

83. Charles Murray, *Human Accomplishment: The Pursuit of Excellence in the Arts and Sciences, 800 BC to 1950* (New York: HarperCollins, 2004), p. 291.

84. Selma C. Berrol, "Education and Economic Mobility: The Jewish Experience in New York City, 1880-1920," *American Jewish Historical Quarterly,* March 1976, p. 261.

85. Stanley Feldstein and Lawrence Costello, *The Ordeal of Assimilation* (New York: Anchor Books, 1974), pp. 122-123. See also Irving Howe and Kenneth Libo, *How We Lived* (New York: Richard Marek Publishers, 1979), p. 204.

86. Clark S. Knowlton, "The Social and Spatial Mobility of the Syrian and Lebanese Community in Sào Paulo, Brazil," p. 298; Luz Maria Martinez Montiel, "The Lebanese Community in Mexico: Its Meaning, Importance and the History of its Communities," Ibid., pp. 380, 385.

87. H. L. van der Laan, *The Lebanese Traders in Sierra Leone*, p. 249.

88. Victor Purcell, *The Chinese in Southeast Asia*, p. 452.

89. Ibid., p. 46.

90. David Nicholls, "Lebanese of the Antilles: Haiti, Dominican Republic, Jamaica, and Trinidad," *The Lebanese in the World*, p. 354.

91. Peter Pulzer, *The Rise of Political Anti-Semitism in Germany and Austria* (Cambridge, Massachusetts: Harvard University Press, 1988), p. 11.

92. James R. Flynn, *Asian Americans: Achievement Beyond IQ* (Hillsdale, New Jersey: Lawrence Erlbaum, 1991).

93. Feroz Ahmad, "Unionist Relations with the Greek, Armenian, and Jewish Communities of the Ottoman, 1908-1914," *Christians and Jews in the Ottoman Empire*, pp. 411, 412.

94. Alec Nove and J. A. Newth, *The Soviet Middle East: A Communist Model for Development* (New York: Frederick A. Praeger, 1967) p. 83.

95. Boutros Labaki, "Lebanese Emigration During the War (1975-1989)," *The Lebanese in the World*, p. 625.

96. Clark S. Knowlton, "The Social and Spatial Mobility of the Syrian and Lebanese Community in Sào Paulo, Brazil," p. 305.

97. See, for example, Bill C. Malone, "Neither Anglo-Saxon Nor Celtic: The Music of the Southern Plain Folk," *Plain Folk of the South Revisited,* edited by Samuel C. Hyde, Jr. (Baton Rouge: Louisiana State University Press, 1997), p. 21.

98. Victor A. Mirelman, *Jewish Buenos Aires, 1890-1930: In Search of an Identity* (Detroit: Wayne State University Press, 1990), pp. 197-204.

99. Albert S. Lindemann, *Esau's Tears*, p. 289.

100. Bernard Lewis, *The Muslim Discovery of Europe* (New York: W. W. Norton, 1982), p. 189; Daniel Evans, "Slave Coast of Europe," *Slavery and Abolition*, May 1985, p. 46; Murray Gordon, *Slavery in the Arab World* (New York: New Amsterdam Books, 1989), p. 107; Solomon Grayzel, *A History of the Jews,* pp. 280-281; David Brion Davis, *Slavery and Human Progress* (New York: Oxford University Press, 1984), pp. 91-93; Lord Kinross, *The Ottoman Centuries: The Rise and Fall of the Turkish Empire* (New York: William Morrow, 1977), p. 146.

101. A. van der Kraan, "Bali: Slavery and the Slave Trade," *Slavery, Bondage and Dependency in Southeast Asia*, edited by Anthony Reid (New York: St. Martin's Press, 1983), pp. 328, 330; Bruno Lasker, *Human Bondage in Southeast Asia* (Chapel Hill: University of North Carolina Press, 1950), p. 17.

102. William Gervase Clarence-Smith, "The Economics of the Indian Ocean and Red Sea Slave Trades in the 19th Century: An Overview," *The Economics of the Indian Ocean Slave Trade in the Nineteenth Century*, edited by William Gervase Clarence-Smith, p. 12; Francois Renault, "The Structures of the Slave Trade in Central Africa in the 19th Century," Ibid., pp. 146, 150-152.

103. William Gervase Clarence-Smith, "The Economics of the Indian Ocean and Red Sea Slave Trades in the 19th Century: An Overview," pp. 11-12.

104. Solomon Grayzel, *A History of the Jews* (New York: Mentor Books, 1968), pp. 280-281.

105. Lord Kinross, *The Ottoman Centuries*, p. 146.

106. David Brion Davis, *Slavery and Human Progress*, p. 93.

107. See, for example, William L. Westermann, *Slave Systems of Greek and Roman Antiquity* (Philadelphia: The American Philosophical Society, 1935), pp. 85, 136.

108. See, for example, Saul S. Friedman, *Jews and the American Slave Trade* (New Brunswick, N.J.: Transaction Publishers, 1998), p. 217; David Brion Davis, *In the Image of God: Religion, Moral Values, and Our Heritage of Slavery* (New Haven: Yale University Press, 2001), p. 71; Larry Koger, *Black*

Slaveowners: Free Black Masters in South Carolina, 1790-1860 (Columbia, S.C.: University of South Carolina Press, 1995); David C. Rankin, "The Impact of the Civil War on the Free Colored Community of New Orleans," *Perspectives in American History,* Vol. XI (1977-78), pp. 380, 385; Willard B. Gatewood, *Aristocrats of Color: The Black Elite, 1880-1920* (Bloomington: Indiana University Press, 1990), p. 83; Ira Berlin, *Slaves without Masters* (New York: Pantheon Books, 1974), pp. 124; 386; Eugene D. Genovese, "The Slave States of North America," *Neither Slave Nor Free: The Freedmen of African Descent in the Slave Societies of the New World* (Baltimore: Johns Hopkins University Press, 1972), edited by David W. Cohen and Jack P. Greene, pp. 270; Philip D. Morgan, "Black Life in Eighteenth-Century Charleston," *Perspectives in American History,* New Series, Vol. I (1984), p. 212; Bernard E. Powers, Jr., *Black Charlestonians: A Social History, 1822-1885* (Fayetteville: University of Arkansas Press, 1994), pp. 48-50, 72.

109. Edward A. Alpers, *Ivory and Slaves: Changing Patterns of International Trade in East Central Africa to the Later Nineteenth Century* (Berkeley: University of California Press, 1975), pp. 58-62, 94, 104, 229-230.

110. Scott Peterson, "Ugandan Officials Urge Asian Investors to Return," *The Christian Science Monitor,* March 17, 1992, p. 4.

111. Lord Kinross, *The Ottoman Centuries,* p. 558.

112. David Marshall Lang, *The Armenians: A People in Exile* (London: George Allen & Unwin, 1981), pp. 31, 34. A fuller account of these atrocities can be found in Henry Morgenthau, *Ambassador Morgenthau's Story* (Detroit: Wayne State University Press, 2003), pp. 202-263.

113. Amy Chua, *World on Fire: How Exporting Free Market Democracy Breeds Ethnic Hatred and Global Instability* (New York: Doubleday, 2003), p. 4.

114. Ignacio Klich, "*Crillos* and Arabic Speakers in Argentina: an Uneasy *Pas de Deux,* 1888-1914," *The Lebanese in the World,* edited by Albert Hourani and Nadim Shehadi, pp. 265, 273.

115. Benjamin Braude and Bernard Lewis, "Introduction," *Chris-*

tians and Jews in the Ottoman Empire: Volume I: The Central Lands (New York: Holmes & Meier, 1982), p. 21.

116. Edna Bonacich, "A Theory of Middleman Minorities," *American Sociological Review*, October 1973, pp. 583-594.

117. Ibid., pp.584-585.

118. Ibid., p. 586.

119. Eric Hoffer, *The True Believer: Thoughts on the Nature of Mass Movements* (New York: Perennial Classics, 2002), p. 91.

120. Charles Murray, *Human Accomplishment: The Pursuit of Excellence in the Arts and Sciences, 800 B.C. to 1950* (New York: HarperCollins, 2003), p. 282.

The Real History of Slavery

1. Simon Robinson and Nancy Palus, "An Awful Human Trade," *Time,* April 30, 2001, pp. 40-41; Andrew Cockburn, "21st Century Slaves," *National Geographic*, September 2003, pp. 2-24; "Slave Trade in Africa Is Highlighted by Arrests," *New York Times,* August 10, 1997, International section, p. 5.

2. Robert C. Davis, *Christian Slaves, Muslim Masters: White Slavery in the Mediterranean, the Barbary, and Italy, 1500-1800* (New York: Palgrave Macmillan, 2003), p. 23.

3. R. W. Beachey, *The Slave Trade of Eastern Africa* (New York: Harper & Row, 1976), p. 137.

4. Orlando Patterson, *Slavery and Social Death: A Comparative Study* (Cambridge Mass.: Harvard University Press, 1982), pp. 406-407; W. Montgomery Watt, *The Influence of Islam on Medieval Europe* (Edinburgh: Edinburgh University Press, 1972), p. 19; Bernard Lewis, *Race and Slavery in the Middle East*, p. 11; Daniel Evans, "Slave Coast of Europe," *Slavery and Abolition*, May 1985, p. 53, note 3; William D. Phillips, Jr., *Slavery From Roman Times to the Early Transatlantic Trade* (Minneapolis: University of Minnesota Press, 1985), p. 57.

5. Martin A. Klein, "Introduction: Modern European Expansion and Traditional Servitude in Africa and Asia," *Breaking the Chains: Slavery, Bondage, and Emancipation in Modern Africa and Asia*, edited by Martin A. Klein (Madison: Uni-

versity of Wisconsin Press, 1993), p. 8; R. W. Beachey, *The Slave Trade of Eastern Africa* p. 137.

6. Martin A. Klein, "Introduction," *Breaking the Chains*, pp. 19, 20. As of 1840, there were still more slaves in India than those emancipated by the British in the Caribbean. David Brion Davis, *The Problem of Slavery in the Age of Revolution, 1770-1823* (Ithaca: Cornell University Press, 1975), p. 63.

7. Martin A. Klein," Introduction," *Breaking the Chains*, p. 11.

8. Lord Kinross, *The Ottoman Centuries: The Rise and Fall of the Turkish Empire* (New York: William Morrow, 1977), pp. 48, 50-51; Ehud R. Toledano, "Ottoman Concept of Slavery in the Period of Reform, 1830s-1880s," *Breaking the Chains*, p. 39. However, the great majority of Ottoman slaves were female, black and domestic servants. Ibid., p. 42.

9. Daniel Evans, "Slave Coast of Europe," *Slavery and Abolition*, Vol. 6, No. 1 (May 1985), p. 42.

10. Robert C. Davis, *Christian Slaves, Muslim Masters*, p. 59.

11. Daniel J. Boorstin, *The Americans*, Vol. II: *The National Experience* (New York: Random House, 1965), p. 203.

12. Philip Nobile, "Uncovering Roots," *Village Voice*, February 23, 1993, p. 34. Another devastating critique of *Roots* is that of Bary B. and Elizabeth Shown Mills, "Roots and the New 'Faction'," *The Virginia Magazine of History and Biography*, Vol. 89, No. 1 (January 1981), pp. 3-16.

13. See, for example, Thomas Sowell *Conquests and Cultures* (New York: Basic Books, 1998), pp. 101-109.

14. See, for example, Orlando Patterson, *Freedom in the Making of Western Culture* (New YOrk: Basic Books, 1991), Chapter 20.

15. Anthony Reid, "The Decline of Slavery in Nineteenth-Century Indonesia," *Breaking the Chains*, p. 71.

16. Abraham Lincoln to Albert G. Hodges, April 4, 1864, reprinted in *The Collected Works of Abraham Lincoln*, ed. Roy P. Basler (New Brunswick, N.J.: Rutgers University Press, 1953), vol. 8, p. 281.

17. Martin A. Klein, "Introduction," *Breaking the Chains,* p. 14.

18. R. W. Beachey, *The Slave Trade of Eastern Africa*, p. 229.

19. Ehud R. Toledano, *The Ottoman Slave Trade and Its Suppression, 1840-1890* (Princeton: Princeton University Press, 1982), p. 93. See also the similar response of the Sultan of Zanzibar: R. W. Beachey, *The Slave Trade of Eastern Africa*, pp. 51-52.

20. Jared Diamond, *Guns, Germs, and Steel: The Fates of Human Societies* (New York: W. W. Norton & Co., 1997), pp. 53-54.

21. R. W. Beachey, *The Slave Trade of Eastern Africa*, pp. 51-52.

22. Ibid., p. 62.

23. Robert Conrad, *The Destruction of Brazilian Slavery 1850-1888* (Berkeley: University of California Press, 1972), pp. 247, 252.

24. Ibid., pp. 251-252; George Reid Andrews, *Blacks and Whites in São Paulo, Brazil, 1888-1988* (Madison: University of Wisconsin Press, 1991), p. 39.

25. George Reid Andrews, *Blacks and Whites in São Paulo*, p. 41.

26. R. W. Beachey, *The Slave Trade of Eastern Africa*, p. 157.

27. Ehud R. Toledano, *The Ottoman Slave Trade and Its Suppression*, pp. 66-67.

28. Ibid., pp. 140.

29. Alex Haley, *Roots: The Saga of An American Family* (New York: Dell Publishing, 1976), pp. 135-136, 165.

30. Martin A. Klein, "Introduction," *Breaking the Chains*, p. 10.

31. R. W. Beachey, *The Slave Trade of Eastern Africa*, p. 189.

32. Ibid., p. 198.

33. Irving Kaplan, et al., *Tanzania: A Country Study* (washington: The American University, 1978), p. 40.

34. R. W. Beachey, *The Slave Trade of Eastern Africa*, p. 183.

35. Ibid., p. 262.

36. Ibid., p. 82.

37. David Brion Davis, *The Problem of Slavery in Western Culture* (Ithaca: Cornell University Press, 1966), pp. 183-184.

38. Claudia Dale Goldin, "The Economics of Emancipation," *Journal of Economic History*, March 1973, p. 71n.

39. Ibid., p. 81.

40. David Brion Davis, *The Problem of Slavery in the Age of*

Revolution, 1770-1823, pp. 68-69; R.W. Beachey, *The Slave Trade of Eastern Africa*, pp. 87, 100-101; W.E.B. Du Bois, *The Suppression of the African Slave Trade to the United States of America, 1638-1870* (Baton Rouge: Louisiana State University Press, 1969), p. 141.

41. R.W. Beachey, *The Slave Trade of Eastern Africa*, p. 119.

42. Ibid., p. 22.

43. Ibid., pp. 21-23.

44. Ibid., p. 41.

45. Ibid., p. 75.

46. Ibid., p. 76.

47. Ibid., p. 84.

48. Raymond C. Howell, *The Royal Navy and the Slave Trade* (London: Croom Helm, 1987), p. 41.

49. Ibid., pp. 43-44.

50. Ibid., p. 56.

51. Reginald Coupland, *The Exploitation of East Africa 1856-1890: The Slave Trade and the Scramble* (Evanston: Northwestern University Press, 1967), pp. 139-140.

52. R.W. Beachey, *The Slave Trade of Eastern Africa*, p. 123.

53. Ibid., pp. 95, 128.

54. Ibid., pp. 172, 174.

55. Ibid., p. 135.

56. Ibid., p. 173.

57. Ibid., p. 140.

58. See, for example, Lewis Cecil Gray, *History of Agriculture in the Southern United States to 1860* (Gloucester, Mass.: Peter Smith, 1958), Vol. I, p. 528; Larry Koger, *Black Slaveowners: Free Black Masters in South Carolina, 1790-1860* (Columbia, S.C.: University of South Carolina Press, 1995); David C. Rankin, "The Impact of the Civil War on the Free Colored Community of New Orleans," *Perspectives in American History*, Vol XI (1977-78), pp. 380, 385; Willard B. Gatewood, *Aristocrats of Color: The Black Elite, 1880-1920* (Bloomington: Indiana University Press, 1990), p. 83; Ira Berlin, *Slaves without Masters: The Free Negro in the Antebellum South* (New York: Pantheon Books, 1974), pp. 124, 386; Eugene D. Genovese, "The Slave States of North Amer-

ica," *Neither Slave Nor Free: The Freedman of African Descent in the Slave Societies of the New World*, edited by David W. Cohen and Jack P. Greene (Baltimore: Johns Hopkins University Press, 1972), p. 270; Philip D. Morgan, "Black Life in Eighteenth-Century Charleston," *Perspectives in American History*, New Series, Vol. I (1984), p. 212; Bernard E. Powers, Jr., *Black Charlestonians: A Social History, 1822-1885* (Fayetteville: University of Arkansas Press, 1994), pp. 48-50, 72.

59. Willard B. Gatewood, *Aristocrats of Color: The Black Elite, 1880-1920* (Bloomington: Indiana University Press, 1990), p. 83; Ira Berlin, *Slaves without Masters*, pp. 124, 386; David C. Rankin, "The Impact of the Civil War on the Free Colored Community of New Orleans," *Perspectives in American History*, Vol XI (1977-78), pp. 380, 385.

60. See, for example, Jerome S. Handler and Arnold A. Sio, "Barbados," *Neither Slave Nor Free*, pp. 245-246; Léo Elisabeth, "The French Antilles," Ibid., pp. 165-166.

61. Carl N. Degler, *Neither Black Nor White* (New York: Macmillan Publishing Co., 1971), p. 86.

62. Martin A. Klein, "Introduction," *Breaking the Chains*, p. 15.

63. David Brion Davis, *The Problem of Slavery in the Age of Revolution, 1770-1823*, p. 44.

64. David Hackett Fischer, *Albion's Seed:* Four British Folkways in America (Oxford: Oxford University Press, 1989), p. 602.

65. R. W. Beachey, *The Slave Trade of Eastern Africa*, pp. 28, 229, 231, 242-244, 252.

66. Eric Williams was perhaps the best known advocate of the position that the antislavery crusade was based on economic self-interest but scholarly critics have devastated his claim. David Brion Davis made the more amorphous—and hence less testable—claim that the anti-slavery movement "reflected the needs and values of the emerging capitalist order." David Brion Davis, *The Problem of Slavery in the Age of Revolution, 1770-1823*, p. 350.

67. John Stuart Mill, "The Contest in America," *Collected Works of John Stuart Mill*, Vol. XXI: *Essays on Equality, law, and Education*, edited by John M. Robson (Toronto: University of Toronto Press, 1984), p. 127.

68. R. W. Beachey, *The Slave Trade of Eastern Africa*, pp. 162-169; Ehud R. Toledano, *The Ottoman Slave Trade and Its Suppression, 1848-1890*, pp. 41, 53.
69. R. W. Beachey, *The Slave Trade of Eastern Africa*, p. 70.
70. Ibid., pp. 56, 75.
71. Martin A. Klein, "Introduction," *Breaking the Chains*, pp. 16, 17.
72. Ibid., pp. 21-22.
73. Martin A. Klein, "Slavery and Emancipation in French West Africa," *Breaking the Chains*, p. 177.
74. William Gervase Clarence-Smith, "Cocoa Plantations and Coerced Labor in the Gulf of Guinea, 1870-1914," *Breaking the Chains*, p. 153.
75. "Where Dutch authority was less well established, the local officials did not even pretend to carry out the antislavery policy." Anthony Reid, "The Decline of Slavery in Nineteenth-Century Indonesia," *Breaking the Chains*, p. 78.
76. Martin A. Klein, "Slavery and Emancipation in French West Africa," *Breaking the Chains*, p. 174.
77. Raymond C. Howell, *The Royal Navy and the Slave Trade* (London: Croom Helm, 1987), p. 205.
78. Anthony Reid, "The Decline of Slavery in Nineteenth-Century Indonesia," *Breaking the Chains*, p. 64.
79. An exception to this condemnation of slavery within the United States was that of the slaves held by American Indians. David Brion Davis characterized this slavery as being "often of a mild, domestic nature," though admitting that sometimes slaves were treated with great cruelty and occasionally an Indian slaveowner "would cut a foot or ankle to prevent escape." David Brion Davis, *The Problem of Slavery in Western Culture*, p. 168n. A mere "cut" would hardly prevent escape, unless it was a serious maiming, in which case "cut" would be a euphemism.
80. See, for example, Martin A. Klein, "Introduction: Modern European Expansion and Traditional Servitude in Africa and Asia," *Breaking the Chains*, pp. 4-6.
81. Anthony Reid, "The Decline of Slavery in Nineteenth-Century Indonesia," *Breaking the Chains*, p. 67; William Gervase

Clarence-Smith, "Cocoa Plantations and Coerced labor in the Gulf of Guinea, 1870-1914," Ibid., p. 156.

82. See the narratives in *White Slaves, African Masters: An Anthology of American Barbary Captivity Narratives,* edited by Paul Baepler (Chicago: University of Chicago, 1999). See also Robert C. Davis, *Christian Slaves, Muslim Masters*, Chapters 5, 6.

83. Robert C. Davis, *Christian Slaves, Muslim Masters*, p. 55.

84. Ibid., pp. 59-61.

85. Ibid., p. 76.

86. Ibid., p. 75.

87. Ibid., p. 4.

88. Ibid., p. 7.

89. Paul Baepler, "Introduction," *White Slaves, African Masters*, p. 9.

90. Robert C. Davis, *Christian Slaves, Muslim Masters*, pp. 43-44.

91. Thomas Jefferson, *Writings*, edited by Merrill D. Peterson (New York: Library Classics of America, 1984), p. 264.

92. "Introduction," *The Republic of Letters: The Correspondence between Thomas Jefferson and James Madison 1776-1826*, edited by James Morton Smith (New York: W.W. Norton, 1995), p. 21.

93. Clement Eaton, *The Freedom-of-Thought Struggle in the Old South* (New York: Harper & Row, 1964), p. 194.

94. Lewis Cecil Gray, *History of Agriculture in the Southern United States to 1860* (Gloucester, Massachusetts: Peter Smith, 1958), Vol. II, p. 656.

95. Calhoun argued against the statement in the Declaration of Independence that "all men are created equal" on grounds that only two people were created and everyone else was born. Moreover, "Men are not born. Infants are born. They grow to be men." John C. Calhoun, "Speech on the Oregon Bill, 27 June 1848" *John C. Calhoun: Selected Writings and Speeches*, edited by H. Lee Cheek, Jr. (Washington: Regnery Publishing, 2003), p. 641. Garrison refused to countenance any objections to his particular plan of emancipation, based on its anticipated consequences, saying, "the question of

expedience has nothing to do with that of right." Elsewhere he called expediency "the deadliest word in our language." Henry Mayer, *All on Fire: William Lloyd Garrison and the Abolition of Slavery* (New York: St. Martin's Press, 1998), pp. 72, 129. How far Garrison would carry his belief in principles over consequences was demonstrated when a fellow abolitionist who was lynched by a mob tried to defend himself, instead of remaining pacifist to the end: "Garrison was 'shocked' that Lovejoy and his coadjutors had allowed the provocations to justify taking up arms in self-defense." Ibid., p. 237.

96. Ibid., p. 176. Such bluntness was rare at the time, but Randolph saw the stark realities of the issues raised by slavery as not being something to be ignored or politely evaded. He said: "Sir, it is a thing which cannot be hid; it is not a dry rot, which you can cover with a carpet until the house tumbles about your ears; you might as well try to hide a volcano in full eruption; it cannot be hid; it is a cancer in your face." Ibid.

97. Fredericki Law Olmsted, *The Cotton Kingdom: A Traveller's Observations on Cotton and Slavery in the American Slave States* (New York: Modern Library, 1969), p. 565.

98. Henry Mayer, *All on Fire*, Chapter 10.

99. James M. McPherson, *The Struggle for Equality: Abolitionists and the Negro in the Civil War and Reconstruction* (Princeton: Princeton University Press, 1964), p. 3.

100. Thomas F. Harwood, "British Evangelical Abolitionism and American Churches in the 1830s," *Journal of Southern History*, August 1962, p. 302; Henry Mayer, *All on Fire*, p. 303.

101. James M. McPherson, *The Struggle for Equality*, p. 12.

102. Ibid., Chapter XII.

103. Henry Mayer, *All On Fire*, p. 372.

104. Ibid., *All on Fire*, p. 72.

105. Edmund Burke, *The Correspondence of Edmund Burke*, Vol VII, edited by P.J. Marshall and John A. Woods (Cambridge: Cambridge University Press, 1968), p. 123.

106. Ibid., p. 124.

107. Edmund Burke, *The Correspondence of Edmund Burke*,

Vol. VIII, edited by R. B. McDowell (Chicago: University of Chicago Press,1969), p. 451.

108. Henry Wiencek, *An Imperfect God: George Washington, His Slaves, and the Creation of America* (New York: Farrar, Straus and Giroux, 2004), p., 5.

109. Edmund Burke, *The Correspondence of Edmund Burke*, Vol. VII, edited by P.J. Marshall and John A. Woods, p. 125.

110. Edmund Burke, *Burke's Politics: Selected Writings of Edmund Burke on Reform, Revolution, and War*, edited by Ross J. S. Hoffman and Paul Levack (New York: Alfred A. Knopf, 1949), p. 58.

111. Russell Kirk, *John Randolph of Roanoke: A Study in American Politics* (Indianapolis: Liberty Press, 1978), p. 174.

112. C. Vann Woodward, *The Future of the Past* (New York: Oxford University Press, 1989), p. 149

113. Henry Wiencek, *An Imperfect God*, p. 160.

114. William H. Freehling, "The Founding Fathers and Slavery," *American Historical Review*, Vol. 77 (1972), p. 87.

115. Ibid., p. 88.

116. Ibid., p. 91.

117. Lewis Cecil Gray, *History of Agriculture in the Southern United States to 1860*, Vol. I, pp. 514, 526.

118. Ulrich B. Phillips, *American Negro Slavery: A Survey of the Supply, Employment and Control of Negro Labor As Determined by the Plantation Regie* (Baton Rough: Louisiana State University Press, 1966), p. 426. In addition, laws in many places became more protective of the slave and less restrictive of "free persons of color" in the years following the American revolution. See, for example, Lewis C. Gray, *History of Agriculture in the Southern United States to 1861*, Vol. I., pp. 514, 526.

119. Daniel J. Boorstin, *The Americans*, Vol. II: *The National Experience* (New York: Random House, 1965), 187.

120. Lewis Cecil Gray, *History of Agriculture in the Southern United States*, p. 526.

121. E. Franklin Frazier, *The Negro in the United States,* revised edition (New York: The Macmillan Co., 1971), p. 62.

122. Clement Eaton, *The Freedom of Thought Struggle in the Old South* (New York: Harper & Row, 1964), pp. 127, 212,

220, 228-229, 231-232.

123. William F. Freehling, *The Road to Disunion: Secessionists at Bay 1776-1854* (New York: Oxford University Press, 1990), p. 159.

124. Even within Africa and Asia, most freed slaves tended to stay where they were, rather than return to some home of which they had no memory or, in the case of colonial Malaya, to the backward hills from which they had been captured. Martin A. Klein, "Introduction: Modern European and Traditional Servitude in Africa and Asia," *Breaking the Chains,* edited by Martin A. Klein, p. 25.

125. David Brion Davis, *The Problem of Slavery in the Age of Revolution 1770-1823*, p. 49.

126. Russell Kirk, *John Randolph of Roanoke*, p. 163; John Randolph, *Collected Letters of John Randolph of Roanoke to Dr. John Brockenbrough, 1812-1833* (New Brunswick, N.J.: Transaction Books, 1988), p. 19.

127. Russell Kirk, *John Randolph of Roanoke*, p. 160.

128. John Randolph, *Collected Letters of John Randolph of Roanoke to Dr. John Brockenbrough, 1812-1813*, p. 11.

129. Quoted in John C. Calhoun, *John C. Calhoun: Selected Writings and Speeches*, p. 670.

130. Carter G. Woodson, *The Education of the Negro Prior to 1861* (New York: Arno Press, 1968), p. 378.

131. Richard Brookhiser, *Founding Father: Rediscovering George Washington* (New York: The Free Press, 1996), p. 183.

132. Henry Wiencek, *An Imperfect God*, pp. 4-5.

133. Thomas G. West, *Vindicating the Founders: Race, Sex, Class, and Justice in the Origins of America* New York: Rowman & Littlefield, 1997), p. 5.

134. Richard Brookhiser, *Founding Father*, pp. 179, 180.

135. Ibid., p. 181.

136. Ibid., p. 182.

137. Ibid.

138. Whittington B. Johnson, *Black Savannah: 1788-1864* (Fayetteville: University of Arkansas Press, 1996), pp. 111, 180.

139. Helen Tunnicliff Catterall, *Judicial Cases Concerning Amer-*

ican Slavery and the Negro (New York: Octagon Books, 1968),Vol. I, p. 205. John Randolph's older brother Richard, who also inherited slaves as part of a mortgaged estate, expressed very similar views and similarly freed his slaves in his will. See Robert Davidoff, *The Education of John Randolph* (New York:W.W. Norton, 1979), p. 49.

140. William Cabell Bruce,*John Randolph of Roanoke 1773-1833* (New York: Octagon Books, 1970),Vol. II, p. 49.

141. John Randolph, *Collected Letters of John Randolph to Dr. John Brockenbrough*, p. 150.

142. W. E. B. Du Bois, *The Suppression of the African Salve Trade to the United States of America, 1638-1870* (Baton Rouge: Louisiana State University Press, 1969), p. 191.

143. John R. Spear, *The American Slave-Trade:An Account of Its Origin, Growth and Suppress* (New York: Charles Scribner's Sons,1900), pp. 218-219.

144. Russell Kirk,*John Randolph of Roanoke*, p. 160.

145. Ibid., p. 169.

146. See, for example, Lewis C. Gray, *History of Agriculture in the Southern United States to 1860*,Vol I, p. 521; Ibid.,Vol. II, p. 660.

147. Peter Kolchin,*A Sphinx on the American Land:The Nineteenth-Century South in Comparative Perspective* (Baton Rough: Louisiana State University Press, 2003), p. 16.

148. William C. Davis, *Look Away! A History of the Confederate States of America* (New York:The Free Press, 2002), pp. 98, 106, 131.

149. Peter Kolchin,*A Sphinx on the American Land*, p. 19.

150. William C. Davis, *Look Away!*, p. 130.

151. Ralph Austen, "The Trans-Saharan Slave Trade:A Tentative Census," *The Uncommon Market: Essays in the Economic History of the Atlantic Slave Trade*, edited by Henry A. Gemery and Jan S. Hogendorn (New York: Academic Press,1979), pp. 68-69.

152. See Bernard Lewis, *Race and Slavery in the Middle East*, pp. 10, 84.

153. Robert C. Davis, *Christian Slaves, Muslim Masters*, p. 25.

154. Martin A. Klein, "Introduction," *Breaking the Chains*, p. 9.

155. Ibid., p. 7.
156. Roger Anstey, "The Volume and Profitability of the British Slave Trade, 1675-1800," *Race and Slavery in the Western Hemisphere*, edited by Stanley L. Engerman and Eugene D. Genovese, pp. 22-23.
157. Henry A. Walker, "Black-White Differences in Marriage and Family Patterns," *Feminism, Children and the New Families*, edited by Sanford M. Dornbusch and Myra H. Strober (New York: The Guilford Press, 1988), p. 91.
158. Stephan Thernstrom and Abigail thernstrom, *America in Black and White: One Nation, Indivisible* (New York: Simon & Schuster, 1997), p. 239.
159. James Q. Wilson, *The Marriage Problem: How Our Culture Has Weakened Families* (New York: HarperCollins, 2002), p. 115.
160. U.S. Bureau of the Census, *Changing Characteristics of the Negro Population* by Daniel O. Price (Washington: Government Printing Office, 1969), p. 224.
161. U.S. Bureau of the Census, *Current Population Reports* P-23-197: *Trends in Premarital Childbearing 1930 to 1994* (Washington: U.S. Bureau of the Census, 1999), p. 2.
162. Henry Wiencek, *An Imperfect God*, p. 5.
163. Adam Smith, *The Theory of Moral Sentiments* (Indianapolis: Liberty Classics, 1976), p. 380.
164. LaWanda Cox, *Lincoln and Black Freedom: A Study in Presidential Leadership* (Columbia, S.C.: University of South Carolina Press, 1981), p. 13.
165. Ibid.
166. Roger Anstey, "A Re-Interpretation of the Abolition of the British Slave Trade, 1806-1807," *The English Historical Review*, April, 1972, pp. 323-324.
167. Ibid., p. 331.
168. LaWanda Cox, *Lincoln and Black Freedom*, 17.
169. Henry Mayer, *All on Fire*, p. 542.
170. LaWanda Cox, *Lincoln and Black Freedom*, pp. 9-19.
171. William D. Phillips, Jr. *Slavery From Roman Times to the Early Transatlantic Trade* (Minneapolis: University of Minnesota Press, 1985), p. 3.

172. David Eltis,"Europeans and the Rise and Fall of African Slavery in the Americas:An Interpretation," *American Historical Review*, December 1993, p. 1400.

173. See, for example, Charles Murray, *Human Accomplishment: The Pursuit of Excellence in the Arts and Sciences, 800 B.C. to 1950* (New York: HarperCollins, 2003), p. 306.

174. *Abraham Lincoln: His Speeches and Writings*, edited by Roy P. Basler (Cleveland: Kraus Reprint, 1981), p. 445.

175. Thomas Jefferson, *Writings* (New York: Library Classics of the United States, 1984), p. 1202.

176. Ibid., pp. 269-270.

177. Ibid., p. 270.

178. Ibid., p. 982.

179. Frederick Law Olmsted, *The Cotton Kingdom*, p. 569.

Germans and History

1. Roy E. Mellor and E.Alistair Smith, *Europe:A Geographical Survey of the Continent* (New York: Columbia University Press, 1979), p. 24.

2. Winston S. Churchill, *Churchill Speaks:Winston S. Churchill in Peace and War, Collected Speeches, 1897-1963*, edited by Robert Rhodes James (New York: Chelsea House, 1980), p. 882, 890.

3. Hugh LeCaine Agnew, *Origins of the Czech National Renascence* (Pittsburgh: University of Pittsburgh Press, 1993), pp. 179, 180, 181, 183, 193, 195. In the eighteenth century, Czech scholars "wrote mostly in German or Latin" while the people "read only Czech." (*Ibid.*, p. 212) Even scholarly studies of Czech literary history were written in Latin or German. (*Ibid.*, p. 116).

4. Robert J. Kaiser, *The Geography of Nationalism in Russia and the USSR* (Princeton: Princeton University Press, 1994), p. 41.

5. Iván T. Berend and György Ränki, *The European Periphery and Industrialization 1780-1914*, translated by Éva Pálmai (Cambridge: Cambridge University Press, 1982), pp. 15, 16.

6. "We're Doing All Right, But What About You?" *The Economist*,August 16, 2003, p. 43.

7. Jean W. Sedlar, *East Central Europe in the Middle Ages, 1000-1500* (Seattle: University of Washington Press, 1994), p. 7.

8. Ibid., p. 86. See also Roy E. H. Mellor and E. Alistair Smith, *Europe: A Geographical Survey of the Continent*, p. 100; Robert Bartlett, *The Making of Europe: Conquest, Colonization and Cultural Change, 950-1350* (Princeton: Princeton University Press, 1993), pp. 150-151; Sidney Pollard, *Marginal Europe: The Contributions of the Marginal Lands Since the Middle Ages* (Oxford: Oxford University Press, 1997), p. 156.

9. Robert Bartlett, *The Making of Europe*, pp. 117-132; Sidney Pollard, *Marginal Europe*, pp. 152-153. There were, in fact, a variety of German laws dominating different parts of East Central Europe. See Paul Robert Magocsi, *Historical Atlas of East Central Europe* (Seattle: University of Washington Press, 1993), pp. 37-41.

10. Peter Gunst, "Agrarian Systems of Central and Eastern Europe," *The Origins of Backwardness in Eastern Europe: Economics and Politics from the Middle Ages Until the Early Twentieth Century* (Berkeley: University of California Press, 1989), p. 64. German law was not the only foreign law to prevail in particular enclaves. Dutch and Flemish migrants who came to Eastern Europe to apply the drainage techniques in which they were skilled were likewise governed by Dutch and Flemish law. Sidney Pollard, *Marginal Europe*, pp. 156-157.

11. Ibid., p. 235.

12. N. J. G. Pounds, *An Historical Geography of Europe, 1800-1914* (Cambridge: Cambridge University Press, 1985), p. 179; Peter F. Sugar, *Southeastern Europe under Ottoman Rule, 1354-1804* (Seattle: University of Washington Press, 1993), pp. 179-180.

13. Ibid., pp. 50, 53, 90, 92, 131, 135.

14. John A. Armstrong, "Mobilized Diaspora in Tsarist Russia," *Soviet Nationality Policies and Practices* (New York: Praeger Publishers, 1978), ed. Jeremy R. Azrael, p. 68; Richard Sallet, *Russian-German Settlements in the United States,*

translated by LaVern J. Rippley and Armand Bauer (Fargo, N.D.: North Dakota Institute for Regional Studies, 1974), p. 14.

15. Carlo M. Cipolla, *Literacy and Development in the West* (New York: Penguin Books, 1969), p. 17, It was much the same story when the empire was broken down regionally. Only about 15 percent of the children in Bosnia-Herzegovina were attending schools in 1880, but 67 percent were in Dalmatia and at least 95 percent in Austria and the Czech territories. Iván T. Berend and György Ránki, *The European Periphery and Industrialization 1780-1914*, p. 57.

16. Ibid., p. 127.

17. Ibid., pp. 115, 127.

18. Hugh LeCaine Agnew, *Origins of the Czech National Renascence*, p. 113.

19. John A. Armstrong, "Mobilized Diaspora in Tsarist Russia,", *Soviet Nationality Policies and Practices*, ed. Jeremy R. Azrael, p. 69.

20. See, for example, Richard Sallet, *Russian-German Settlements in the United States*, p. 3.

21. Fred C. Koch, *The Volga Germans: In Russia and the Americas, from 1763 to the Present* (University Park: Pennsylvania State University Press, 1978), p. 195.

22. Jean W. Sedlar, *East Central Europe in the Middle Ages, 1000-1500* (Seattle: University of Washington Press, 1994), p. 86.

23. Robert Bartlett, *The Making of Europe*, pp. 54, 200, 274-277; Hugh LeCaine Agnew, *Origins of the Czech National Renascence*, p. 52; Charles A. Price, *Southern Europeans in Australia* (Canberra: Australian National University Press, 1979), p. 55.

24. Karl Stumpp, *The German-Russians: Two Centuries of Pioneering* (Bonn: Edition Atlantic-Forum, 1966), pp. 140-141.

25. Robert Bartlett, *The Making of Europe*, pp. 228, 236-238.

26. Gary B. Cohen, *The Politics of Ethnic Survival: Germans in Prague, 1861-1914* (Princeton: Princeton University Press, 1981), p. 3.

27. Robert A. Kann and Zdenek V. David, *The Peoples of the*

Eastern Habsburg Lands, 1526-1918 (Seattle: University of Washington Press, 1984), pp. 201-202, 215, 245, 249, 265, 267.

28. Anders Henriksson, *The Tsar's Loyal Germans: The Riga German Community, Social Change and the Nationality Question, 1855-1905* (New York: Columbia University Press,1983), pp. 15, 35, 54.

29. Gary B. Cohen, *The Politics of Ethnic Survival*, pp. 24-26; Anders Henriksson, *The Tsar's Loyal Germans*, pp. 2, 37; Roger P. Bartlett, *Human Capital* (Cambridge University Press, 1979), p. 35. Earlier, there was anti-Latvian discrimination. Ibid, p. 89.

30. Ibid., pp. 20, 22-26.

31. Anthony T. Bouscaren, *International Migrations Since 1945* (New York: Frederick A. Praeger, 1963), p. 58.

32. Ibid., Chapter 6.

33. Fernand Braudel, *The Mediterranean and the Mediterranean World in the Age of Philip II* (New York: Harper & Row), Vol. I, p. 189.

34. Ronald C. Newton, *German Buenos Aires, 1900-1933* (Austin: University of Texas Press, 1977), p. 9.

35. Victor Wolfgang von Hagen, *The Germanic People in America* (Norman: University of Oklahoma Press, 1976), p. 326; Alfred Dolge, *Pianos and Their Makers* (Covina, California: Covina Publishing Company, 1911), pp. 172, 264; Edwin M. Good, *Giraffes, Black Dragons, and Other Pianos: A Technological History from Cristoforito the Modern Concert Grand* (Stanford: Stanford University Press, 1982), p. 137n; W. D. Borrie, "Australia," *The Positive Contribution by Immigrants*, edited by Oscar Handlin (Paris: United Nations Educational, Scientific and Cultural Organization, 1955), p. 94.

36. Karl Stumpp, *The German-Russians*, pp. 8-9.

37. Victor Wolfgang von Hagen, *The Germanic People in America*, pp. 13, 14, 17.

38. Christopher Hibbert, *The English: A Social History 1066-1954* (New York: W.W. Norton & Co., 1987), p. 175;

Wolfgang von Hagen, *The German People in America*, p. 75.

39. Victor Wolfgang von Hagen, *The Germanic People in America*, p. 77; Virginia Brainard Kunz, *The Germans in America* (Minneapolis: Lerner Publications, 1966), pp. 19-20; Daniel J. Boorstin, *The Americans*, Vol. I: *The Colonial Experience* (New York: Random House, 1958) , pp. 350-351.

40. Adam Giesinger, *From Catherine to Khruschev: The Story of Russia's Germans* (Lincoln, Nebraska: American Historical Society of Germans from Russia, 1974), pp. 143-144.

41. Larry V. Thompson, Book Review, *Journal of Latin American Studies*, May 1976, p. 159. See also Victor Wolfgang von Hagen, *The Germanic People in America*, pp. 242-243, 270; Ronald C. Newton, *German Buenos Aires, 1900-1933*, pp. 7-8, 22.

42. Albert Bernhardt Faust, *The German Element in the United States* (New York: Arno Press, 1960), Vol. I, pp. 320-327; Virginia Brainard Kunz, *The Germans in America*, pp. 48-51, 55, 60-61.

43. T. N. Dupuy, *A Genius for War: The German Army and General Staff, 1807-1945* (Englewood Cliffs, N.J.: Prentice-Hall, Inc., 1977), p. 4.

44. Ian Harmstorf and Michael Cigler, *The Germans in Australia* (Melbourne: Australasian Educa Press, 1985), pp. 28, 62.

45. Kathleen Neils Conzen, "The Germans," *Harvard Encyclopedia of American Ethnic Groups* (Cambridge, Mass.: Harvard University Press, 1980), edited by Stephan Thernstrom, et al, p. 420.

46. Albert Bernhardt Faust, *The German Element in the United States*, Volume I, pp. 447-448.

47. Richard Sallet, *Russian-German Settlements in the United States*, p. 30.

48. Carl Wittke, *We who Built America: The Sage of the Immigrant* (Cleveland: The Press of Case Western Reserve University, 1964), pp. 225-226.

49. Ibid., pp. 499-500.

50. Ibid., pp. 102-103.

51. I bought a copy in the hotel where I was staying in 1988.

52. Ian Harmstorf and Michael Cigler, *The Germans in Australia*, p. 82.

53. Ibid., p. 70.

54. Iris Barbara Graefe, "Cultural Changes Among Germans from Russia in Argentina, 1967-1977," *Germans from Russia in Colorado* (The Western Social Science Association, 1978), p. 58.

55. Theodore Huebener, *The Germans in America* (Philadelphia: Chilton Company, 1962), p. 84; Hildegard Binder Johnson, "The Location of German Immigrants in the Middle West," *Annals of the Association of American Geographers*, March 1951, pp. 24-25.

56. Joseph Wandel, *The German dimension of American History* (Chicago: Nelson-Hall, Inc., 1979), p. 56.

57. LaVern J. Rippley, "Germans from Russia," *Harvard Encyclopedia of American Ethnic Groups*, ed. Stephan Thernstrom, et al., p. 427.

58. Jean Roche, *La Colonisation Allemande et le Rio Grande do Sul* (Paris: Institut des Hautes Études de L'Amérique Latine, 1969), pp. 445, 457, 459, 460.

59. Charles H. Anderson, *White Protestant Americans* (Englewood Cliffs, New Jersey: Prentice-Hall, Inc., 1970) p. 85; U.S. Bureau of Census, *Current Population Reports*, series P-20, no. 221 (Washington, D.C.: U.S. Government Printing Office, 1971), p. 7.

60. "Germans," *The Australian People: An Encyclopedia of the Nation, Its People and Their Origins*, edited by James Jupp (North Ryde, Australia: Angus and Robertson Publishers, 1988), p. 485; R.B. Walker, "Some Social and Political Aspects of German Settlement in Australia," *Journal of the Royal Australian Historical Society*, March 1975, pp. 36-37.

61. Jean Roche, *La Colonisation Allemande et le Rio Grande do Sul*, pp. 551-575, 587.

62. T. Lynn Smith, *Brazil: People and Institutions* (Baton Rouge: Louisiana State University Press, 1972), p. 134.

63. Thomas W. Merrick and Douglas H. Graham, *Population and Economic Development in Brazil 1800 to the Present* (Bal-

timore:The Johns Hopkins University Press, 1979), p. 111.

64. Victor Wolfgang von Hagen, *The Germanic People in America*, p. 322.

65. Ibid., p. 21.

66. W. O. Henderson, *The Rise of German Industrial Power, 1834-1914* (Berkeley: University of California Press, 1975), p. 23.

67. Ibid., pp. 24, 25, 26, 27, 29.

68. Ibid., pp. 25, 44.

69. Ibid., pp. 53, 57.

70. Ibid., pp. 53, 55.

71. Ibid., p. 49.

72. B. R. Mitchell, *European Historical Statistics, 1750-1970* Abridged edition (New York: Columbia University Press, 1975), p. 223-225.

73. "Victory in Europe," *Time*, May 14, 1945, p. 15.

74. William L. Shirer, *The Rise and Fall of the Third Reich: A History of Nazi Germany* (New York: Simon and Shuster, 1960), pp. 597-598.

75. Ibid., pp. 593-595.

76. Valdis O. Lumans, *Himmler's Auxiliaries: The Volksdeutsche Mittelstelle and the German Minorities* (Chapel Hill: University of North Carolina Press, 1993), p. 22.

77. Ibid., Chapters 1, 2.

78. Ibid., Chapter 4.

79. Ibid., pp. 88-93, 104.

80. Ibid., p. 91.

81. Ibid., pp. 129-130.

82. Charles A. Price, *German Settlers in South Australia* (Melbourne: Melbourne University Press, 1945), Chapter VI; G. Kinne, "Nazi Stratagems and Their Effects on Germans in Australia up to 1945," *Journal of the Royal Australian Historical Society*, June 1980, pp. 1-19.

83. Jean Roche, *La Colonisation Allemande et le Rio Grande do Sul*, pp. 541-542; Richard F. Behrendt, "Germans in Latin America," *Inter-American Monthly*, April 1943, p. 23; G. Kinne, "Nazi Stratagems and Their Effects on Germans in

Australia up to 1945," *Journal of the Royal Australian Historical Society*, June 1980, p. 16.

84. Adam Giesinger, *From Catherine to Khrushchev*, p. 311.

85. Ibid., pp. 313-314.

86. James R. Flynn, "Massive IQ Gains in 14 Nations: What IQ Tests Really Measure," *Psychological Bulletin*, Vol. 101, pp. 271-291; James R. Flynn, "IQ Gains Over Time: Toward Finding the Causes," *The Rising Curve: Long-Time Gains in IQ and Related Measures,* edited by Ulric Neisser (Washington: American Psychological Association, 1998), pp. 25-66.

87. Sarah Gordon, *Hitler, Germans, and the "Jewish Question"* (Princeton, N. J.: Princeton University Press, 1984), p. 8.

88. Raphael Patai, *The Vanished Worlds of Jewry* (New York: Macmillan Publishing Co., Inc., 1980), p. 57. See also Daniel L. Niewyk, *The Jews in Weimar Germany* (Baton Rouge: Louisiana State University Press, 1980), p. 98; Gary B. Cohen, *The Politics of Ethnic Survival*, pp. 76, 82, 96.

89. Carl Wittke, *We Who Built America*, p. 329; Eric E. Hirshler, "Jews from Germany in the United States," *Jews from Germany in the United States*, edited by Eric E. Hirshler (New York: Furrow, Straus and Cudahy, 1955), pp. 42-45; Frederick C. Luebke, *Germans in the New World: Essays in the History of Immigration* (Urbana: University of Illinois Press, 1990), p. 170.

90. Judith Laikin Elkin, *Jews of the Latin American Republics* (Chapel Hill: University of North Carolina Press, 1980), p. 37; Ezra Mendelsohn, *The Jews of East Central Europe between the World Wars* (Bloomington: Indiana University Press, 1983), p. 133.

91. Michael Brenner, *The Renaissance of Jewish Culture in Weimar Germany* (New Haven: Yale University Press, 1996), p. 32.

92. Albert Bernhardt Faust, *The German Element in the United States*, Vol I, p. 45. Frederick C. Luebke, *Germans in Brazil: A Comparative History of Cultural Conflict During World War I* (Baton Rouge: Louisiana State University, 1987), p. 81. There has been challenge to the idea that Germans in the United States had amicable relations with blacks, or were

abolitionist in their view of slavery. See, for example, the papers in *States of Progress: Germans and Blacks in America Over 300 Years*, edited by Randall M. Miller (The German Society of Pennsylvania, 1989). However, the issue is not whether the Germans met some absolute standard in either their relations with blacks or in their views of slavery. The point is that their record compares favorably with that of other contemporary whites. Even this volume devoted to re-assessing the history of Germans' relations with blacks in the United States, and their attitudes toward slavery, does not claim that the Germans were more racist than other whites, and some of the historical facts cited in that volume include the admission of some blacks as members of German churches in colonial Pennsylvania and the Moravians' missionary work among slaves (p.6), the inclusion of blacks in a predominantly German union in Chicago at the beginning of the twentieth century (pp. 17-18), and the fact that it would be difficult "to find any significant German leaders who were advocates of slavery" during the antebellum era (p. 57).

93. Clement Eaton, *The Freedom-of-Thought Struggle in the Old South* (New York: Harper & Row, 1964), pp. 33, 239, 247.

94. Ibid., pp. 113-114.

95. Virginia Brainard Kunz, *The Germans in America*, p. 50.

96. Albert Bernhardt Faust, *The German Element in the United States*, Vol. I, pp. 98-99, 103, 112, 213, 240; Ibid., Vol. II, p. 423; Joseph Wandel, *The German Dimension of American History*, pp. 15, 16, 20, 27, 51, 65; R. L. Biesle, "The Relations between the German Settlers and the Indians in Texas, 1844-1860," *Southwestern Historical Quarterly*, July 1927, pp. 116-129.

97. Philip Raine, *Paraguay* (New Brunswick, N.J.: Scarecrow Press, 1956), p. 304.

98. Ian Harmstorf and Michael Cigler, *The Germans in Australia*, pp. 49, 80-81.

99. R. W. Beachey, *The Slave Trade of Eastern Africa* (New York: Harper & Row, 1976), p. 229.

100. Sarah Gordon, *Hitler, Germans, and the "Jewish Question,"* pp. 30-31.
101. Ibid., p. 32.
102. Ibid., p. 129.
103. Ibid., pp. 79-80.
104. Ibid., pp. 120-121.
105. Ibid., pp. 175-186.
106. Ibid., p. 182.
107. Ibid., p. 183.
108. Ibid., p. 8.
109. Ibid., Chapter 6.
110. Ibid., p. 196.
111. Bartosz Jalowiecki, "Lies the Germans Tell Themselves," *Commentary*, January 2004, p. 43. This $55 billion was not only for Jews but also for other victims of the Nazi regime and, while this article was highly critical of contemporary trends in Germany, it did *not* deal with pre-Hitler Germans.
112. Harry Leonard Sawatsky, *They Sought a Country: Mennonite Colonization in Mexico* (Berkeley: University of California Press, 1971), p. 365.

Black Education: Achievements, Myths and Tragedies

1. *Report of the Board of Trustees of Public Schools of the District of Columbia to the Commissioners of the District of Columbia: 1898-1899* (Washington: Government Printing Office, 1900), pp. 7, 11.
2. Henry S. Robinson, "The M Street School," *Records of the Columbia Historical Society of Washington, D.C.*, Vol. LI (1984), p. 122.
3. The specific data can be found in my "Black Excellence: The Case of Dunbar High School," *The Public Interest*, Spring 1974, p. 8.
4. Ibid., p. 141.
5. My detailed statistical data were filed with the National Technical Information Service, U.S. Department of Commerce, Springfield, Virginia 22161. The Accession Number was PB265 8.13 and the codes for Dunbar High School Students were 0508 (graduates) and 0598 (dropouts). In the course of collecting these data, I had a separate hand tabu-

lation done of maids and doctors among the parental occupations. However, in the computerized data, there are broader occupational categories, though parents with high-level professional occupations such as doctors are sufficiently few to show that the notion that Dunbar students were the children of such professional was false.

6. Mary Gibson Hundley, *The Dunbar Story: 1870-1955* (New York: Vantage Press, 1965), p. 31.

7. Jacqueline Goggin, *Carter G. Woodson: A Life in Black History* (Baton Rouge: Louisiana State University Press, 1993), p. 30.

8. E. Delorus Preston, Jr., "William Syphax, A Pioneer in Negro Education in the District of Columbia," *Journal of Negro History*, October 1935, p. 463; Henry S. Robinson, "The M Street High School, 1891-1916," *Records of the Columbia Historical Society of Washington, D.C.*, Vol. LI (1984), p. 137.

9. Mary Church Terrell, "The History of the High School for Negroes in Washington." *Journal of Negro History*, Vol. II, No. 3 (July 1917), pp. 255-256.

10. Ibid., p. 256.

11. Ibid., p. 261.

12. Mary Gibson Hundley, *The Dunbar Story*, 13, 65.

13. See the numerous references listed in Thomas Sowell, *Inside American Education* (New York: The Free Press, 1993), p. 322, footnote 99.

14. Mary Gibson Hundley, *The Dunbar Story*, p. 24.

15. Ibid., pp. 74, 131, 132, 147; Henry S. Robinson, "The M Street School," *Records of the Columbia Historical Society of Washington, D.C.*, Vol. LI (1984), p. 127.

16. Henry S. Robinson, "The M Street School," *op.cit.*, p. 122.

17. Louise Daniel Hutchison, *Anna Cooper: A Voice from the South* (Washington: Smithsonian Institution Press, 1981) p. 59.

18. Mary Gibson Hundley, *The Dunbar Story*, pp. 149-150.

19. Stephen Birmingham, *Certain People: America's Black Elite* (Boston: Little, Brown and Co., 1977), p. 279.

20. See Mary Gibson Hundley, *The Dunbar Story*, p. 75.

21. Ibid., p. 78; Mary Church Terrell, "The History of the High School for Negroes in Washington," *Journal of Negro History*, Vol. II, No. 3 (July 1917), p. 262.

22. Mary Gibson Hundley, *The Dunbar Story*, pp. 39, 74.

23. Robert N. Mattingly, *Autobiographic Memories 1897-54: M Street-Dunbar High School* (Washington, D.C.: privately published by Robert N. Mattingly, May 1974), p. 9.

24. *Black Americans in Defense of Our Nation* (U.S. Department of Defense, 1985), p. 153.

25. Mary Church Terrell, "The History of the High School for Negroes in Washington," *Journal of Negro History*, Vol. II, No. 3 (1917), p. 264.

26. Louise Daniel Hutchison, *Anna J. Cooper: A Voice from the South*, p. 62.

27. The unnamed individuals were, respectively, William H. Hastie, Benjamin O. Davis, Sr., Robert C. Weaver, Edward W. Brooke, and Charles Drew.

28. Mary Gibson Hundley, *The Dunbar Story*, p. 57.

29. Ibid., pp. 32-33.

30. Stephen Birmingham, *Certain People: America's Black Elite*, pp. 144-145.

31. Jervis Anderson, "A Very Special Monument," *The New Yorker*, March 20, 1978, p. 113.

32. Ibid., p. 92.

33. *Brown vs. Board of Education*, 347 U.S. 483.

34. Thomas Sowell, "Black Excellence: The Case of Dunbar High School," *The Public Interest*, Spring 1974, p. 8.

35. See data in Thomas Sowell, "Assumptions versus History in Ethnic Education," *Teachers College Record*, Vol. 83, No. 1 (Fall 1981), pp. 47, 49, 51.

36. Ibid., p. 54.

37. Jervis Anderson, "A Very Special Monument," *The New Yorker*, March 1978, p. 105.

38. Tucker Carlson, "From Ivy League to NBA," *Policy Review*, Spring 1993, p. 36.

39. Thomas Sowell, "Assumptions versus History in Ethnic Education," *Teachers College Record*, Fall 1981, pp. 40, 41.

40. Philip E. Vernon, *The Abilities and Achievements of Orien-*

tals in North America (New York: Academic Press, 1982), p. 98.

41. Lance T. Izumi, et al, *They Have Overcome: High-Poverty, High Performing Schools in California* (San Francisco: Pacific Research Institute, 2002), p. 9; Samuel Casey Carter, *No Excuses: Lessons from 21 High-Performing, High-Poverty Schools* (Washington: The Heritage Foundation, 2000), pp. 43-44.

42. Samuel Casey Carter, *No Excuses*, pp. 96-97.

43. For a chilling account of the lawless atmosphere in some minority schools, see Joshua Kaplowitz, "How I Joined Teach for America and Got Sued for $20 Million," *City Journal*, Winter 2003, pp. 16-26.

44. Samuel Casey Carter, *No Excuses*, pp. 41-42.

45. Ibid., 49-50.

46. Ibid., 51-52.

47. Ibid., 95-96. See also pp. 85-96 for the KIPP School in the Bronx.

48. Ibid., 39.

49. Tania Li, *Malays in Singapore: Culture, Economy, and Ideology* (Singapore: Oxford University Press, 1989), p. 134.

50. Stephen Cole and Elinor Barber, *Increasing Faculty Diversity: The Occupational Choices of High-Achieving Minority Students* (Cambridge, Massachusetts: Harvard University Press, 2003), p. 169.

51. Eric A. Hanushek, et al, "New Evidence About Brown v. Board of Education: The Complex Effects of School Racial Composition on Achievement," National Bureau of Economic Research, Working Paper 8741 (Cambridge, Massachusetts: National Bureau of Economic Research, 2002), Abstract.

52. Ellis B. Page and Timothy Z. Keith, "The Elephant in the Classroom: Ability Grouping and the Gifted," *Intellectual Talent: Psychometric and Social Issues*, edited by Camilla Persson Benbow and David Lubinski (Baltimore: The Johns Hopkins University Press, 1996), p. 208.

53. John Ogbu, *Black American Students in an Affluent Suburb: A Study of Academic Disengagement* (Mahwah, NJ: Lawrence Erlbaum Associates, 2003).

54. Robert Higgs, *Competition and Coercion: Blacks in the*

American Economy, 1865-1914 (Cambridge: Cambridge University Press, 1977), p. 120.

55. Some have argued that, linguistically, such ways of talking are just as valid as any other language. But that misses the point entirely, when it comes to the *social* consequences of talking one way rather than another. A passage from Thomas Hardy's novel, *The Mayor of Casterbridge* made the point. After a girl said, "Bide where you be a minute, father!" this exchange ensued:

> "Bide where you be," he echoed sharply. "Good God, are you only fit to carry wash to a pig-trough, to use such words as those?" She reddened with shame and sadness. "I meant, 'Stay where you are, Father' " she said in a low, humble voice. "I ought to have been more careful."

David Hackett Fischer, *Albion's Seed: Four British Folkways in America* (Oxford: Oxford University Press, 1989), p. 260.

56. Nathan Glazer and Daniel Patrick Moynihan, *Beyond the Melting Pot*, second edition (Cambridge, Mass.: MIT Press, 1970), p. 241.

57. Data from the College Board.

58. Arthur Jensen, "How Much Can We Boost IQ and Scholastic Achievement?" *Harvard Educational Review*, Vol. 39, No. 1 (1969), p. 116. The answer that Professor Jensen offered to the question in his title was that we can boost scholastic achievement a lot, even if we cannot boost IQ very much.

59. Ibid., p. 117. All of this from Jensen's key 1969 article has long since been lost sight of during decades of acrimonious controversy, essentially fighting against other arguments by other people who did use theories of racial differences to depict blacks as uneducable. Professor Jensen's arguments are by no means above criticism but he should be confronted for what he said, not for what others have said. Again, history has to have its own integrity, if it is to be of any use other than as a projection into the past of current ideological visions.

60. The College Board, *SAT Scores for Each Ethnic Group by Highest Level of Parental Education, 1994* (Princeton), p. 16.

61. See data and sources cited on pages 42, 44, and 46 of my

article "Assumptions versus History in Ethnic Education," *Teachers College Record*,Vol. 83, No. 1 (Fall 1981).

62. My own experiences in this regard can be found in my memoir, *A Personal Odyssey* (New York:The free Press, 2000), pp. 154-161, 187-188, 221-223.

63. Horace Mann Bond, *A Study of Factors Involved in the Identification and Encouragement of Unusual Academic Talent among Underprivileged Populations* (U.S. Department of Health, Education, and Welfare, January 1967), p. 147. [Contract No. SAE 8028, Project No. 5-0859].

64. Kent Mommsen, *Career Patterns of Black Doctorates*, doctoral dissertation in sociology, Florida State University, 1970, p. 13.

65. See, for example,Theodore Dalrymple, *Life at the Bottom: The Worldview That Makes the Underclass* (Chicago: Ivan R. Dee, 2001).

66. Henry Reid Hunter, *The Development of the Public Secondary Schools of Atlanta, Georgia, 1845-1937* (Atlanta: Office of the School Historian,Atlanta Public Schools, 1974), p. 52.

67. James M. McPherson, *The Abolitionist Legacy: From Reconstruction to the NAACP* (Princeton: Princeton University Press, 1975), p. 31.

68. Gunnar Myrdal, *An American Dilemma* (New York: Harper & Row, 1944), p. 950n.

69. Bulletin, 1916, No. 38, U. S. Department of the Interior, Bureau of Education, *Negro Education:A Study of the Private and Higher Schools for Colored People in the United States*, (Washington: Government Printing Office, 1917), p. 41.

70. Ibid., p. 42.

71. Henry Reid Hunter, *The Development of the Public Secondary Schools of Atlanta, Georgia 1845-1937*, p. 21.

72. Gunnar Myrdal, *An American Dilemma*, p. 950n.

73. Ibid., p. 950.

74. Ibid., p. 201.

75. James M. McPherson, *The Abolitionist Legacy*, p. 159.

76. Ibid., p. 367.

77. Ibid., p. 206.
78. Conor Cruise O'Brien, *Memoir: My Life and Themes* (London: Profile Books, Ltd, 1998), p. 277.
79. W. E. B. Du Bois, "The Hampton Idea," *The Education of Black People: Ten Critiques, 1906-1960*, edited by Herbert Aptheker (Amherst: University of Massachusetts Press, 1973), pp. 6-7.
80. W. E. B. Du Bois, *The Philadelphia Negro: A Social Study* (New York: Schocken Books, 1970), p. 395.
81. W.E.B. Du Bois, *The Souls of Black Folk* (New York: Gramercy Books, 1994), p. 53.
82. Booker T. Washington, *Up From Slavery: An Autobiography* (Garden City, N.Y.: Doubleday & Co., 1951), pp., 223-224.
83. "Nearly sixteen millions of hands will aid you in pulling the load upward, or they will pull against you the load downward." Ibid., p. 222.
84. C. Eric Lincoln, "The Negro College and Cultural Change," *Daedalus*, summer 1971, p. 614.
85. W. E. B. Du Bois, "Education and Work," *The Education of Black People*, edited by Herbert Aptheker, p. 68.
86. Louis R. Harlan, *Booker T. Washington: The Wizard of Tuskegee 1901-1915* (New York: Oxford University Press, 1983), p. 138.
87. Booker T. Washington, *The Future of the American Negro* (New York: The New American Library, Inc., 1969), pp. 80-81.
88. Willard B. Gatewood, *Aristocrats of Color: The Black Elite, 1880-1920*(Bloomington: Indiana University Press, 1990), p. 266.
89. Louis R. Harlan, *Booker T. Washington: The Wizard of Tuskegee 1901-1915*, p. 280.
90. Booker T. Washington, *Up From Slavery*, p. 93.
91. Ibid., p. 203.
92. Booker T. Washington, *The Future of the American Negro*, p. 80.
93. Booker T. Washington, *Up From Slavery*, p. 93.
94. Booker T. Washington, *The Future of the American Negro*, p. 141.

95. Louis R. Harlan, *Booker T. Washington*, pp. 291, 297-298, 302-303; *idem., Booker T. Washington: The Wizard of Tuskegee, 1901-1915* (New York: Oxford University Press, 1983), p. 244-250.

96. James M. McPherson, *The Abolitionist Legacy*, pp. 352-363.

97. Louis R. Harlan, *Booker T. Washington: The Wizard of Tuskegee*, p. 361.

98. Ibid., p. 134.

99. A fuller discussion of Booker T. Washington can be found in my article, "Up from Slavery" in the December 5, 1994 issue of *Forbes* magazine, as well as in the already cited two-volume biography of Booker T. Washington by Louis R. Harlan.

100. Kelly Miller, "Washington's Policy," *Booker T. Washington and His Critics: The Problem of Negro Leadership* edited by Hugh Hawkins (Lexington: D.C. Heath and Co., 1962), p. 51.

101. Booker T. Washington, *Up from Slavery*, p. 270.

102. Conor Cruise O'Brien, *Memoir: My Life and Themes*, p. 277.

103. James M. McPherson, "White Liberals and Black Power in Negro Education, 1865-1915," *American Historical Review*, Vol. 75, No. 5 (June 1970), p. 1362.

104. Ibid., p. 1362. A very similar view was taken by William Syphax, founder of the institution that would later be called Dunbar High School. Half of the first 50 teachers hired were white and Syphax said that those who hired teachers "deem it a violation of our official oath to employ inferior teachers when superior teachers can be had for the same money." R. Delorus Preston, Jr., "William Syphax, A Pioneer in Negro Education in the District of Columbia," *Journal of Negro History*, October 1935, pp. 458, 464.

105. James M. McPherson, "White Liberals and Black Power in Negro Education, 1865-1915," *American Historical Review*, Vol. &5, No. 5 (June 1970), p. 1375.

106. E. Franklin Frazier, *The Negro in the United States*, revised edition (New York: The Macmillan Co., 1971), p. 558.

107. James M. McPherson, *The Abolitionist Legacy*, p. 295.

108. Michael R. Winston, "Through the Back Door: Academic

Racism and the Negro Scholar in Historical Perspective," *Daedalus*, Vol. 100, No. 3 (Summer 1971), pp. 702-703.

109. Helen Allen Bullock, "The Black College and the New Black Awareness," *Daedalus*, Vol. 100, No. 3 (Summer 1971), p. 585.

110. One of my mentors at Howard University, Professor Sterling A. Brown, once described the process by which faculty members had been paid at some black colleges. Their paychecks would be slid across a table to them, face down, to be signed on the back. Then they would slide the check back to the person who counted out the cash to them. It could cost them their jobs if they turned those checks over to see what salary they were officially being paid, which is to say, how much was being skimmed off by the administration. E, Franklin Frazier reported: "in one state institution the president paid his teachers with a personal check, altered at will their monthly salaries, which were based upon verbal agreements, and would discharge them in the middle of the month if he became dissatisfied with them." E. Franklin Frazier, *The Negro in the United States*, p. 478n.

111. E. Franklin Frazier, *Black Bourgeoisie: The Rise of a New Middle Class in the United States* (New York: Collier Books, 1962), p. 73.

112. E. Franklin Frazier, *The Negro in the United States*, p. 480.

113. E. Franklin Frazier, *Black Bourgeoisie*, p. 74.

114. Ibid., p. 74.

115. Carter G. Wooodson, *The Education of the Negro Prior to 1861* (New York: The Arno Press, 1968), pp. 274, 276, 277.

116. See, for example, Thomas Sowell, *Inside American Education: The Decline, the Deception, the Dogmas* (New York: The Free Press, 1993), pp. 140-146.

117. Ibid., Chapter 6.

118. See Thomas Sowell, *Civil Rights: Rhetoric or Reality?* (New York: William Morrow and Co., 1984), p. 49.

119. E. Franklin Frazier, *The Negro in the United States*, pp. 558-559.

120. U.S. Bureau of the Census, *Historical Statistics of the*

United States: Colonial Times to 1970 (Washington: U.S. Government Printing Office, 1975), p. 381.

121. Stephan Thernstrom and Abigail Thernstrom, *America in Black and White: One Nation, Indivisible* (New York: Simon & Schuster, 1997), p. 233.

122. Ibid.

123. James M. McPherson, *The Abolitionist Legacy*, p. 72.

124. Ralph Ellison, *Shadow and Act* (New York: Random House, 1964), p. 87.

125. Quoted in Jervis Anderson, "A Very Special Monument," *The New Yorker*, March 20, 1978, pp. 107-108.

History versus Visions

1. John Perazzo, *The Myths That Divide Us* (Briarcliff Manor: World Studies Books, 199), p. 17.

2. R. Bayly Winder, "The Lebanese in West Africa," *Comparative Studies in Society and History*, Vol. 4 (1967), pp. 309-310.

3. Donald R. Snodgrass, *Inequality and Economic Development in Malaysia* (Kuala Lumpur: Oxford University Press, 1980), p. 4.

4. Amy L. Freedman, "The Effect of Government policy and Institutions on Chinese Overseas Acculturation: The Case of Malaysia," *Modern Asian Studies*, Vol. 35, No. 2 (2001), p. 416.

5. Andrew Tanzer, "The Bamboo Network," *Forbes*, July 18, 1994, pp. 138-145.

6. Peter S. Li, "Income Achievement and Adaptive Capacity: An Empirical Comparison of Chinese and Japanese in Canada," *Visible Minorities and Multiculturalism in Canada,* edited by K. Victor Ujimoto and Gordon Hirabayash (Toronto: Buttersworth, 1980), p. 365; Thomas Sowell, *Ethnic America: A History* (New York: Basic Books, 1981), p. 5; Teiiti Suzuki, *The Japanese Immigrant in Brazil* (Tokyo: University of Tokyo Press, 1969), p. 91.

7. Eric Woodrum et al., "Japanese American Economic Behavior: Its Types, Determinants and Consequences," *Social Forces,* June 1980, pp. 1237, 1238; Daniel O Price, *Changing Characteristics of the Negro Population* (Washington, D.C.: U.S. Government Printing Office, 1969), p. 45.

8. S.W. Kung, *Chinese in American Life: Some Aspects of Their History, Status, Problems, and Contributions* (Seattle: University of Washington Press, 1962), p. 57.

9. Rupert B.Vance, *Human Geography of the South: A Study in Regional Resources and Human Adequacy* (Chapel Hill: University of North Carolina Press, 1932), p. 203.

10. Stanley Feldstein and Lawrence Costello, *The Ordeal of Assimilation* (New York: Anchor Books, 1974), pp. 122-123. See also Irving Howe and Kenneth Libo, *How We Lived* (New York: Richard Marek Publishers, 1979), p. 204.

11. Arthur Herman, *How the Scots Invented the Modern World* (New York: Crown Publishers, 2001), p. 20.

12. E. Franklin Frazier, *Black Bourgeoisie: The Rise of a New Middle Class in the United States* (New York: Collier Books, 1962), p. 74.

13. Eric Richards, "Scotland the Uses of the Atlantic Empire," *Strangers with the Realm: Cultural Margins of the British Empire*, edited by Bernard Bailyn and Philip D. Morgan (Chapel Hill: University of North Carolina Press, 1991), p. 84.

14. James Buchan, *Crowded with Genius: The Scottish Enlightenment, Edinburgh's Moment of the Mind* (New York: HarperCollins, 2003), p. 129.

15. Eric Richards, "Scotland and the Uses of the Atlantic Empire," *Strangers within the Realm*, edited by Bernard Bailyn and Philip D. Morgan, p. 86.

16. Ned C. Landsman, *Scotland and Its First American Colony, 1683-1765* (Princeton: Princeton University Press, 1985), p. 82.

17. Irokawa Daikichi, *The Culture of the Meiji Period* (Princeton: Princeton University Press, 1985), p. 7.

18. E. Franklin Frazier, *The Negro in the United States* revised edition (New York: The Macmillan Co., 1971), pp. 568, 592. See also Gunnar Myrdal, *An American Dilemma: The Negro Problem and Modern Democracy* (New York: Harper & Brothers, 1944), p. 142.

19. See Thomas Sowell, *Civil Rights: Rhetoric or Reality?* (New York: William Morrow and Co., 1984), p. 49.

20. Willard B. Gatewood, *Aristocrats of Color: The Black Elite, 1880-1920* (Bloomington: Indiana University Press, 1990), pp. 186-187, 332; Allan H. Spear, *Black Chicago* (Chicago: University of Chicago Press, 1967), p. 168; E. Franklin Frazier, *The Negro in the United States*, pp. 284-285; Florette Henri, *Black Migration: Movement North, 1900-1920* (New York: Anchor Books, 1976), pp. 96-97; Gilbert Osofsky, *Harlem: The Making of a Ghetto* (New York: Harper & Row, 1966), pp. 43-44; Ivan H. Light, *Ethnic Enterprise in America: Business and Welfare Among Chinese, Japanese, and Blacks* (Berkeley: University of California Press, 1972), Figure 1 (after p. 100); W.E.B. Du Bois, *The Black North in 1901: A Social Study* (New York: Arno Press, 1969), p. 25.

21. Lorelle Savage, "Who Should Change—Them or Us?" *National Outlook* (Australia), October 1996, p. 4.

22. James M. McPherson, "Deconstructing Affirmative Action," *Perspectives* (Newsmagazine of the American Historical Association), Vol. 41, No. 4 (April 2003), p. 6.

23. Ibid.

24. Angelo Codevilla, *The Character of Nations* (New York: Basic Books, 1997), p. 50.

25. See, for example, my *Conquests and Cultures*, pp. 175-184.

26. "A Nervous New Arrival on the European Union's Block," *The Economist*, August 30, 2003, p. 17.

27. David B. Abernethy, *The Dynamics of Global Dominance: European Overseas Empires 1415-1980* (New Haven: Yale University Press, 2000), p. 86.

28. Orlando Patterson, *Freedom*, Vol. I: *Freedom in the Making of Western Culture* (New York: Basic Books, 1991), p. 8.

29. Noel B. Gerson, *Harriet Beecher Stowe: A Biography* (New York: Praeger Publishers, 1976), pp. 110-111.

30. Lord Kinross, *The Ottoman Centuries: The Rise and Fall of the Turkish Empire* (New York: William Morrow and Co., 1977), p. 115.

31. Pierre L. van den Berghe, "Asian Africans Before and After Independence," *Kroniek van Afrika* (Netherlands), Vol. 3, No 6 (1975), p. 202.

32. Howard Zinn, *A People's History of the United States* (New York: Harper & Row, 1980), p. 10.

33. Elizabeth Wiskemann, *Czechs and Germans: A Study of the Struggle in the Historic Provinces of Bohemia and Moravia* (London: Oxford University Press, 1938), pp. 142, 148.

34. Nicholas D. Kristof and Sheryl WeDunn, *Thunder from the East: Portrait of a Rising Asia* (New York: Vintage Books, 200), p. 237.

35. Ivan Light and Charles Choy Wong, "Protest or Work: Dilemmas of the Tourist Industry in American Chinatowns," *American Journal of Sociology*, May 1975, p. 1359.

36. Gunnar Myrdal, *An American Dilemma: The Negro Problem and Modern Democracy* (New York: Harper & Row, 1944), p. 964.

37. Anyone can verify this by accessing the raw data, which are available from National Technical Information Service, U.S. Department of Commerce, Springfield, Virginia 22161, Accession Number PB265 8.13. The school codes for Dunbar High School are 0508 (students who graduated) and 0598 (students who attended without graduating).

38. Edmund Burke, *Reflections on the Revolution in France* (London: J. M. Dent & Sons, Ltd., 1967), p. 137.

Index

123, 126, 127, 128, 133, 136, 139, 143, 146, 147, 148, 150, 153-154, 157, 158, 160, 166, 180, 181, 182, 183, 184, 186, 191, 193, 194, 253, 154, 259, 260-263, 266, 269, 271, 274, 275, 280, 282, 283, 286, 288, 290

Universalism, 272-273

Urbanization, 41, 42, 47, 48, 174, 175

Victimhood, 57, 213, 225, 254, 279-280

Violence (see Crime and Violence)

Virginia, 3, 4, 11, 16, 17, 19, 21, 22, 23, 24, 25, 27, 28, 35, 37, 41, 139, 141, 145, 146, 153, 166, 195

Wales and the Welsh, 5, 10, 21

Washington, Booker T., 37, 229, 231-235, 352 (note 99)

Washington, D.C., 21, 39, 40, 41, 42, 47, 48, 154, 204, 206, 207, 209-211, 214, 224, 231, 243, 288

Washington, George, 140, 145, 147, 149-151, 163, 165, 166, 279

West Indians: 32-33

White Liberals, 51-59, 63, 261

White Southerners, x, 1-27, 61, 299-300 (note 116)
    ancestors: 3, 8, 13, 15, 16, 18, 19, 21-22, 24, 25, 27, 28, 29,-30, 59
    business: 18-21
    carelessness: 16-17
    cleanliness: 4, 20
    contrasts with Northerners: 2-3, 14, 18, 20-21, 22, 23-27, 27-28, 59-60, 166
    education: 4, 22-23
    elites: 22
    gambling: 19
    enterprise: 17-18, 21
    mental tests: 23, 31, 300 (note 119)
    oratory: 6
    poor whites: 11, 13
    pride: 6, 7-13, 13, 18, 56
    recklessness: 11-12
    recreation: 6
    religion: 24-27
    sex: 6, 23-24, 26
    self-restraint: 6, 14